A JOURNEY THROUGH THE BIBLE

A JOURNEY THROUGH THE BIBLE

Volume 2
Job to Malachi

DENIS LYLE

Christian Year Publications

ISBN-13: 978 1 912522 37 8

Typeset by John Ritchie Ltd., Kilmarnock
Printed by Bell & Bain Ltd., Glasgow

"But continue thou in the things which thou hast learned and hast been assured of, knowing of whom thou hast learned them; And that from a child thou hast known the holy scriptures, which are able to make thee wise unto salvation through faith which is in Christ Jesus. All scripture is given by inspiration of God, and is profitable for doctrine, for reproof, for correction, for instruction in righteousness: That the man of God may be perfect, thoroughly furnished unto all good works."

2 Timothy 3:14-17

Contents

Foreword

I have had the privilege of knowing Denis for over 40 years. In fact, I officiated at his marriage to Catherine who has been his faithful wife and co-labourer in the Gospel for many years. Since that time, Denis has been a fervent and faithful preacher of the glorious Gospel of Jesus Christ and a distinguished Bible teacher.

As a boy, he received Jesus Christ as his Saviour and as a young man he responded to God's call to full-time service. In 1998, Denis became the pastor of Lurgan Baptist Church. I attended this church as a young teenager and listened to the godly William Mullan who skilfully taught the Word in his famous weekly Bible Classes. During a ministry that has spanned 45 years, Denis has had a real burden to win souls for Christ and his expository teaching of God's Word has taken him to various countries of the world, including USA, Australia, Romania and South Africa.

His preaching of the Word of God manifests a fervent love for his Master and an earnest desire that those who profess faith in Christ will "*grow in grace, and in the knowledge of our Lord and Saviour Jesus Christ*" (2 Peter 3:18).

Having read Volume 1 of Denis' latest writings, *'A Journey through the Bible'*, I count it an honour to be asked to write this short *Foreword* to Volume 2. I genuinely commend these Volumes as a must for your personal library. They flow from our brother's Tuesday night Bible Classes and are aimed at the encouragement and instruction of God's people. It is clearly evident that Denis has accumulated a wealth of scriptural knowledge through his years of prayerful study of God's precious Word and your soul will been enriched and edified as you carefully read these Volumes with your open Bible before you. Remember, these Volumes are to assist your understanding of God's Word, not a substitute for it. In his preparation for this series of Bible Studies at Lurgan Baptist Church, Denis, no doubt, read various faithful Bible expositors and found much enlightenment from their writings.

Whether you are a preacher, Sunday School teacher or just a believer with a yearning to know more about our wonderful Lord, you will find these studies refreshing and uplifting. Let '*A Journey through the Bible*' be a real blessing to your soul as you face many challenges in your walk with God.

God's Word is amazing and exciting and as you read and study it, you will appreciate the wonders of God's grace and goodness.

Dr William McCrea
Calvary Free Presbyterian Church
Magherafelt
Northern Ireland

Preface

I am delighted to see the publication of this second volume of **'A Journey Through the Bible'.** These books are the outcome of a series of studies conducted in Lurgan Baptist Church on Tuesday evenings. They began in the autumn of 2013 and concluded in the spring of 2017. On this Journey, I took one book of the Bible each night and sought to give an overview of it.

Some people suggested that I should spend more than one week on particular books and I understood why they made such a suggestion. However, my exercise was to devote the same time to each of the sixty six books – to the well-known as well as to the more obscure and to the large as well as to the small.

It was a great encouragement to me to see so many gather Tuesday by Tuesday with such an evident interest in the Word of God. It has also been very encouraging to have received so many positive comments since the publication of Volume 1. As I have travelled throughout Ulster and further afield, I have been constantly asked when Volume 2 would be published.

I am delighted to know that Christians have been blessed by reading my chapters on Genesis to 2 Chronicles and it is my prayer that you will be blessed by reading these chapters on Job to Malachi.

Over the course of my ministry, I have preached on many different subjects. However, the series preached on *'A Journey Through the Bible'* was the series I found most difficult. To aid my understanding, I drew widely from all sorts of writers. Their books on the Bible enlightened me, enriched me and encouraged me and some of their content is found in these Volumes. That is my disclaimer to plagiarism.

As I wrote in my *Preface* to Volume 1, I trust that as you ponder the pages of *'A Journey Through the Bible'* that you will have a new appreciation of the written Word and a fresh appreciation of our wonderful Saviour, of whom this Book so eloquently speaks.

Denis Lyle
Moira
Northern Ireland
June 2018

Bibliography

Unlocking the Bible: J. David Pawson - Collins
Willmington's Guide to the Bible: H.L. Willmington - Tyndale House, Wheaton, Illinois
Wiersbe's Expository Outlines on the New Testament: Warren Wiersbe - Victor Books
The Bible Exposition Commentary: Warren Wiersbe - Victor Books
The Message of the Old Testament: Mark Dever - Crossway Books
The Message of the New Testament: Mark Dever - Crossway Books
The MacArthur Bible Handbook: John MacArthur - Thomas Nelson
Adventuring Through the Bible: Ray Steadman - Discovery House Publishers
God's Wonderful Word: Trevor Knight - Young Life
A Sure Foundation: Alan Cairns - Ambassador
Bible Survey Outlines: Roland V. Hudson - Eerdmans Publishing Company
Explore The Book: J. Sidlow Baxter - Zondervan Publishing House
The Bible Book by Book: Raymond Brown - Collins
Know your Bible: Graham Scroggie - Pickering & Inglis
From Cover to Cover: Brian Harbour - Broadman Press
Exploring the Old Testament Book by Book: John Phillips - Kregel
Exploring the New Testament Book by Book: John Phillips - Kregel
The Old Testament: Gareth Crossley - Evangelical Press
Jensen's Survey of the Old Testament: Irving Jensen - Moody Press
A Survey of the New Testament: Robert H. Gundry - The Paternoster Press
The Collected Writings of J.B. Hewitt: Gospel Tract Publications
Basic Bible Study Notes: Ian Brown (Martyrs Memorial Free Presbyterian Church, Belfast)
An Introduction to the New Testament: Lamoyne Sharpe - Printed in U.S.A.
Books of the Bible: Steve Wagers

CHAPTER 1

Job

'Why?' How often that question comes in life! How difficult it is to find an answer! Why does a good God allow tragedy to come to His children? Why should that young, beautiful girl be stricken with an incurable disease? Why should the innocent child of devoted parents be born intellectually disabled? Several years ago, I stood in a country cottage in County Antrim and gazed at the bullet holes that had shattered that home. I.R.A. terrorists had earlier surrounded the cottage, determined to shoot the son of the family. He was a policeman. In the midst of all the confusion, the Christian mother had been shot dead through her bedroom window. As I gazed at the tear-stained faces of her daughters, the question I asked was: *"Why?"*

The subject of the book of Job is - the problem of suffering, especially as it bears upon the life of a believer.

Why do the godly suffer and why is God silent?

Job and his friends wrestle with these problems, but arrive at no satisfactory conclusion. It is not until the Lord speaks that the true answers are found. In fact, Job did not find the answers to what he was asking, but by the end of the book he had lost his questions!

Christopher Morley says:

"I had a million questions to ask God, but when I met Him they all fled my mind and it didn't seem to matter".

There are over 300 questions in the book of Job. Many of them are asked by Job himself, but when Job met God, he said: "B*ehold, I am vile; what shall I answer Thee? I will lay mine hand upon my mouth"* (Job 40:4) and *"I have heard of Thee by the hearing of the ear: but now mine eye seeth Thee. Wherefore I abhor myself, and repent in dust and ashes"* (Job 42:5-6).

What a remarkable man Job was! His name may have come from the Hebrew word for *"persecution"*, thus meaning *"persecuted one"* or from an Arabic word meaning *"repent"*, thus meaning *"repentant one"*. Whatever the meaning of his name, Job was a real historical character. Whenever I think of this book, I think of the word:

1. Authenticity

You see, the authenticity of this book has been questioned. Do you recall the Protestant division of the Old Testament? The 39 books of the Old Testament are divided into 5 categories.

1. *The Law or Pentateuch:* Genesis to Deuteronomy
2. *History:* Joshua to Esther
3. *Wisdom or Poetry:* Job to the Song of Solomon
4. *The Major Prophets:* Isaiah to Daniel
5. *The Minor Prophets:* Hosea to Malachi

The Hebrew Old Testament is divided differently. It groups all of the Old Testament books into three major sections: *The Law, the Prophets and the Writings* (see Luke 24:27, 44).

In our English Bibles, the book of Job begins the section on poetry which embraces Job, Psalms, Proverbs, Ecclesiastes and the Song of Solomon.

It has been argued by some that the book of Job is not history or that is only partly history, yet in Ezekiel 14 verse 14 God Himself is recorded as saying: *"Though these three men, Noah, Daniel, and Job were in it (i.e. Jerusalem), they should deliver but their own souls by their righteousness"*. Then again, in the book of James, the writer declares: *"Ye have heard of the patience of Job, and have seen the end of the Lord; that the Lord is very pitiful, and of tender mercy"* (James 5:11).

If this book was inspired by God - and we believe it was - then we accept the *authenticity* of the book of Job. Although found within the poetical books of the Old Testament, the events recorded in this book are historically true. Then there is the word:

2. <u>Antiquity</u>

Many Bible scholars regard this as the oldest book in the Bible. Why? Well, for one thing there was his age. You see, he lived for another 140 years after the experiences described in this book (Job 42:16), placing him in the days of the patriarchs, Abraham, Isaac and Jacob (see, for example, Genesis 11:10-26 and 25:7). Then again, Job acted as high priest in his family in the manner of Abraham (Job 1:4-5). This was not allowed after the Exodus. Moreover, Job's wealth was measured in livestock rather than gold and silver (Job 1:3 and 42:12). All of these things indicate that Job lived before or during the period of Abraham, making this book the most ancient book in the Bible. There is then the word:

3. <u>Adversity</u>

God's people do suffer. Bad things happen many times to good people, so one cannot judge a person's spirituality by his painful circumstances or successes. Job's three friends said Job suffered because he had sinned - and that was not true. Elihu said that God was chastening Job to make him a better man - and that was only partly true.

But the fundamental reason for Job's suffering was to silence the blasphemous accusations of Satan and prove that this man would honour God even though he had lost everything.

This was a battle in the heavenlies (see Ephesians 6:12), but Job did not know it. Job's life was a battlefield where the forces of God and Satan were engaged in a spiritual struggle to decide the question: *"Is God worthy of man's worship?"*

Sidlow Baxter says:

"Such suffering as we learn from the book of Job is not judicial but remedial, not punitive but corrective, not retributive but disciplinary, not a penalty but a ministry. This is the interim solution. The final solution will be given in that promised day, when instead of seeing through a glass darkly we shall see *'face to face'*, and shall *'know even as we are known'*".

So, as we come to this book we are faced with the question: ***"Why?"***

Why do the righteous suffer? Where is God when tragedy strikes? If God is all-loving, how can He allow human suffering? Why do bad things happen to good people? Does God not care? Is the Lord worthy of 'worship in the tough times'? Or - *Must the Lord buy worshippers with blessings?*

These are difficult questions.

In the words of this very book of Job: *"Man is born unto trouble, as the sparks fly upward"* (Job 5:7) and *"Man that is born of a woman is of few days, and full of trouble"* (Job 14:1). So this book is dealing with one of the oldest problems in the world - suffering. Years ago, people did not really understand the problem of suffering. Today, it is much the same.

Written largely in poetic prose, the book divides itself into three sections:

(1) <u>THE PROLOGUE: Job's Dilemma - Chapters 1-3</u>

Job hailed from the land of Uz - and there has been much discussion as to where this was. Some place it near Edom, close to Midian (Lamentations 4:21). Others say that the Edomites conquered this country and many talk about Uz as east of Israel in the Arabian Desert, the present day borderland of Jordan, Iraq and Saudi Arabia.

Job was a great, gracious and godly man who was universally

loved and respected both on earth and in Heaven. These opening chapters describe:

(a) THE PROSPERITY OF JOB

In every way, Job was a rich man. He was:

<u>*Rich in Character*</u>

The book begins: *"There was a man in the land of Uz, whose name was Job; and that man was perfect and upright, and one that feared God, and eschewed evil"*. The word *'perfect'* means *'blameless'* and the word *'eschewed'* means *'to turn away'*. Job was not sinless, but he was blameless. When it came to sin or any form of wickedness, Job got as far away from it as he possibly could. Job could sing with Charles Albert Tindley:

> *"Nothing between my soul and my Saviour,*
> *Naught of this world's delusive dream;*
> *I have renounced all sinful pleasure;*
> *Jesus is mine; there's nothing between."*

Job was like this because he feared God. *"The remarkable thing about fearing God"*, says Oswald Chambers, *"is when you fear God, you fear nothing else; whereas if you do not fear God, you fear everything else"*.

<u>*Rich in Family*</u>

In those days, a large family was seen as a blessing from God. No doubt his seven sons and three daughters met frequently to enjoy each other's company. But do you notice the spiritual concern Job had for them? (see Job 1:5) That does not mean that their celebration was wicked. It only shows that Job was a godly man and wanted to be sure his family were right with God. How fortunate these children were to have such a godly father! By the way, how will your children remember you? Do they ever see you on your knees before God? Do they recognise in you a man of God? Notice that Job was also:

Rich in Possessions

Living in a day when wealth was measured primarily in terms of land, animals, and servants, Job had all three in abundance. But although he was rich, he did not turn from God. Job acknowledged that the Lord had given this wealth to him (Job 1:21) and he used his wealth generously for the good of others (see Job 29:12-17 and 31:16-32). You see, God had blessed Job and he was not slow to thank God for all that He had done. Paul wrote: *"I know both how to be abased, and I know how to abound"* (Philippians 4:12). Most of us have no problems trusting God when we are *"abased"*, and things are going wrong, but how difficult it is to serve God and remember Him when things are prosperous! Job did not permit his money and his possessions to take the place of God. Do you? Job was also:

Rich in Friends

Look at Chapter 2 verse 11: *"Now when Job's three friends heard of all this evil that was come upon him, they came every one from his own place"*. Now while it is true that his three friends hurt him deeply and wronged him greatly, they were still his friends. *"My best friend"*, said Henry Ford, *"is the one who brings out the best in me"*, but Job's friends brought out the worst in him. However, in the end, I like to think that Job and his friends were reconciled (see Job 42:7-10) and I like to think that their relationship became even deeper than before. To have true friends is to be wealthy indeed. So, there is ***the prosperity of Job,*** then look at:

(b) THE ADVERSITY OF JOB

In Chapter 2 verse 13, we read: *"his grief was very great"*. His grief was exceedingly great. During the Great Depression of 1929, the stock market crashed on Black Tuesday. Then there was the Black Monday of 1987 when stock markets around the world crashed. Well, Job, had the blackest of all days. In one day, he lost *his fortune* (Job 1:13-17). Then he lost *his family* (Job 1:18-19). In one day, Job lost those that he loved and he lost the things that he loved. Then he lost *his fitness* (Job 2:7-8) and, to add insult to injury, he even lost *his friends.* He says: *"My kinsfolk have failed, and my familiar friends have forgotten me"* (Job 19:14). In one day, he went from sunshine to rain, from joy to pain. He went from blessedness to brokenness, from insulation to isolation, from happiness to heartache.

King Solomon was right when he said: *"Man also knoweth not his time: as the fishes that are taken in an evil net, and as the birds that are caught in the snare; so are the sons of men snared in an evil time, when it falleth suddenly upon them"* (Ecclesiastes 9:12). Now Job knew *what* had happened, but he did not know *why* it had happened - and that is the crux of the matter. Job was not meant to know the explanation of his trial and on this simple fact everything hangs. If Job had known the explanation, there would have been no place for faith - and the man would never have come forth as gold purified in the fire. Suppose the Lord had come to Job and had said: *"Listen, the Devil is going to attack you and will do some terrible things to you, but I want you to know that I am going to take care of you and you will get double of everything you lose"*. Tell me, would that have been a test of Job's faith? Hardly! You see, this book was written to help us understand that we do not always have to understand.

There are things that are going to happen in your life that you will not understand this side of Glory. But you do not have to understand what God is doing, if you can trust God always to do what is right.

We are allowed in this book to visit the throne room of Heaven and hear God and Satan speak. We know who causes this destruction and why he was allowed to cause it. But if we did not have the opening chapters of this book, we would probably take the same approach as Job's friends and blame Job for the tragedy. Look at Chapter 1 verses 8 to 11 and notice some interesting things about the Devil here. We learn that Satan does not have:

The Presence of God

Satan is not omnipresent. He can only be in one place at a time. When believers say that Satan is troubling them, because something trivial has gone wrong, they are mistaken. He generally has more important work to do with other people!

The Perception of God

"And the LORD said unto Satan: 'Hast thou considered My servant Job?" (Job 1:8) You see, God knew Job's heart, but Satan did not. Satan cannot read your mind. He cannot know your thoughts, for only God knows the heart.

The Power of God

Look at what the Devil says in Chapter 1 verses 9 and 10. He refers to a hedge that had been made by God about Job and his house. He says that God had blessed Job. How did he know that God had put a hedge about Job? Well, he knew it because he had tried to get to Job, but he could not because Job was protected by the Lord. The Devil and all of his demons in Hell can attack you, but they cannot touch you without the permission of the Lord. The Psalmist says: *"The angel of the LORD encampeth round about them that fear Him, and delivereth them"* (Psalm 34:7).

Now in the midst of all this, Satan asked a very good question: *"Doth Job fear God for nought?"* (Job 1:9) Satan's accusation is that nobody is good without a cause. Nobody just loves God for the sake of loving God. His assertion was that Job served God only because God served Job.

The Devil said in effect: *"Oh, I know why Job serves You! Job serves You because You have blessed him. Job serves You because You have been so good to him. But You take away his wealth, his health, and then You will see whether or not Job serves You"*. Satan's accusation against Job is really an attack against God. Satan is saying: *"The only reason Job fears You is because You pay him to do it. You are not a God worthy of worship. You have to pay people to worship You"*.

Is the Lord to be worshipped because of who He is - or because of the things He gives? If God never gave you one blessing, would you still serve the Lord Jesus? You have to ask yourself: *"If the Lord did not bless me spiritually, materially, domestically, would I still be as excited about worshipping the Lord, loving the Saviour, reaching the lost?"* Here is a legitimate question. Would you worship, love, serve the Lord, if there was nothing in it for you?

The story is told about a mother, exasperated with her little five-year-old boy who had been giving her trouble all afternoon. She said: *"Would you please straighten up and be good?"* Her son replied: *"I will, if you will give me $5.00"*. She looked at him and said: *"Why can't you be good for nothing like your Daddy?"* Well, the reason why Satan attacked Job was to prove that he wasn't good for nothing!

So Job's life becomes the battlefield where the forces of God and Satan engage in a spiritual struggle to decide this question: *"Is God worthy of worship even though a man loses everything?"* The prosperity of Job and the adversity of Job – and then there is:

(c) THE FIDELITY OF JOB

How would you react if you lost your *Home*? Job's response is wonderful. He worshipped God and uttered a tremendous statement of faith. He looked *Backward: "Naked came I out of my mother's womb"* (Job 1:21). Everything Job owned was given to him by God and the same God who gave it had the right to take it away. He looked *Forward: "Naked shall I return thither,"* He looked *Upward: "Blessed be the name of the LORD"*. Instead of cursing as Satan said Job would do, Job blessed the Lord. It takes real faith in the midst of sorrow and suffering to so speak.

How would you react if you lost your *Health*? (Job 2:7-8) Job had a disease called elephantiasis, so called because the limbs become jointless lumps like an elephant's legs. Some say it belongs to the leprosy family.

Job lost his home and his health, but he never lost his faith in God. He could testify: *"Though He slay me, yet will I trust in Him"* (Job 13:15) and *"But He knoweth the way that I take: when He hath tried me, I shall come forth as gold"* (Job 23:10). Chapter 1 concludes with these words: *"In all this Job sinned not, nor charged God foolishly"*.

There was the prosperity and the adversity and the fidelity of Job, and then there was:

(d) THE MISERY OF JOB

You see, the Lord allowed Satan to attack *Job's Possessions:* *"And the LORD said unto Satan, Behold, all that he hath is in thy power"* (Job 1:12). Then He allowed Satan to attack *Job's Person:* *"And the LORD said unto Satan, Behold, he is in thine hand; but save his life"* (Job 2:6). Job's suffering was so intense that he wished he had never been born. Time and again he asks - Why? (Job 3:11-12, 23) Yet note what he says in Chapter 2 verse 10: *"Shall we receive good at the hand of God, and shall we not receive evil?" (Job 2:10)* That word *'evil'* can be translated *'adversity'. You see, whether we like it or not, God not only comforts the afflicted, He afflicts the comfortable.* He not only brings us good, but He brings us adversity. Do you want to know why? Because God is not so much interested in your *happiness* as He is in your *holiness*. Was Job not a better man for going through what God allowed? Indeed, though he lost a great deal through this soul-crushing experience, he gained far more than he lost (See Job 42:12-16). Through this furnace of affliction he perseveres and becomes an even stronger, more mature believer. (See Job 42:5).

Are there not times when we just have to rest in the faithfulness of God? - Knowing that God is too wise to make mistakes, too loving to be unkind, too powerful to be denied in His purpose.

Well, that is the Prologue. Then there is:

(2) THE DIALOGUE: Job's Debate - Chapters 4-37

Look at Chapter 2 verse 11. When they heard of his situation, Job's three friends came to him. Times of prosperity bring out people who want to be your friend. Times of adversity show the true colour of those you thought were your friends. So along came Job's friends. We can almost picture Job as he saw them coming. He must have groaned. He knew these men, knew them only too well. They would say that they had come to *sympathize,* but they really had come to *scrutinize* and then to *sermonize.*

Now the discussions between Job and his three friends go in three cycles. Eliphaz, Bildad and Zophar take turns in presenting their arguments. Right after each contribution, there is an account of Job's reply. One friend speaks: Job replies. The second friend speaks: Job replies. The third friend speaks: Job replies. This procedure is followed three times, except that in the final round Zophar does not offer any further contribution. Instead, Job makes a final response to all three friends.

Now these debates at times are heated and they centre around futile speculations concerning the mystery of suffering. The arguments presented by Job's three friends are basically the same. They say: *"Job, we know what your problem is. There is sin in your life!"* They were, in effect, saying Job's great suffering was because Job was a great sinner and a great hypocrite. Now let's look at:

(a) THE OLD FRIENDS

You see, all three of them were old (see Job 32:6). They were older than Job (see Job 15:10), and we assume from the order in Chapter 2 verse 11 that Eliphaz was the oldest; Bildad was the second oldest and Zophar was the youngest of the three. Note in:

(a) Eliphaz: Voice of Philosophy: Mysticism

Eliphaz is the type of person who tries to help you in your troubles by telling you about his experiences. He is the man with the exotic experience. He liked to talk about spirits and visions. Do you see what he says in Chapter 4 verses 12 to 17? He claims that God gave him a vision or experience. If you have not had his experience, then you evidently have missed out in your spiritual life. No doubt he has many spiritual heirs in the church today! Eliphaz suggested that Job must have been a great sinner, otherwise these things would not have happened to him. Listen to what he says: *"Remember, I pray thee, who ever perished, being innocent? Or where were the righteous cut off? Even as I have seen, they that plow iniquity, and sow wickedness, reap the same"* (Job 4:7-8).

(b) Bildad: Voice of History: Traditionalism

Bildad has been described as *"the champion of orthodoxy"*. He is *"the look to the past"* type. (See Job 8:8-10). Bildad supposed that Job was a sinner (Job 8:3, 6 and 11-13). He is pitiless in his approach - for he was the only one to mention Job's children (see Job 8:4). He was the kind of person who has a pat answer, a pet proverb and a pertinent verse for every occasion.

(c) Zophar: Voice of Orthodoxy: Legalism

Zophar was callous. You see, he bluntly said that Job was a sinner and he said it in the harshest of terms. Look at his cutting speech in Chapter 11 verses 5 and 6, culminating in: *"God exacteth of thee less than thine iniquity deserveth"*. Do you see what he is saying? *"Job, if you were getting what you deserved, you would not only be diseased, you'd be dead, and not only dead, but damned! You'd be in hellfire at this moment!"*

Now, all these three men are committed to the same theory of life, namely that suffering is always the direct outcome of sin. You see, they believed in a ***"health and wealth gospel"***. They believed that if a man loved the Lord enough and trusted the Lord enough, he would be healthy, wealthy, and wise. Their theology taught that suffering is always a result of sin. In effect, they believed that *if you are not rich, then you are not right; if you are not healthy, then you are not holy.*

I want to stress that I believe if you are a child of God, you are going to suffer if you sin. David, for example, suffered. He suffered physically, emotionally, domestically and spiritually. For twelve months he carried around in his heart unconfessed sin. Then, in Psalm 51, he beats out his confession and he says: *"Make me to hear joy and gladness; that the bones which Thou hast broken may rejoice"* (Psalm 51:8). You see, if you are bound to sin, you are bound to suffer. Suffering follows sin, just as night follows day. But, listen carefully: *Even though sin always causes suffering, suffering is not always caused by sin.* (See John 9:3) The Lord Jesus never sinned, but He suffered more than any other man in history. You see, suffering is not always a sign that you are *not* right with God. In

Job's case, it was a sign that he *was* right with God. *God did not pick on a sinning man. God picked on a sanctified man.*

Now, what Job's so-called ***'friends'*** were really saying was this: *"If you would be like us and be as good as we are, you would not be suffering. Because you are suffering, there must be some real sin in your life"*. Do you know what Job called his three friends? Job called them: *"miserable comforters"* (Job 16:2). They were the greatest help when they said nothing! When you go to sympathize with a person, be careful not to sermonize.

When Job's three friends had finished, Job replied. He made a number of speeches and in those speeches he basically said that God was responsible for his suffering, and that he had sought to live pure in God's sight. So now the Old Friends step aside and,

(b) THE YOUNG FRIEND

Takes the stage. Now, Elihu is on better ground than the other friends. The other three had kept harping on about some supposed sin in the past. Elihu, by contrast, is concerned with a wrong attitude in the present. Job's actions may have been right. He was *not the sinner* his three friends described him to be, but his attitude was wrong. He was *not the saint* Job saw himself to be. Job was slowly moving toward a defiant, self-righteous attitude that was not at all healthy. It was this *"know it all"* attitude that God exposed and destroyed when He revealed Himself to Job. That brings us to the final section of the book:

(3) <u>THE EPILOGUE: Job's Deliverance: Chapters 38-42</u>

Job had challenged God. He had said: *"Then call Thou, and I will answer: or let me speak and answer Thou me"* (Job 13:22). God now responded to Job's challenge. In Chapter 38, the court of Heaven is called to order. The audience is called to rise as the gavel goes down on the bench, and God shows up and speaks up.

Dr James Merritt from the U.S.A. whose work I continually draw from brings out four pertinent points. Firstly:

(a) *GOD REVEALED JOB'S FAULT*

For 37 chapters, the Lord is silent. Throughout all of Job's questions, the Lord has remained silent. He just watches and listens. But then, beginning at Chapter 38, God hurls a series of majestic questions at Job concerning the wonders of creation. You see, the answer to Job's problems was not an *explanation* from God, but a *revelation* of God. When God displayed His majesty and power, it humbled Job and brought him to a place of silent submission before God. That was the turning point.

Warren Wiersbe says:

"The whole purpose of this interrogation was to make Job realise his own inadequacy and inability to meet God as an equal and defend his cause."

You see, the Lord gives Job a test, a quiz, and he missed every question. First of all God reminds Job of:

1. His Pre-eminence

God says: *"Where wast thou when I laid the foundations of the earth? declare, if thou hast understanding"* (Job 38:4). He said: *"Job, I created this world. I can do anything in it and through it that I choose to do"*.

2. His Power

Job confesses: *"I know that Thou canst do every thing"* (Job 42:2). Job now understands that God not only has the *right* to do everything, but He has the *resource* to do everything. God sets the record straight once and for all. Job is reminded of how little he is and how big God is.

God asks:
"Where wast thou when I laid the foundations of the earth?" (Job 38:4)
"Hast thou commanded the morning since thy days?" (Job 38:12)
"Doth the eagle mount up at thy command?" (Job 39:27)

Job could not answer a single question. In effect, God was saying to Job: *"Job, you have had a great deal to say about things. But you do not know how I do things in the material universe, so how can you possibly know how I do things in the moral and spiritual universe?"*

3. His Purpose

Job says: *"I know that ... no thought can be withholden from Thee"* (Job 42:2). Now Job understands that not only has God the *right* to do anything and the *resource* to do anything, but He has a *reason* for what He does. God has a purpose and a plan for your life - and for this universe. Do you know something? When God finishes talking with him, Job says: *"I have heard of Thee by the hearing of the ear: but now mine eye seeth Thee. Wherefore I abhor myself, and repent in dust and ashes" (Job 42:5-6).* You see, the bottom line is that imperfect man has no right to question the motives and methods of a perfect God. *"Job, just because you don't see Me, you can't hear Me and you're not able to understand Me, doesn't mean that I am any less God. I am the One who created it all, controls it all, conducts it all and completes it all."*

(b) GOD RENEWED HIS FELLOWSHIP

God accepts Job. (See Job 42:8) Indeed, Job is brought to the point where he rests in God Himself - apart from explanations. Do you need to be brought there? Like Job, have you been questioning God? Arguing with God? Debating with God? Do you not realise that *God is too kind to do anything cruel, too wise to make a mistake and too deep to explain Himself.*

(c) GOD REBUKED HIS FRIENDS

Do you remember Eliphaz, the voice of *Philosophy* that said: "Job, you're a Foolish Heathen?" Do you remember Bildad, the voice of *History* that said: "Job, you're a Fake Hypocrite?" Do you remember Zophar, the voice of *Orthodoxy* that said: "Job, you're a Fortunate Human?" Well, they are back in Job. They re-appear in Chapter 42. Do you see verses 7 and 8? These three men have played the part of spiritual know-it-alls in their critique of Job's life. Job has been down, and they have kicked him while he was down. Now the Lord says: *"My wrath is kindled against you. Get Job to pray for you"*. Can you picture it? They walk up to Job, clear their throats and say: *"Brother Job, uh, would you mind praying for us?"* What a turn of events. We are reminded of the words of the Lord Jesus in Matthew 5 verses 44-45: *"Love your enemies, bless them that curse you, do good to them that hate you, and pray for them which despitefully use you, and persecute you; that ye may be the children of your Father which is in Heaven"*.

If people are talking about you, mistreating you, tearing you down, discouraging you, or accusing you, you need not race to the telephone and talk to Mr. Forked-Tongue, or Mrs. Dirty-Laundry Lips. You need to talk to the Lord about it. Charles Stanley, an outstanding Bible teacher in the U.S.A, said that when he was being unfairly criticised at a point in his ministry, he learned that people cannot fight three things. *They cannot fight silence. They cannot fight prayer. They cannot fight love.* Did you know that the greatest way to handle criticism is not to handle it all, but to let God handle it?

(d) GOD RESTORED HIS FORTUNE

"And the LORD turned the captivity of Job, when he prayed for his friends: also the LORD gave Job twice as much as he had before" (Job 42:10). He had double the number of sheep, camels, oxen and asses – but only the same number of children that he originally had. Can I suggest that the reason Job did not receive double the number of children is because he did not lose the first children. They were dead, but not lost. Job knew exactly where they were. In glory!

Someone has well said: ***"God often digs the wells of joy with the spades of sorrow"***. That is true. *All's well that ends well*! The book of Job tells us that eventually, whether here on earth or up in Heaven, all will end well for the child of God.

You may never know the reason, but when you cannot trace God's hand, you can trust God's heart.

Have you ever read the remarkable novel *"Treasure Island"* by Robert Louis Stevenson? His father was a chief engineer, establishing lighthouses up and down the coast of Scotland. While he was just a boy, his father took him on an ocean voyage inspecting the lighthouses along the coast of England. They were not out for long when a terrible storm came upon them. For over 24 hours, they fought for their lives. During the course of the storm, the father made his way to the top deck, telling his son to stay below in the cabin. There was only one man up there, the captain of the ship. The storm was so fierce that he had taken a rope and strapped himself to the mast of the ship in case he would be swept overboard. When the father made it to where the captain was, he took one long look into the face of the captain. Without saying a word, he went back downstairs to his cabin.

When his little boy saw him, he said: *"Daddy, are we going to drown? Is the ship going down?"*

His father picked him up in his arms, held him close and said: *"No! We are going to make it through the storm".*

"But, Daddy, how can you be so sure?"

"I looked into the captain's face and everything is going to be all right!"

Job looked into the face of the captain of his salvation and realised that he could endure the storm of suffering.

I can just imagine Job, years later, sitting on the front porch of his house, talking to his grandchildren, and he recounts to them all the things that the Lord had taught him in that time in his life. All of a sudden he bursts out into a song:

"I've had many tears and sorrows,
I've had questions for tomorrow,
There've been times I didn't know right from wrong:
But in every situation, God gave blessed consolation,
That my trials come to only make me strong.

Through it all, through it all,
I've learned to trust in Jesus,
I've learned to trust in God.
Through it all, through it all,
I've learned to depend upon His Word.

I thank God for the mountains,
And I thank Him for the valleys,
I thank Him for the storms He brought me through:
For if I'd never had a problem, I wouldn't know that He could solve them,
I'd never know what faith in God could do."

Will you do that? Trust in God and depend upon His Word?

CHAPTER 2

Psalms

Throughout history, when the hearts of God's people have been right before Him, there has been singing and music. When God brought His people out of captivity in Egypt and delivered them from Pharaoh's pursuing army, they sang a song to the Lord (Exodus 15:1). When God gave Israel victory over Jabin, the king of Canaan, under the leadership of Deborah and Barak, they sang (Judges 5:1). When David brought up the ark of the covenant into Jerusalem, there was much joy expressed through singing and music (1 Chronicles 15:25-28). When King Hezekiah restored the Temple worship in Jerusalem, the Levites sang praises to the Lord (2 Chronicles 29:30). At the conclusion of the Lord's Supper, just before Christ and the disciples went out to the Mount of Olives where He would be betrayed and arrested, they sang a hymn (Mark 14:26), which commentators agree was the Hallel - Psalms 113-118. When Paul and Silas were unjustly thrown into jail in Philippi, with their backs beaten and their feet in the stocks, they sang hymns of praise to God (Acts 16:25).

Since the days of the New Testament, God's people have continued to sing. In A.D. 112, Pliny wrote a letter to the Emperor Trajan which reported, among other things, that the Christians sang hymns *"to Christ as God"*. A Psalm was the expression of joy uttered by Augustine at his conversion and a Psalm was the consolation on his lips as he lay on his deathbed. John Chrysostom comforted himself in exile by quoting the Psalms. John Huss had a Psalm on his lips as he was burned at the stake. Reciting a Psalm, Luther entered the Diet of Worms prepared to defy the church and stand by faith alone. The great revivals under the Wesleys in the 18th Century and under Moody and Sankey in the 19th Century were also marked by an upsurge in hymn-writing and singing. One day in Heaven, we will all be gathered around the throne of God, singing praises to the Lamb that was slain (Rev. 5:9; 14:3 and 15:3).

Whenever God's people have their hearts right before Him, there has been, there is, and there will be singing and music. *It should come as no surprise, then, that the longest book in the Bible, the Old Testament book quoted most frequently in the New Testament, is a hymn-book, the book of Psalms.* God loves to hear His people sing His praises and so He included the Psalms as a major part of His inspired Word.

The book of Psalms is probably the most loved and the best known part of the Bible. This book has been valued throughout the history of the church. Martin Luther called it: *"a Bible in miniature"*. He said: *"In the Psalms we look into the heart of every saint"*. John Calvin declared: *"In the Psalms, we look into a mirror and see our own heart"*. A.C. Gaebelein used to say: *"A Psalm a day keeps worry away"*. A modern commentator put it this way: *"Every Psalm seems to have my name and address on it"*.

The book of Psalms is the book of human emotions. No matter what mood you may be in, there is a Psalm to give expression to that mood. The book of Psalms is the hymn book and prayer book of Israel in the Old Testament. The Psalms is probably the most unusual book of the Bible. For example:

The Psalms is the largest book in the Bible, containing 150 Psalms.

Psalm 119 is the longest chapter in the Bible. Containing 176 verses, it has more verses than many other short books of the Bible.

Psalm 117 is the shortest chapter of the Bible, containing only two verses. It's also the middle chapter of the Bible, the very centre of the 1189 chapters found in Genesis through Revelation. The book of Psalms is written by more authors than any other book in the Bible.

The Psalms is the most quoted Old Testament book in the New

Testament. There are 360 Old Testament quotations in the New Testament. Do you know how many are from the Psalms? 112 are from the book of Psalms.

The book of Psalms contains more Messianic prophecies than any other Old Testament book, other than possibly Isaiah.

It reveals the Messiah, the Lord Jesus as the Son of God (Psalm 2) and Son of Man (Psalm 8). It speaks about Him in His obedience (Psalm 40:6-8); betrayal (Psalm 41:9); crucifixion (Psalm 22); resurrection (Psalm 16); ascension (Psalm 68:18) and enthronement (Psalm 110).

No wonder various Christians have said: *"This is the book where I have found help in the crises of life"* and *"If I could only take one book of the Bible with me to a desert island, it would be the book of Psalms"*.

Like a hymn book, the Psalms is very difficult to analyse, but let us notice firstly:

(1) THE TITLE - THE PSALMS

(a) THE HEBREW TITLE

The Hebrew title is *"Tehillim"* which means **"Praises"**. Another Hebrew title is *"Tephiloth"* which means **"Prayers"**. This title is taken from Psalm 72 verse 20 where we read: *"The prayers of David the son of Jesse are ended"*. So, Psalms is both a hymn book and a prayer book. It can be used in private life or public worship. It shows the saint on his knees in every mood of life, amidst trials and triumphs, burdens and blessings. Although sometimes he is penitent, sometimes pleading, sometimes praising, he is nevertheless always praying and so should we. So the entire collection of Psalms is entitled *"Praises"* in the Hebrew text. But:

(b) THE GREEK TITLE

The Septuagint (LXX), the Greek translation of the Old Testament, labelled it: *"Psalms"* (See Luke 20:42 and Acts 1:20). The word *"psalms"* comes from a Greek word which means *"the plucking of strings"*. It means a song to be sung to the accompaniment of a plucked or stringed instrument such as a harp or lyre. So, the Psalms is a collection of worship songs sung to God by the people of Israel with musical accompaniment. This collection of 150 Psalms constituted Israel's ancient God-breathed (2 Timothy 3:16) *"hymn book"* which defined the proper spirit and content of worship. The Psalms is the *"book of Praises"* given to assist believers in the proper worship of God. This book is the irreplaceable devotional guide, prayer book and hymnal of the people of God. Note, then, the title of the book: The Psalms.

(2) THE TIMING OF THE PSALMS

Can we put this book of Psalms into some sort of historical setting? Well, the Psalms cover a long period of Jewish history - from the time of Moses about 1410 B.C. to the time of the return from the Babylonian exile about 430 B.C. So these Psalms were composed over a span of almost 1,000 years. You see, we can ascertain the timing of these Psalms by:

(a) THE BACKGROUND

Look at Psalm 90 verse 1. Now do you see here the superscription at the beginning? **"A Prayer of Moses the man of God."** About 116 Psalms have a superscription like this. The superscription can identify its author, historical context and how it should be sung. Although these superscriptions were not part of the original text, they are considered accurate and reliable. Psalm 90 was probably the first Psalm written. It was composed by Moses during Israel's forty years of wilderness wanderings - 1445-1405 B.C. - perhaps around 1410 B.C.

Psalm 90 is likely the first Psalm, but what was the last Psalm? Look at Psalm 126. Do you see the opening verse? *"When the LORD turned again the captivity of Zion, we were like them that dream."* This is thought to have been recorded after the time of Israel's Babylonian captivity, during their return to the land of Judah about 430 BC. So the first Psalm was composed by Moses;

the last Psalm recorded after Israel's time in Babylon. But the vast majority of Psalms were written during the Kingly reigns of David (1020-970 B.C.) and Solomon (970-931 B.C.) around 1000 B.C.

Can you see the span of years that are covered by the Psalms? From about 1400 B.C. - the time of Moses - to about 430 B.C. - the time of Ezra.

So we can see the timing of these Psalms by considering the *Background* but also by considering:

(b) THE BOOKS

The book of Psalms is actually five books in one and divides into five sections, every one with its own theme. Each of these five books in the book of Psalms ends with a doxology and each corresponds to the five books of Moses. So, sometimes folk refer to the book of Psalms as *"the Pentateuch of David"*, because they are thought to mirror the first five books of the Bible, which are known as *"the Pentateuch of Moses"*.

The Hebrew scholar Delitzsch has said: *"The Psalter is also a Pentateuch, the echo of the Mosaic Pentateuch, from the heart of Israel. It is the fivefold book of the congregation to Jehovah as the Law is the fivefold book of Jehovah to the congregation."*

So what are we saying? We are saying that these five books of the Psalms correspond to the first five books of Moses. Let us consider this for a moment.

Book 1: Psalm 1 to 41
Do you see how Book 1 ends with a doxology? Psalm 41 verse 13: *"Blessed be the LORD God of Israel from everlasting, and to everlasting. Amen, and Amen"*. Now because this first book highlights God's power in creation (for example, Psalms 8 and 19) and is dominated by the theme of sin and salvation, it is easy to see how it could correspond to the book of *Genesis*.

Book 2: Psalm 42 to 72
Do you see how Book 2 ends? Psalm 72 verse 19: *"Blessed be His glorious name for ever: and let the whole earth be filled with His glory; Amen and Amen"*. Bible scholars have noted that this second book of Psalms focuses on Israel's ruin and redemption and this can be said to correspond to the book of *Exodus,* which tells us about Israel's redemption from Egyptian bondage.

Book 3: Psalm 73 to 89
Do you see how Book 3 ends? Psalm 89 verse 52: *"Blessed be the LORD for evermore. Amen, and Amen"*. The Psalms in Book 3 concentrate primarily on the holiness of Israel's sanctuary - and this coincides with the concern of the book of *Leviticus* with the tabernacle and holiness.

Book 4: Psalm 90 to 106
Do you see how Book 4 ends? Psalm 106 verse 48: *"Blessed be the LORD God of Israel from everlasting to everlasting: and let all the people say, Amen. Praise ye the LORD"*. Now, these Psalms clearly correspond to *Numbers,* the fourth book of Moses. This group of Psalms begins with the one written by Moses and ends with one that recounts Israel's rebellions in the wilderness.

Book 5: Psalm 107 to 150
Do you how Book 5 ends? Psalm 150 verse 6: *"Let every thing that hath breath praise the LORD. Praise ye the LORD"*. Now this fifth book focuses on the sufficiency of God's Word (Psalm 119) and the universal praise of God's name (Psalm 146-150). Is this not the emphasis of the book of *Deuteronomy* which is the fifth book of Moses? It is all about God and His Word.

So the book of Psalms is actually five hymn books grouped together. But, who wrote these Psalms? Well, Psalms is one of the rare books of the Bible written by several people. They wrote from many different experiences of life. For example, *David, "the sweet psalmist of Israel"* (2 Samuel 23:1) is the chief author of the Psalms. He is credited with writing 75 of the 150 Psalms. (Compare Psalm 2 with Acts 4:25 and Psalm 95 with Hebrews 4:7.) The *sons of Korah,* a guild of singers, are also credited with writing ten psalms - Psalms 42, 44-

49, 84-85 and 87. *Asaph,* a priest who served as a worship leader of ancient Israel, wrote twelve Psalms - Psalms 50 and 73-83. *Solomon* also wrote some Psalms - Psalms 72 and 127. Quite a number of the Psalms are anonymous, though *Ezra,* who was a scribe and priest of Israel, is thought to be the author of some of the anonymous Psalms. Now, as we have seen, many of these Psalms have roots which are deep in Hebrew history so one good way of studying them is to observe the circumstances that gave them birth.

(3) THE TYPES OF PSALMS

There are three basic ways to study the Psalms:

1. By Book Division

We have seen that each of the five books ends with a doxology.

2. By Authorship

We have noted that the Psalms have a variety of authors.

3. By Subject Matter

We can classify certain Psalms according to their subject matter. For example, there are:

(a) THE DEVOTIONAL PSALMS

These contain personal and precious promises which all believers can feed upon. These Psalms include both sobbing and singing. The authors at times will pout, doubt and shout! Here the naked soul of man is revealed as perhaps in no other writings.

Let us look for a moment at Psalm 13:

"How long wilt Thou forget me, O LORD? for ever? how long wilt Thou hide Thy face from me?
2 How long shall I take counsel in my soul, having sorrow in my heart daily? how long shall mine enemy be exalted over me?

3 Consider and hear me, O LORD my God: lighten mine eyes, lest I sleep the sleep of death;
4 Lest mine enemy say, I have prevailed against him; and those that trouble me rejoice when I am moved.
5 But I have trusted in Thy mercy; my heart shall rejoice in Thy salvation.
6 I will sing unto the LORD, because He hath dealt bountifully with me."

Do you ever feel like that? That the Lord has forgotten or forsaken you? One popularly-held misconception about the Bible is that its heroes were men who differed entirely from other men. They never suffered defeat; they never became discouraged; they were at all times successful, saintly and supremely happy. Nothing could be further from the truth! The fact is that all of them were *"subject to like passions as we are"* (James 5:17). These men all bore the bitter burden of defeat. They were at times overwhelmed with despair.

Look at Psalm 56. Do you see verse 8? *"Thou tellest my wanderings: put Thou my tears into Thy bottle: are they not in Thy book?"* Fancy that! God puts our tears into His bottle. You see, when Jewish people wanted to express their sympathy at the death of someone they loved, they did not send flowers or wreaths to the funeral. *Do you know what they did?* They had glass bottles about four inches high which they could hold under their eyes and weep into. They would then send the bottle of tears to the bereaved relatives as an expression of sympathy. Do you know something? God is able to do the same for us. God puts your tears into His bottle. He sympathises with you. Burdened believer, do you realize that:

Standing somewhere in the shadows you'll find Jesus,
He's the Friend who always cares and understands.
Standing somewhere in the shadows you will find Him
And you'll know Him by the nail prints in His hands.

(b) THE PENITENTIAL PSALMS

These are the Psalms of penitence or the "sorry psalms". Psalms 6, 32, 38, 51, 102, 130 and 143 are all penitential Psalms. Look at the best known of them - Psalm 51.

"Have mercy upon me, O God, according to Thy lovingkindness:
according unto the multitude of Thy tender mercies blot out my
transgressions.
2 *Wash me throughly from mine iniquity, and cleanse me from my sin.*
3 *For I acknowledge my transgressions: and my sin is ever before me.*
4 *Against Thee, Thee only, have I sinned, and done this evil in Thy*
sight: that Thou mightest be justified when Thou speakest, and be clear
when Thou judgest.
5 *Behold, I was shapen in iniquity; and in sin did my mother conceive*
me.
6 *Behold, Thou desirest truth in the inward parts: and in the hidden part*
Thou shalt make me to know wisdom.
7 *Purge me with hyssop, and I shall be clean: wash me, and I shall be*
whiter than snow.
8 *Make me to hear joy and gladness; that the bones which Thou hast*
broken may rejoice.
9 *Hide Thy face from my sins, and blot out all mine iniquities.*
10 *Create in me a clean heart, O God; and renew a right spirit within*
me.
11 *Cast me not away from Thy presence; and take not Thy holy Spirit*
from me.
12 *Restore unto me the joy of Thy salvation; and uphold me with Thy*
free Spirit.
13 *Then will I teach transgressors Thy ways; and sinners shall be*
converted unto Thee.
14 *Deliver me from bloodguiltiness, O God, Thou God of my salvation:*
and my tongue shall sing aloud of Thy righteousness.
15 *O Lord, open Thou my lips; and my mouth shall shew forth Thy*
praise.
16 *For Thou desirest not sacrifice; else would I give it: Thou delightest*
not in burnt offering.
17 *The sacrifices of God are a broken spirit: a broken and a contrite heart,*
O God, Thou wilt not despise.
18 *Do good in Thy good pleasure unto Zion: build Thou the walls of*
Jerusalem.
19 *Then shalt Thou be pleased with the sacrifices of righteousness, with*
burnt offering and whole burnt offering: then shall they offer bullocks
upon Thine altar."

Do you know what this is all about? The consequences of sin in the life of a believer! When a Christian sins, it affects him spiritually and mentally and physically. Look at verse 8 and then verse 12. David did not say: *"Restore unto me Thy salvation"*. He had not lost his salvation, but he did lose the joy of it. *You see, when God saved you, He did not fix you up so that you could not sin anymore. He just fixed you up so that you could not sin and enjoy it.* The most miserable man on earth is not an unsaved man. The most miserable man on earth is a man out of fellowship with God. He has lost the joy.

Dr Adrian Rogers asks: How would you like to take a test and find out if you are backslidden or not? Is there in your heart this moment *"joy unspeakable and full of glory"*? There is only one thing that can take the joy out of your heart. Not two, or three, or four, but one. What? Sin! Furthermore, only one kind of sin. Would you like to know what kind? Yours! *"Make me to hear joy and gladness"* (verse 8). When there is unconfessed sin in our lives, nothing we hear sounds good. We attend church and we lash out. The singing was flat; the leaders were unfriendly, the preacher was too long. Everything we hear is wrong. Do you know why? It's because *we* are wrong. *You* are wrong. The joy is gone. I wonder, do you need to pray? *"Restore unto me the joy of Thy salvation."*

(c) THE IMPRECATORY PSALMS

To *imprecate* is to *pray against* or to *invoke evil* on someone or something. Some of the Psalms that fall into this category are Psalms 35, 55, 58 and 59. There are many more. Look at Psalm 35.

"Plead my cause, O LORD, with them that strive with me: fight against them that fight against me.
2 Take hold of shield and buckler, and stand up for mine help.
3 Draw out also the spear, and stop the way against them that persecute me: say unto my soul, I am thy salvation.
4 Let them be confounded and put to shame that seek after my soul: let them be turned back and brought to confusion that devise my hurt.
5 Let them be as chaff before the wind: and let the angel of the LORD chase them.

[6] *Let their way be dark and slippery: and let the angel of the LORD*
persecute them.
[7] *For without cause have they hid for me their net in a pit, which*
without cause they have digged for my soul.
[8] *Let destruction come upon him at unawares; and let his net that he*
hath hid catch himself: into that very destruction let him fall.
[9] *And my soul shall be joyful in the LORD: it shall rejoice in His*
salvation.
[10] *All my bones shall say, LORD, who is like unto Thee, which*
deliverest the poor from him that is too strong for him, yea, the poor and
the needy from him that spoileth him?
[11] *False witnesses did rise up; they laid to my charge things that I knew*
not.
[12] *They rewarded me evil for good to the spoiling of my soul.*
[13] *But as for me, when they were sick, my clothing was sackcloth: I*
humbled my soul with fasting; and my prayer returned into mine own
bosom.
[14] *I behaved myself as though he had been my friend or brother: I bowed*
down heavily, as one that mourneth for his mother.
[15] *But in mine adversity they rejoiced, and gathered themselves together:*
yea, the abjects gathered themselves together against me, and I knew it
not; they did tear me, and ceased not:
[16] *With hypocritical mockers in feasts, they gnashed upon me with their teeth.*
[17] *Lord, how long wilt Thou look on? rescue my soul from their*
destructions, my darling from the lions.
[18] *I will give Thee thanks in the great congregation: I will praise Thee*
among much people.
[19] *Let not them that are mine enemies wrongfully rejoice over me:*
neither let them wink with the eye that hate me without a cause.
[20] *For they speak not peace: but they devise deceitful matters against*
them that are quiet in the land.
[21] *Yea, they opened their mouth wide against me, and said, Aha, aha,*
our eye hath seen it.
[22] *This Thou hast seen, O LORD: keep not silence: O Lord, be not far*
from me.
[23] *Stir up Thyself, and awake to my judgment, even unto my cause, my*
God and my Lord.
[24] *Judge me, O LORD my God, according to Thy righteousness; and let*
them not rejoice over me.

25 Let them not say in their hearts, Ah, so would we have it: let them not say, We have swallowed him up.
26 Let them be ashamed and brought to confusion together that rejoice at mine hurt: let them be clothed with shame and dishonour that magnify themselves against me.
27 Let them shout for joy, and be glad, that favour my righteous cause: yea, let them say continually, Let the LORD be magnified, which hath pleasure in the prosperity of His servant.
28 And my tongue shall speak of Thy righteousness and of Thy praise all the day long."

Now some Christians have difficulty with these Psalms. They say: *"How can we reconcile these Psalms with the teaching of Christ?"* Did not the Lord Jesus say: *"Love your enemies, bless them that curse you, do good to them that hate you, and pray for them which despitefully use you, and persecute you"?* (Matthew 5:44) Therefore, people say: *"Why do these Psalms sound so violent, while the New Testament seems to talk about love and forgiveness?"* Well, if we put ourselves in the place of the Psalmist, we will see that the enemies he faced are the same enemies we face today. The New Testament tells us: *"We wrestle not against flesh and blood"* (Ephesians 6:12). Sometimes we forget who our real enemy is. We think that the person who opposes our plans, attacks our reputation or exasperates us in some way is our enemy. No, people may hurt us, but people are not our true enemies. Our battle is against *Satan* and his forces. A second foe is the *world*. Says John: *"Love not the world"* (1 John 2:15). Then there is another enemy we face, not external but internal. Do you know what it's called? *The flesh!* (Gal. 5:19). The flesh will war against us as long as we dwell in these mortal bodies. Now, do you see who our real enemy is? The world, the flesh and the devil. The world is our external enemy. The flesh is our internal enemy. The devil is our infernal enemy. Do we not need to deal severely with these enemies? Are these imprecatory Psalms not a picture of the way we must deal with the real enemies - Satan, the world system he controls and our own fallen flesh? So, there are devotional Psalms and penitential Psalms and imprecatory Psalms. Then there are:

(d) THE ASCENT PSALMS

"The Songs of Ascents" take in Psalms 120-134. Look for a moment at Psalm 121.

"A Song of degrees.

"I will lift up mine eyes unto the hills, from whence cometh my help.
2 My help cometh from the LORD, which made heaven and earth.
3 He will not suffer thy foot to be moved: He that keepeth thee will not slumber.
4 Behold, He that keepeth Israel shall neither slumber nor sleep.
5 The LORD is thy keeper: the LORD is thy shade upon thy right hand.
6 The sun shall not smite thee by day, nor the moon by night.
7 The LORD shall preserve thee from all evil: He shall preserve thy soul.
8 The LORD shall preserve thy going out and thy coming in from this time forth, and even for evermore."

Do you see the important words at the top of the Psalm? *"A Song of Degrees" or "A Song of Ascents"*. Now, what does that mean? Well, the Hebrew word *"Degrees"* or *"Ascents"* comes from a root that means *"to go up"*, as ascending a stairway. You see, in those ancient days, the Israelites would travel to Jerusalem – a city about 2700 feet in elevation - for the three annual feasts. (See Exodus 23:14-19). Coming from whatever distant town they called home, the pilgrims would make the long journey by foot, walking with their family and friends and enjoying their holiday travel. They were eager for good times in the Holy City, seeing friends again over the feast and making sacrifices to the Lord. *Now, as they journeyed to Jerusalem, they would sing these Psalms together.* Has your family ever enjoyed a sing-along during a holiday journey in the car? Have you ever sung on your way to church, preparing your hearts for worship? It must have been a great comfort for them to be reminded of God's care for them as they travelled. What about *our* spiritual journey? These Psalms are not limited to ancient history, but rather contain essential truths for our journey through this life, to our eternal home.

(e) THE HALLELUJAH PSALMS

These six Psalms – from Psalm 113 to Psalm 118 - known also as the *"Hallel Psalms"* were sung on the night of the Passover. The Jews sang Psalms 113 and 114 before the meal and before drinking the second festal cup. Then, at the close of the meal, at the time the fourth cup was filled, they sang Psalms 115 to 118. Can you picture the Lord Jesus at the head of the table, gazing into the wine that spoke so eloquently of His blood soon to be shed? Can you hear His rich voice as He raises the tune and rings out the words of Psalm 113?

"Praise ye the LORD. Praise, O ye servants of the LORD, praise the name of the Lord.
2 *Blessed be the name of the LORD from this time forth and for evermore.*
3 *From the rising of the sun unto the going down of the same the LORD'S name is to be praised.*
4 *The LORD is high above all nations, and His glory above the heavens.*
5 *Who is like unto the LORD our God, who dwelleth on high,*
6 *Who humbleth Himself to behold the things that are in heaven, and in the earth!*
7 *He raiseth up the poor out of the dust, and lifteth the needy out of the dunghill;*
8 *That He may set him with princes, even with the princes of His people.*
9 *He maketh the barren woman to keep house, and to be a joyful mother of children. Praise ye the LORD."*

Isaac Watts penned a hymn based on this Psalm:

Ye servants of the Almighty King,
In every age His praises sing,
Where'er the sun shall rise or set,
The nations shall His praise repeat.

Above the earth, beyond the sky,
Stands His high throne of majesty;
Nor time nor place His power restrain,
Nor bound His universal reign.

Which of the sons of Adam dare,
Or angels, with their God compare?
His glories how divinely bright,
Who dwells in uncreated light!

Behold His love! He stoops to view
What saints above and angels do;
And condescends yet more to know
The mean affairs of men below.

From dust and cottages obscure,
His grace exalts the humble poor;
Gives them the honour of His sons,
And fits them for their heav'nly thrones.

So do you see now that there are different types of Psalms?

The Lord Jesus sang Psalms in the Upper Room. He quoted them on the Cross. Accordingly, when we mediate on the Psalms, we are pondering pages loved by our Lord. Indeed, this brings us naturally to the fourth thing we want to say about the Psalms:

(4) THE TESTIMONY OF THE PSALMS

The Psalms testify of Christ. Do you remember what the Risen Lord said to His disciples in the Upper Room? *"All things must be fulfilled which were written in the law of Moses, and in the prophets, and in the psalms, concerning Me"* (Luke 24:44). The Psalms reveal the person and work of Jesus Christ. Such Psalms are called the **Messianic Psalms** and there are about fifteen of them.

As Irving Jensen says:

"Some of the Old Testament's most minute prophecies of Christ are found here. They are about His person (God and man); His character (righteous and holy); His work (death and resurrection) and His offices (priest, judge and king)".

These Messianic Psalms foretell the two comings of Christ. They speak about:

(a) CHRIST'S COMING TO REDEEM

Look at Psalm 22. It begins:

"My God, my God, why hast Thou forsaken Me? why art Thou so far from helping Me, and from the words of My roaring?
2 *O My God, I cry in the day time, but Thou hearest not; and in the night season, and am not silent.*
3 *But Thou art holy, O Thou that inhabitest the praises of Israel.*
4 *Our fathers trusted in Thee: they trusted, and Thou didst deliver them.*
5 *They cried unto Thee, and were delivered: they trusted in Thee, and were not confounded.*
6 *But I am a worm, and no man; a reproach of men, and despised of the people.*
7 *All they that see Me laugh Me to scorn: they shoot out the lip, they shake the head, saying,*
8 *He trusted on the LORD that He would deliver Him: let Him deliver Him, seeing He delighted in Him.*
9 *But Thou art He that took Me out of the womb: Thou didst make Me hope when I was upon My mother's breasts.*
10 *I was cast upon Thee from the womb: Thou art My God from My mother's belly.*
11 *Be not far from Me; for trouble is near; for there is none to help."*

What a graphic picture we have here of crucifixion! Now, it is important to remember that Christ did not quote David. Rather, David quoted Christ, for the Spirit of Christ told David the words the Saviour would utter 1,000 years before the event. Is that not amazing? Moreover, is it not amazing that this Psalm speaks of *"pierced hands and feet"* (verse 16) centuries before the Romans used crucifixion as a method of execution? One of the greatest *"I am"* statements of Christ occurs in this Psalm. Do you see verse 6? *"But I am a worm, and no man."* Christ stooped so low to lift so little!

Surely as we read this Psalm, we have to say with the hymn writer:

"But none of the ransomed ever knew,
How deep were the waters crossed,
Nor how dark was the night that the Lord passed through,
Ere He found His sheep that was lost."

(b) CHRIST'S COMING TO REIGN

Psalm 16 prophesies His resurrection; Psalm 68 speaks of His ascension into Heaven; Psalm 110 speaks of the priesthood of Christ and Psalm 2 speaks of His coming to reign. Look at Psalm 2:

"Why do the heathen rage, and the people imagine a vain thing?
2 *The kings of the earth set themselves, and the rulers take counsel together, against the LORD, and against His anointed, saying,*
3 *Let us break Their bands asunder, and cast away Their cords from us.*
4 *He that sitteth in the heavens shall laugh: the Lord shall have them in derision.*
5 *Then shall He speak unto them in His wrath, and vex them in His sore displeasure.*
6 *Yet have I set My king upon My holy hill of Zion.*
7 *I will declare the decree: the LORD hath said unto Me, Thou art My Son; this day have I begotten Thee.*
8 *Ask of Me, and I shall give Thee the heathen for Thine inheritance, and the uttermost parts of the earth for Thy possession.*
9 *Thou shalt break them with a rod of iron; Thou shalt dash them in pieces like a potter's vessel.*
10 *Be wise now therefore, O ye kings: be instructed, ye judges of the earth.*
11 *Serve the LORD with fear, and rejoice with trembling.*
12 *Kiss the Son, lest He be angry, and ye perish from the way, when His wrath is kindled but a little. Blessed are all they that put their trust in Him."*

Here is a Psalm that predicts the destruction of the heathen in the time of the Tribulation, and the Millennial Reign of Jesus Christ.

Can you see here:

Christ's Sonship: Verse 7
Christ's Sovereignty: Verse 8
Christ's Severity: Verse 9

One moment the Beast will be strutting across the world and the armies of mankind will be drawn to Megiddo to oppose Christ's coming reign. It will be East and West and West against East, but all of them against Christ. The next moment the Beast and his armies will be gone and *"Jesus will reign!"*

What about:

(5) THE THEMES OF THE PSALMS

There are a number of themes that run throughout the Psalms. Let me limit myself to three. There is:

(a) THE WORSHIP OF GOD

The Psalms are all about the worship of God. Now what is worship? A.W. Tozer said: *"Worship is the missing jewel in the evangelical church"*. The English word *"worship"* derives from *"worth-ship"*, that is the one who is worthy. The Greek word *"axios"* meaning *"worthy, deserving"* was the cry of the spectators at the Greek games when the victor appeared. Surely we can re-echo the words of the twenty four elders in the book of Revelation: *"Thou art worthy, O Lord, to receive glory and honour and power: for Thou hast created all things, and for Thy pleasure they are and were created"* (Revelation 4:11). You see, God is to be worshipped:

1. For Who He is: His Attributes

The Psalms tell us a lot about God's *attributes*, that is – who He is. Do you recall verse 1 of Psalm 48? *"Great is the LORD, and greatly to be praised."* Do you know verse 1 of Psalm 115? *"Not unto us, O LORD, not unto us, but unto Thy name give glory, for Thy mercy, and for Thy truth's sake."* Do you recall Psalm 139? Here is a Psalm that describes God's *Omnipotence*: He is all-powerful. It describes God's *Omniscience*: He is all-knowing. It describes God's *Omnipresence*:

He is everywhere. As we prepare for worship, let us not forget who God is. Do you not think that if we were mindful of who God is, there would be a spirit of reverence among us?

2. <u>For What He has done: His Actions</u>

The Psalms tell us a lot about God's *actions,* that is - what He does. In verses 3 and 4 of Psalm 8, the Psalmist says: *"When I consider Thy heavens, the work of Thy fingers, the moon and the stars, which Thou hast ordained; What is man, that Thou art mindful of him?"* In Psalm 78 and verse 12, the Psalmist says: *"Marvellous things did He in the sight of their fathers, in the land of Egypt".* Continually we hear about two major acts in the Psalms - **Creation and Redemption**.

Now, is this not the benchmark of true worship? God is to be worshipped for Who He is and for What He has done. However, if modern day worship is to be judged by this criteria, there is a lamentable lack. So many modern songs are self-centred and experience-orientated. Then again, in conservative churches so often we exhibit a low view of worship when we rush through *"the preliminaries"* to reach the message as soon as possible. Do we not need to take time to *"be still and know that He is God" (Psalm 46:10)*?

(b) THE WALK WITH GOD

There are Psalms for every occasion of life.

If you are happy and want to express your *joy,* try Psalm 66.
If you are grateful and want to express your *thanks,* pray the words of Psalm 40.
If you are troubled by *fear,* read Psalm 91.
If you are *discouraged,* read Psalm 42.
If you feel *lonely,* read Psalm 62.
If you are *worried,* try Psalm 37.
If you are struggling with *bitterness,* try Psalm 94.
If you feel *forsaken,* immerse yourself in the comfort of Psalm 88.

Most people recognise Psalm 46 as the basis for Martin Luther's marvellous hymn: *"A Mighty Fortress is our God"*. That hymn was published in 1529 at a critical time in Martin Luther's life. You see, during the traumatic days of the Reformation, Luther often became discouraged, sufferings bouts of despair and even depression. The entire world he felt was against him. But, in those dark and difficult hours, he would turn to his co-worker Philip Melanchthon and say *"Come, Philip, let us sing the Psalms"*. They would often sing a version of Psalm 46 set to music.

> *"A sure stronghold our God is He,*
> *A timely shield and weapon,*
> *Our help He'll be and set us free,*
> *From every ill can happen."*

The Psalms encouraged, strengthened and fortified Luther in his daily walk with God.

Do you have trouble knowing how to *pray*? Well, take the Psalms and pray them back to God.

Do you have difficulty overcoming *doubt and depression*? Go and live for a while in the Psalms.

Do you have a fear of *death*? The Psalms will help you put death where it belongs.

Use the Psalms in your walk with God.

(c) THE WORD FROM GOD

The largest chapter in the Bible is Psalm 119, with its 176 verses. Here is a Psalm that extols the Word of God. There are twenty two sections with eight verses each. Each section begins with a different letter of the Hebrew alphabet. Here is a man who is bound to the Word of God, not by the chains of *law,* but by the magnetic attraction of *love*. You show me a man who loves the Lord and I will show you a man who loves the Word. Tell me, is the Bible your greatest treasure?

We have noticed that the Psalms fall into different groups. Let me give you a *"Psalm Sandwich"* as we conclude our examination of the book of Psalms. You see Psalms 22-24 form a very important group. They are like a sandwich - though people tend to lick the jam out and leave the bread! What do I mean? Well these three Psalms belong together:

Psalm 22 is the Psalm of the **Cross**.
Psalm 23 is the Psalm of the **Crook**.
Psalm 24 is the Psalm of the **Crown**.

In **Psalm 22** we see our **Substitute**.
In **Psalm 23** we see our **Shepherd**.
In **Psalm 24** we see our **Sovereign**.

In **Psalm 22** we see our Substitute as He **Pardons**.
In **Psalm 23** we see our Shepherd as He **Protects**.
In **Psalm 24** we see our Sovereign as He **Prevails**.

In **Psalm 22** we have the **Good Shepherd Dying** for the sheep.
In **Psalm 23** we have the **Great Shepherd Living** for the sheep.
In **Psalm 24** we have the **Chief Shepherd Coming** for the sheep.

In **Psalm 22** Christ died to care of the **Penalty** of sin.
In **Psalm 23** Christ rose to take care of the **Power** of sin.
In **Psalm 24** Christ is coming to take care of the **Presence** of sin.

In **Psalm 22** Christ takes care of our **Past**.
In **Psalm 23** He takes care of our **Present**.
In **Psalm 24** He takes care of our **Future**.

David could say: *"The Lord is my Shepherd ... and I will dwell in the house of the Lord for ever"*.

Does that not want to make you shout: *"Hallelujah, what a Saviour"*?

In the words of the Psalmist: *"Praise ye the LORD"* (Psalm 150:6).

CHAPTER 3

Proverbs

"Do you know of a good book of advice for young men?" a gentleman asked an aged pastor.

"Certainly", was his immediate reply, *"I recommend the book of Proverbs. It is full of truest wisdom and the most priceless helps for the conduct of life. It will decide every question, solve every problem, meet every perplexity, and help to build up a noble, manly Christian character."*

Now, as we approach this book, I want to think about:

ITS PROVERBS

Our English speaking world has many proverbs. Do you recall some of them? *"A stitch in time saves nine"*; *"Make hay while the sun shines"*; *"Look before you leap"* and *"A penny saved is a penny earned"*. We recognize these sayings instantly. They are proverbs - pithy sayings that in a few pungent words give the results of years of human experience. Our English word *"proverb"* is actually made up of two Latin words, *'pro'* ('instead of') and *'verba'* ('words'). So, a proverb is a sentence that is *"instead of many words"*. It is a short sentence that summarises a wise principle. The English word *'proverb'*, as the title of this book, is a translation of the Hebrew word *'mashal'* and *'mashal'* has been defined as *"a brief, pithy saying which expresses wisdom"*. But keep in mind that these proverbs are included in the literature which is *"given by inspiration of God"* (2 Timothy 3:16). This is wisdom from God!

These proverbs or maxims set out what is right and what is wrong in the sight of the Lord. They show the practical outworking of godliness in the spiritual, moral and social spheres. Here the wise man is the one who lives his life according to the revealed will of God. He walks in the way of truth and righteousness and consequently he is blessed by the Lord. You see, what Psalms is to our *devotional life,* Proverbs is meant to be to our *practical life.*

Psalms tells us how to *worship,* Proverbs tells us how to *walk.*

Psalms was the Hebrew *hymnbook,* Proverbs was the Hebrew *handbook.*

The one is chiefly concerned with *what I believe;* the other is chiefly concerned with *how I behave.*

It has been said:

"Here are laws from heaven for earth. Here are counsels from above for conduct here below. Here are the words of the wise on the ways of the world. Here is prudence through precept."

ITS PERSONALITIES

There are a number of personalities who are credited with uttering these proverbs. Do you see how the book begins? *"The proverbs of Solomon the son of David, king of Israel."* Likewise Chapter 10 begins: *"The proverbs of Solomon".* Yet again Chapter 25 begins: *"These are also proverbs of Solomon, which the men of Hezekiah ... copied out".* So the book itself testifies to the authorship of Solomon. It was King Solomon, son of King David who *"spake three thousand proverbs"* (1 Kings 4:32). From this vast number of proverbs, the Spirit of God led him to choose a much smaller collection for the instruction of believers in all ages. You see, Solomon was wiser than all the philosophers of his day. How did Solomon acquire this wisdom? Well, in the earlier days of his life, the Lord appeared to him at Gibeon and said: *"Ask what I shall give thee"* (1 Kings 3:5). Aware of the great responsibility of being a king over Israel, he said *"Give therefore Thy servant an understanding heart to judge Thy people, that I may discern between good and bad: for who is able to judge this Thy so great a people?"* (verse 9). The Lord was pleased with this request and responded by giving him *"a wise and an understanding heart"* (verse 12).

But other servants, guided by God's Spirit, were also involved in producing this book. *"The men of Hezekiah"* referred to at the start of Chapter 25 were a group of scholars in King Hezekiah's day who compiled the material in Chapters 25 to 29 and in Proverbs 30 and 31 you meet *"Agur the son of Jakeh"* and *"King Lemuel"* whom many scholars think was another name for Solomon. But most of this book came from the hand of Solomon.

Solomon thus wrote three books of the Bible:

He wrote the Song of Solomon when he was *young and in love.* It is a book of the **heart**.

He wrote Proverbs when he *was middle-aged and his intellectual powers were at their zenith.* It is a book of the **will**.

He wrote Ecclesiastes when he was *old, disappointed and disillusioned with the carnality of much of his life.* It is a book of the **mind**.

ITS PERIOD

King Solomon ruled Israel from 971-930 B.C. Taking into account *"the men of Hezekiah"* we are looking at a time period that spans from 971 to 686 B.C.

ITS PROBLEM

The problem is this. *Many of us have treated these proverbs as if they were promises.* You see, Hebrew proverbs are general statements of what is usually true in life - and they must not be treated like promises. For example, Proverbs 17 verse 17 says: *"A friend loveth at all times"*, but sometimes even the most devoted friends have disagreements. Take another proverb: *"A soft answer turneth away wrath"* (Proverbs 15:1). In most instances, this is true, but our Saviour's lamb-like gentleness did not deliver Him from shame and suffering.

Take another proverb: *"The fear of the LORD prolongeth days: but the years of the wicked shall be shortened"* (Proverbs 10:27). Generally speaking, this is true but some godly saints have died very young while more than one rebel has had a long life. David Brainerd, missionary to the American Indians, died at twenty-nine. Robert Murray McCheyne died just two months short of his thirtieth birthday. Henry Martyn, missionary to India and Persia, died at thirty one. William Borden, who gave away all his fortune to the work of the Lord, was only twenty five years of age when he died in Egypt on his way to China.

"The righteous is delivered out of trouble, and the wicked cometh in his stead" or *"and it comes on the wicked instead"* says Proverbs 11 verse 8. This certainly happened to Mordecai in Esther 7 and to those who accused Daniel in Daniel 6, but millions of Christian martyrs would testify to the fact that the statement is not an absolute in this life.

So, keep in mind that a proverb is not a promise. It is a guideline not a guarantee.

Now, this book of Proverbs falls into three main sections, each division beginning with the phrase: *"The proverbs of Solomon"*. Notice:

(1) THE FIRST SECTION OF THE BOOK - CHAPTERS 1 to 9

Proverbs is unusual among the books of the Bible in that it tells us why it was written. The prologue says that learning from proverbs will lead us to wisdom. Look at Chapter 1 verses 1 to 3. The theme of the book of Proverbs is **wisdom**.

Abraham Lincoln said on one occasion: *"I don't think much of a man who is not wiser today than he was yesterday"*. Surely one of the greatest needs of modern man is wisdom. Think about this for a moment. In many ways, our generation is the most prolific of all generations. We have more college graduates. In our day and age it is not enough to have a simple degree. It is increasingly important to have master's degrees to excel in our chosen professions.

Knowledge is exploding. We travel farther and fly higher than any previous generation in history. We accumulate data as never before. The computer age is advancing in such a way that information becomes outdated with virtually every passing minute.

But while such knowledge is increasing, wisdom is often lacking. Many lives are in shambles. Suicide rates are higher than ever before. Morals are at a record low. Divorce is ever on the increase. In many ways, the world is on the brink of chaos. And yet to such a generation the book of Proverbs says: Here is wisdom!

This first section of the book talks about:

(a) OUR WISDOM

Look at Chapter 2 verses 10 and 11: *"When wisdom entereth into thine heart, and knowledge is pleasant unto thy soul; discretion shall preserve thee, understanding shall keep thee"*. Now we commonly think of wisdom as the ability to use knowledge in the right way - and this is a practical definition. But, in the Bible, wisdom means so much more. It is a matter of the heart not the mind alone. It is a spiritual matter. There is a *"wisdom of this world"* (see 1 Corinthians 2:1-8 and James 3:13-18) and there is a divine wisdom from above. Well, what is wisdom? Look at the key verse that unlocks the book: *"The fear of the LORD is the beginning of knowledge"* (Proverbs 1:7). This statement is amplified in Chapter 9 verse 10: *"The fear of the LORD is the beginning of wisdom: and the knowledge of the holy is understanding"*.

Two major themes overlap in the book of Proverbs and they are ***wisdom*** and ***folly***. In the book of Proverbs, wisdom is actually pictured as a lovely woman who calls to men to follow her into a life of blessing and success. Folly is pictured as a wicked woman who tempts the foolish and leads them to Hell.

So what is wisdom? *"The fear of the LORD."* Fifteen times over, Solomon uses this phrase in his book. If we truly fear the Lord then we will acknowledge from our hearts that He is the Creator and we are the creatures; He is the Father and we are His children; He is the Master and we are the servants. Do you fear God like that? Do you respect Him for who He is? Do you listen carefully to what He says? Do you obey His Word? *"The fear of the LORD"* is not the fear that God might hurt us, but rather the fear that we might hurt Him. In other words, it is the fear that something we do might offend Him or grieve His loving heart. In this sense *"fear"* means reverence or respect - and it is this kind of loving respectful fear that is the beginning of wisdom.

Now please notice something important. ***The fear of the Lord is not the end of wisdom.*** It is not all that is required for being wise. It is only the beginning! True wisdom is not only built on the fear of the Lord. It is also built on the Word of the Lord.

Solomon was the wisest of men and yet in his latter years, he did not live out the wisdom he taught. In Solomon we see the fulfilment of the maxim which says: *"Do as I say, not as I do"*. Here we see him pleading with his son Rehoboam to pursue a life of godliness as he talks about:

(b) OUR WALK

Solomon says: *"My son, walk not thou in the way with them"* (Proverbs 1:15). You see, bad companionships lead to debased behaviour. When you read these opening chapters, it is like the advice of an affectionate father to his son before he goes up to the wicked city. Look at Chapter 2 verses 10 to 22. Did you ever say anything like that to your son or daughter? Did you ever say to them as they were about to start work or study in the city: *"There will be the bright lights, the evil companions, the sexual sins, the demon drink, the godless colleagues - keep close to the Lord, keep yourself pure and fear the Lord"*?

You see, this book presents wisdom as a ***moral*** choice rather than a ***mental*** one. When the world speaks of fools, it means people whose IQ is not very high. But, in the Bible, someone who is intelligent can be very foolish.

Someone can be mentally clever and morally silly.

Do you recall what the Devil told Eve? That eating the fruit would lead to wisdom, but in fact it only led to independence from God, the source of all wisdom. Worldly wisdom seeks to find the most profitable option, but Biblical wisdom seeks what is best for your character.

Look at Proverbs 6 verses 20 to 29. Today's society is permissive. John Phillips tells us that by the time the average American child has reached the age of eighteen, he has spent 20,000 hours before the television. That is more time than he spends at school. What is he watching? Drug and alcohol abuse, violence, sex, greed and gambling. Meanwhile, so many mothers are being brainwashed by the 'soaps' - and what are they watching? Abortion, pre-marital sex, extra-marital sex, drugs, and sexual perversion of every kind.

Do we not need to get back to the first nine chapters of the book of Proverbs? Do we not need to heed what is said about our wisdom and our walk? But, the book also speaks about:

(c) OUR WORDS

A key subject in the book of Proverbs is the tongue. Look at Chapter 6 verses 16 to 19: *"These six things doth the LORD hate: yea, seven are an abomination unto Him: A proud look, a lying tongue, and hands that shed innocent blood, An heart that deviseth wicked imaginations, feet that be swift in running to mischief, A false witness that speaketh lies, and he that soweth discord among brethren"*.

Go through the book of Proverbs sometime and write the dozen or more references to the phrase: *"abomination to the LORD"*. Do you see the things the Lord detests? Here are seven abominations to the Lord. Snobbery, lies, murder, conspiracy, mischief, perjury and gossip. The tongue figures in four of those. So sins of speech are a major topic throughout the book. What is in the heart comes out of the mouth. (See, for example, Proverbs 4:20-27 and 6:1-5) Do you know something? *Our tongues are a barometer of whether we are living a life that is pleasing to God or not.* The tongue is a dangerous weapon. Some believers use their tongues for *Blasting:* they gossip. Some use it for *Blistering:* they tear down others. Some use it for

Boasting. Few use it for Blessing. Have we not all at times used our tongues and said things that were unkind, unjust, untrue, unfair and unloving?

The story is told of a lady who was a notorious gossip. She would spend most of her day on the phone, sharing titbits with any and with all who would listen. She came to the pastor one day and said: *"The Lord has convicted me of my sin of gossip. My tongue is getting me and others into trouble."*

Well, the preacher knew she was not sincere - because she had gone through this routine before. Guardedly, he asked: *"What do you plan to do?" "I want to put my tongue on the altar"*, she replied. Calmly, he responded: *"There isn't an altar big enough!"*

Is it not time that your tongue was under the control of the Spirit of God? Then, Proverbs gives instructions about:

(d) OUR WORK

Do you know what they say? Enjoy hard work! We live in an age of benefits when it seems, at times, that laziness is encouraged and hard work is shunned. In this book of Proverbs, the idle man or woman is despised. Look at Chapter 6 verses 6 to 11 where the ant is used as an illustration and then comes the intimation: *"Yet a little sleep, a little slumber, a little folding of the hands to sleep: so shall thy poverty come"*. Later on, we read: *"The soul of the sluggard desireth, and hath nothing: but the soul of the diligent shall be made fat"* (Proverbs 13:4). Do you bring your best to your daily work? Do you *"do it heartily, as to the Lord, and not unto men"* (Colossians 3:23)?

(2) THE FURTHER SECTION OF THE BOOK - CHAPTERS 10 to 24

Now remember the three divisions come where the book ascribes the authorship to Solomon. Look at Chapter 10 verse 1: *"The proverbs of Solomon"*. Now this part of the book is full of advice about relationships especially family relationships. There are:

(a) ISSUES RELATING TO PARENTHOOD

Do you know the proverb? *"Spare the rod and spoil the child."* Where do you think it comes from? Let us examine the Holy Spirit's views on parental discipline. Look at Proverbs 13 verse 24: *"He that spareth his rod hateth his son: but he that loveth him chasteneth him betimes"*. To chasten means: *"carefully seeks discipline for him"*. Do you know what this book says? *"Foolishness is bound in the heart of a child; but the rod of correction shall drive it far from him"* (Chapter 22:15). *"Withhold not correction from the child: for if thou beatest him with the rod, he shall not die. Thou shalt beat him with the rod, and shalt deliver his soul from hell"* (Chapter 23:13-14).

Is this not diametrically opposed to today's philosophy which says: *"Wee Johnny is basically good and will turn out well if given the right environment!"* Is that what this book of Proverbs says? No! It says that if you do not punish your children quickly when they are doing wrong, you do not love them.

Some years ago, a columnist in one of Chicago's daily newspapers printed a letter he had received from a distraught mother of a rebellious teenage son. She said: *"My son is running around with the wrong crowd and breaking my heart. He will not listen to me and he defies me to my face. What can I do about it?"*

Jack Mabley's answer was short and to the point: *"Shrink him down to seventeen months and begin all over again!"* In other words, for this lad the mother's awakening had come too late. Will it be too late for you? Then there are:

(b) ISSUES RELATING TO PROSPERITY

We are living in a materialistic age, the wisdom of which is to get rich and stay rich. Nor are most people too concerned as to how they acquire their wealth. Do you recall that Solomon was one of the wealthiest men in the world? His wealth was the talk of every kingdom and tribe of his day. His ships plied the trade lines of the Mediterranean; his camels crossed the desert spreading his fame far and wide and returning with riches for the king. But here is what he said about wealth: *"Treasures of wickedness profit nothing"* (Proverbs 10:2). *"Riches profit not in the day of wrath"* (Chapter 11:4). *"In the house of the righteous is much treasure: but in the revenues of the wicked is trouble"* (Chapter 15:6). Wealth is not wrong if you get it honestly and use it wisely. Remember what the Bible says: *"But thou shalt remember the LORD thy God: for it is He that giveth thee power to get wealth"* (Deuteronomy 8:18). When we give to the Lord, remember that it was never ours in the first place. We are simply giving to God what He has already given to us.

Parenthood and prosperity. Then there are:

(c) ISSUES RELATING TO POLITICS

Remember that Solomon was a king and he was a capable and successful administrator. He knew all about diplomacy, politics and the matters of the state. His observations on practical government should be a handbook for all in office today. He says: *"When it goeth well with the righteous, the city rejoiceth: and when the wicked perish, there is shouting"* (Proverbs 11:10). He says: *"Righteousness exalteth a nation: but sin is a reproach to any people"* (Chapter 14:34).

There was a time when the secret of England's (and the United Kingdom's) greatness was the open Bible, but not now! During World War II, King George VI called the nation to prayer. Just after the end of the War, W. E. Vallance wrote a book entitled: ***"The War, the Weather and God"*** in which the author showed that God honoured those national days of prayer - with one exception. That was when the British Government ignored the King's call and urged workers, in view of the national emergency, to put in longer hours on the very day the King had requested a day of prayer. Sadly, we have been like that ever since. Do we not need in government today men who *"fear the Lord"*? Men who have the *"wisdom from above,"* because they fear the Lord more than they fear the press, the public and their peers?

Finally, there are:

(d) ISSUES RELATING TO PIETY

Are you beginning to see what this book of Proverbs is all about? It is describing life as it really is! Not life in church, but life in the street, the office, the shop and the home. Proverbs is interested in where most of our waking life is lived. Proverbs is all about *"where the rubber hits the road"*. That is why Solomon deals so much with lying. *"The lip of truth shall be established for ever: but a lying tongue is but for a moment"* (Chapter 12:19).

In Chapter 18, Solomon deals with **Tale-bearing**. He says: *"The words of a talebearer are as wounds, and they go down into the innermost parts of the belly"* (verse 8). Do you know what a talebearer is? One who runs from person to person telling matters that ought to be concealed, whether they are true or false. (See Chapter 10:12)

In Chapter 26, Solomon deals with **Flattery**. He says: *"A flattering mouth worketh ruin"* (verse 28). Do you know what flattery is? Insincere praise given by one who has selfish motives. *"Flatter"* and *"flutter"* belong to the same family of words, and you can just see the flatterer as he *"flutters"* over all his victims trying to impress. Absalom *"fluttered"* all over the men of Israel (2 Samuel 15:5), stole their hearts and divided the kingdom. Beware of the flatterer indeed! Proverbs says: *"Meddle not with him that flattereth with his lips"* (Chapter 20:19).

(3) THE FINAL SECTION OF THE BOOK - CHAPTERS 25 to 31

In this final section, observe:

(a) THE VARIOUS PICTURES

This section draws scores of little word pictures, little illustrations, that glow like little sections in a stained glass window. Here are a few examples: *"A word fitly spoken is like apples of gold in pictures of silver"* (Chapter 25:11); *"As the cold of snow in the time of harvest, so is a faithful messenger to them that send him: for he refresheth the soul of his masters"* (Chapter 25:13). Words can be like lovely fruit and refreshing cold water from the mountain snows. Using the right words, presenting them in the right way, at the right time, what a blessing they are when *"fitly spoken"*.

Now, if you look at these chapters, you will find lots of these word pictures.

(b) THE VIRTUOUS WOMAN

Dr. Sidlow Baxter calls her: **"Mrs. Far Above Rubies"**. Here is an example of what God intended when He created Eve. She was fashioned out of Adam's rib to show that she is to be *at his side, not on his back, or under his feet.* Solomon has talked about *"wicked women"* in Chapters 1 to 9. He has talked about *"brawling women"* or *"nagging wives"* (See Chapters 21:9 and 25:24), but the book closes with a tribute to the godly dedicated wife who brings honour to God and joy to her family.

Next to making a decision for Christ, the most important decision a Christian will make is the choice of a life's partner. The book of Proverbs says: *"A virtuous woman is a crown to her husband"* (Chapter 12:4); *"Whoso findeth a wife findeth a good thing, and obtaineth favour of the LORD"* (Chapter 18:22) and *"A prudent wife is from the LORD"* (Chapter 19:14).

Do you notice her fine qualities here?

1. Her Spirituality

The King's mother is teaching her son the things of God. She is warning Lemuel about sinful companions, strong drink, and failure to obey the Word of God. Tell me, do you have a God-fearing mother? If so, have you thanked God for her?

2. Her Loyalty

Look at Chapter 31 verse 10 to 12 – and particularly the opening words of verse 11: *"The heart of her husband doth safely trust in her"*. The two key words are *heart* and *trust*. Love and faith! Is this not what marriage is all about? It is a matter of the heart for there must be true love between a husband and his wife.

3. Her Industry

Look at Chapter 31 verse 22: *"She maketh herself coverings of tapestry"*. This priceless woman is a worker. Whether it be sewing or cooking or helping her husband in the family business, she is faithfully doing her share. Did you notice that she works *willingly? "She seeketh wool, and flax, and worketh willingly with her hands"* (Chapter 31:13). She is up early. *"She riseth also while it is yet night"* (Chapter 31:15). She is not one of these women that lie in bed all day.

4. Her Modesty

Have a look at verses 23 to 26 of Proverbs 31. Her husband is known in the gates and she is known for her faithfulness at home. You see, husband and wife have a place in the economy of God, and when one steps out of place there is trouble and confusion. The New Testament teaches that the husband is the head of the home, the wife is the heart of the home and the children are the hub of the home. Can you see that she does not depend on fancy clothing? Rather, according to verse 25, *"strength and honour are her clothing"*. The law of kindness rules her tongue.

5. Her Piety

Look at verse 30: *"Favour is deceitful, and beauty is vain: but a woman that feareth the LORD, she shall be praised"*. Is this not the secret of her life? No doubt she would meet with the Lord in the morning. She would pray for her husband and family, and though the years might mark her body, her beauty in the Lord only grows greater.

She is a Good **Woman** (verse 25); She is a Good **Wife** (verse 12); She is a Good **Mother** (verse 21); She is a Good **Neighbour** (verse 20).

Thus, while the early chapters of this book have much to say about the bad woman and her temptations, the final chapter has much to say about the good wife and her trustworthiness. I wonder, are these qualities found in you? Are you Spiritual? Loyal? Industrious? Modest? Godly?

This then is the Book of Proverbs, an excellent book to read and re-read on a regular basis.

Since it has 31 chapters, you may want to read it through one month each year.

If you do, you will discover this:

Reading a proverb takes seconds, memorizing a proverb takes minutes, applying a proverb takes a lifetime.

CHAPTER 4

Ecclesiastes

An old European fable tells of the downfall of a spider. One day, it descended on a single thread from a barn's lofty rafters and alighted near the corner of a window. From there, it wove its web. This corner of the barn was very busy with insects and soon the spider waxed fat and prosperous. One day in his prosperity as he surveyed his web he noticed the strand that reached up into the unseen. He had forgotten its significance and thinking it a stray thread, he snapped it. *Instantly, his whole world collapsed around him!*

Solomon had a strand that connected him to Heaven. Solomon had a relationship with the Lord, but somewhere in life he got so fat, so interested in the things of this life, that he cut the living link between himself and God.

Is this where you are today? Once, you walked close with the Lord, but then you got materially fat, felt you could do without the Lord and now your cry is:

"Where is the blessedness I knew,
When first I saw the Lord?
Where is the soul-refreshing view,
Of Jesus and His Word?"

Now, you will recognize that the words of Ecclesiastes are the words of King Solomon, the son of the great king David. Do you see how the book begins? *"The words of the Preacher, the son of David, king in Jerusalem."* Who else could have described himself as *"the son of David, king in Jerusalem"?*

Here we have the words of a man who because of his privileged position has sampled all that life has to offer. But, he is also King and carries the responsibility of ruling others. In addition, he takes upon himself the responsibility of teaching them and calls himself: *"The Preacher"*. That is what the Greek term *'Ecclesiastes'* means. It can be translated: *"preacher"* or *"philosopher"* or *"lecturer"*. Some feel the best translation is: *"speaker"*. What do you call the person who presides over the debates in the House of Commons? ***The Speaker***. So this book is written in the style of an old man presiding over a debate, a debate that is going on in his own mind. Like every good speaker, he allows the pros and cons to be given equal opportunity. So, the motion that life is not worth living is followed by a motion, proclaiming that it is.

According to Jewish tradition, Solomon wrote the *Song of Solomon* in his early years, expressing *a young man's love*. He wrote the book of *Proverbs* during his middle age years, revealing *a mature man's wisdom*. But, he wrote the book of *Ecclesiastes* in his declining, latter years, disclosing *an old man's sorrow*. Here is the record of Solomon's regret for his grave moral lapses. Remember the opening verse of 1 Kings 11: *"But King Solomon loved many foreign women"*.

Someone has said that while the Song of Solomon is a book of **sweet romance** and Proverbs is a book of **sacred regulations**, Ecclesiastes is a book of **sad retrospect.**

Here is an old man who has come to the end of life, having lived a wasted life, and he preaches a sermon. Solomon says: *"I want to preach you a sermon on the purpose and meaning of life. I want to tell you what it is to live your life apart from a vital relationship with the Lord"*. So Ecclesiastes is a very:

<u>Relevant Book</u>

In a world full of disillusioned people, Solomon speaks as one who has tasted all that the world has to offer - the best of pleasures, the height of power, the ultimate in prestige, worldwide popularity - and still he remains unsatisfied. Solomon has tried it all. Is there not a search for satisfaction in this old world? There are people today who are trying everything. They are looking for something that will address the deepest needs of their heart. The problem is they are looking in the wrong place.

Secondly, it is also a very:

Philosophical Book

It seeks to answer key questions. What is life all about? What does it mean? Why are we here? What is our purpose in life? Where is it all going? Is life worth living? So Ecclesiastes examines the question: ***"Is there life before death?"***

A Jewish writer once described life as *"a blister on top of a tumour and a boil on top of that"*. The American poet Carl Sandburg compared life to *"an onion, you peel it off one layer at a time and sometimes you weep"*. Some time ago in the city of Chicago, a sewer worker and a well-known agnostic were being interviewed. They were asked about their personal philosophy of life. The agnostic said this: *"There is a statement in the Bible which summarises my life, 'We have toiled all night and have taken nothing'"*. The man who worked on the sewer said this: *"I digge de ditch to gette de money to buy de food to gette de strength to digge de ditch!"* I wonder - is that how you feel?

Thirdly, it is a very:

Depressing Book

It is a book that at times can be very pessimistic. One particular phrase appears twenty-seven times in the book. Do you know what it is? *"Under the sun."* This defines the outlook of the writer as he looks at life from a human perspective and not necessarily from Heaven's point of view. Solomon is applying his own wisdom and experience to complex situations and he is trying to make some sense out life. Now, of course, Solomon writes under the inspiration of the Holy Spirit. 2 Timothy 3 verse 16 teaches that *"all Scripture is given by inspiration of God"* and towards the end of his book Solomon declares: *"The preacher sought to find out acceptable words: and that which was written was upright, even words of truth"* (Ecclesiastes 12:10). What he wrote is what God wanted His people to have. But please keep in mind Solomon's viewpoint. He is examining life *"under the sun"*.

Campbell Morgan perfectly summarises Solomon's outlook when he says:

"This man had been living through all these experiences under the sun, concerned with nothing above the sun ... until there came a moment in which he had seen the whole of life - and there was something over the sun. It is only as a man takes account of that which is over the sun as well as that which is under the sun that things under the sun are seen in their true light."

Fourthly, it is a very:

<u>**Valuable Book**</u>

You see, if our vision is limited to this earth and this life, we will never understand what life is all about and what makes it worth living. Is this not where the value of this book can be seen? It concludes that only God can satisfy the deepest hungers of the human heart. Thus while much of the book is pessimistic, it ends on a note of assurance. Beyond *"the sun"* is a living God who can fill the hearts of those who will let Him.

Now, as has been said, Ecclesiastes is actually a sermon. Solomon is saying: *"I want to preach you a sermon on the purpose and meaning of life. I want to tell you what it is to live your life apart from the Lord."* The result is the book of Ecclesiastes. As we examine this book, there are three things we should consider:

(1) <u>THE START OF HIS SERMON: Chapter 1 verses 1 to 11</u>

This book is a sermon. As Sidlow Baxter observed:

"There is the announcement of a theme, a brief introduction, a developing of the theme and a practical application in conclusion."

Do you see here:

(a) *THE PREACHER'S TEXT*

It is interesting to notice that Solomon has put the key to this book right at the front door. He says in verse 2 of Chapter 1: *"Vanity of vanities, saith the Preacher, vanity of vanities; all is vanity"*. Just in case we missed it, he put the same key at the back door. *"Vanity of vanities, saith the preacher; all is vanity"* (Chapter 12:8). Do you see that word *"vanity"*? It does not refer to egotism. Today, we connect vanity with a self-inflated ego. The story is told of the woman who said to her pastor: *"When I confess my sins, I confess the sin of vanity most of all. You see, every morning, I admire myself in the mirror for half an hour."* The pastor replied: *"My dear lady, that isn't the sin of vanity. You are suffering from the sin of imagination!"*

Solomon was not suffering from a self-inflated ego. No! He had been there, done that, and, as they say, even had the T-shirt! But he was only left with the conclusion: *"If this is all that there is, then it is all vanity, empty, futile and meaningless"*. The word *"vanity" ('hevel')* here means: *"something without substance which quickly passes away"*. One Hebrew professor described *"hevel"* as: *"whatever is left after you break a soap bubble"*.

Do you realise that is what life without the Lord is? I wonder, where did Solomon find this text for his sermon? Maybe one day Solomon was at the library in the Royal Palace. Perhaps he pulled down some books written by his father, King David. Maybe it was the book of Psalms. Could it be that as he was thumbing through those Psalms he came across Psalm 39? If so, as he read that Psalm he came to verse 5 which says: *"Behold, Thou hast made my days as an handbreadth; and mine age is as nothing before Thee: verily every man at his best state is altogether vanity. Selah"*.

Could it be that when Solomon read that verse, he said: *"That is the verse that describes my life. It is so brief and I have come to understand that the things in this world are only vanity. They are emptiness. They are meaningless. They are only puffs of smoke."* Solomon has found the text which describes his life. I wonder, is there a verse in the

Bible that describes your life? If the Lord would write down one verse that would describe the story of your life, what would it be? Solomon says: *"Here is the story of my life – 'Vanity of vanities, all is vanity' saith the preacher"*. Do you see the Preacher's text? Then there is:

(b) THE PREACHER'S TOPIC

Do you see that phrase again: *"Under the sun"*? That expression, used for the first time in Ecclesiastes 1 verse 3, means life lived without reference to the Lord. However, life for the believer is not to be lived *"under the sun"*. Life for the Christian is rather to be lived *"in the heavenlies"* (see Ephesians 1:3). Is this not Solomon's topic? Life without God in the centre of our lives is utterly futile. Now to illustrate that Solomon tells us that:

1. Life without the Lord is Meaningless

Dr Warren Wiersbe, one of my favourite Bible commentators and to whom I owe so much, says that *it is like an Unending Cycle*. *"One generation passeth away, and another generation cometh"* (Ecclesiastes 1:4). In other words, one generation is always passing off the scene and another generation is always coming on the scene. This is not a fatalistic approach to life - this is a realistic approach to life without the Lord. We get up, go to work, come home, eat dinner, watch TV, read a book, and go to bed - only to repeat that again and again until our retirement. Then we die! Well, is this not how a lot of folk view life? Solomon is saying: *"On the surface, life looks a hamster running on a wheel! What's the point?"* Is this how you view life?

Then, again according to Wiersbe, *it is like an Unchanging Cycle.* Solomon talks about the sun rising, (Chapter 1:5); the wind blowing (verse 6), and the rivers running (verse 7). His point is that nature does not change. *There is motion but not promotion.* Life is just like a merry-go-round. Solomon says: *"Round and round and round we go, like a merry-go-round. There is no meaning to life, no purpose to it."* Is that how you feel today? What would be the text of the sermon of your life? Well, Solomon said: *"My life without the Lord has been meaningless."* Meaningless – and also:

2. Life without the Lord is Monotonous

Everything is boring, utterly boring. Is that not what he says in verse 8 of Chapter 1? *"The eye is not satisfied with seeing, nor the ear filled with hearing."* We can never see enough or hear enough to bring satisfaction. Everything ultimately brings weariness and boredom, forcing us to constantly seek new things. Do you see what Solomon is saying? A life lived without the Lord is not fulfilling. Tennis star, Boris Becker, was at the very top of the tennis world, yet he was on the brink of suicide. He said: *"I had won Wimbledon twice before, once as the youngest player. I was rich. I had all the material possessions I needed. It's the old song of movie stars and pop stars who commit suicide. They have everything, and yet they are happy with nothing. I had no inner peace. I was a puppet on a string."* You may look for a new toy, a new talent or a new treasure for satisfaction, but you will never find it.

Do you know why? Because God has *"set the world in their hearts"*. He has *"put eternity in your heart"* (Chapter 3:11) and no-one can find peace and satisfaction apart from Him. A life lived to oneself, on oneself, by oneself, and for oneself is where *"there is no remembrance of former things; neither shall there be any remembrance of things that are to come with those that shall come after"* (Chapter 1:11).

If you make the tragic mistake of living your life *"under the sun"*, with no regard for the Lord, then one day you will be a Solomon. You will look back over your life with sadness and forward with fear to the grim ghost of death. The text of your life will be: *"Vanity of vanities; all is vanity"*.

(2) THE SUBSTANCE OF HIS SERMON: Chapter 1 verse 12 to Chapter 10 verse 20

Keep in mind that Solomon is describing *"life under the sun"*, life lived without any reference to the Lord. Notice:

(a) THE THINGS THAT SOLOMON HAD SOUGHT

Opening his heart, he tells us how he had experimented with

every element in the laboratory of life, trying to unlock the secret of life and make life worth living. Do you notice that Solomon experimented in:

1. <u>The Intellectual World</u>

Look at what he says in Chapter 1 verse 13: *"I gave my heart to seek and search out by wisdom concerning all things that are done under heaven"*. What he is saying is that he gave himself to study. *"I decided that I would find wisdom. I would find satisfaction in education."* Solomon was given a gift of wisdom from the Lord. Do you recall what the Lord said to him? *"Ask what I shall give thee"* (1 Kings 3:5). God just gave him a blank cheque. To his credit Solomon said: *"Give me wisdom so I will know how to lead these people"*. The Bible says that God filled this man Solomon with supernatural wisdom so that he became the wisest man who ever lived. In fact, the Queen of Sheba came to visit Solomon. The Bible says: *"She came to prove him with hard questions"* (1 Kings 10:1). When he answered all her questions, she exclaimed: *"The half was not told me!"* (1 Kings 10:7).

He was a wise man. He was an educated man. In the book of Kings, we learn some of things that he did. *"He spake three thousand proverbs: and his songs were a thousand and five"* (1 Kings 4:32).That same chapter goes on to say: *"He spake of trees"* (verse 33) - so he was an expert in ***botany.*** He also spoke of beasts – so he was an expert in ***zoology.*** He spoke of fowl - so he was an expert in ***ornithology.*** He spoke of creeping things – so he was an expert in ***entomology.*** If you wanted to know anything about any realm or field of study, all you had to do was ask Solomon, for he was a very educated man. He thought he would find satisfaction in the stimulation of his mental faculties. But notice what he says in Chapter 1 verses 17 and 18: *"I gave my heart to know wisdom, and to know madness and folly: I perceived that this also is vexation of spirit. For in much wisdom is much grief: and he that increaseth knowledge increaseth sorrow"*.

The more he learned, the less he knew, and the less he liked what he learned. Human knowledge can answer the questions of time, but it cannot answer the questions of eternity. Philosophy can answer the question about man's mind, but it cannot answer the question about man's soul. Science can answer the question: *"How does a man die?"*, but it cannot answer the question: *"If a man dies, will he live again?"* Ethics can answer the question: *"How can a man be right with other men?"*, but it cannot answer the question: *"How can a man be right with God?"*

Solomon is saying: *"Take it from me, I had all the education a man could ever hope for, but it produced no satisfaction"*. Now, I am not putting a premium on a lack of education. I am not minimizing the importance of education. For it *is* important. You do not have to be ignorant. The story is told about an old boy who got up in church and prayed: *"Lord, I thank Thee for my ignorance, and I pray that Thou wilt make me ignoranter!"* We must not belittle education, but it is possible to have a head full and a heart empty.

Solomon also explored:

2. <u>The Material World</u>

He sets before us his financial portfolio in this very passage. He says: *"I made me great works; I builded me houses"* (Chapter 2:4). Solomon became interested in architectural design. *"I planted me vineyards"* - he became an expert in agriculture. He says: *"I made me gardens and orchards"* - he got interested in horticulture. Then he says: *"I got me servants and maidens ....also I had great possessions"*. Here was a man swimming in a sea of opulence and affluence. Do you know what the Word of God says? *"The weight of gold that came to Solomon in one year was six hundred threescore and six talents of gold"* (1 Kings 10:14). Do you know how much that is worth? $304 million. But that is only the gold! The silver was so abundant that it was not even counted. (See 1 Kings 10:21) So, we could safely round up the $304 million to about $500 million a year.

Did that bring contentment? No, for Solomon says: *"All was vanity and vexation of spirit"* (Ecclesiastes 2:11). Solomon discovered that you can have a lot in your purse and have nothing in your person.

You can be a prince on the outside and a pauper on the inside. As Christians, do we have a stewardship perspective on all that God has given us? We should recall what David, Solomon's father, said as he prayed: *"All things come of Thee, and of Thine own have we given Thee"* (1 Chronicles 29:14).

Solomon knew much about the intellectual world and the material world – and also:

3. The Physical World

He says in Chapter 2 verse 8 that he tried: *"the delights of the sons of men"*. That means that Solomon tried sexual pleasure. In fact, did you know that the Bible says that Solomon had seven hundred wives and three hundred concubines (1 Kings 11:3)? A thousand women! Can you imagine how it was when all the in-laws came round to the palace at the weekend? Seven hundred mothers-in-law!

Of course, we are living now in the days of sexual liberation. The idea that the gift of sex is something for the confines of holy matrimony – see 1 Corinthians 6 verse 13 - is ridiculed. The idea of keeping yourself pure is scorned. We live in an age of sexual permissiveness - and what has it brought us? It has brought us broken homes. It has brought us scarred boys and girls. It has brought us sexually transmitted diseases, A.I.D.S. So much for your sexual revolution! ***Young folk, will you remember that you are more than just a physical being?*** The world tells us, that we came from animals, that we will die like animals, and, therefore, you can live like animals. The world says, it does not matter if you commit sexual immorality, as that is the way the animals are. It does not matter if you live in the barnyards of life. But, I need to tell you this - **you are more than a physical being**. God created you with a soul, and your soul will spend eternity in Heaven or Hell, and the only thing that will make the difference is your relationship with Jesus Christ. Now, do you see that Solomon had it all as far as this world is concerned? But look at how he sums it up: *"Therefore I hated life; because the work that is wrought under the sun is grievous unto me: for all is vanity and vexation of spirit"* (Ecclesiastes 2:17).

(b) THE THINGS THAT SOLOMON HAD SEEN

Having failed to find the answer to life's longings in the things that he had sought, he began to observe life more carefully. He sees everything as it unfolds around him. Time and again he refers to what he had seen: *"And moreover I saw under the sun"* (Chapter 3:16); *"Then I returned, and I saw vanity under the sun"* (Chapter 4:7); *"There is an evil which I have seen under the sun"* (Chapter 6:1). Solomon records the vanity of everything he saw. As John Phillips says, he had seen the vanity of

1. Time without Eternity: (3:1-11)
2. Mortality without Immortality: (3:18-22)
3. Might without Right: (4:1-3)
4. Plenty without Peace: (4:4-8)
5. Prosperity without Posterity: (4:9-12)
6. Sovereignty without Wisdom: (4:13-16)
7. Religion without Reality: (5:1-6)
8. Wealth without Health: (5:7-20)
9. Treasure without Pleasure: (6:1-10)
10. Life without Length: (6:11-12)

Do you see what he says in Chapter 3 verse 11? *"He hath set the world in their heart."* That word *"world"* means *"the ages"* or as some have suggested, *"eternity"*. The cry wrung from the empty heart of Solomon was echoed by the immoral Augustine before he found Christ: *"Thou hast made us for Thyself and our hearts are restless until they rest in Thee"*. You see, God has made the human soul for eternity and there is nothing big enough *"under the sun"* to fill it.

(c) *THE THINGS THAT SOLOMON HAD STUDIED*

"I returned and considered", he says at the start of Chapter 4 and then in verses 4 and 15, *"I considered"*. Now, keep in mind, he is pointing out life *"under the sun"*. He is telling us how the man of the world looks at life. Solomon is backslidden and he is a picture of all that folk aspire to be without the Lord. In Chapters 7 to 10, Solomon is cynical. Do you see what he says in Chapter 7 verse

15? *"All things have I seen in the days of my vanity: there is a just man that perisheth in his righteousness, and there is a wicked man that prolongeth his life in his wickedness."* In other words, what is the use of even trying to be good?

Do you see what he says about women in verses 26 to 28 of Chapter 7? *"I find more bitter than death the woman, whose heart is snares and nets, and her hands are bands: whoso pleaseth God shall escape from her; but the sinner shall be taken by her"* (verse 26). Roaming his harem, listening to the babble of foreign voices, aware of the intrigue and plots that went on and of the petty squabbles among his many wives, Solomon groaned because he could not find a single one compatible with him. *"One man among a thousand have I found; but a woman among all those have I not found"* (verse 28).

Increasingly, he became obsessed with the fact of death, with the fact that death awaits everyone. Almost in every chapter he touches on death. Solomon keeps talking about death. Have you ever heard the expression: *"the fly in the ointment"*? It is taken right out of this section: *"Dead flies cause the ointment of the apothecary to send forth a stinking savour"* (Chapter 10:1). Do you know something ? It is a *dead* fly. That is the fly in the ointment for every person only living for this life. Sooner or later, death will come and end it all. Here is an old man looking back over a wasted life and he realised he only has one thing to do - and that is to sit there and wait for death.

Solomon began well, but it is not how we begin but rather how we finish that really matters. When I was pastor in the Iron Hall, Belfast, there was an elder who prayed for believers who were passing from time into eternity like this: *"Lord, may they be at peace with You; may they be at peace with the family, and may they be at peace with the brethren"*.

As we think about Solomon, the words of that old gospel song come to mind:

> *"Wasted years, wasted years, Oh how foolish,*
> *As you walk on in darkness and fear,*

Turn around, turn around, God is calling,
He's calling you from a life of wasted years."

Are *you* like Solomon? Are you *wasting* your years? Or, are you investing them? Are you living life *"under the sun"* or are you living life *"beyond the sun"*?

(3) THE SUMMARY OF HIS SERMON: Chapters 11 and 12

In the last couple of chapters in the book, Solomon wraps his sermon up. He talks about:

(a) THE CHALLENGES OF LIFE

In the first six verses of Chapter 11, he talks about the challenge of *Life's Prospects;* in verses 7 and 8, he talks about the challenge of *Life's Presence* and in the final two verses, he talks about the challenge of *Life's Past.*

There is an underlying theme in these opening verses. It is the matter of sowing seed and winning people to the Lord. Do you notice how we are to sow the seed? We should:

1. Sow Confidently
"Cast thy bread upon the waters: for thou shalt find it after many days" (verse 1). The picture here is sowing rice on the water. This was a custom in Egypt. Sow it confidently and it will come back. Somewhere in the future, there will be a harvest.

2. Sow Liberally
"Give a portion to seven, and also to eight; for thou knowest not what evil shall be upon the earth" (verse 2). Not every seed is going to come up. Some of the seed will not come up. But sow liberally and the more seed you sow, the more will come up.

3. Sow Intelligently
"If the clouds be full of rain, they empty themselves upon the earth: and if the tree fall toward the south, or toward the north, in the place where the tree falleth, there it shall be" (verse 3). There are principles of nature.

Clouds empty rain. There are certain eternal principles that we can depend on as we sow the seed.

4. <u>Sow Diligently</u>
"He that observeth the wind shall not sow; and he that regardeth the clouds shall not reap" (verse 4). What he is saying is that we ought not let circumstances and conditions hinder us in sowing seed. There is really never a good time, so far as circumstances are concerned. We are to make opportunities. We are to be instant in season and out of season.

5. <u>Sow Believingly</u>
"As thou knowest not what is the way of the spirit, nor how the bones do grow in the womb of her that is with child: even so thou knowest not the works of God who maketh all. In the morning sow thy seed, and in the evening withhold not thine hand: for thou knowest not whether shall prosper, either this or that, or whether they both shall be alike good" (verses 5 and 6). We do not understand how a child is formed in a mother's womb. We might know a great deal more than Solomon did, but it is still a mystery. The point is, just as we do not understand the work of God in certain physical realms, neither do we understand the work of God in certain spiritual realms. So we are to sow trustfully. Trust God to do what He can do. The challenge is - Are we sowing the seed of God's Word and trusting God to give the increase?

The Challenges of Life, and then:

(b) THE COMMANDS FOR LIFE

Notice the *"Rs"* in Chapters 11 and 12.

The first one is *"Rejoice"*: *"Rejoice, O young man, in thy youth; and let thy heart cheer thee in the days of thy youth, and walk in the ways of thine heart, and in the sight of thine eyes: but know thou, that for all these things God will bring thee into judgment"* (Chapter 11:9).

The second one is *"Renounce"*: *"Therefore remove sorrow from thy heart, and put away evil from thy flesh: for childhood and youth are vanity"* (Chapter 11:10).

The final one is *"Remember": "Remember now thy Creator in the days of thy youth"* (Chapter 12:1). Now, of course, *"to remember"* means far more than simply to recall that there is a Creator. It means: *"to pay attention to"*. The word signifies commitment. This is Solomon's version of the words of Christ: *"But seek ye first the kingdom of God, and His righteousness"* (Matthew 6:33). You see, to remember the Lord is to commit ourselves to Him. Have you done that?

Of course, Solomon is speaking here to young people, but remember that growing up soon gives way to growing old. Benjamin Disraeli, the famous Jewish statesman who helped make Britain great, wrote: *"Youth is a blunder, manhood a struggle and old age a regret"*. The picture here of age and decay is that of a house falling apart and returning to dust. The days of service will soon be over, the opportunities will be past and we will be called to give an account at the Judgment Seat of Christ.

Challenges, Commands and then:

(c) THE CLIMAX IN LIFE

What is the most decisive moment in life? Well, do you see how Solomon closes the book? *"Let us hear the conclusion of the whole matter: Fear God, and keep His commandments: for this is the whole duty of man. For God shall bring every work into judgment, with every secret thing, whether it be good, or whether it be evil"* (Chapter 12:13-14). Here is the answer to disillusionment, cynicism and meaninglessness: *"Fear God and keep His commandments"*.

At last, Solomon lifted his head and got his eyes on the world to come. Do you need to do that?

Even as Christians, we become so earthbound. Life for us under the sun can become a struggle. What we need to do is keep our eye on eternity, on life above the sun.

Stephen Olford was called home to Glory on 29th August 2004. In his younger days, he was particularly gifted in the field of mechanical engineering. He enrolled in the Devonport Technical College and sought to further his dream of a promising career. He had been saved at the age of 12 and answered the call to preach at the age of 17, but he came to the place where he was disappointed and disillusioned with other believers. *So he turned his back on the church and became a thoroughgoing backslider.* He wanted to see what the world had to offer him. So he turned his back on the call of God and the home of missionary parents.

One night, Stephen was coming home from a motorcycle race and he suffered a terrible accident. He lay on an icy road for hours, which ultimately led to an extremely advanced stage of pneumonia. *He was sent to the hospital and after a few hours the doctors said that there nothing else they could do, so they sent him home to die.* Stephen Olford lay in a recovery bed for several months. He testified later that it was during that time that the Lord began to deal with his heart about his future. One day, his mother came in and dropped a note on his bed. It was a note from his father, who was on the mission field in Africa.

The amazing thing was that in those days it took three months for a letter to arrive in England from Africa, thus his father had no idea of his accident and that he had been sent home to die. After his mother left the room, Stephen with a heart cold towards the Lord, opened the letter from his father. In it were but a few simple words that read:

"Dear Stephen,

Only one life
'Twill soon be past
Only what's done for Jesus
Will last."

It was at that moment that Stephen Olford bowed his head, humbled his heart, and determined that his **"only one life"** would be lived for the Saviour who loved him and gave Himself for him.

Is that what you need to do?

CHAPTER 5

The Song of Solomon

Many people are surprised to find the Song of Solomon included in the Bible. It is one of only two books in the Bible where the name of God is not even mentioned once. Esther is the other. In fact, there is no mention of anything distinctly spiritual in it from beginning to end. There is no reference to God; no mention of sin, nor any religious theme at all, yet the Jews have revered this poem as unique. The Jews compare Proverbs to the outer court of the temple; Ecclesiastes to the holy place, and the Song of Solomon to the most holy place.

There are several things we should notice about this book. Consider:

1. <u>The Introduction to the Book</u>

(a) <u>Look at Its Name</u>

The book opens with the words: *"The song of songs, which is Solomon's"*. Do you how many songs Solomon wrote? According to 1 Kings 4 verse 32, he wrote 1005 songs but this one is *"the song of songs"*. It is the greatest of all songs. It is also sometimes called *"Canticles"* which is derived from the Latin for: *"a series of songs"*. You see, just as the *"Holy of Holies"* is the highest place and the *"King of kings"* is the highest of all kings, so the *"song of songs"* is the greatest of all songs. There is none like it for excellence!

Ecclesiastes mournfully testified:

"I tried the broken cisterns, Lord,
But, ah, the waters failed!
E'en as I stooped to drink, they fled,
And mocked me as I wailed."

The Song of Solomon lifts us to a higher note:

"Now none but Christ can satisfy,
None other name for me;
There's love and life and lasting joy,
Lord Jesus, found in Thee."

(b) Look at Its Author

"The song of songs, which is Solomon's" or *"which is of Solomon"* or *"which is about Solomon"*. This means that it was written by him or written about him. Solomon was the son of David and Bathsheba - his birth is recorded in 2 Samuel 12 verse 24. His name appears in the book seven times. (Chapters 1:1, 5, 3:7, 9, 11; 8:11, 12)

Now do you recall that Solomon wrote three books of the Bible?

He wrote the Song of Solomon when he was young and in love. *It is a book of the heart.*

He wrote Proverbs when he was middle-aged and his intellectual powers were at their zenith. *It is a book of the will.*

He wrote Ecclesiastes when he was old, disappointed and disillusioned with the carnality of much of his life. *It is a book of the mind*.

In other words, Solomon wrote this book when he was in a healthy spiritual state, before his tragic decline recorded in 1 Kings 11. According to verses 3 and 4 of that Chapter, his many wives turned away his heart after other gods. Some think that the book was composed around 965 B.C. If this is correct, this would place it about the time of the building of the first Temple in Jerusalem - 966-959 B.C.

(*c*) <u>*Look at Its Story*</u>

What is it all about? Well, it is *"a love story"* and the main characters of the story are Solomon, a Shulamite woman and a group called *"the daughters of Jerusalem"*. Now, some Bible students see another character in the story - a shepherd lover. In verse 7 of Chapter 1, the question is posed: *"Tell me, O thou whom my soul loveth, where thou feedest, where thou makest thy flock to rest at noon"*. These students say that from the affection of the shepherd lover, Solomon tries to lure the Shulamite woman away.

Whatever view you take, it is good to keep in mind the words of John Phillips:

"The abiding value of the Song of Solomon is clear, whichever view is taken. As human life finds its highest fulfilment in the love of man and woman, so spiritual life finds its highest fulfilment in the love of Christ and His church."

If we take the first view, what is the story here?

King Solomon had a vineyard in the hill country of Ephraim about 50 miles north of Jerusalem. According to verse 11 of Chapter 8, he let it out to keepers. The family of keepers consisted of a mother, two sons (see Chapter 1:6) and two daughters - the Shulamite (Chapter 6:13) and a little sister (Chapter 8:8). The Shulamite seems to have been *"the Cinderella"* of the family. She declares: *"I am black, but comely"* (Chapter 1:5). She was naturally beautiful but went unnoticed. Her brothers, who were probably her half-brothers (*"my mother's children"* - Chapter 1:6) made her work hard tending the vineyards, so that she had little opportunity to care for her personal appearance.

She pruned the vines and set traps for the little foxes (see Chapter 2:15). She also kept the flocks (Chapter 1:8), but being out in the open so much, she was burned by the sun (Chapter 1:5). One day, a handsome stranger came to the vineyard. It was Solomon, but he was disguised. He showed an interest in her and she became embarrassed concerning her personal appearance. *"Look not upon me, because I am black, because the sun hath looked upon me"* (Chapter 1:6). She took him for a shepherd and asked about his flocks. *"Tell me, O thou whom my soul loveth, where thou feedest, where thou makest thy flock to rest at noon"* (Chapter 1:7). He answered her evasively: *"If thou know not, O thou fairest among women, go thy way forth by the footsteps of the flock, and feed thy kids beside the shepherds' tents"* (Chapter 1:8), but also spoke loving words to her: *"Thy cheeks are comely"* (verse 10). He promised rich gifts for the future. *"We will make thee borders of gold with studs of silver"* (verse 11). He won her heart and left with the promise that one day he would return. She dreamed of him at night and sometimes thought that he was near. Chapter 3 opens with her words: *"By night on my bed I sought him whom my soul loveth: I sought him, but I found him not"*. Finally, he did return, not as a shepherd but as the King to make her his bride (see Chapter 3:6-7). Now that, in essence, is the setting of the story.

2. The Interpretation of the Book

It is when we move from the introduction to the book to the interpretation of the book that we find ourselves in difficulty. You see, there are numerous interpretations, with arguments for and against by a host of Christian scholars. We are left with the Saviour's challenge in Luke 10 verse 26: *"How readest thou?" "What is your reading of it?"* Well, we could look at this book in at least four ways. We could view it:

(a) LITERALLY

Some of the expressions in this book are such that Jewish leaders advised their young people not to read it before the age of thirty, but what we have here is a precious love story. On the one hand, this book denounces asceticism and, on the other hand, it denounces lust. What does it tell us? That there is a God-ordained place for the enjoyment of physical love. That place is between a husband and wife. There is no other place for physical love, except in the confines of the covenant of marriage. In a day when sexual love is debased, exploited and publicly paraded, there is a need for Christian married couples to know that physical relationships can be pure and holy. Hebrews 13 verse 4 captures the heart of this song:

"Marriage is honourable in all, and the bed undefiled: but whoremongers and adulterers God will judge".

The love of a man and wife ought to be a beautiful experience, as described in this book, but sin can destroy this beautiful gift. Back in the book of Proverbs, Solomon warns against sexual sins; here in the Song of Solomon, he extols the beauty and joy of married love.

(b) HISTORICALLY

From the earliest days, the Jews saw in this story a picture of the relationship between Jehovah God and Israel. Israel was *"wedded"* to the Lord at Mount Sinai, when the nation accepted the Law. Do you recall the words of Isaiah? *"Thy Maker is thine husband; the LORD of hosts is His name; and thy Redeemer the Holy One of Israel"* (Isaiah 54:5). God says through Jeremiah: *"Turn, O backsliding children; for I am married unto you"* (Jeremiah 3:14). As depicted in the story of Hosea, Israel was not faithful to her divine husband and *"played the harlot"* with the idolatrous nations of the world. She turned her back on her Beloved. However, there will come a day when Israel will return home and be restored to her Beloved.

(c) TYPICALLY

The marriage relationship is used in the New Testament (Ephesians 5:23-33) to describe the relationship between Christ and the church.

In searching for the true interpretation of the Song of Solomon, we should be like the Ethiopian eunuch. Do you recall what he asked when he was reading Isaiah 53? *"Of whom speaketh the prophet this? Of himself, or of some other man?"* (Acts 8:34) The Ethiopian eunuch was questioning Philip about the subject of Isaiah's prophecy. Was Isaiah speaking about himself or about someone else? Philip shows him that the subject of Isaiah 53 was not Isaiah but the Lord Jesus: *"Then Philip opened his mouth ... and preached unto him Jesus"* (verse 35). In just the same way, in this Song of Solomon the author is speaking about Christ. If we expect to find Christ in this book on the basis that Christ is to be found *"in all the Scriptures"* (Luke 24:27), we shall not be disappointed.

It has to be acknowledged that there are some who feel that Solomon cannot be a fitting type of the Heavenly Bridegroom. How shall we answer this?

Well, look at Psalm 45. Do you see the title to the Psalm? *"A Song of Loves"* or *"A Song of Love."* But we can go further, for this is a song of royal love. This is a song of praise to the King on his wedding day. It appears that the bride was a foreign princess. In verse 10, the instruction is given: *"Forget also thine own people, and thy father's house"*. Can you see the international prominence of the King? Many dignitaries are coming to this festive occasion, bringing their costly gifts. *"The daughter of Tyre shall be there with a gift"* (verse 12). You see, this is a royal marriage hymn and it refers to Solomon. 1 Kings 3 verse 1 tells us that Solomon took Pharaoh's daughter and brought her into the city of David. However, while the primary reference is to Solomon, the ultimate reference is to Christ. Look at verses 6 and 7: *"Thy throne, O God, is for ever and ever: the sceptre of Thy kingdom is a right sceptre. Thou lovest righteousness, and hatest wickedness: therefore God, Thy God, hath anointed Thee with the oil of gladness above Thy fellows"*. Do you know where that is quoted? In the Hebrew epistle - for that book takes those verses and applies them directly to Christ. Therefore, as Solomon is a type of Christ in his wisdom and in his wealth, so, here in Psalm 45, he is a type in this marriage union. Thus this Psalm goes hand in hand with the Song of Songs.

(d) DEVOTIONALLY

This book presents a vivid picture of faithful love and deepening communion. The intimate terms used only illustrate the wonderful love between Christ and the Christian.

Robert Murray McCheyne often preached from this book. He said:

"No book furnishes a better test than does the Song of the depth of a man's Christianity. If his religion be in his head only, a dry

form of doctrines, or if it hath place merely in his fancy like Pliable in Pilgrim's Progress, he will see nothing here to attract him. But if his religion hath a hold on his heart, this will be a favourite portion of the Word of God."

At the heart of Christianity is a very personal relationship. Christianity is grasping the truth of Paul's words: *"The Son of God … loved me, and gave Himself for me"* (Galatians 2:20).

The Apostle Paul grasped it – and so too did Charles Wesley. He expressed it like this:

"O Love Divine, how sweet Thou art
When shall I find my willing heart
All taken up by Thee?
I thirst, I faint, I die to prove
The fulness of redeeming love,
The love of Christ to me."

It is said that Samuel Rutherford could spend a whole night in prayer. His wife would miss him during the night and would get up and go looking for him. Even on cold nights, she would find him on his knees praying, and she would take his big overcoat and throw it around him.

Men like D. L. Moody, Robert Murray McCheyne and Charles Spurgeon really knew close communion with the Saviour.

This is not some kind of second experience, as some people try to describe it. It is more than an experience. *It is a personal relationship with Jesus Christ, seeing how wonderful He is, how glorious He is.* You see, we need to come to the place where the words of 1 John 4 verse 19 can truly be said of us: *"We love Him, because He first loved us"*.

To open up this little book will be like the breaking of Mary's alabaster box of ointment in John 12. May the fragrance of it fill our lives and spread out to others!

Many see three sections in the book:

(1) Courtship Days: Chapter 1 verse 2 to Chapter 3 verse 5
(2) The Wedding: Chapter 3 verse 6 to Chapter 5 verse 1
(3) Married Life: Chapter 5 verse 2 to Chapter 8 verse 14.

However, if we try to fit Christian experience into this pattern, we will be left with many problems. Accordingly, let us just try and look at the three sections literally, typically and devotionally.

(1) COURTSHIP: Chapter 1 verse 1 to Chapter 3 verse 5 – Events Preceding the Wedding

With no explanation of who she is or what wonderful things have happened to her, the Shulamite launches into a statement about her love for the King. Notice:

(a) THE APPEAL FOR LOVE

She yearns for expressions of his love. *"Let him kiss me with the kisses of his mouth: for thy love is better than wine"* (Chapter 1:2). The expressions of love include *touch* ('kisses'), *taste* ('wine') and *smell* ('ointment'). No wonder she cries out: *"Take me with you!" "Draw me, we will run after thee"* (verse 4).

True love is likened to a banquet. Frequently in the Song of Solomon, you will find love compared to the enjoyment of food and drink. There are references to fruit (Chapter 2:3); wine (Chapters 1:2 and 5:1) and honey and milk (again, Chapter 5:1). Do you recall that Scripture compares the future reign of Christ to a great marriage feast? (See, for example, Isaiah 25:6, Matthew 8:11, Luke 13:29 and Revelation 19:6-9) Here, Solomon's love draws her to his chambers where a great banquet has been prepared. It is here that she confesses her unworthiness: *"Look not upon me"* (Chapter 1:5-6). He extols her beauty and calls her: *"my love"* (Chapter 1:15; 2:2, 10, 13; 4:1, 7; 5:2; 6:4).

Is this not what the Christian life is all about? Being a Christian is being in love with the Lord! Being a believer is not merely going to church, reading a Bible, or engaged in service. ***It is a heart relationship with the Lord Jesus.*** The question that the Risen Lord asked Peter is the one He asks you: *"Lovest thou Me?"* (John 21:16).

George Müller of Bristol considered it the first and most important duty of the day to get his own soul happy in the Lord. You see, if we keep our hearts singing in His love, our minds filled with thoughts of Him, and our wills enslaved to His, then the world will not get very far with us.

How important to note the appeal of love! Then there is:

(b) THE AWAKENING OF LOVE

It seems that, after the banquet, the King left the scene. We assume that his courtiers escorted the Shulamite safely home to her house in the north. She went back to her normal life, but her eyes and ears were always open as she anticipated his return. Love was awakening in her heart. Do you remember when you were in love? All you could do was think about him and talk about him and talk to him. Look at this Shulamite maid. Can you see the awakening of love in her heart? Well:

<u>She testified: "I love Him"</u>

She referred to him as *"him whom my soul loveth"* (Chapter 3:1). All she can do is think about him; all she can do is talk about him. Are you so in love with your King that all you can do is think about Him and talk about Him?

<u>She testified: "I listen for Him"</u>

In verse 8 of Chapter 2, she declares: *"The voice of my beloved!"* What does he say? *"My beloved spake, and said unto me, Rise up, my love, my fair one, and come away"* (verse 10). He wanted her to leave her work and go with him for an adventure in the country. She is clearly listening for the sound of his voice. Do you recall the words of the Lord Jesus? *"My sheep hear My voice, and I know them, and they follow Me"* (John 10:27). Do you know where you can hear His voice? In His Word. Are you listening to His voice as He speaks to you though His Word?

<u>She testified: "I live for Him"</u>

She declares: *"My beloved is mine, and I am his"* (Chapter 2:16). She was saying: *"He belongs to me and I belong to Him. I exist for him. My world is Him."*

Incidentally, as a married couple, do you live for each other? You certainly do before you get married, but sometimes things change!

One girl told her mother: *"John spends so much money on me! I wish I could think of some way to get him to quit spending so much."*
Do you know what her mother said? *"Marry him!"*

But, tell me, are you living for your King? Can you say with Paul: *"For to me to live is Christ"* (Philippians 1:21)?

<u>She testified: "I look for Him"</u>

In the opening verses of Chapter 3, she goes to bed and has a dream about her lover. She is looking for him.

What about us? Are we, are you: *"Looking for that blessed hope, and the glorious appearing of the great God and our Saviour Jesus Christ"* (Titus 2:13)?

It is said that every evening Horatius Bonar looked into the darkness of the night and said: *"Perhaps tonight, Lord!"* and opened the curtains in the morning with: *"Perhaps today, Lord!"*

So ends the first part in this Song.

(2) <u>RELATIONSHIP: Chapter 3 verse 6 to Chapter 5 verse 1 - Events Accompanying the Wedding</u>

Can you picture this? One day, she is out in the fields and notices horses and chariots and a great cloud of dust appearing. She asks her brothers who it is. They tell her it is the landlord, King Solomon. He has come from Jerusalem to visit his estates. They get ready to bow down low before the King. *She has never seen him and so she takes a look, only to find that the King in the big chariot is her young man.* So she leaves the farm and travels south to live in the city. They are married and set up home together. Now I want you to notice here:

(a) THE BRIDEGROOM

Look at Chapter 3 verses 6 and 7: *"Who is this that cometh out of the wilderness like pillars of smoke, perfumed with myrrh and frankincense, with all powders of the merchant? Behold his bed, which is Solomon's; threescore valiant men are about it, of the valiant of Israel"*. Keep in mind that Solomon was both a king (Chapters 1:4, 12; 3:9) and a shepherd (Chapters 1:7-8; 2:16; 6:2-3).

In Old Testament days, rulers were called shepherds (see Jeremiah 23:4 and Ezekiel 34:2). The eastern sheik was the father of a household, the shepherd of a flock and a king over a realm. (It is delightful that these three images are contained in Luke 12 verse 32 where the Lord Jesus gives a promise: *"Fear not, little flock; for it is your Father's good pleasure to give you the kingdom"*.) But, look, here is the King coming to claim his bride.

Can you see something of *His Pomp*? Chapter 3 verse 6 refers to *"pillars of smoke"* and to *"myrrh and frankincense"*.

Can you see something of *His Power*? Chapter 3 verses 7 and 8 refer *to "valiant men"* and to *"swords"* and *"war"*.

Can you see something of *His Prosperity*? Chapter 3 verse 9 and 10 refer to the *"wood of Lebanon"* and to *"silver"* and to *"gold"* and to *"purple"*.

The daughters of Jerusalem get excited and sing to each other: *"Go forth, O ye daughters of Zion, and behold king Solomon with the crown wherewith his mother crowned him in the day of his espousals"* (Chapter 3:11).

The bride has her attendants, the King has joy in his heart and the time has finally come for the wedding to take place. Do we not have here a reminder of the coming of the King of Kings to claim His bride, the church?

(b) THE BRIDE

We all know that in modern marriages the bride is the centre of attention. *"What did the bride wear?"* is the big question that is always asked.

I want you to see here that the King is more concerned with her own beauty than with her dress. He has claimed her for himself and it is now their wedding night. She will lay aside her veil as a symbol that she belongs to him and that she has nothing to hide.

To the Ephesian believers, Paul said three things about the church:

He compared the church to a Building. That has to do with the Foundation of the church.

He compared the church to a Body. That has to do with the Function of the church.

Finally, he compared the church to a Bride. That has to do with the Fidelity of the church.

Do you see how the groom opens his speech? *"Behold, thou art fair, my love"* (Chapter 4:1).

Do you see how he closes his speech? *"Thou art all fair, my love"* (Chapter 4:7). He says: *"You are beautiful!"*

What a day that will be when we shall be presented *"to Himself a glorious church, not having spot, or wrinkle, or any such thing; but that it should be holy and without blemish"* (Ephesians 5:27).

As J. N. Darby wrote:

"And is it so! I shall be like Thy Son?
Is this the grace which He for me has won?
Father of glory - thought beyond all thought!
In glory, to His own blest likeness brought."

(c) THE BLISS

Wedding bliss! Is this not what God intended when He brought Adam and Eve together? *"Therefore shall a man leave his father and his mother, and shall cleave unto his wife: and they shall be one flesh. And they were both naked, the man and his wife, and were not ashamed"* (Genesis 2:24-25).

Do you know what God's kind of marriage is? ***It is a total commitment of the total person with another person until death.*** *An exclusive relationship and an enduring relationship.* Incidentally, did you notice that Solomon rejoiced that his bride was a virgin? Look at Chapter 4 verse 12: *"A garden enclosed is my sister, my spouse; a spring shut up, a fountain sealed"*. These are terms of exclusiveness. A walled garden is one that only the owner of the garden can enter. Solomon's bride did not give herself to anyone but only to him.

Then, in verse 16 of Chapter 4, she portrays herself as an *"open garden"*. In other words, it was not until she was married that they could enjoy physical love.

Do you know something? God wants us to stay sexually pure. People today speak of safe sex. The only safe sex is within the confines of the marriage bond. So here the marriage is consummated. They are enjoying *"a mountain top"* experience as they share their love.

(3) FELLOWSHIP: Chapter 5 verse 2 to Chapter 8 verse 14 - Events Following the Wedding

Are you aware what a Jewish wedding was like? It could last for a week and, during the week of the marriage celebration, the bride and groom were treated like a King and a Queen. They were treated like royalty. Modern couples have a *"honeymoon"* and usually travel to some place where they can be left alone. But, eventually, the couple have to return to life with its problems and duties - and so did Solomon and his wife. You will notice that the Shulamite had another disturbing dream. Look at:

(a) HER DREAM

"I sleep, but my heart waketh: it is the voice of my beloved that knocketh, saying, Open to me, my sister, my love" (Chapter 5:2). Apparently, she had locked the door and gone to bed without him. She is asleep, but the voice of her beloved comes from outside the door. He wants her to share her love with him, but she is too lazy to get up. Do you see what she says? *"I have put off my coat ... I have washed my feet"* (verses 3 and 4). It is as though she says: *"Please, don't bother me, I am too comfortable."* Then she sees his hand (verse 4) and she realises her sin. Remember His hands are pierced! She then rises, but, alas, her beloved has gone.

Are there times when the Lord wants to fellowship with you but you are too busy? Like Martha, are you troubled about *"many things"*, but have you neglected that *"one thing"* (Luke 10:38-42)? God wants to have holy tryst with us!

Some Christians who would not think of missing the Lord's Supper make that observance the sum total of their commitment to the local church! They think they can sit back and relax after that they have *"washed their feet"*, so to speak.

Realising her mistake, the Shulamite sought him. She called, but he did not answer, so she went seeking him. In contrast to the events of Chapter 3, this time the city guards did not co-operate with her. In fact, they smote her and wounded her. Then she spoke to the daughters of Jerusalem and told them that she was faint from love. *"I charge you, O daughters of Jerusalem, if ye find my beloved, that ye tell him, that I am sick of love"* (Chapter 5:8). They asked her what made her beloved so special and in reply we see:

(b) HER DESCRIPTION

Do you see how she describes her beloved? She talks about:

His Purity

"My beloved is white and ruddy" (verse 10). White is the symbol of purity and holiness; ruddy is the symbol of glowing health. The Bible says Christ knew no sin. He did no sin. In Him is no sin. He is the flawless, faultless, sinless, spotless One.

His Position

He is the *"chiefest among ten thousand"* (verse 10). Christ is the chiefest, not merely of ten thousand, but the chiefest among every ten thousand that the heart can conceive or the mind can imagine!

His Person

Notice that she describes everything about Him and comes to this conclusion: *"Yea, he is altogether lovely. This is my beloved, and this is my friend, O daughters of Jerusalem"* (verse 16).

It is now daylight and the women of Jerusalem offer to help her to find her husband, but do you see:

(c) HER DISCERNMENT

The Shulamite knows him well and knows where he has gone. *"My beloved is gone down into his garden, to the beds of spices, to feed in the gardens, and to gather lilies"* (Chapter 6 verse 2).

How well do you know your spouse? One of the important elements in a marriage is getting to know each other - so that we can read each other's minds and anticipate actions and words.

Solomon was not lost to her, even though they were not together. He was feeding his flock in the garden and she knew where to go.

And the moment he saw her, he began to speak about:

(d) HER DELIGHTFULNESS

"Thou art beautiful, O my love, as Tirzah, comely as Jerusalem" (Chapter 6 verse 4). Tirzah was the capital of the northern kingdom of Israel before Samaria was built. It was situated in a beautiful part of the country. The very name *"Tirzah"* means *"delightful"*. What Solomon was saying was this: *"You are fit for a king!"*

In verses 4 to 7 of this Chapter, he tells her that she is **Fair**. In verse 9, he tells her that she is **First**. You see, in the eyes of the Shulamite, Solomon was *"altogether lovely"* - beautiful - and in Solomon's eyes, his wife was the only one of her kind, unique. Even the daughters of Jerusalem praised the Shulamite for her beauty. They blessed her. They praised her.

In Chapter 7, they express their mutual love. She can say: *"I am my beloved's, and his desire is toward me"* (verse 10), and then we see:

(e) HER DESIRE

She wants to make a visit to the country. This is something Solomon had wanted to do previously, but she had - in Chapter 2 verses 8 to 17 - refused. Sometimes, visiting another place gives a freshness to a married couple, and she gives promises to give him her love. *"Let us get up early to the vineyards ... there will I give thee my loves"* (Chapter 7:12).

In the final section of the book, the daughters of Jerusalem see the couple returning home from their honeymoon trip to the villages and they notice:

(f) HER DEPENDENCE

The question is asked: *"Who is this that cometh up from the wilderness, leaning upon her beloved?"* (Chapter 8:5). She is leaning on her beloved.

The hymnwriter knew the joy of dependence on the Lord Jesus:

"What have I to dread, what have I to fear,
Leaning on the everlasting arms?
I have blessed peace with my Lord so near,
Leaning on the everlasting arms."

The book closes with the Shulamite in her garden, conversing with some friends. Her husband calls to her, because he wants to hear her voice. You see, there is a place for other friends, but no-one must replace the spouse God gives to us.

How does the bride respond to her groom? Do you see:

(g) HER DECLARATION

She tells him, in effect, to hurry up! *"Make haste, my beloved, and be thou like to a roe or to a young hart upon the mountains of spices"* (Chapter 8:14). She is waiting to experience his love.

So this love song ends, where the book of Revelation ends, where the Bible itself ends. *"Even so, come, Lord Jesus"* (Revelation 22:20).

Does this book not ultimately speak of Christ? Can we not say of Him: *"My beloved is mine, and I am His"* and *"Yea, He is altogether lovely"*?

I am bound to Him by the *old cord of Creation* - He created me.
I am bound to Him by the *strong cord of election* - He chose me.
I am bound to Him by the *red cord of redemption* - He redeemed me.
I am bound to Him by the *new cord of decision* - I responded to His love.

In the words of Dr. Sidow Baxter:

"Sweet wonder, all Divine,
That He should now be mine!
The rapture, who can tell
Where He has cast His spell?

Perfection's crown is He,
The sum of bliss to me,
My endless Heaven to be
Is Jesus."

In September 2014, Ulster lost one of its most renowned preachers - Ian Paisley. Here is how Dr. Paisley spoke of Christ in meetings at Ballymena at which some of our family were saved:

'He is purity without alloy. He is beauty without defect. He is loveliness without flaw. Every way our Saviour is viewed He is altogether lovely.

He is altogether lovely in His Person.
He is altogether lovely in His Passion.
He is altogether lovely in His Pardon.
He is altogether lovely in His Peace.
He is altogether lovely in His Provision.
He is altogether lovely in His Priesthood.
He is altogether lovely in His Power.

We exalt Him. We adore Him. We worship Him. We bless Him. We praise Him. We gaze upon Him. We love Him. We want no other. We desire no other. We will have no other. We will cling to no other. We will seek no other. We will look to no other. We will love no other. *"My beloved is mine and I am His." "Yea, He is altogether lovely."'*

CHAPTER 6
Isaiah

Ray Stedman tells the story that during World War II an American pilot was flying near the South Pacific island of Guadalcanal when he encountered a squadron of enemy planes. The enemy attacked him and, in the ensuing dogfight, his plane was hit and seriously damaged. Though he was uninjured, his plane was going down. The pilot managed to nudge his plane away from the enemy-held island to a tiny island not far away. He bailed out, his parachute opened and he floated down toward the little jungle island. During his pre-flight briefing, he had been told that some of the neighbouring islands were inhabited by cannibals. His boots had no sooner hit the sand than a group of islanders came running toward him. The island people surrounded him and took him back to their village.

To his amazement, he discovered that a number of them spoke English - and they were not cannibals. *They were Christians.* The pilot was an atheist. Though relieved that he was not *'on the menu'*, he was convinced that these islanders had simply traded tribal myths for Christian myths. Since he had a long wait before being rescued, he had plenty of time to talk with the islanders about their beliefs. One day, he noticed one of the villagers sitting near a cooking fire, reading his Bible. *"Do you believe the stories in that book?"* the American asked. The villager pointed to the black pot over the cooking fire: ***"If it were not for this book,"*** he replied, ***"you would be in that pot!"***

The Bible is a powerful force for changing human lives. As the Hebrew epistle declares: *"The word of God is quick, and powerful, and sharper than any twoedged sword, piercing even to the dividing asunder of soul and spirit, and of the joints and marrow, and is a discerner of the thoughts and intents of the heart"* (Hebrews 4:12).

Most begin their Christian experience by reading the New Testament - and that is understandable. Sadly, however, many never get round to reading the Old Testament. Do you recall that the 39 Old Testament books are divided into 5 categories?

1. *The Law or Pentateuch: Genesis to Deuteronomy*
2. *History: Joshua to Esther*
3. *Wisdom or Poetry: Job to Song of Solomon*
4. *The Major Prophets: Isaiah to Daniel*
5. *The Minor Prophets: Hosea to Malachi*

Isaiah was the greatest of the prophets! The book of Isaiah is found in the middle of the Bible and it has often been called *"a miniature Bible"*. How many books does the Bible have? 66! How many books are there in the Old Testament? 39! In the New Testament? 27! Well, the book of Isaiah divides in exactly the same way. The first part of the book has 39 chapters. There is a distinct division at Chapter 40 so that the remaining 27 chapters constitute the second part of this book. Thus the book of Isaiah is a kind of Bible all in itself.

Even more remarkable is that fact that Chapters 40 to 66 divide clearly into three sections, each of nine chapters and the first two end with the same solemn phrase: *"There is no peace, saith the LORD, unto the wicked"* (Isaiah 48:22) and *"There is no peace, saith my God, to the wicked"* (Isaiah 57:21). But do not stop there, for each of these nine chapters divide into three sections of three chapters. If you take the middle section of the three, the three sections are Chapters 49-51, 52-54 and 55-57. Now, take the middle section - Chapters 52-54 - and take the middle verse of the middle chapter of the middle section. Where are we? We are at the Cross. *"But He was wounded for our transgressions, He was bruised for our iniquities: the chastisement of our peace was upon Him; and with His stripes we are healed"* (Chapter 53:5).

At the centre of this tremendous book, God has put the Lamb. He is the crux, the centre and the heart. Let us keep the Lamb where God has put Him - in the centre!

Now, when we come to Isaiah there are certain things we must keep before us. The first is:

1. THE PROPHET

Think of his Name.

Isaiah means: *"The Lord is salvation"*, and salvation or deliverance is the key theme of his book.

As Warren Wiersbe says:

"Isaiah spoke of the deliverance of Judah from Assyrian invasion - Chapters 36-37. He spoke of the deliverance of the nation from Babylonian captivity - Chapter 40. He spoke of the future deliverance of the Jews from worldwide dispersion among the Gentiles - Chapters 11-12. He spoke about the deliverance of lost sinners from judgment - Chapter 53 - and he spoke of the deliverance of creation from the bondage of sin when the Kingdom is established - Chapters 60 and 66."

Isaiah was a prophet. He is described as such in, for example, John 12 verse 38. Now, what was a prophet? Well, whenever a prophet appeared in Israel, it was always a sign that apostasy and rebellion were predominant in the nation. So the primary ministry of a prophet was to deliver a message from God calling the nation back to God. In Deuteronomy 18, Moses predicts the coming of a particular prophet – the Lord Jesus Himself. He adds that God had said: *"I will put My words in His mouth; and He shall speak unto them all that I shall command Him"*. You say: *"I thought a prophet was someone who foretold the future!"* Well, he *was* a *"foreteller"*, but he was first of all a man with a message from God for his own generation. A ***"forthteller"*** rather than a *"foreteller"*.

The fact that the Old Testament refers to Isaiah as *"the son of Amoz"* thirteen times has led some to believe that Isaiah's father was a man of some prominence.

Isaiah was called to his ministry *"in the year that King Uzziah died"* - see Chapter 6 verse 1. That year was 739 B.C. and Isaiah's ministry spanned a period of about 50 years. Jewish tradition believes that Isaiah was born into nobility and that he mixed freely with royalty. Tradition also says that the wicked King Manasseh killed Isaiah by having him sawn in half. Hebrews 11 verse 37 refers to those who were *"sawn asunder"*. Amongst those was, it seems, Isaiah.

2. THE PRINCES

Various kings are mentioned in Chapter 1 verse 1. Isaiah prophesied during the reigns of these four kings – Uzziah, Jotham, Ahaz and Hezekiah. He was martyred in the reign of a fifth.

You will recall that the nation divided after the death of Solomon. Ten tribes in the north organized as Israel and two tribes in the south as Judah. The capital of Israel was Samaria and the capital of Judah was Jerusalem.

Isaiah ministered in Jerusalem but his messages touched both the north and the south. Isaiah lived to see Israel, the northern kingdom, decline and go into captivity to Assyria.

3. THE POWERS

In that day, various powers were all vying for position. The empires of Egypt, Assyria, Babylon and Persia overshadow the whole prophetic era, with the empires of Greece and Rome colouring the visions of Daniel. The power struggles of these nations form the historical background against which the prophets poured their warnings, their wooings, and their woes.

The prophet, the princes, the powers, and what about:

4. THE PROBLEM

The Problem of Isaiah! In recent years, this book has been subjected to criticism in relation to its unity and authorship. As wicked King Manasseh took the saw and divided Isaiah into two, so there are those today who would take the saw of criticism and modernism and divide this book into two or perhaps three sections. They talk of a *"Deutero-Isaiah"* (*'Deutero'* means second). Some even talk of a *"Trito-Isaiah* (*'Trito'* means third). So now we have 'three Isaiahs'! You see, what these critics are basically saying is that God does not know the future - and so they contend that various prophetical sections of the book are actually historical sections. But, our God *does* know the future and He is able to predict the future. Why, in this very book He says: *"I am God, and there is none like Me, declaring the end from the beginning, and from ancient times the things that are not yet done"* (Chapter 46:9-10). Moreover, the New Testament puts its stamp of approval on this book. John, in Chapter 12 of his Gospel, speaks of Isaiah the prophet. There are further references in Romans 9 verses 27 and 29 and Chapter 10 verses 16 and 20. Different verses from different sections of Isaiah are quoted - and yet attributed to the one prophet, Isaiah. This is enough for me!

The book falls into three distinct parts. The keynote of the first part is *Condemnation;* the keynote of the second part is *Confiscation,* and the keynote of the last part is *Consolation.* In the first part, *Assyria* is central; in the third part, it is *Babylon,* and the second part *points back to the one and forward to the other.*

Section 1: CONDEMNATION - Chapters 1-35: PROPHETIC

Isaiah has been called *"the evangelical prophet"* and the *evangelical message* of this prophet cannot be fully appreciated and applied until sin is exposed for what it really is. So, in this section:

(a) SERMONS ARE PREACHED

The book opens with a series of sermons denouncing the personal sins of the people (Chapters 1-6) and the national sins of the leaders (Chapters 7-12). These sermons or prophecies of Isaiah were given against a backdrop of peace and prosperity. The first four chapters of the book seem to belong to the closing years of Jotham's reign. (See Chapter 6:1 and 7:1.) This was a reign that had known some prosperity. 2 Chronicles 27 verse 6 records that he *"became mighty"*. However, along with the prosperity came pride and indulgence. There was an *"every man for himself"* attitude. The poor were oppressed and injustice was common, hence the instruction: *"Seek judgment, relieve the oppressed, judge the fatherless, plead for the widow"* (Chapter 1:17).

One of the great concerns of Isaiah was that religion had become a ritual. The people went through the routine of worship, but their hearts remained cold toward the Lord. God declares: *"To what purpose is the multitude of your sacrifices unto Me?"* (Chapter 1 verse 11). The Lord Jesus was equally concerned about an outward empty show. He applied Isaiah 29 verse 13 to the Pharisees and scribes of His day. *"Well hath Esaias prophesied of you hypocrites, as it is written, This people honoureth Me with their lips, but their heart is far from Me"* (Mark 7:6). Before passing judgment on the worshippers of a bygone day, perhaps we should confess the *"sins of the worshipping church"*. Do we worship with a full heart? What about our minds? Where are they as we enter the presence of God? The nation, Judah, was a disappointment to God. He intended them to be fruitful - and in the opening verses of Chapter 5, they are likened to a vineyard - but they brought forth wild grapes.

One of the other great concerns of Isaiah was foreign alliances. Because of the increasing power of Assyria, Rezin the king of Syria and Pekah the king of Israel tried to persuade Ahaz, the king of Judah, to join them. When Ahaz refused, they attacked Judah. Isaiah told Ahaz to trust in the Lord, but he refused and turned to Assyria for help. The sad story is told in 2 Chronicles 28 verses 16 to 25. You see, instead of trusting God, they made alliances with whichever power seemed able to provide the best protection at the time. *"Woe to them that go down to Egypt for help"* (Isaiah 31:1). The Lord did not get a look in!

I wonder whether in that time of crisis *you* were trusting the Lord. You see, when you fear the Lord, you do not need to fear the people or the circumstances.

(b) SENTENCES ARE PROCLAIMED

In Chapters 13 to 23, sentences of judgment are passed on the nations. Isaiah called these prophetic utterances: *"burdens"*. Look at Chapter 13 verse 1: *"The burden of Babylon"*; Chapter 15 verse 1:

"The burden of Moab"; Chapter 17 verse 1: *"The burden of Damascus"*; Chapter 19 verse 1: *"The burden of Egypt"*; Chapter 21 verse 11: *"The burden of Dumah"* and Chapter 23 verse 1: *"The burden of Tyre"*. The Hebrew word *"burden"* means *"to lift up"*. You see, the prophet was carrying a heavy weight because of the solemn nature of his message. He was announcing judgments that involved the destruction of cities and the slaughter of thousands of people.

Is it not wonderful to know in the words of Isaiah: *"Behold, the nations are as a drop of a bucket ... And the inhabitants thereof are as grasshoppers"* (Chapter 40:15, 22)?

Here is an interesting quote! *"Whether you like it or not, history is on our side. We will bury you."*

Do you know who said that?

The Premier of the Soviet Union, Nikita Khrushchev, made that statement to a group of Western diplomats on 18th November, 1956. But Khrushchev is dead and the Soviet Union no longer exists! His boastful prophecy was not fulfilled. Do you know why? *"The most High ruleth in the kingdom of men, and giveth it to whomsoever He will."* (Daniel 4:32).

God is still on the throne. *"History is His story!"* And so we see here:

(c) SONGS ARE PRESENTED

There are songs of future glory for the nation in Chapters 24 to 27. You see, Israel is going to be redeemed through the world being judged. Isaiah speaks of a particular day in his prophecy. Do you know what he calls it? He calls it *"the day of the LORD"* - see Chapter 13 verse 6 and Chapter 24 verses 21 to 23. This is that period of time when God will send judgment to the nations and purify Israel in preparation for the coming of His King to reign in Jerusalem. The *"day of the Lord"* is described by John in Revelation Chapters 6 to 19. It is described by the prophets - for example, Joel 1 verse 15; Zephaniah 1 verse 7 and Zechariah 14 verse 1 - and it is described by the Lord Jesus in the Olivet

Discourse of Matthew 24 and 25. It is going to be a time of terrible suffering. The environment will be devastated. Millions of people will die. True believers in the Lord Jesus, however, will not be on the earth when this judgment comes. They are going up! They will see Jesus Christ - and not the Antichrist.

To the prophets, *"the day of the Lord"* was foreshadowed by events in their own day. Assyria's conquest of the northern kingdom and the Babylonian captivity of Judah both picture *"the coming day of the Lord"*. But Isaiah not only foresaw a *"grim"* day, he foresaw a *"glorious"* day when Israel would be singing again. *"In that day shall this song be sung in the land of Judah"* (Chapter 26:1). In the previous chapter - Chapter 25 - there is a prophecy, a picture of the Lord Himself making a *"feast of fat things, a feast of wines on the lees"*. The people are saved by God. They are glad and rejoice in His salvation. For the Old Testament Jew, a feast was a picture of the Kingdom Age when Messiah would reign over Israel and all the nations of the world.

There are three comings of the nation of Israel into the promised land:

The first time they came into the land, it was from Egypt - and they gave the world *the Bible.* The second time they came into the land, it was from Babylon - and they gave the world *the Saviour.* The third time is what is being prophesied here, after the purging of the nation in the fires of the great tribulation - they will give the world *the Millennium.*

And:

Jesus shall reign where'er the sun
Does his successive journeys run,
His kingdom stretch from shore to shore
Till moons shall wax and wane no more.

For Him shall endless prayer be made,
And endless praises crown His head;
His name, like sweet perfume, shall rise
With ev'ry morning sacrifice.

People and realms of ev'ry tongue
Dwell on His love with sweetest song;
And infant voices shall proclaim
Their early blessings on His name.

(d) SINS ARE PORTRAYED

Here we have a series of *"woes"* that focus primarily on Jerusalem. Do you know what Isaiah is seeking to do here? He is trying to get the rulers of Judah to stop trusting *"power politics"* and international treaties and instead start trusting the Lord.

Let us look at one of these *"woes"*, quoted already: *"Woe to them that go down to Egypt for help"* (Chapter 31:1). Their faith was in men not in God. Going to Egypt for help had always been a temptation to the Jews. (see Exodus 13:17 and 14:11-12; Numbers 11:5 and 14:3.)

Was there any reason why they should fear the Assyrians? Well, does a lion fear a flock of sheep? Do eagles fear as they hover over their young in the nest? In one single night, as described in Isaiah 37 verse 36, the Assyrian army was wiped out. Think of the money Judah would have saved and the distress they would have avoided had they only rested in the Lord. But, they trusted the words of the Egyptians and not the Word of God.

As we face our enemies and challenges, the temptation is always to turn to the world or to the flesh for help. But, we need to trust the Lord! Do you know what faith is? Here is one definition: *Faith is living without scheming.*

That is what Isaiah was saying to Judah and Jerusalem - and that is what he is saying to us today!

Section 2: CONFISCATION - Chapters 36-39: HISTORIC

To *confiscate* is *"to seize"*. By this time, Assyria had swooped down on the Northern Kingdom of Israel and had taken them into captivity. After that took place - in 722 B.C. - Judah had constant problems with Assyria. 2 Kings 18 describes how Hezekiah finally rebelled against Assyria. When Sennacherib threatened to attack, Hezekiah tried to bribe him. Sennacherib accepted the bribe, but he broke the treaty and invaded Judah in 701 B.C.

When we come to Hezekiah, we are looking at one of the godliest kings in Judah. Do you know what the Bible says of Hezekiah? *"He trusted in the LORD God of Israel; so that after him was none like him among all the kings of Judah, nor any that were before him. For he clave to the LORD, and departed not from following Him, but kept His commandments, which the LORD commanded Moses"* (2 Kings 18:5-6).

Former U.S. Secretary of State, Dr. Henry Kissinger, once told the New York Times: *"There cannot be a crisis next week. My schedule is already full!"* Crises come, whether schedules permit them or not, and sometimes crises seem to pile up.

How do we handle them? One of my favourite Bible commentators, Warren Wiersbe, says:

"What life does to us depends on what life finds in us. A crisis does not make a person. It shows what a person is made of!"

Hezekiah faced three crises involving three enemies in a short space of time.

There was an *International Crisis*: the invasion of the Assyrian army.

There was a *Personal Crisis*: his sickness and near-death experience.

There was a *National Crisis*: the visit of the Babylonian envoys.

He came through the first two victoriously, but the third tripped him up. Notice then:

(a) HEZEKIAH'S PROBLEM

Problems often come when circumstances seem to be at their best. Hezekiah had led the people in a great reformation and the people were reunited in the fear of the Lord. But, instead of *"receiving blessing"*, they found themselves *"facing battles"*. *"And thus did Hezekiah throughout all Judah, and wrought that which was good and right and truth before the LORD his God ... after these things, and the establishment thereof, Sennacherib king of Assyria came, and entered into Judah"* (2 Chronicles 31:20 and Chapter 32:1).

Had the Lord turned a blind eye and a deaf ear to all that Hezekiah had done? Of course not! But the Assyrian invasion was a part of the discipline of the Lord to teach them to trust Him alone. Do you recall that even Hezekiah had at first put his trust in treaties and treasures? 2 Kings 18 verses 15 and 16 record how Hezekiah gave silver and treasures and gold to the king of Assyria. Judah's attempt to get help from Egypt was an act of unbelief. They decided to *"strengthen themselves in the strength of Pharaoh, and to trust in the shadow of Egypt"* (Isaiah 30:2).

Hezekiah and his people needed to learn what we still need to learn. To use that definition again: *"faith is living without scheming"*. Are you also facing a problem of great proportions? Are you trusting God for it?

(b) HEZEKIAH'S PRAYER

Look at Chapter 37 verses 14 to 20: *"And Hezekiah received the letter from the hand of the messengers, and read it: and Hezekiah went up unto the house of the LORD, and spread it before the LORD. And Hezekiah prayed unto the LORD, saying, O LORD of hosts, God of Israel, that dwellest between the cherubims, Thou art the God, even Thou alone, of all the kingdoms of the earth: Thou hast made heaven and earth. Incline Thine ear, O LORD, and hear; open Thine eyes, O LORD, and see: and hear all the words of Sennacherib, which hath sent to reproach the living God. Of a truth, LORD, the kings of Assyria have laid waste all the nations, and their countries, And have cast their gods into the fire: for they were no gods, but the work of men's hands, wood and stone: therefore they have destroyed them. Now therefore, O LORD our God, save us from his hand, that all the kingdoms of the earth may know that Thou art the LORD, even Thou only."*

Do you see how saturated it is with Biblical theology? Did you notice that Hezekiah recognised God as the <u>Creator?</u> *"Thou has made heaven and earth."* He recognized God as the <u>only true and living God.</u> *"Thou art the God, even Thou alone."* He recognised God as the <u>Covenant God of Israel.</u> He recognised God as the *"LORD of hosts,"* that is the *"Lord of the armies"*. Did you notice the real basis for prayer? *"That all the kingdoms of the earth may know that Thou art the LORD, even Thou only."* You see, the glory of God was his chief concern. Sometimes, when we pray it is for our own glory - or the glory of the family or the nation or the church. We should seek glory for the Lord.

How did God respond? *"Then the angel of the LORD went forth, and smote in the camp of the Assyrians a hundred and fourscore and five thousand: and when they arose early in the morning, behold, they were all dead corpses"* (Chapter 37:36).

Do you believe that God is *"able to do exceeding abundantly above all that we ask or think"* (Ephesians 3:20)?

But it was not all good news, for notice:

(c) HEZEKIAH'S PAIN

He experienced physical suffering. Although this took place before the Assyrian invasion, that invasion was impending. Can you imagine how the people of Judah reacted when they heard that their king was going to die and Assyria was on the march?

Hezekiah cried to the Lord and was given 15 more years of life, but he did not use the time well, for do you notice:

(d) HEZEKIAH'S PRIDE

What happened is told in Isaiah 39 and what happened is this - the Babylonians arrived with a *"Get well"* card from the son of the King of Babylon. Hezekiah was pleased that someone so far away was thinking about him. He showed the visitors around his palace so that they would tell their King what a wonderful king Hezekiah was. But, when Isaiah heard what happened, he was horrified and told Hezekiah that one day the King of Babylon would take everything the visitors of Babylon had seen.

When Satan as the roaring lion (1 Peter 5:8) cannot defeat us, he comes as the deceiving serpent. (2 Corinthians 11:3). What Assyria could not do with weapons, Babylon could do with gifts.

Do we not need to stay humble before the Lord? In the words of the Psalmist: *"a broken and a contrite heart, O God, Thou wilt not despise"* (Psalm 51:17).

Isaiah – a book of Condemnation and Confiscation, but notice finally:

Section 3: CONSOLATION - Chapters 40-66: MESSIANIC

In these chapters, Isaiah is looking far ahead. He sees Babylon destroying Jerusalem and the Jews going into captivity. But, he sees God forgiving His people, delivering them from captivity, and taking them back to Jerusalem to rebuild the Temple and restore the nation. As always, the prophet's vision is filled with the vision of Christ. **Isaiah sees His two comings - His coming to redeem and His coming to reign.** But while he saw these two aspects of Christ's coming, he did not see the church age which lay between. *Isaiah saw two mountain ranges of truth, one behind the other, but he could not see the valley in between.*

Now, as you study these chapters, keep in mind that they were originally addressed to a group of discouraged refugees who faced a long journey home and a difficult task when they got there. These last 27 chapters divide into three sections. Firstly, there is brought before us:

(a) THE GREATNESS OF GOD - Chapters 40-48

The emphasis here is on *God the Father.* Do you see:

The Greatness of His Person: Chapter 40

Look at Chapter 40 verses 18-22:

"To whom then will ye liken God? or what likeness will ye compare unto Him? The workman melteth a graven image, and the goldsmith spreadeth

it over with gold, and casteth silver chains. He that is so impoverished that he hath no oblation chooseth a tree that will not rot; he seeketh unto him a cunning workman to prepare a graven image, that shall not be moved. Have ye not known? have ye not heard? hath it not been told you from the beginning? have ye not understood from the foundations of the earth? It is He that sitteth upon the circle of the earth, and the inhabitants thereof are as grasshoppers; that stretcheth out the heavens as a curtain, and spreadeth them out as a tent to dwell in."

How could this feeble remnant of Jews ever return to their land? The answer is in one word. *God. "Behold your God"* says the prophet. He is the Creator of the universe. Is He not able to strengthen and sustain you?

"Hast thou not known? hast thou not heard, that the everlasting God, the LORD, the Creator of the ends of the earth, fainteth not, neither is weary? there is no searching of His understanding. He giveth power to the faint; and to them that have no might He increaseth strength. Even the youths shall faint and be weary, and the young men shall utterly fall: But they that wait upon the LORD shall renew their strength; they shall mount up with wings as eagles; they shall run, and not be weary; and they shall walk, and not faint." (Chapter 40:28-31)

The Greatness of His Purpose: Chapter 41

Jehovah is not simply the God of the Jews. He is the Controller of the nations. He would raise up Cyrus from the east (verse 2) - Persia - but bring him down from the north - (verse 25). You see, Israel did not have anything to fear: *"Fear thou not; for I am with thee: be not dismayed; for I am thy God: I will strengthen thee; yea, I will help thee; yea, I will uphold thee with the right hand of My righteousness"* (verse 10). God was with them and, in the words of Romans 8 verse 28, was working out His purpose. He was working all things together for good.

The Greatness of His Pardon: Chapters 42-43

Here we are introduced to the Lord Jesus: *"Behold, My servant, whom I uphold; Mine elect, in whom My soul delighteth"* (Chapter

42:1). These words are quoted in Matthew 12 verses 18 to 21. We see His first coming in humility and grace and then His second coming in power and judgment. Of course, between these two events we have the entire church age. Here Isaiah chides the nation for having forgotten God: *"Thou hast not brought Me the small cattle of thy burnt offerings; neither hast thou honoured Me with thy sacrifices"* (Chapter 43:23). However, in His grace He would forgive their sins. *"I, even I, am He that blotteth out thy transgressions for Mine own sake, and will not remember thy sins"* (verse 25).

What a God we have! Time and again God says to His people: *"Fear not!"*

"But now thus saith the LORD that created thee, O Jacob, and He that formed thee, O Israel, Fear not: for I have redeemed thee, I have called thee by thy name; thou art Mine. When thou passest through the waters, I will be with thee; and through the rivers, they shall not overflow thee: when thou walkest through the fire, thou shalt not be burned; neither shall the flame kindle upon thee. For I am the LORD thy God, the Holy One of Israel, thy Saviour: I gave Egypt for thy ransom, Ethiopia and Seba for thee. Since thou wast precious in My sight, thou hast been honourable, and I have loved thee: therefore will I give men for thee, and people for thy life. Fear not: for I am with thee" (Chapter 43:1-5).

Are you fearful? Fearful, because of the circumstances before you, the enemy around you, and the inadequacy within you? God says: *"Fear not"*.

The Greatness of His Promises: Chapters 44-45

Read these chapters and notice how many times God repeats two words in these chapters. Do you know what they are? *"I will."*

In Chapter 44, God promises to restore Israel to their land, bless the land and reign as their King.

In Chapter 45, God promises to go before Cyrus as he captures the invincible fortress of Babylon. Do you know how Cyrus did it? He dried up the rivers that flowed into the city and went into the city under the gates. History records this event, but prophecy announced it hundreds of years before it happened.

The Greatness of His Power: Chapters 46-48

These chapters describe the utter ruin of Babylon. Is this not amazing? When Isaiah wrote this, Babylon was not yet a world power, so some of the Jews must have wondered what they were reading. However, Babylon *did* become a world power and they *did* conquer Judah, but one day *God would conquer them.*

Do you see here again the futility of idols? *"They bear him upon the shoulder, they carry him, and set him in his place, and he standeth; from his place shall he not remove: yea, one shall cry unto him, yet can he not answer, nor save him out of his trouble"* (Chapter 46:7). Instead of the heathen gods carrying their people, the people would carry the gods!

But, God would carry His people. He would bring salvation to Zion.

"Hearken unto me, O house of Jacob, and all the remnant of the house of Israel, which are borne by Me from the belly, which are carried from the womb: And even to your old age I am He; and even to hoar hairs will I carry you: I have made, and I will bear; even I will carry, and will deliver you" (Chapter 46:3-4).

(b) THE GRACE OF GOD: Chapters 49-57

The emphasis here is on *God the Son,* the suffering Servant.

At the heart of this section is Isaiah 52 verse 13 to Chapter 53 verse 12. The Servant that Isaiah describes is the Messiah and the New Testament affirms that this Servant-Messiah is Jesus Christ, the Son of God. (See, for example, Matthew 8:17 and Acts 8:27-40).

So we have found the central section of the book and we have found the central chapter. What then is the central statement? Look at Isaiah 53 verses 5-6: *"But He was wounded for our transgressions, He was bruised for our iniquities: the chastisement of our peace was upon Him; and with His stripes we are healed. All we like sheep have gone astray; we have turned every one to his own way; and the LORD hath laid on Him the iniquity of us all."*

There it is! Isaiah the evangelical prophet; Isaiah the great Gospel preacher of the Old Testament; Isaiah whose very name means *"Jehovah saves"* brings us step by step to Calvary and leaves us standing as guilty sinners before the One who loved us enough to die for us. It was this very sentence that the Ethiopian eunuch was reading in his chariot when Philip led him to Christ in Acts 8. That is what this great book of Isaiah is all about. It is about Christ. God's answer to man's desperate need.

Years ago, the great evangelist D. L. Moody was boarding a train. He had been conducting evangelistic meetings. Many had been saved. There was one man, however, who had kept putting it off. He knew he was a sinner. He knew he was lost. He knew he needed to be saved. He had intended to go forward and get the matter settled, but he had put it off and put it off. Now the meetings were over and D. L. Moody - the man who had been used of God to hammer away at his conscience - was leaving town. The man rushed off to the station, hoping to have a word with the preacher before he left, but he arrived just as the train was about to leave the station. He spotted D. L. Moody waving goodbye to a group of friends. He rushed down the platform. *"Mr. Moody, Mr. Moody,"* he cried. *"What must I do to be saved?"* The train was beginning to move and the desperate man ran alongside the coach. D. L. Moody looked at him. What could he say to point a man to Christ in just five seconds as the train was gathering speed? ***"Isaiah 53:6"***, he called. ***"Go in at the first 'all' and go out at the last one."***

The man went home, found his Bible and turned to Isaiah 53 verse 6. He went in at the first all. *"**All** we like sheep have gone astray." "Yes!"* he said, *"that's me alright. I have gone astray"*. He went out at the last all. *"All we like sheep have gone astray; we have turned every one to his own way; and the LORD hath laid on Him the iniquity of us **all**." "Thank God"*, he said. *"I am a sinner, but Jesus died for me"*.

That is the Gospel of Isaiah. That is the Gospel story of the Old Testament. That is the same Gospel we find in the New Testament.

"I am a sinner, but Jesus died for me."

Have you gone in at the first 'all' and come out at the last 'all'?

(c) THE GLORY OF GOD: Chapters 58-66

The emphasis here is on *God the Spirit.*

"So shall they fear the name of the LORD from the west, and His glory from the rising of the sun. When the enemy shall come in like a flood, the Spirit of the LORD shall lift up a standard against him" (Chapter 59:19).

"As for Me, this is My covenant with them, saith the LORD; My spirit that is upon thee" (Chapter 59:21).

"The Spirit of the LORD God is upon Me" (Chapter 61:1).

"But they rebelled, and vexed His holy Spirit: therefore He was turned to be their enemy, and He fought against them. Then He remembered the days of old, Moses, and His people, saying, Where is He that brought them up out of the sea with the shepherd of His flock? where is He that put His holy Spirit within him? That led them by the right hand of Moses with His glorious arm, dividing the water before them, to make Himself an everlasting name? That led them through the deep, as an horse in the wilderness, that they should not stumble? As a beast goeth down into the valley, the Spirit of the LORD caused him to rest: so didst Thou lead Thy people, to make Thyself a glorious name" (Chapter 63:10-14).

Now, one of the challenges of this book is this. *Will Isaiah's prophecies receive literal fulfilment or not?* Has the Lord abandoned national Israel and permanently replaced the nation with the church, meaning that there is no future for Israel? The answer is: *"No!"* and at least for two reasons.

The first is - the literal fulfilment of many of Isaiah's prophecies have already occurred.

John MacArthur says: *"To contend that those yet unfulfilled will see non-literal fulfilment is biblically groundless".*

A-Millennial teaching accepts literally all the prophecies relating to Christ's First Coming and then spiritualises and allegorises all the prophecies related to Christ's Second Coming!

The second is - Isaiah has much to say about God's faithfulness to Israel, that He would not reject the people He has created and chosen. Why, this nation is engraved on the palms of His hands! Jerusalem's walls are ever before His eyes! (Chapter 49:16) God is bound by His own Word to fulfil the promises He has made to Israel and in the closing section of Isaiah we see the glory of the coming kingdom.

"But be ye glad and rejoice for ever in that which I create: for, behold, I create Jerusalem a rejoicing, and her people a joy. And I will rejoice in Jerusalem, and joy in My people: and the voice of weeping shall be no more heard in her, nor the voice of crying.There shall be no more thence an infant of days, nor an old man that hath not filled his days: for the child shall die an hundred years old; but the sinner being an hundred years old shall be accursed. And they shall build houses, and inhabit them; and they shall plant vineyards, and eat the fruit of them. They shall not build, and another inhabit; they shall not plant, and another eat: for as the days of a tree are the days of My people, and Mine elect shall long enjoy the work of their hands.They shall not labour in vain, nor bring forth for trouble; for they are the seed of the blessed of the Lord, and their offspring with them. And it shall come to pass, that before they call, I will answer; and while they are yet speaking, I will hear. The wolf and the lamb shall feed together, and the lion shall eat straw like the bullock: and dust shall be the serpent's meat. They shall not hurt nor destroy in all My holy mountain, saith the Lord." (Isaiah 65:18-25)

What a picture of the blessings of the kingdom when Jerusalem will be the centre of the earth. At that time, the prayer *"Thy kingdom come"* will be answered. Christ will reign in righteousness, justice, truth and peace.

What should our response be to that coming crowning day?

Well, what was Isaiah's response to the glory of the Lord? To the call of the Lord?

"Here am I; send me" (Chapter 6:8).

"Mine are the hands to do the work,
My feet shall run for Thee,
My lips shall sound the glorious news,
Lord, Here am I, send me!"

The King is coming, but before He comes to redeem the nation, He is coming to rapture, to take from the world His own.

When that day dawns, may we not be ashamed before Him at His coming.

CHAPTER 7

Jeremiah

Ray Stedman tells the story that during the German occupation of Denmark in World War II, King Christian X demonstrated remarkable courage in the face of Nazi oppression. One morning, the King looked out of his window, and saw the hated Nazi flag flying over a public building in Copenhagen. He called for the German commandant and angrily demanded that the flag be removed.

The amused commandant refused: *"We Germans do not take orders"*, he replied. *"We give them."*

"If you do not have it removed this instant", said the King, *"a Danish soldier will take it down."*.

"Then he will be shot", said the Nazi officer.

"Fire away then", said the King, *"for I shall be that soldier"*.

The Germans removed the flag.

That is a profile in courage, the courage to stand up for a higher cause than life itself.

Now there are many pictures of courage throughout the Old and New Testaments - men and women who took a courageous and costly stand for the Lord. One of the most courageous of all was Jeremiah. *Jeremiah was a unique spiritual leader and one of the most outstanding personalities of the Old Testament.* Jeremiah recounts more of his life than any other prophet, telling of his ministry, the reactions of his audiences, his testings and his personal feelings. The name *"Jeremiah"* means *"Jehovah throws"*, in the sense of laying down a foundation, or *"Jehovah appoints, establishes, or sends"*.

Now while Jeremiah is one of the best-known of all the prophets, his book seems to have been neglected. How often have we heard a series of messages from this prophecy? People have neglected this book and perhaps for one of three reasons:

1. It is a Big Book

It is 52 chapters long, second only to Isaiah's 66 chapters. *Legend says that Jeremiah visited the Republic of Ireland, kissed the Blarney Stone and received the gift of the gab!* The length of the book reflects the number of prophecies in his 40 year ministry (627 - 586 B.C.). Some or all of them may have been dictated to his secretary Baruch - see Chapter 36 verse 4. It appears that for some it is too big a book to tackle.

2. It is a Hard Book

It is a difficult book to analyse, because it is not in chronological order. It is like a collection of sermons recorded at random.

Young says:

"Jeremiah's prophecies may seem to be somewhat scattered, but their arrangement enables the prophet to emphasize repetition. The themes of Jeremiah are recurring ones: the sinfulness of the nation and the approaching doom. Into his book, he weaves these thoughts and as we read on we meet them over and over again until the impression which they have made upon us is truly powerful and tremendous."

It *is* difficult to outline this book, but we could do it like this:

1. Before the Fall of Jerusalem: Chapters 1-33
2. During the Fall of Jerusalem: Chapters 34-39
3. After the Fall of Jerusalem: Chapters 40-52

The climax of the book is the fall of Jerusalem. Everything that goes before, which includes Jeremiah's prophecies, points to that hour of tragedy. This means:

3. It is a Sad Book

There seems to be nothing but bad news for Judah, and Jeremiah was feeling the pain at what was happening to the nation.

However, in spite of all these difficulties, this is a wonderful book. Imagine for a moment you are Jeremiah the preacher. You live during the last days of a decaying nation. You preach to the nation and call people to repentance, but no-one listens. You are threatened and opposed at every turn. You have no wife, no companionship because the days are evil and the Lord has told you not to marry. *"Thou shalt not take thee a wife"* (Chapter 16:2). You feel abandoned and alone, your friends have turned away from you. You wish you could quit, but you cannot. The Word of God burns in your bones and you have to speak it regardless of the consequences.

You love your nation and your people, but you see disaster looming. You see the enemy massing on the border ready to conquer your land and carry out the judgment of God and you are powerless to prevent it.

"Instead of heeding your warnings of coming judgment, the nation turns on you and seeks to destroy God's man in a day of crisis!"

In essence, that is Jeremiah.

The message and the man are inseparable and we should notice:

(1) THE TIMES OF HIS MINISTRY

In his book: *"Jeremiah – Prophet of Crisis"*, Dr Ted Rendall, from whom I gleaned much in this study, reminds us that Jeremiah lived and died in a century of crisis. His 40 year ministry took place during the reigns of Judah's final five kings: Josiah (640-609

B.C.); Jehoahaz (609 B.C.); Jehoiakim (609-598 B.C.); Jehoiachin (598-597 B.C.) and Zedekiah (597-586 B.C.). Thus we see that Jeremiah served in a time of:

(a) INTERNATIONAL CONFLICT

Egypt (2 Kings 23:29), Assyria, (2 Kings 17:6) and Babylon (2 Kings 20:12) were the great world powers all vying for supremacy in this part of the ancient world. Israel often became the cockpit of the nations in their struggle. When this young prophet began his ministry, Babylon was but a cloud, the size of a man's hand, on the horizon of the future. However, Jeremiah lived to see that ruthless nation descend on his people and destroy the capital city of Jerusalem and the splendid Temple of Solomon, the dwelling place of Jehovah, the God of Israel. 2 Kings 25 verse 9 records how the house of the Lord and the King's house and all the houses of Jerusalem were burned with fire.

We, too, live in an age of international conflict. Two major World Wars are behind us, but we do not know when we shall be plunged into the whirlpool of a third. Are we not living in the era of passenger jets being shot out of the sky? A crisis in Ukraine, in Iraq, in Syria, in Gaza and in Israel, to name just a few. Where in the world is there peace?

(b) NATIONAL DECLINE

As Dr. Ted Rendall says:

"Jeremiah lived in the midst of a crumbling society, rotting within, and fast falling apart at the seams. Like a vessel caught in the storm, Judah was fast breaking up."

For Israel, the law of Moses was the national code. Tested by that standard, the wall of Judah was crooked and was marked for demolition. Think of the record of Judah in Jeremiah's time. There was:

Idolatry: the worship of a whole series of pagan deities and this entailed involvement in immoral practices and sinful rites. *"Thy children have forsaken Me, and sworn by them that are no gods"* (Chapter 5:7).

Immorality: *"They were as fed horses in the morning: every one neighed after his neighbour's wife"* (Chapter 5:8); *"I have seen also in the prophets of Jerusalem an horrible thing: they commit adultery"* (Chapter 23:14).

Injustice: *"They judge not the cause, the cause of the fatherless, yet they prosper; and the right of the needy do they not judge"* (Chapter 5:28).

Covetousness: *"The itch to be rich!"* characterised them. *"From the least of them even unto the greatest of them every one is given to covetousness"* (Chapter 6:13 – and repeated in Chapter 8:10)

Dishonesty: *"Their tongue is as an arrow shot out; it speaketh deceit"* (Chapter 9:8).

Violence: *"As a fountain casteth out her waters, so she casteth out her wickedness: violence and spoil is heard in her"* (Chapter 6:7).

These were the sins of Jeremiah's age and these were the sins that made God's people the *"generation of His wrath"* (Chapter 7:29).

We need hardly point out the fact that these are the sins of our society as well! Can we hope, therefore, to escape the righteous judgment of God?

(c) FORMAL WORSHIP

The people believed they could sin as they pleased and pay mere lip service to the Lord!

In Jeremiah's day there was, of course, a tremendous reformation. This was initiated by Josiah, a very godly King. The divine assessment of him is found in 2 Kings 23 verse 25: *"Like unto him was there no king before him, that turned to the LORD with all his heart, and with all his soul, and with all his might, according to all the law of*

Moses; neither after him arose there any like him". In his day, the sins of idolatry, sodomy and inhumanity were dealt with. (See 2 Kings 23:5, 7 and 10). Sadly, however, Josiah's reformation proved to be superficial and did not produce true spiritual worship of Jehovah.

All that Judah had was a formal religion. *"The priests say not, Where is the LORD? And they that handle the law knew Me not: the pastors also transgressed against Me, and the prophets prophesied by Baal, and walked after things that do not profit"* (Chapter 2:8). In Chapter 3 verse 10, God declares: *"Judah hath not turned unto Me with her whole heart, but feignedly"*. Formal worship! Is there not a warning here for us? Do you ever feel that we are just going through the motions? Do you ever feel that we are just going through the mechanics of worship? Is it not easy to *'traffic in unfelt truth'* and offer formal and perfunctory prayers?

(d) CONTINUAL APOSTASY

The land was full of false prophets and blind leaders. God spoke to Jeremiah and said: *"The prophets prophesy lies in My name: I sent them not, neither have I commanded them, neither spake unto them: they prophesy unto you a false vision and divination, and a thing of nought"* (Chapter 14:14). While the faithful prophet, Jeremiah, was delivering faithful sermons, these false prophets were offering false security. Thus in Chapter 28, Hananiah predicted the speedy return of Jeconiah and the captives. Who do you think they believed? What an age it was! A time when the servant of God was despised and the Word of the Lord was disobeyed. A time when it was said: *"truth is perished"* (Chapter 7:28).

Is Jeremiah's age not a picture of ours? An era when God's Word is rejected, resisted and reviled - even by those who profess His name. And what of those who speak in the name of the Lord? Are they not branded fanatics? Of course, this age climaxed in:

(e) PROVIDENTIAL JUDGMENT

Indeed, is this not the theme of the book? The judgment of the Lord upon Jerusalem and Judah. The Lord announced this judgment as early as the first chapter: *"I will utter My judgments against them touching all their wickedness, who have forsaken Me"* (Chapter 1:16). Time and time again, God's judgment is declared as the consequence of the people's sin and disobedience. Sin cannot be left unpunished. The nation had to be purified and purged.

These were the leading characteristics of Jeremiah's age.

(2) THE TERMS OF HIS MINISTRY

By *"terms"* is meant *"the conditions of an agreement"*. Here the Lord enters into an agreement with Jeremiah and He lays down the conditions. Notice:

(a) THE SELECTION

It is generally agreed that Jeremiah was born in 645 B.C. He was born in a small village called Anathoth (Chapter 1:1) which is today called Anata. It lies about three miles north-east of Jerusalem. Naturally timid and sensitive, Jeremiah shrank from the gigantic task to which God called him.

Look at verse 5 of Chapter 1. Pastor Bill Freel points out four telling phrases:

"I formed thee." Jeremiah is responsible to God physically. You see, God gave him the genetic structure He wanted him to possess. We are reminded in the New Testament - 1 Corinthians 6 verse 19 - that the Christian's body is the temple of the Holy Spirit. We must not defile or abuse that body.

"I knew thee." Jeremiah is responsible to God intellectually. God gave Jeremiah his I.Q. We have to love the Lord our God with all our *"minds"*.

"I sanctified thee." Jeremiah is responsible to God spiritually. The idea of sanctification is to be separated to God, to be in a God-given place. God sets us apart spiritually.

"I ordained thee." Jeremiah is responsible to God vocationally. He is called to be a prophet not a priest. Jeremiah should have followed in his father's footsteps. At this time, the priesthood was hereditary, but God had another plan. Has God another plan for you? Is God setting you apart for special service?

Remember what a prophet was. The Hebrew word probably comes from an Arabic root that means *"to announce"*. For example, in Exodus 7 verses 1 and 2, Moses spoke to Aaron and Aaron was his spokesman (*"prophet"*) before Pharaoh.

Prophets did more than reveal the future, for their messages applied to the nation at that time. They were *forthtellers* more than *foretellers*, exposing, as they did, the sin of the nation and calling the people back to their covenant responsibilities before God.

This was the task for which Jeremiah was set apart. Selected for service. Is that you? Is God putting His hand on your life? A veteran missionary once gave the following advice to prospective missionaries: *"Do not go to the field unless you can look the Devil straight in the face and say, 'I have a perfect right to be here.'"*

There was the Selection – and then there was:

(b) THE OBJECTION

Jeremiah's response to the call of God was: *"Ah, Lord God! behold, I cannot speak: for I am a child"* (Chapter 1:6). If you look at verse 2 of Chapter 1, you can date Jeremiah's call. It came in the thirteenth year of the reign of Josiah. This would have been 627 B.C. - so Jeremiah was about 18 years of age when he received the call of God, a mere child according to the notions of his day. No wonder he hesitated! When he looked at the *work* before him and the *wickedness* around him and the *weakness* within him, Jeremiah was sure that he was not the man for the job.

Dr. Rendall reminds us:

"When Moses was called by the Lord, he pled his Inability (Exodus

4:10). When Gideon was called by the Lord, he pled his Inferiority (Judges 6:15). When Isaiah was called by the Lord, he pled his Impurity (Isaiah 6:5). When Jeremiah was called by the Lord, he pled his Immaturity."

"Ah, Lord God! behold, I cannot speak." The strange thing about Jeremiah's plea is that he called God *"Lord"*, but he did not submit to His Lordship. He is either Lord of all or not Lord at all! Is this not the crux of the matter when it comes to excuses? You see, any time we offer an excuse for not coming to church, not fulfilling a position, not witnessing to some soul, or simply not doing what God says, we are not submitting to His Lordship. You may sing *"He is Lord"*, but is He really your Lord?

Jeremiah shrank from the work thrust upon him by God, but God would not take his *"No!"* for an answer. So He gave young Jeremiah three instructions: *"Go where I send you, speak what I command you, and be not afraid of their faces"* (See Chapter 1:7-8). He then promised: *"I am with thee to deliver thee"*. Now, that was:

(c) THE PROTECTION

As we have noted, Jeremiah was about 18 years of age when he began to preach. He was very, very nervous. <u>So God reassures him</u>: *"Jeremiah, you have My presence, I am with you"*. He knew that the Lord was with him. As you face that difficult assignment, do you realize that the Lord is with you? *"He hath said, I will never leave thee, nor forsake thee. So that we may boldly say, The Lord is my helper, and I will not fear what man shall do unto me"* (Hebrews 13:5-6). God, firstly, reassures him.

But that is not all. <u>God</u>, secondly, <u>reinforces him</u>: Look at the promise of verse 18: *"For, behold, I have made thee this day a defenced city, and an iron pillar, and brazen walls against the whole land, against the kings of Judah, against the princes thereof, against the priests thereof, and against the people of the land"*. In other words, none of the hostile looks or comments of the people would intimidate him. Anyone who has spoken in public will know what that means! We call Jeremiah *"the weeping prophet"*. He was that, for we hear him say:

"Oh that my head were waters, and mine eyes a fountain of tears, that I might weep day and night for the slain of the daughter of my people" (Chapter 9:1). He was, however, also a courageous man who faced many dangers and trials and yet remained true to the Lord.

Is the Lord calling *you* to special service? Like Jeremiah, are you fearful, nervous, and uncertain? Learn this lesson - the God who calls, equips (Chapter 1:5); the God who equips, encourages (Chapter 1:8) and the God who encourages, will fortify you to do His work.

(3) <u>THE THEMES OF HIS MINISTRY</u>

Jeremiah's message was twofold: Destruction and construction. Do you notice that in verse 10 of Chapter 1: *"Root out, and to pull down, and to destroy, and to throw down, to build, and to plant"*.

When you study the Old Testament prophets, there are a few truths that stand out:

1. ***Past Sin***: for the appearance of a prophet was always a sign that apostasy and rebellion were predominant in the nation. The nation had disobeyed God's law.

2. ***Present Responsibility***: the people must repent or God will send judgment.

3. ***Future Hope***: the Lord will come one day and establish His glorious kingdom.

The Lord did not give Jeremiah a joyful message of deliverance. Can you imagine listening to a preacher for 40 years hammering away at the same message? Judgment! Judgment! Judgment! Now, we notice here:

(a) JUDGMENT ON THE SINNING NATION: Chapters 2-45

In this section, Jeremiah predicts that Judah's punishment was coming very quickly. He appealed to his countrymen to repent and avoid God's judgment by an invader. *"Amend your ways and your doings, and I will cause you to dwell in this place ... If ye throughly amend your ways and your doings; if ye throughly execute judgment between a man and his neighbour; if ye oppress not the stranger, the fatherless, and the widow, and shed not innocent blood in this place, neither walk after other gods to your hurt; Then will I cause you to dwell in this place, in the land that I gave to your fathers, for ever and ever"* (Chapter 7:3-7).

Once invasion was certain after Judah refused to repent, he pleaded with them not to resist the Babylonian conqueror in order to prevent total destruction. *"Bring your necks under the yoke of the king of Babylon, and serve him and his people, and live"* (Chapter 27:12). Can you imagine how that went down? Jeremiah was regarded as a traitor. He was misunderstood, misrepresented, persecuted, arrested, imprisoned and more than once his life was in danger. The people then, just like the people now, did not want to hear the truth, but Jeremiah told them plainly that they were defying the Lord, disobeying the law, and destined for judgment. (See Chapter 4:6 and Chapter 12:14)

In Chapter 1, the Lord gave Jeremiah two signs about what would happen. There was:

1. *The Sign of the Almond Tree*: verses 11-12. The almond tree is the first to awaken after the winter's sleep, and this sign symbolized the nearness of events that were to come.

2. *The Sign of the Boiling Pot*: verses 13-15. This symbolized the eruption of the Babylonians into the Land.

Yet, beyond this doom and gloom comes a ray of hope. Some of the most positive prophecies about the future of Israel are found in Jeremiah. Bible scholars call Chapters 30-33: *"The Book of Consolation"*. It is the dawning of a new day for the people of Israel, not only for the exiles in Babylon but also for the Jewish people in the latter days before the Lord returns.

Do you know what it would take to destroy Israel?

"Thus saith the LORD, which giveth the sun for a light by day, and the ordinances of the moon and of the stars for a light by night, which divideth the sea when the waves thereof roar; The LORD of hosts is His name: If those ordinances depart from before Me, saith the LORD, then the seed of Israel also shall cease from being a nation before Me for ever" (Chapter 31:35-36).

If the sun quits rising and the moon quits shining and the waves of the sea roll no more, then Israel will cease to exist. The fact that the name *"Israel"* is back on the map today is proof that God keeps His promises. There will always be an Israel!

(b) JUDGMENT ON THE SURROUNDING NATIONS: Chapters 46-51

Do you recall that Jeremiah was called to be *"a prophet unto the nations"* (Chapter 1:5). He had spoken to his people for over forty years, but they would not listen. Now he speaks to the nations related in some way to the Jewish people. One by one, he predicted judgment from God on various nations. In the closing chapters of this book, there are messages for Egypt, Philistia, Moab, Ammon, Edom, Damascus and Elam as well as Babylon. There is a phrase that is repeated in these chapters time and time again. Do you know what it is? *"I will."* Do you know something? *"History is His story."* Benjamin Franklin said: *"I have lived a long time and the longer I live the more convincing proofs I see of this truth, that God governs in the affairs of men"*. Do you believe that?

God sees what the nations do - and He rewards them justly. Have the nations of our day acted any better than the nations of Jeremiah's day? Abortion, the abuse of children, genocide, international terrorism and a host of other sins have stained the hands of nations with blood. What will they do when the Judge becomes angry and starts to avenge the innocent? Says Hebrews 10 verse 31: *"It is a fearful thing to fall into the hands of the living God"*.

(4) THE TRIALS OF HIS MINISTRY

John MacArthur points out that Jeremiah faced major trials. There was:

1. Trial by Death Threats (Chapter 11:18-23)
2. Trial by Isolation (Chapter 15:15-21)
3. Trial by Stocks (Chapter 19:14 - Chapter 20:18)
4. Trial by Arrest (Chapter 26:7-24)
5. Trial by Challenge (Chapter 28:10-16)
6. Trial by Destruction (Chapter 36:1-32)
7. Trial by Violence and Imprisonment (Chapter 37:15)
8. Trial by Starvation (Chapter 38:1-6)
9. Trial by Chains (Chapter 40:1)
10. Trial by Rejection (Chapter 42:1 - 43:4)

Consider the second of these trials – Chapter 15 verses 15-21.

"O LORD, Thou knowest: remember me, and visit me, and revenge me of my persecutors; take me not away in Thy longsuffering: know that for Thy sake I have suffered rebuke. Thy words were found, and I did eat them; and Thy word was unto me the joy and rejoicing of mine heart: for I am called by Thy name, O LORD God of hosts. I sat not in the assembly of the mockers, nor rejoiced; I sat alone because of Thy hand: for Thou hast filled me with indignation. Why is my pain perpetual, and my wound incurable, which refuseth to be healed? wilt Thou be altogether unto me as a liar, and as waters that fail?

Therefore thus saith the LORD, If thou return, then will I bring thee again, and thou shalt stand before Me: and if thou take forth the precious from the vile, thou shalt be as My mouth: let them return unto thee; but return not thou unto them. And I will make thee unto this people a fenced brasen wall: and they shall fight against thee, but they shall not prevail against thee: for I am with thee to save thee and to deliver thee, saith the LORD. And I will deliver thee out of the hand of the wicked, and I will redeem thee out of the hand of the terrible."

Jeremiah here is under severe strain. He is under tremendous pressure. Why? Well, as Dr. Ted Rendall reminds us, there was:

(a) UNCEASING OPPOSITION

Look at his prayer in verse 15. He speaks about suffering persecution. That persecution was fanned into flame by his own townspeople.

The people of Anathoth, Jeremiah's hometown, attempted to assassinate the prophet. (See Chapter 11:21) It injured their family pride that this teenager was going around upsetting the whole of Jerusalem. From then on, he was branded a traitor. He was rejected by the prophets, because they were false prophets. He was shunned by the priests, because he spoke against the priests' job, the Temple and the sacrifices. The kings regarded him as a political traitor and the people hated him, hatching various plots to end his life. You talk about opposition! Jeremiah knew all about it.

The famous preacher John Henry Jowett said on one occasion: *"Preaching that costs nothing, accomplishes nothing"*. That certainly applies to Jeremiah. If ever an Old Testament servant had to take up his cross in order to follow the Lord, it was Jeremiah.

Could it be that *you* are facing opposition because of your witness? Is that stand against you coming from your own family? Your own town? Your neighbours? Perhaps like Jeremiah you feel like quitting.

(b) UNRESPONSIVE CIRCUMSTANCES

Did you know that discouragement can come from two causes? It can arise from a sense of our own inability or it can come from the unresponsive circumstances in which we labour. Jeremiah had conquered the first but was suffering the second, at least for a time. It was the failure of his people that brought Jeremiah to a place of discouragement. Why was the word he was preaching not bearing fruit and changing the nation? Was it really worth it all staying there and ministering to such a hard-hearted people? Why was Jeremiah unable to reach and win them? He said at one time: *"A wonderful and horrible thing is committed in the land; the prophets prophesy falsely, and the priests bear rule by their means, and My people love to have it so"* (Chapter 5:30-31).

Do *you* know something about this test? Are you preaching away with an apparent lack of success? Do you feel that in that Sunday School class, that work with the elderly, that ministry in the community that it is all in vain?

(c) UNRELIEVED ISOLATION

As he recounts his past experience in verse 16 of Chapter 15, he says: *"Thy words were found, and I did eat them"*, no doubt referring to his call in Chapter 1. He then mentions the cost of answering that call: *"I sat not in the assembly of the mockers, nor rejoiced; I sat alone because of Thy hand"*. Do you know what Jeremiah experienced? Social suffering. God did not allow him to marry. *"The word of the LORD came also unto me saying, Thou shalt not take thee a wife, neither shalt thou have sons or daughters in this place"* (Chapter 16:1-2). Coupled with that, the Lord said to Jeremiah: *"For thus saith the LORD, Enter not into the house of mourning, neither go to lament nor bemoan them"* (Chapter 16:5).

Jeremiah was to maintain a thorough separation from the ordinary and legitimate functions of social life.

He was told there was no point in settling down to a comfortable lifestyle because judgment was near. Can you imagine the terrible sense of isolation and aloneness that must have gripped Jeremiah during those dark years?

Is his fortitude not so relevant for our age? With our nation seemingly "hell-bent" on undermining every moral law based on the Scriptures, with religious denominations denying the fundamentals of the faith, with modernism dominating many evangelical churches, the sense of aloneness and pressure for conformity is almost unbearable. In Chapter 8 verse 12, the people are accused of not being ashamed when they committed abomination. *"Neither could they blush."* As Gareth Crossley says: *"Religious leaders of our day do not know how to blush"*.

There was also the trial of:

(d) UNANSWERED PRAYER

Jeremiah is forced to cry out in verse 18 of Chapter 15: *"Why is my pain perpetual, and my wound incurable, which refuseth to be healed?"* Indeed, he is laying the blame for his circumstances at God's door. He is openly accusing God of having failed him in the hour of his spiritual need, in the time of his spiritual thirst. Jeremiah got so low that he wanted to quit. He said: *"I will not make mention of Him, nor speak any more in His name"* (Chapter 20:9).

Is that you? Do you feel like quitting? Remember - *It is always too soon to quit.* Who are you doing it for anyhow? Could it be that Jeremiah forgot his calling? One thing is certain, in the last chapter of his life we are confronted with:

(5) THE TRIUMPHS OF HIS MINISTRY

You see:

(a) He was Encouraged to Continue his Ministry

Look at Chapter 15 verse 19: *"Therefore thus saith the LORD, If thou return, then will I bring thee again, and thou shalt stand before Me: and if thou take forth the precious from the vile, thou shalt be as My mouth: let them return unto thee; but return not thou unto them".*

The Lord was going to reinstate him.

W.G. Blaikie has paraphrased this verse like this: *"If thou returnest to Me and givest up these doubts and reproaches, I will take thee back as My servant, to stand before Me, and if thou bringest forth in thy heart, good, instead of unworthy thoughts of Me, thou shalt be My mouth".*

I wonder, do *you* need to be reinstated?

The Lord was going to empower him: Jeremiah was going to be like a wall of brass to withstand the attacks of his people (see Chapter 15:20).

The Lord was going to be with him: *"For I am with thee to save thee and to deliver thee, saith the LORD"* (Chapter 15:20).

Have you stumbled in your ministry? Have you forgotten your calling? The Lord wants to reinstate you, empower you and be with you. He was with Jeremiah so much so that:

(b) He was Enabled to Complete his Ministry

All that Jeremiah predicted came true. The nation was taken captive to Babylon. After 586 B.C. Jeremiah was forced to go with a fleeing remnant to Egypt. Some say he was stoned to death there for preaching the truth. Whatever it was that happened to him, Jeremiah finished well.

Imagine preaching for over 40 years and in the end seeing everything fall apart. But God did not call Jeremiah to be successful. He did not call him to win a popularity contest.

Measured by human standards, he was a failure, but measured by the will of God, he was a great success.

Do we not need men and women of Jeremiah's calibre in our churches today?

Christians who consider faithfulness more than fame, loyalty more than popularity, the praise of God more than the praise of men.

Are you such a person? Perhaps you are saying: *"There's a price to pay!"* There certainly is! But there is a crown to win, there is a Christ to please and there is a commendation to hear. *"Well done, thou good and faithful servant"* (Matthew 25:21).

What does the hymn-writer encourage us to do?

Go, labour on, 'tis not for naught;
Thy earthly loss is heavenly gain;
Men heed thee, love thee, praise thee, not;
The Master praises - what are men?

CHAPTER 8

Lamentations

Bart Ehrman is supposed to be one of America's leading Bible scholars, and yet he is a non-believer. He used to consider himself a "born again Christian", but, as he writes in his book: *"God's Problem"*, he came to a point where he felt compelled to leave the Christian faith.

He explains:

"The problem of suffering became for me the problem of faith. If God is all-powerful, then He is able to do whatever He wants and can, therefore, remove suffering. If He is all-loving, then He obviously wants the best for people and, therefore, does not want them to suffer. And yet people suffer! How can that be explained?" (quoted in: *"Adventuring through the Bible"*, by Ray Stedman, page 369)

Is there any other solution to the problem of evil? Well, Jeremiah in the book of Lamentations shows us another solution. A solution that is rooted in and consistent with our faith in a loving and powerful God.

The full name of this book is: *"The Lamentations of Jeremiah"*. This is one of the saddest books in the Bible, for it contains the prophet's tear-stained reflections on the city of Jerusalem followings its destruction by Nebuchadnezzar of Babylon.

In the *Septuagint,* the Greek translation of the Hebrew Old Testament, there is a little note which states that Jeremiah uttered these lamentations as he sat on the hillside overlooking the city.

As you read this book, you can almost see the tears dropping onto to the page and making the ink run. Here is a man weeping his heart out. Indeed the *Septuagint* calls this book: *"Tears"*.

The book of Lamentations takes its English title from the Latin *Vulgate* - the Latin version of the Bible. *"Lamentations"* means: *"a funeral dirge or a funeral song"*.

In the Hebrew Bible, it takes its title from the first word of Lamentations. Our English version translates it: *"How"*. Do you see it? *"How doth the city sit solitary, that was full of people!"* It is the Hebrew word *"eykah"*. It could be translated: *"Alas"*. One paraphrase puts it this way: *"Oh, oh, oh"*. It is a word of mourning. It is a word of sorrow. It is a word of grief. *"Alas, the city sits desolate that was full of people."* It is a picture of mourning for the city of Jerusalem which has fallen. The city of Jerusalem has been taken, and now we are going to read a funeral dirge. Indeed, there are five funeral songs in the book of the Lamentations, one in each chapter.

It is important for us to link the book of Lamentations with the book of Jeremiah. In Jeremiah 52, we have the historical account of the fall of the city of Jerusalem. This chapter records the *facts of history*. The book of Lamentations records *the feelings of the heart,* the emotions involved in seeing this city fall, and seeing its citizens carried away into captivity.

As you read this book, you will discover that it is an eye-witness account, the record of someone who actually saw all of these events take place. Jeremiah is now sitting down and writing a series of these funeral songs.

Jeremiah should remind us of Jesus! Do you recall the question He asked His disciples? *"Whom do men say that I the Son of Man am? And they said, Some say that Thou art John the Baptist: some, Elias; and others, Jeremias, or one of the prophets"* (Matthew 16:13-14).

Jeremiah weeps over the city of Jerusalem: Jesus weeps over the city of Jerusalem. *"And when He was come near, He beheld the city, and wept over it"* (Luke 19:41).

Jeremiah realized that Jerusalem was going to fall in his day. Jesus realized that Jerusalem was going to fall in His day as well.

On the north side of Jerusalem is a cave which in Jewish tradition is known as "Jeremiah's Grotto". It is believed that this is where Jeremiah went to pray when he was lonely and hurt and in pain. That grotto is a cave in a hill called Golgotha where we believe that Christ died on the cross. So, when you think of Jeremiah, think of Jesus. The Lord Jesus was *"a man of sorrows, and acquainted with grief"* (Isaiah 53:3) and those sufferings and sorrows are echoed here in the book of Lamentations.

Now, this book has an interesting structure. There is a specific way in which these funeral songs are put together. Lamentations is written in what is called an acrostic form. What is meant by that? Chapters 1, 2 and 4 all have 22 verses based on the 22 letters of the Hebrew alphabet, each verse beginning with a letter in the order of the alphabet. (Chapter 5 also contains 22 verses, but it is not written as an acrostic.) When you come to Chapter 3, you will notice that instead of 22 verses, this chapter has 66 verses. What you have in Chapter 3 is that every letter of the Hebrew alphabet has three verses to it. So, the first three verses begin with the first letter of the Hebrew alphabet, the next three verses begin with the second letter of the alphabet, the next three verses begin with the third letter of the alphabet, and so on. So it takes 66 verses to run through the full 22 letters. Somebody might ask: *"Why did the Holy Spirit lead Jeremiah to write these songs in this form?"* Well, this was an aid to memory. An apt reminder that God wants His people to hide His Word in their hearts. He wants us to be able to say with the Psalmist: *"Thy word have I hid in mine heart, that I might not sin against Thee"* (Psalm 119:11).

As has been said, Lamentations is a funeral dirge. It is a series of funeral songs, lamenting and mourning and grieving over the fall of Jerusalem. What you have here is a complete picture of misery and grief and sorrow. This method helps to express Jeremiah's complete grief, his *"A to Z"* of grief. He is telling a story of grief all the way from the beginning to the end. Lamentations can be described as *"the Wailing Wall"* of the Bible. It is like an elegy written in a graveyard. It is perhaps the saddest book in all of the Bible.

Can you picture the scene? The city of Jerusalem is now in ruins. The stench of death is in the air. Jeremiah begins to walk through the city. Over here, he sees little children crying. Over there, he hears the piercing wail of women who have been widowed. There are piles of dead bodies everywhere. This is the atmosphere as Jeremiah begins his lament. Remember each chapter contains one of the five songs that are beautifully and carefully put together. Let us look at these songs briefly and notice:

CHAPTER 1 - THE REALITY OF THEIR SUFFERING

What we have here in the first chapter is *"the funeral of a city"*. The city, Temple, palace, houses and walls all lie in ruins. God's altars had been thrown down and the holy places desecrated and burned with fire. Jerusalem is compared here to a rich princess or queen who had suddenly been left alone and robbed of all her wealth and beauty. Once she had been full, now she was empty. Once she was honoured, now she was disgraced. Her joy has been replaced by tears, her great victories are now lost in defeat.

Why has this happened? The answer is this - instead of loving Jehovah, she had courted many lovers and the false gods of the heathen nations. Now those heathen nations had become her enemies. Can you see:

(a) JEREMIAH'S SORROW

He had seen it coming. He had warned and pleaded with the apostate people whom he had loved dearly. *"It shall come to pass, when ye shall say, Wherefore doeth the LORD our God all these things unto us? Then shalt thou answer them, Like as ye have forsaken Me, and served strange gods in your land, so shall ye serve strangers in a land that is not yours"* (Jeremiah 5:19). His dire predictions had all been fulfilled. The rulers of Jerusalem had called him a traitor for preaching unconditional surrender to Babylon. He had been persecuted and abused. His written prophecies had been cut to ribbons and flung in the fire. But, they had come true and now Jeremiah weeps his heart out over the desolate city. *"No comforter, no comforter!"* he cries again and again (Chapter 1:2, 9, 16, 17, 21). Sin always brings sorrow and tragedy!

Some years ago, a prison chaplain noticed one of the prisoners sewing a covering on a pair of overalls. Greeting the man cheerfully, he said: *"Good morning friend, Sewing?"*

"No Sir", replied the prisoner with a grim smile, *"Reaping!"*

Is this not what Jeremiah is saying? Look at verse 18: *"The LORD is righteous; for I have rebelled against His commandment"*. Jeremiah is saying: *"We are reaping what we have sown"*. The awful judgments that came were only what the city and the nation deserved.

Rebellion always leads to discipline. *"For whom the Lord loveth He chasteneth, and scourgeth every son whom He receiveth"* (Hebrews 12:6). When God chastens us, the experience is not an easy one. Sometimes we blame the Lord for whatever happens to us. Our attitude is: *"I do my best and still these things happen! It's not fair! Since God is in charge of justice, then it must be His fault that unfair things happen to me."* But is God unfair? Paul says: *"God forbid: yea, let God be true, but every man a liar"* (Romans 3:4). It is impossible – always impossible - for God to be wrong and often we are simply reaping what we sow. As Jeremiah looks out over the ruins of Jerusalem, with the tears streaming down his face, he realizes that this destruction is a sign that God is right and His judgment is unerring. There was Jeremiah's sorrow and there was:

(b) JERUSALEM'S SORROW

Do you recall that around 1000 B.C. David had established his capital in Jerusalem? Thus, for nearly 400 years God had blessed this beloved city. He had allowed the Northern Kingdom to be carried away by the Assyrians in 722 B.C. However, Jerusalem had been spared for over another 100 years. But, all this mercy, longsuffering and patience had been in vain for Judah continued provoking the Lord through constant sinning. The end had now come. Indeed so critical was Jerusalem's destruction that the facts are recorded in four separate Old Testament chapters: 2 Kings 25; 2 Chronicles 36; Jeremiah 39 and Jeremiah 52. Do you see how the *"weeping prophet"* puts it in verse 17 of this chapter? *"The LORD hath commanded concerning Jacob, that his adversaries should be round about him."* Their suffering was real. The question needs to be asked: If God did not hesitate to judge His beloved people - *"the apple of His eye"*, to quote Deuteronomy 32 verse 10 - what will He do to the nations of the world who reject His Word?

CHAPTER 2 - THE REASON FOR THEIR SUFFERING

Why did God allow His people to be judged by Babylon? Because of their sin!

There was:

(a) THE SINFULNESS OF THE PEOPLE

Do you recall the sins that marked Jeremiah's age? Idolatry; Immorality; Injustice; Covetousness; Dishonesty and Violence. For Israel, the law of Moses was the national code and tested by that standard the wall of Judah was crooked and marked for demolition. Sin cannot be left unpunished. The nation had to be purified and purged - and God's judgment fell. The people were taken to Babylon, an idolatrous nation, and never again have the Jewish people bowed down to idols!

Do you realize that sin has consequences, even for a Christian? If you grievously sin, God will forgive you, but that forgiveness is not going to eliminate some of the consequences. You use drugs and get hooked on them and then you ask God to forgive you. He does and He saves you. Then your little baby is born a cocaine baby. That is the consequence of sin.

The story is told about young boy who was just constantly disobeying his father. His father eventually said: *"Son, you just disobey me all the time. I want to show you just how bad your behaviour is"*.

He went out in the back garden and said: *"Son, do you see that post there? Every time you disobey me and do something that you should not, I am going to drive a nail into that post."*

It did not take long before that post was just full of nails. The father said: *"Son, do you see all those nails?"*

The boy said: *"I do, Dad. It breaks my heart"*.

The father said: *"I'll tell you what. Every time you do good now, I am going to pull out one of those nails"*.

The boy caught on to that. They started pulling out those nails. It was not long until all the nails were gone. The father went out there one day and his boy was crying. He said: *"Son, why are you crying? All the nails are out of the post"*.

He said: *"I know, Dad. But the marks are still there!"*

That is the way it is with us. God forgives, but the consequences, the scars, are still there.

Here is Judah and they are experiencing the consequences of their sin!

(b) THE FAITHLESSNESS OF THE PROPHETS

The spiritual leaders had given the people a false message and they had been believed. Says verse 14 of Chapter 2: *"Thy prophets have seen vain and foolish things for thee: and they have not discovered thine iniquity, to turn away thy captivity"*. Do you know what these false prophets preached? *"Peace, peace, when there is no peace"* (Jeremiah 6:14; 8:11). They preached a popular message that the people wanted to hear - *"Ye shall not serve the king of Babylon"* (Jeremiah 27:9) - while Jeremiah preached the Lord's message and was rejected and persecuted. For over forty years, Jeremiah had openly opposed these false prophets. He compared them to deceitful physicians (Jeremiah 6:14); empty wind (Jeremiah 5:13); peddlers of chaff (Jeremiah 23:28) and toxic people spreading deadly infection (Jeremiah 23:15).

Do you need to be reminded that we have "false prophets" with us today. People who want to be popular with the crowd instead of pleasing to the Lord. Tell me, which concerns you most - the praise of man or the praise of God?

(c) THE TRUTHFULNESS OF THE LORD

They were suffering God's judgment because God is faithful to His promises. *"The LORD hath done that which He had devised; He hath fulfilled His word that He had commanded in the days of old"* (Chapter 2:17). Now what word was that? Come back to the book of Deuteronomy and to Chapter 28. Do you know what the Lord is doing here? He is giving the nation two choices. God says: *"If you obey Me, I will bless you"* (verses 1-14), but: *"If you disobey Me, I will curse you"* (verses 15-68). Obedience is the key to blessing!

Look at what God says in verses 56 and 57 of that chapter in Deuteronomy. He speaks about women eating their own children! Is this not an awful prediction? Yet, this is exactly what happened in the siege of Jerusalem. *"The hands of the pitiful women have sodden their own children: they were their meat in the destruction of the daughter of my people"* (Lamentations 4:10). You see, the famine was so severe that the mothers even killed and ate their own children.

For forty years Jeremiah had warned the people that their sin would find them out, yet the nation would not listen. How long will it take *us* to learn that we cannot disobey God's Word and escape? God is not playing games with us in the Bible. When God tells us to do something, we must do it or pay the price - for God is faithful to His Word. You know, some Christians have the notion that God will not do what He says. He will not really judge sin! He will not really hold us accountable! But, God will, for He is true to His Word!

CHAPTER 3 - THE RESPONSE TO THEIR SUFFERING

We should observe how personal this chapter is. The pronouns: *"He"* and *"His"* referring to God and *"I"* and *"me"* referring to Jeremiah are predominant in this chapter.

Here we are confronted with:

(a) THE MISERY OF THE PROPHET

Think of it! Jeremiah had faithfully proclaimed God's message for forty years and yet the nation had turned a deaf ear. Is it any wonder he suffered? Do you notice:

He is affected *spiritually*. He says: *"Also when I cry and shout, He shutteth out my prayer"* (verse 8).

He is affected *physically*. He says: *"My flesh and my skin hath He made old, He hath broken my bones"* (verse 4).

He is affected *socially*. He says: *"I was a derision to all my people; and their song all the day"* (verse 14).

He is affected *emotionally*. He says: *"Thou hast removed my soul far off from peace"* (verse 17).

Moreover, the tears of Jeremiah fell copiously. He says: *"For these things I weep; Mine eye, Mine eye runneth down with water"* (Chapter 1:16). *"Mine eyes do fail with tears, my bowels are troubled"* (Chapter 2:11). One Bible scholar says: *"Our Western tendency to admire people who do not weep comes from Greek rather than Hebrew thinking. In modern Israel a man can never get to be Prime Minister unless he can weep over the grave of an Israeli soldier"*.

Jeremiah wept because of the sin, the stubbornness, the suffering of his people.

Nehemiah was called to build the walls, but first he had to weep over the ruins (Nehemiah 1:4).

I wonder, is my ministry marked by tears?

Think of the tears of Jeremiah, the tears of Nehemiah, the tears of *Paul*, the tears of *Christ*.

Think of the tears of *Robert Murray McCheyne* for his parish in Dundee.

The tears of *William Burns* as *"the thud of Christless feet on their road to Hell"* broke his heart.

Does the thought of Christless feet on the way to Hell break *your* heart? If so, we will see to it that we are at the weekly Prayer Meeting!

Samuel Hadley was a great soul winner in New York City. One night he was overheard as he prayed: *"Oh God, the sin of this city is breaking my heart!"*

What is the exhortation of the hymn-writer?

"Let me look at the crowd as my Saviour did,
Till my eyes with tears grow dim,
Let me look till I pity the wandering sheep,
And love them for love of Him."

Jeremiah was burdened for his people, but in his brokenness there shines a ray of light, for he turned from contemplating his misery to contemplating:

(b) THE MERCY OF THE LORD

This gave him hope. Jeremiah realized that God could have wiped out all the people in His anger, but instead He had sent them to Babylon. Thus they were still alive and the nation was still a nation. Jeremiah believed that it was because of God's mercy that they had not been entirely consumed. He says: *"It is of the LORD'S mercies that we are not consumed, because His compassions fail not. They are new every morning: Great is Thy faithfulness"* (Chapter 3:22-23).

Somehow, in the midst of his hopelessness, Jeremiah finds a thread of hope. Somewhere, in the midst of being ready to give up, Jeremiah finds a reason to look up.

He has looked *out* and become distressed.
He has looked *in* and become depressed.
But, he looks *up* and becomes blessed.

Do you need to look up? Look up to a good God, a compassionate God - and a faithful God. The faithfulness of God!

Have you ever thought about the things the Bible says that God is faithful to do?

God is faithful to chasten. The Psalmist says: *"I know, O LORD, that Thy judgments are right, and that Thou in faithfulness hast afflicted me"* (Psalm 119:75).

God is faithful to *forgive*. John says: *"If we confess our sins, He is faithful and just to forgive us our sins, and to cleanse us from all unrighteousness"* (1 John 1:9).

God is faithful to *sympathize*. *"Wherefore in all things it behoved Him to be made like unto His brethren, that He might be a merciful and faithful high priest in things pertaining to God, to make reconciliation for the sins of the people. For in that He Himself hath suffered being tempted, He is able to succour them that are tempted"* (Hebrews 2:17-18).

God is faithful to *deliver*. *"There hath no temptation taken you but such as is common to man: but God is faithful, who will not suffer you to be tempted above that ye are able"* (1 Corinthians 10:13).

Peter says: *"Wherefore let them that suffer according to the will of God commit the keeping of their souls to Him in well doing, as unto a faithful Creator"* (1 Peter 4:19).

Is it not good to know that we live in a world where we have a faithful God who is good? No matter what the enemy may say to us, we need to remind ourselves that the Lord is good and He is never closer to us than when He chastens us.

So, here in Chapter 3, the Misery of the Prophet and the Mercy of the Lord – and then:

(c) THE MESSAGE FOR THE PEOPLE

Do you notice Jeremiah's counsel? *"Let us search and try our ways, and turn again to the LORD"* (verse 40). You see, while faithfulness marked God, unfaithfulness marked the people. Therefore there needs to be:

1. **A Reviewing of our Lives:** *"Let us search"*
2. **A Recognition of our Failures:** *"And turn again"*
3. **A Retracing of our Steps:** *"To the Lord"*

David failed Morally. Can you see him? He stands within his fine palace, healthy, handsome and hawk-like in his gaze. He can have anything he wants and he wants Bathsheba. We all know the outcome. He failed morally - and so did Judah.

Elijah failed Spiritually. He had taken his eyes off the Lord and cried: *"O LORD, take away my life; for I am not better than my fathers"* (1 Kings 19:4). He failed spiritually - and so did Judah.

Jonah failed Vocationally. There are only two roads in the Christian life. One leads to Nineveh; the other to Tarshish. The way to Nineveh is the way to *revival;* the way to Tarshish is the way to *ruin*. He failed vocationally - and so did Judah.

Like Judah, do you need to review your life? Have you failed the Lord morally, spiritually or vocationally? Do you need to turn again to the Lord?

CHAPTER 4 - THE RECOLLECTION IN THEIR SUFFERING

In this Chapter, we see:

(a) THE CONTRAST BETWEEN TWO PERIODS

The former glory of Israel is contrasted with her present misery. Jeremiah is in the acrostic mode again. Each of these twenty two verses starts with a successive letter of the Hebrew alphabet. Do you see how it begins? *"How"* – it is the same word again! *"Alas is the gold become dim! How is the most fine gold changed!"* (verse 1). Jeremiah is talking about gold and jewels and these stand for the people of Israel. The tribes of Israel were represented as jewels set in gold on the breastplate of the high priest and also on his shoulders. (See Exodus 28 and 39) But, their sins had cheapened them and they had lost their beauty.

Look at Israel now:

The children's tongues stick to the roof of their mouths for thirst – Chapter 4 verse 4.

The rich and pampered were in the streets begging for bread – Chapter 4 verse 5.

The women had cooked and eaten their own children – Chapter 4 verse 10.

The false prophets and priests were staggering through the streets covered with blood – Chapter 4 verse 14.

The king - Zedekiah - had been captured and blinded and carried off to captivity – Chapter 4 verse 20.

What a contrast all this was to Israel in her former glory! Do you see how low sin can bring you?

(b) THE CONTRAST BETWEEN TWO PARTIES

The Edomites, the descendants of Esau, rejoiced at the destruction of Jerusalem and encouraged the Babylonians. They may have even assisted them in their work. (See Psalm 137:7; Ezekiel 25:12-14 and Obadiah.)

Israel had drunk the bitter cup of God's wrath, but one day the cup would be handed to Edom and their time of judgment would come. (See Jeremiah 25:15, 21 and 49:7,22.) When someone wrongs you, do not seek revenge. God says: *"Vengeance is Mine; I will repay"* (Romans 12:19).

Now that brings us to the last chapter:

CHAPTER 5 - THE REQUEST FROM THEIR SUFFERING

This chapter has twenty two verses, but it is not an acrostic. Here the prophet is praying for himself and the suffering remnant who had survived the invasion. His prayer contained four elements:

(a) THE ELEMENT OF REMEMBRANCE

He asked the Lord to: *"Remember, ... Consider, and behold"* (verse 1). Jeremiah knew that the Babylonian captivity would not end for seventy years - Jeremiah 25:11 - but he asked the Lord to be merciful to the poor people in the land and the exiles in Babylon.

(b) THE ELEMENT OF REPENTANCE

Do you see it in verse 16? *"The crown is fallen from our head: Woe unto us, that we have sinned!"*

What was the cause of all this trouble, loss and pain? The Babylonian army? The wrath of God? No, the sins of His people! Jeremiah confessed this: *"We have sinned"*.

But, bless God, the book does not end there. Though the throne of Judah was destroyed, Jeremiah saw the living and unchanging God on His throne in heaven and that gave him courage. There was:

(c) THE ELEMENT OF RECOGNITION

"Thou, O LORD, remainest for ever; Thy throne from generation to generation" (verse 19), and finally:

(d) THE ELEMENT OF RENEWAL

In verse 21, Jeremiah cries: *"Turn Thou us unto Thee, O LORD, and we shall be turned; Renew our days as of old"*. Yes, they felt forsaken and forgotten. *"Wherefore dost Thou forget us for ever, and forsake us so long time?"* (verse 20), but they knew God would return to them if they returned to Him. That had been promised way back in the opening verses of Deuteronomy 30.

The final prayer of this funeral dirge will yet be fulfilled. *"Renew our days as of old"* - verse 21 - and Israel will be supreme among the nations. Then will their troubles be over forever!

Like Jeremiah, does your life seem to be falling apart at the seams? Does your ministry seem to be a failure?

Will you look up to the God who is *faithful* (Chapter 3:23); the God who is *good* (Chapter 3:25) and the God who is *unchanging* (Chapter 5:19)?

To put it very simply - you can count on the Lord.

When from my life the old-time joys have vanished,
Treasures once mine, I may no longer claim,
This truth may feed my hungry heart, and famished:
Lord, Thou remainest! Thou art still the same!

When streams have dried, those streams of glad refreshing -
Friendships so blest, so rich, so free;
When sun-kissed skies give place to clouds depressing,
Lord, Thou remainest! Still my heart hath Thee!

When strength hath failed, and feet, now worn and weary,
On gladsome errands may no longer go,
Why should I sigh, or let the days be dreary?
Lord, Thou remainest! Couldst Thou more bestow?"

Thus through life's days - whoe'er or what may fail me,
Friends, friendships, joys, in small or great degree,
Songs may be mine, no sadness need assail me,
Since Thou remainest! Still My heart hath Thee!
James Danson Smith

CHAPTER 9
Ezekiel

A well-known business man in the U.S.A. said some time ago that, in spite of all his wealth and fame, he was a troubled man. He worried about the future of the planet. He feared a nuclear holocaust, a disaster caused by pollution or a disease that would be resistant to all known medicine. However, the Christian does not share that man's fears that all will end with a catastrophe. The Bible reveals that an unseen God is in control and that the future will unfold according to the predictions of the prophets of Israel. Ezekiel is one of those prophets who speaks strangely but eloquently to the fears and hopes that mark our day. His words are both timely and insightful for our age, but Ezekiel's book is one of the most neglected in the whole of Scripture.

How can we bring it to life and see that it is relevant for our day? Well, let us think about:

1. THE PERSON

"Ezekiel" means *"strengthened by God"* which indeed he was for the prophetic ministry to which God called him. God declared unto him: *"Behold, I have made thy face strong against their faces"* (Chapter 3:8). Ezekiel was born in the year 622 B.C. during the reign of good King Josiah (640 - 609 B.C.) and he was taken into captivity into Babylon in the year 597 B.C.

Like Jeremiah, he was called from being a priest to being a prophet. He was thirty years of age at the time of his call (Chapter 1:1). According to the opening verses of Numbers 4, this was the normal age for a priest to begin his ministry.

2. *THE PLACE*

The book opens with Ezekiel among the captives by the river of Chebar. Ezekiel and his wife were among 10,000 Jews taken captive to Babylon in 597 B.C. The story of their captivity is told in 2 Kings 24. They lived in Tel-Abib on the bank of the Chebar river, southeast of Babylon. So you can see right away that Ezekiel was an exilic prophet. He was God's man with God's message to the exiles or captives in Babylon.

Ezekiel was a contemporary of Jeremiah and Daniel. *Jeremiah* was God's prophet mainly to the Jews in Jerusalem before the city of Jerusalem fell. *Daniel* was God's prophet, mainly to the court of Nebuchadnezzar, in the land of Babylon. *Ezekiel* was God's prophet to the exiles in Babylon before and after the fall of the city of Jerusalem. So Ezekiel was the prophet of the captivity.

3. *THE PERIOD*

We should try to grasp the timeline of the book. It will be helpful if we remember that there were distinct phases in the Babylonian captivity:

In 605 B.C. Daniel and other individuals of noble birth were carried away - see Daniel 1:1-3 and 2 Chronicles 36:6-7.

In 597 B.C. King Jehoiachin and Ezekiel, along with many others, were taken to Babylon – see 2 Kings 24:10-16.

In 586 B.C. after a long siege, Judah's last king Zedekiah was carried away, the walls of Jerusalem were destroyed and both Temple and City were burned – see 2 Kings 25:1-7.

The events recorded in the first part of this book - that is, until Chapter 24 - take place between the second and third phases. Ezekiel was taken into captivity in 597 B.C. when he was twenty five years of age. He received his call to preach five years later. All this was six years before the destruction of Jerusalem.

Can you grasp this? Can you see this? Six years before the destruction of Jerusalem, Jeremiah is ministering to his people in Jerusalem and Ezekiel is preaching to the Jews in captivity in Babylon. They are both saying the same thing. Judgment is coming!

Yet the amazing thing is that though these Jews had already witnessed the Babylonians coming twice and taking people into captivity, they still refused to believe that God would allow His city to be destroyed. There were, in fact, false prophets both in Jerusalem and in Babylon who were explicitly saying: *"Jerusalem will not be destroyed!"* You see, there were some people who were *living in denial*. Even though they were in captivity, even though they were in dire circumstances, they really refused to see the situation they were in.

Does that not remind you of our nation? All of the things that are taking place around us, in our government, in our land! Yet, many refuse to believe that ahead for our own nation is the judgment of God.

So to these people in Babylon who living in denial, Ezekiel is going to deliver a message of judgment. So, in the first 24 chapters of the Book we have the fate of Judah.

But there is another group of people who are in exile! While there are those who are living in denial, those who do not see the signs around them of the judgment of God, those who are just going deeper and deeper into idolatry, there are, on the other hand, people who are *living in despair*. They feel that God has totally deserted them. They see the signs of the times. They see the dire circumstances they are in. They know that it is a judgment of God upon them. So they are living in despair. They are the ones who declare: *"By the rivers of Babylon, there we sat down, yea, we wept, when we remembered Zion"* (Psalm 137:1). So, to that group of people, God is calling Ezekiel to deliver a message of hope. What is that message? Well, in Chapters 33 to 48, we have a preview of God's return to His people in great splendour and glory.

Ezekiel thus has a two-pronged message: a message of judgment to those who are in denial and a message of hope to those who are in despair. In between the two messages - in Chapters 25-32 - we have the foes of Judah. There are prophecies concerning the nations all around them.

One of the key phrases of the book is: *"the glory of the LORD"* (see Chapter 1:28; 3:12, 23; 10:4, 18; 11:23; 43:4-5 and 44:4). Wherever God is, there is glory. *"Glory"* means *"the radiance or brightness of God"*. Ezekiel is the book of God's glory. The book begins with Heavenly Glory in the opening vision - Chapter 1. It ends with Earthly Glory in the vision of the New Order - Chapters 40-48. In between it tells of Departing Glory – Chapter 8:4; 9:3; 10:4, 18, 19 and 11:22-23. Thus we see:

(4) THE PATTERN

The pattern of the book is emerging before us:

Before the Fall of Jerusalem: Chapters 1-24

During the Fall of Jerusalem: Chapters 25-32

After the Fall of Jerusalem: Chapters 33-48

Here is Ezekiel in distant Babylon able to see events in Jerusalem through the power of the Spirit of God. Notice, firstly, then:

(1) THE FATE OF THE JEWISH PEOPLE: Chapters 1-24

Here is Ezekiel the priest unable to exercise his ministry since he was far away from the Temple and the altar, but now God opens the Heavens and calls him to be a prophet.

Do you see here:

(a) THE CONSECRATION OF THE MAN OF GOD

We read: *"Then I came to them of the captivity at Tel-abib, that dwelt by the river of Chebar, and I sat where they sat"* (Chapter 3:15). In other words, Ezekiel obeyed the Lord. Now, this consecration:

1. Commenced with a Vision

This is very often the case when God calls His men to preach.

Do you remember Isaiah? He says: *"In the year that king Uzziah died I saw also the Lord sitting upon a throne"* (Isaiah 6:1).

Do you recall John on the island of Patmos? The Lord gave John an unfolding view of future events. But, do you remember before all of that, what happens in Chapter 1 of Revelation? John is given a vision of the glorified Lord Jesus.

Before Ezekiel undertakes his discouraging and disheartening ministry, God wants him to get a little glimpse of His glory. We are told what this vision is. *"As the appearance of the bow that is in the cloud in the day of rain, so was the appearance of the brightness round about. This was the appearance of the likeness of the glory of the LORD. And when I saw it, I fell upon my face, and I heard a voice of one that spake"* (Chapter 1:28).

If you do not understand anything else about this vision - and there is much that we may not understand - understand this: what Ezekiel gets in Chapter 1, before he starts his prophetic ministry, is a vision of the glory of the Lord.

What did Ezekiel see that day?

(a) The Whirlwind: Chapter 1:4

Did this not symbolize God's judgment on Jerusalem? Babylon was coming out of the north. The storm cloud with its fiery lightning meant destruction for Jerusalem.

(b) The Cherubims: Chapter 1:5-14

Verse 5 speaks about: *"living creatures"* and Ezekiel identifies these *"living creatures"* later (Chapter 10:20) as the cherubims. Do you know what the cherubims do? One of their duties is to help in the administration of the government of God. (See 1 Samuel 4:4; Psalm 80:1 and Psalm 99:1) The four faces speak of their characteristics:

the intelligence of man, the strength of the lion, the service of the ox and the heavenliness of the eagle.

Some see in these faces the four Gospels:

Matthew*, writing to the Jews, pictures Christ as a Lion, the Messiah.*
Mark, *writing to the Romans, pictures Christ as an Ox, the Servant.*
Luke, *writing to the Greeks, pictures Christ as the perfect Man.*
John, *writing to the whole world, pictures Christ as the Eagle, the mighty God.*

Certainly these creatures could move quickly to accomplish the will of God.

(c) The Wheels: Chapter 1:15-21

Wheels! Wheels within wheels! How strange and mystical. The size and circle of the wheels was vast. They seemed to reach down to earth and touch the very Heaven. They were like a child's gyroscope. They were *"full of eyes"* (Chapter 1:18), picturing the omniscience of God as He rules His creation. Proverbs 15 verse 3 declares: *"The eyes of the LORD are in every place, beholding the evil and the good".* The wheels connected the cherubims with earth, speaking of the government of God. These fearful wheels are the wheels of Divine Government and that government touches both earth and Heaven.

(d) The Firmament: Chapter 1:22-27

This was a beautiful *"platform"* above the wheels and the cherubims, containing the throne of God. God is still on the throne! His will is being accomplished in this world even if we do not always see it.

(e) The Rainbow: Chapter 1:28

There was a rainbow in the storm. Certainly this told Ezekiel that God's mercy and God's covenant would not fail His people.

Warren Wiersbe says:

"Noah saw the rainbow after the storm, John saw it before the storm, but Ezekiel saw it within the storm."
What is this vision of glory all about? It tells us that God is at work in the world judging the sins of His people, but still keeping His covenant of mercy.

Do you see what happened to Ezekiel as the result of this vision? *"And when I saw it, I fell upon my face"* (Chapter 1:28). Is our God not an awesome God? Does He not know *everything*? He is omniscient. Is He not *everywhere*? He is omnipresent. Can He not do *anything*? He is omnipotent. No wonder Ezekiel is on his face! He sees the glory of the Lord and the glory of the Lord is the outward manifestation of the Divine Presence.

This consecration commenced with a vision and then this consecration:

2. *Continued with a Voice*

God *Stands us on our Feet* (Chapter 2:2) and then God *Sends us on our Way* (Chapter 2:3).

God called Ezekiel to be a watchman, a watchman of souls. He fed him with the Word, as in Jeremiah 15 verse 16, and filled him with the Spirit.

Could it be that like Ezekiel *you* also have seen a vision and heard a voice? Is God calling *you* to be a watchman? Will you respond in the words of the hymnwriter?

My eyes look up to Thee;
May I more clearly see,
Thy glorious Throne.
Falling before Thy grace,
Humbled upon my face,
May I Thy call embrace,
Thy Word make known.

And then do you see:

(*b*) *THE CONDEMNATION OF THE CITY OF GOD*

This condemnation takes in a vast number of chapters within the book. From Chapter 4 to Chapter 24, Ezekiel more than any other prophet not only communicated his message verbally, but visually. In other words, Ezekiel was to act out, by signs, that Jerusalem was doomed. For example:

1. In Chapter 4, he was to take a slab of clay, draw a picture of Jerusalem on it and lay siege to it with model battering rams, and so forth. He did this in total silence, watched by the crowds who were doubtless asking: *"What is the prophet doing now?"*

2. Perhaps the hardest thing for Ezekiel concerned the death of his wife. In Chapter 24 verses 15 to 24, she dies and he was not even allowed to mourn, symbolising that when Jerusalem finally fell, the people would be so stunned that they would not be able to believe it and would not even cry.

If in the opening chapter we see the *Glory of God Revealed,* then in these Chapters we see the *Glory of God Removed.*

Why did Jerusalem fall? Well, in Chapter 8, a year after the first vision, God gave Ezekiel another vision, this time of the sins of the people back in Jerusalem. The glory appeared again and God took the prophet in vision to the holy city. There he saw a fourfold view of the sins of the people. He saw, in verse 5, an image set up at the north gate of the Temple, possibly of Astarte, the foul Babylonian goddess. He saw, in verses 6 to 12, secret heathen worship in the hidden precincts of the Temple. Ezekiel then saw, in verses 13 and 14, the Jewish women weeping for Tammuz. Tammuz was said to be the son of Semiramis, Queen of heaven, and he was supposed to die and be raised from the dead each spring. Then, as now in Romish and other religious circles, the favourite deity of women was the virgin and her child. These Jewish women in the Temple were not weeping for their sins nor were they were weeping to the Lord. Rather, they were weeping for Tammuz. Still again, in verses 15 and 16, Ezekiel saw the high priest and the twenty-four courses of priests worshiping the sun.

Is it any wonder God planned to destroy the city? Idolatry, immorality and ingratitude marked its people. Of course, the glory of the Lord could not remain in such a wicked place. Ezekiel saw the glory at the Temple in Chapter 8 verse 4, but in Chapter 9 verse 3 the glory moved to the threshold of the Temple. The throne of glory was now empty. It would become a throne of judgment. Then, in Chapter 10 verse 4, the glory of God moved above the threshold of the house, hovering there before judgment was going to fall. In Chapter 10 verse 18, the glory departed from off the threshold of the house and stood over the cherubims. Then, in the next verse, the glory moved with the cherubims to the eastern gate of the Temple. Finally, in Chapter 11 verses 22 and 23, the glory moved out of the Temple to the top of the Mount of Olives. What was said in 1 Samuel 4 verse 21 needed to be said again: *"Ichabod, the glory has departed"*.

Why was the glory removed? Because God cannot share His glory with another. The idols and the sins of the people had driven Him away! Their sins may have been hidden from the people, but God saw them and God judged them. *"Ichabod, the glory has departed."* Is this not happening today? As you travel around the country, how heart-breaking to see so many church buildings closed, others falling into decay, others sold for bingo halls and so on. Why? The glory has departed and the lampstand has been removed. What a solemn warning to us corporately! Moreover, God will remove His glory and His blessing from our lives unless we serve Him faithfully with honest and pure hearts.

Thus, in the first 24 Chapters, there is brought before us the Fate of the Jewish People. Then, secondly, we see:

(2) *<u>THE FOES OF THE JEWISH PEOPLE</u>*: <u>Chapters 25-32</u>

The background here is important. When Jerusalem fell all the neighbouring countries were thrilled.

David Pawson in his *"Unlocking the Bible"* writes:

"The phrase: 'Hip! Hip! Hooray!' comes from the delighted cry 'Hip Hip' which is made up of the three initial letters of "Jerusalem is fallen!" in the Latin language - so the phrase was an Anti-Semitic celebration."

So many people were delighted by the destruction of Jerusalem. During the great days of their nation, the Jews had been a separated people and this irritated their neighbours. The Jewish claim that Jehovah was the only true and living God meant that the other nations worshipped dead idols. So you can imagine that these nations that surrounded Judah were thrilled with the Babylonian invasion.

A glance at the map will show that Ezekiel dealt first with the nations on the east - Ammon, Moab and Edom - then with those on the west - Philistia, Tyre, and Sidon - and finally with the nation to the south - Egypt.

It is interesting that Ezekiel did not have a message of judgment against Babylon. God used Isaiah - Isaiah 21 verses 1-9 - and especially Jeremiah - Jeremiah 31 and 40 - for that task.

In the closing verse of Psalm 137, the captives in Babylon are recorded saying concerning Babylon: *"Happy shall he be, that taketh and dasheth thy little ones against the stones"*. Someone might respond: *"How awful!"* Well, the Edomites took babies by the ankles and smashed their brains out against the walls of Jerusalem. The Psalmist is crying from the heart: *"We want you to suffer in the same way as we have suffered"*. So this is a description of God paying back these surrounding nations for exploiting the fall of Jerusalem.

Some of these predictions are remarkably detailed. Let us just take one. Ezekiel predicts the downfall of Tyre, located on the eastern coast of the Mediterranean Sea.

Again David Pawson in his book, *"Unlocking the Bible"*, tells us that Tyre was actually two cities, one on the coastline some sixty miles north-west from Jerusalem and the other on an island half a mile out in the Mediterranean Sea. Can you see the *Sin of Tyre* in verse 2 of Chapter 26? Tyre had rejoiced over the fall of Jerusalem, because it meant that her trade caravans going from the north to Egypt in the south would no longer have to pay tax. Can you see the *Judgment of Tyre* in verses 3 to 5? Ezekiel predicts that one day Tyre will be razed to the ground. The whole city will be thrown into the sea and the place where Tyre stood will become a place for fishermen to dry their nets.

Now this is amazing, because no other city has ever been thrown into the sea, neither before nor since. But this prediction came true! In 322 B.C. Alexander the Great came marching down towards Egypt with his great army. The people of Tyre got into fishing boats and went out to the island that lay half a mile from the shore, knowing that Alexander had an army but not a navy. However, Alexander was not called *"The Great"* for nothing. He built a land-bridge leading from the coastline to the island. Do you know how he did it? He threw the debris of the old city into the water, he literally scraped the coastline clean.

Do you see verse 4 of Chapter 26? *"I will also scrape her dust from her."* After this was done, his army went across and defeated the people of Tyre. If you could go to the site of the old city of Tyre today, you will find it is just bare rock, with fishermen spreading their nets on it, just as Ezekiel had prophesied.

Is God's Word not amazing? Here we see a prophecy against the *King of Tyre*. In Chapter 28, in the King of Tyre we see the Devil himself. Is it not great to know that God is still on the throne?

One of the key phrases in the book of Ezekiel is this: *"They shall know that I am the LORD"* (see Chapter 28:22-23). This is the heart of the book! Gentile nations will know that the Lord is God by the judgments they experience and Israel will know that the Lord is God by the captivity they endure.

Do you know something? God achieved His purpose. He sent His people into Babylon the capital of idolatry and the Jews to this very day have never again entered into the worship of foreign gods.

Then, in the third section of the book, there is:

(3) THE FUTURE OF THE JEWISH PEOPLE: Chapters 33-48

Remember that when we come to this final section of the book, Jerusalem has fallen. Verse 21 of Chapter 33 records: *"It came to pass in the twelfth year of our captivity, in the tenth month, in the fifth day of the month, that one that had escaped out of Jerusalem came unto me, saying, The city is smitten"*. After Jerusalem was destroyed in 586 B.C. there was a complete change in Ezekiel's preaching from judgment to joy, from gloom to glory, from pessimism to optimism. Ezekiel predicts Israel's return and restoration. There is a bright future for the nation of Israel.

Now some Christians prefer to interpret Ezekiel Chapters 33 to 48 symbolically. They apply these descriptions *spiritually* to the church today, rather than *literally* to Israel in the future. However, we have been interpreting Ezekiel's words literally up to this point. What right then do we have to change our approach and start interpreting his words symbolically?

As Dr. David Cooper says: *"When the plain sense of Scripture makes good sense, then we need no other sense"*.

Remember Ezekiel is preaching to the exiles in Babylon and he is speaking of a time when God will do a new work and His glory will return to the land. The *Glory of God was Revealed* in the opening chapters. The *Glory of God was Removed* in the middle chapters. The *Glory of God will be Restored* in the final chapters.

Notice in these final chapters:

(a) THE NEW NATION: Chapter 37

Perhaps the most popular passage in the book is Chapter 37, made famous by the Negro spiritual. Do you know it?

> *"Dem bones, dem bones, dem dry bones*
> *Dem bones, dem bones, dem dry bones*
> *Dem bones, dem bones, dem dry bones*
> *Don't you hear the word of the Lord?"*

Now remember that at this time both Israel and Judah were ruined politically. Assyria had scattered Israel and Judah had just been captured by Babylon. Isaiah and Jeremiah predicted a return from captivity, but Ezekiel's vision goes even further down the years. In the vision, he saw very many bones in the valley or battlefield. It was a picture of utter defeat - the bones of the armies drying and unburied. What a picture of the Jewish people! But through the power of *God's Word* (verse 7) and through the power of *God's Spirit* (verse 9) life was given to them.

This Chapter has been used to preach revival to the Church - and it may be so used by way of application. The interpretation, however, relates to Israel.

This Chapter is not about a bodily resurrection or even about the salvation of the Jews. It rather pictures a future revival of the nation when the Jews will be brought out of the Gentile nations where they have been scattered and the old division of the nation into two will be a thing of the past. In verses 16 and 17, two sticks become one! Israel will have its national sovereignty restored.

Now has this not happened? On 14th May 1948, this nation that had lain dormant and dead for two thousand years was raised, and the modern nation of Israel entered the family of nations again.

Of course, Israel is still dead spiritually, but one day when Christ returns *"all Israel shall be saved"* (Romans 11:26).

A New Nation, but notice too:

(b) THE NEW VICTORY: Chapters 38-39

These chapters deal with the famous *"battle of Gog and Magog"*. Now it is important that we do not confuse this war with the Battle of Armageddon in Revelation 19 which takes place at the end of the seven year tribulation period. Nor is it the same battle involving Gog and Magog mentioned in Revelation 20 for that will take place after the thousand year reign of Christ. When then will this battle take place? When the Jews are dwelling safely in their own land (Chapter 38:8, 11, 12, 14) in the *"latter years"* (Chapter 38:8). When will that be?

Keep in mind that when the church is raptured, many events will unfold quickly in the world. It seems that the old Roman Empire will be restored, headed by the Antichrist. He will agree to protect the Jews for seven years - as predicted in Daniel 9 verse 27. Now, during the first three and a half years of the tribulation period, Israel will enjoy rest in the land, protected by the Antichrist. But probably Russia and her satellites will want the great wealth of Israel. (See Chapter 38:12-13) Gesenius, whose Hebrew lexicon has never been superseded, says that *"Gog"* is undoubtedly the Russians. He also identified *"Meshech"* as Moscow and *"Tubal"* as Tobolsk. Will this invasion be put down to Russia's Anti-Semetism? No, they are coming to capture the wealth of Israel and to control the world of the Middle East. However, God will intervene and destroy the army of Russia. So great will be the defeat that, according to verse 12 of Chapter 39, it will take seven months to bury the dead. The Antichrist will hasten to Israel's help only to discover that Russia is no longer a world power, and then he will set himself up in the Jewish temple as the world dictator, thus breaking his covenant with the Jews. This will be *"The Abomination of Desolation"* spoken of by Daniel the prophet.

One thing is certain, there will be a new victory. The northern invader will come to a terrible end on the mountains of Israel.

A New Nation, a New Victory and:

(c) THE NEW TEMPLE: Chapters 40-46

I want you to notice that the temple here could not be the heavenly temple since Ezekiel was taken, in Chapter 40 verse 2, to Israel to see it.

It could not be Zerubbabel's temple since the glory of God was not present there.

It could not be the eternal temple since the Lord and the Lamb are, according to Revelation 21 verse 22, its temple.

Therefore, this must be an earthly millennial temple. Now this is the last of seven great Biblical temples:

1. The Tabernacle of Moses: 1500-1000 B.C. - Exodus 40.

2. The Temple of Solomon: 1000-586 B.C. - 1 Kings Chapters 5-8.

3. The Temple of Zerubbabel: 515 B.C. to A.D. 70 - Rebuilt later by Herod - Ezra 6 and John 2 verse 20.

4. The Temple of the Body of Christ: 4.B.C. to A.D. 30 - John 2 verse 21.

5. The Spiritual Temple: the church - from Pentecost to the Rapture - Acts 2

6. The Tribulation Temple: From the Rapture until Armageddon - Revelation 11.

7. The Millennial Temple - Ezekiel 40-48, Isaiah 2:3 and 60:13; Joel 3:18; Haggai 2:7,9.

What will be its purpose? To provide a dwelling place for the cloud of glory - verse 5 of Chapter 43 describes the glory of the Lord filling the house - and to provide a centre for the King of Glory. *"I will dwell in the midst of the children of Israel for ever"* (Chapter 43:7).

The Lord's promise to occupy a future temple reminds us of our present privilege of being, according to 1 Corinthians 6 verse 19, temples of the Holy Spirit.

(d) THE NEW LAND: Chapters 47-48

The temple has been rebuilt; the glory has returned; rivers of blessing flow from the temple; the tribes are re-gathered and set in the land in order around the sanctuary. The promises made to Abraham will be fulfilled and his descendants will possess and enjoy their land. The Messiah that Israel rejected at His first coming will be received and honoured. God will fulfil every kingdom promise found in the pages of the prophets.

The last words of Ezekiel ring out and will continue to ring out until Christ comes again to make these visions a reality.

Looking at the city and at the temple and at the nation, Ezekiel cries: *"The name of the city from that day shall be, The LORD is there".*

"The LORD is there - Jehovah- shammah."

Is it not great to know that what will be true of this city in a day to come is true of us today? Is it not great to know that the Lord is there with you right now?

One of the names of the Lord our God,
Which speaks of His love and care,
Is called in the Hebrew 'Jehovah-shammah',
And it means: "The Lord is there".

In your hours of sorrow and times of grief,
When your soul seems so filled with despair,
Reflect on the words of 'Jehovah-shammah',
And know in your heart: "He is there".

When you're flat on your back or you're suffering pain,
And you're feeling that life is not fair,
Start counting your blessings from "Jehovah-shammah",
Just think of His love: "He is there".

When your plans go awry or your dreams fall apart,
When your burdens are heavy to bear,
Lean hard on the promise of "Jehovah-shammah",
You are never alone: "He is there".

When the Devil's temptations press hard on your soul,
And he deviously seeks to ensnare,
Run quickly to Jesus, your "Jehovah-shammah",
Then your battle is won: "He is there".

When your heart overflows with thanksgiving and praise,
And you pour out your love in your prayer,
There's rejoicing in Heaven by "Jehovah-shammah",
For He hears and we know: "He is there".

CHAPTER 10

Daniel

From May to September 1787, the American Constitutional Convention met in Philadelphia to develop a system of government for the new nation. By 28th June, progress had been so slow that Benjamin Franklin stood and addressed George Washington, President of the Convention. Among other things he said was this: *"I have lived, Sir, a long time and the longer I live, the more convincing proofs I see of this truth, that God governs in the affairs of men"*. He then moved that they invite some of the local ministers to come to the Convention to lead them in prayer for divine guidance. Though not a professed evangelical believer, Benjamin Franklin believed in a God who is the Architect and Governor of the universe, a conviction that agrees with the testimony of Scripture.

Do you recall that Abraham called God: *"the Judge of all the earth"* (Genesis 18:25)? King Hezekiah prayed: *"Thou art the God, even Thou alone, of all the kingdoms of the earth"* (2 Kings 19:15). In Daniel's day, King Nebuchadnezzar learned the hard way, that *"the most High ruleth in the kingdom of men, and giveth it to whomsoever He will"* (Daniel 4:32).

Graham Scroggie describes the book of Daniel as: *"the greatest book in the Bible on godless kingdoms and the kingdom of God"*. The godless kingdoms referred to are the Gentile nations and the kingdom of God is the Millennial reign centred in Israel. The grand truth which applies to all kingdoms is summed up in four words: *"God rules the world"*. Heaven rules! Is this not the theme of the book of Daniel? The Universal Sovereignty of God. *"God is still on the throne"* – that is the message of the book of Daniel.

Daniel, whose name means *"God is my judge"*, is the fifth and final book of the Major Prophets. Jeremiah influenced the remnant at Jerusalem; Ezekiel influenced the Jews in captivity, and Daniel influenced the kings in the palace at Babylon.

Prophetically, Daniel deals with *"the times of the Gentiles"*, an expression found in Luke 21 verse 24, and that period of time began in 606 B.C. with the fall of Jerusalem. Political control of Jerusalem passed from Jewish to Gentile hands - where it has remained ever since. Although the government of the modern reborn state of Israel is located in Jerusalem and the old city is now in the hands of the Jews, the Dome of the Rock - a Muslim mosque - still stands on the ancient site of Solomon's Temple. The *"times of the Gentiles"* will end when Christ returns to establish His earthly kingdom.

Practically, Daniel encourages us to honour God in an ungodly environment. The principle of 1 Samuel 2 verse 30: *"Them that honour Me, I will honour"* is vividly illustrated in this book.

Personally, Daniel stimulates us to rest on the absolute sovereignty of God: *"There is a God in heaven"* (Daniel 2:28). *"The most High ruleth in the kingdom of men, and giveth it to whomsoever He will"* (Chapter 4:25).

Gareth Crossley states: *"The prophecy of Daniel is a spiritual tonic to all believers of any nation or generation who are bewildered or distressed by national or international events".*

Does the state of the world concern you? Do international events overwhelm you? Well, let this book of Daniel minister to your soul, for *"God is still on the throne".*

Daniel easily divides into two main sections – Chapters 1-6 and then Chapters 7-12.

As John Phillips puts it:

"The first six chapters are *Historical*: the last six chapters are

Prophetical. The first six chapters have to do with Daniel and His Personal Friends: the last six chapters have to do with Daniel and His People's Future."

As in all these studies, we cannot be *exhaustive* but rather *selective*. However, as we seek to overview this book, I trust we will grasp all the salient points:

(1) THE BOOK OF DANIEL IS AUTHENTIC

No other book in the Bible has been subject to such criticism as the book of Daniel. Sir Robert Anderson wrote a book entitled: *"Daniel in the Critics' Den"*, in which he defended the genuineness of this book. No book of the Old Testament has been as mistreated and scorned by critics as the book of Daniel. W. A. Criswell says: *"There is not a liberal theologian in the world, past or present, who accepts the authenticity of the book of Daniel"*. Daniel has been under attack, even more than the book of Genesis. Critics believe that if they can discredit this book, then the entire Bible will come tumbling down like a pack of cards.

What do they say? They say: *"Daniel is a fictitious book. It was not written when it purports to have been written. All of the events which the book of Daniel prophesied were written after they had already come to pass"*. Now, why do they say this? It is because the book of Daniel is a prophecy. God is predicting ahead of time what was going to be. The critics say: *"There is no such thing as God predicting what is going to happen in the future"*. According to Daniel's critics, prophecy is an impossibility. There is no such thing as foretelling events to come. Therefore, a book that contains predictions must have been written after the fact. They deny the supernatural, and that is why the liberals hit this book.

These attacks can be traced back to a man by the name of Porphyry who was born in 233 A.D. in Tyre, Syria. He wrote fifteen books with the revealing title: *"Against the Christians"*. Porphyry became a polytheist - he worshipped many gods. One of his favourite targets was Daniel. He did everything he could to prove that this book was written about 165 B.C. and that all of the events which the book of Daniel predicted were written after they had already come to pass. All of the modern critics have taken Porphyry's arguments and rehashed them.

Why do we not think like them? The explanation for our stance is because of the authenticity of this book. The genuineness of this book:

(a) IS AFFIRMED BY THE SCRIPTURES

This book is affirmed in the Old Testament

Ezekiel mentions Daniel by name in Chapter 14 verse 14 and again in Chapter 28 verse 3 and regards him as such an outstanding person as to link his name with those of Noah and Job. If the critics do not believe Daniel, then they have a problem with Ezekiel also.

This book is affirmed in the New Testament

This book is affirmed in the New Testament by none other than the Lord Jesus Himself. In Matthew 24 verse 15, He mentions Daniel by name and quotes from his prophecy.

The critic says that Daniel is a *forgery*: Christ says that Daniel is a *prophecy* - and we take our stand with the Lord Jesus.

It always amazes me how the critics seem to think they can tell God what He can and cannot do. The Lord Jesus says that there was a Daniel and that he was a prophet. That settles it! Indeed, do you recall how our Lord Jesus proved His Messianic ministry out of the prophecies of the Old Testament?

"And beginning at Moses and all the prophets, He expounded unto them in all the Scriptures the things concerning Himself" (Luke 24:27).

"And He said unto them, These are the words which I spake unto you, while I was yet with you, that all things must be fulfilled, which were written in the law of Moses, and in the prophets, and in the psalms, concerning Me" (Luke 24:44).

This was Christ's way of proving that He was the true Messiah, namely that He was the fulfilment of prophecy. He did so at the outset of His public ministry by quoting from Isaiah 61 - see Luke 4:16-21 – and now, on the day of His resurrection, He does it again.

Is this not how the apostles preached? Paul says: *"Having therefore obtained help of God, I continue unto this day, witnessing both to small and great, saying none other things than those which the prophets and Moses did say should come; that Christ should suffer, and that He should be the first that should rise from the dead, ... King Agrippa, believest thou the prophets? I know that thou believest"* (Acts 26:22, 23, 27).

If the prophecies are not true, Christianity is not true, for to destroy the prophets is to destroy Christ.

Secondly, the genuineness of Daniel is:

(b) IS CONFIRMED BY THE SCIENTISTS

Archaeology confirms the book of Daniel. For example, the opening verses say that Nebuchadnezzar, the ruler of Babylon, took vessels from the Temple at Jerusalem and brought them into the treasury of his god.

"Never heard of such a thing", says the modernist. *"That was a completely unknown custom. We cannot find any reference in ancient history to such a practice."* Can they not? They have now discovered an inscription that proves Nebuchadnezzar always put his choicest spoils into his house of worship. Just one of those peculiar habits of the King!

In the first few verses, there is a reference to a man by the name of Ashpenaz, who was master of the eunuchs. The critic says: *"No-one has ever heard of this fellow! He was just another fictional character out of Daniel's fantasy"*. Do you know something? During the last quarter of a century, the name *"Ashpenaz"* has been found on the monuments of ancient Babylon which are now in the Berlin Museum. It says: *"Ashpenaz, master of eunuchs in the time of Nebuchadnezzar"*. The Dead Sea Scrolls contain eight copies of

Daniel, more than any other manuscript, which affirms the high esteem that was accorded the book by the strict Essenes who hid the scrolls.

What a Bible we have! Accurate to the very last detail.
What a God we have! Able to predict the future.

(2) __THE BOOK OF DANIEL IS HISTORIC__

As a teenager, Daniel was taken into Babylon where he spent the rest of his life. It is probable that the last official task he performed was to prepare the papers authorizing the Jews to return to their own land to rebuild the Temple in 539 B.C. No doubt, he wrote this book shortly after that date. (See Chapter 8:15, 27; 9:2; 10:2, 7 and 12:4-5)

As this book opens, the drums of war are beating in the Middle East. Egypt and Babylon, the two superpowers of the late seventh century before Christ, were competing with each other for control of that part of the world. In the early summer of 605 B.C. the Babylonian army, under the leadership of Nebuchadnezzar, attacked the Egyptian army at Carchemish on the upper Euphrates River and soundly defeated them. The Egyptians were forced to retreat south to their homeland and this opened Judah to the control of the Babylonians. As a result, by August of 605 B.C. Nebuchadnezzar took control of the city of Jerusalem. On the 15th or 16th of the same month, his father, Naboplassar, died in Babylon. Nebuchadnezzar rushed home to claim the throne and on that return home he carried captive with him some of the sacred vessels of the temple of Jehovah in Jerusalem and the cream of the Jewish young men. Daniel and his companions were among those captives.

This is the background from a *secular* point of view, but if you look at the opening verses, you will see the background from a *spiritual* point of view. As the book of Daniel opens, the Southern Kingdom of Judah is about to reap a bitter harvest for long years of disobedience to God's Word. Judgment should not have come as any surprise, for as far back as Moses, the initial dynamic leader of the people, sombre warnings had been clearly sounded. Deuteronomy 28, for example, set out the results of obedience and the results of disobedience. A price would have to be paid for departure from God.

Notice:

(a) THE DEPARTURE IN JUDAH

Two particular sins caused Judah to be taken into captivity.

1. *There was a Departure from the WORD of GOD*

The Mosaic Law specified that every seventh year the land was not to be farmed. It was to be a Sabbatical year, a year of rest for the land, symbolizing the truth that *"the earth is the Lord's"*. The command was given in Leviticus 25 verse 1 to 4 and the consequence of failure to comply with the command in Leviticus 26 verse 32 to 35. This was God's Word to the nation, but they disregarded it and for 490 years the land had no rest.

How long will it take us to learn that we cannot disobey God's Word and escape? God is not playing games with us in the Bible! When God tells us to do something, we must do it or pay the price.

Think of it! 490 years and no Sabbatical years! 70 Sabbatical years ignored! So what did God do? He sent them into captivity for 70 years - see 2 Chronicles 36 verse 21 and Jeremiah 25 verse 11.

Think of the patience of God, lasting for nearly 500 years, a patience which had all but run out. For the Northern Kingdom of Israel, that divine patience was exhausted in 722 B.C. when the Assyrians besieged Israel's capital, Samaria, and carried away captive its leading citizens. Now, more than 100 years later, Babylon came as God's instrument of judgment on Jerusalem. God's patience has limits because He is also a God of justice and He must judge sin. Any nation or individual is foolish to imagine that God will never intervene to judge.

2. *There was a Departure from the WORSHIP of GOD*

Idolatry had become an accepted lifestyle. Israel - the Northern Kingdom - had been by characterized by Jeroboam's calf worship and the worship of Baal. Now in Judah - the Southern Kingdom - the same sordid story was repeated. No wonder we read in verse 2 of Daniel 1: *"And the Lord gave Jehoiakim .... into his hand"*. Says 2 Kings 24 verse 3: *"Surely at the commandment of the LORD came this upon Judah"*.

Now, Babylon was the centre of idol worship. Indeed, idolatrous religion had its origin there. There is a reference in Daniel 1 verse 2 to the land of Shinar, the old word for the land of Babylon. Nimrod the tyrant comes to mind, and visions of the tower of Babel – all as told in Genesis 10 and 11. Thus, when God allowed His people to be taken into captivity in Babylon, He was sending them back to the capital city of idolatry and for 70 years they experienced those idols that they had wanted to serve.

What was the outcome? After their years of captivity in Babylon, they had no more desire for idol worship. To this day, the Jewish people only worship one God, Jehovah. Do you see what happened to them? God put them in the land of Babylon to hate the false idols that they had once loved.

Do you know something? We also had better be careful regarding to what we attach ourselves, for God may let us have our fill of it!

So there was *the Departure in Judah* and, consequently, there was:

(b) THE DEPORTATION OF JUDAH

Look at the *PERIOD* of it:

Chapter 1 and verse 1 is set in the third year of the reign of Jehoiakim. Now keep in mind that this deportation took place in three stages. The first attack took place in 605 B.C. This is the one spoken about in our text, at which time the first group of captives were taken. Among them were Daniel and his friends.

The second invasion was in 597 B.C. when Ezekiel and a much larger number of people were taken.

The third and final invasion was in 586 B.C. when the Temple was destroyed and the city was burned. This final invasion is described in 2 Kings 24 verses 6 to 16.

Look at the *PURPOSE* of it:

Verse 3 refers to: *"certain of the children of Israel, and of the king's seed, and of the princes"*. In verse 4, they are described as: *"children in whom was no blemish, but well favoured, and skilful in all wisdom, and cunning in knowledge, and understanding science"*. By removing *"the cream of the nation"*, Nebuchadnezzar was impoverishing that nation of its future leaders, and at the same time recruiting young men for Babylon. It is probable that Daniel and his three friends were of royal descent.

Look at the *PLACE* of it:

Babylon at this time in history was the number one superpower. This was a ruthless and evil empire. Nebuchadnezzar was the Hitler of the ancient world. Babylon was an awful place to try and live for God, yet it was here that Daniel was taken as a teenager and it was here he remained until the end of his life.

So often believers say: *"It is so difficult to live for the Lord where I work. I think I'll change my job."* Did you ever think of Daniel? As a teenager, in the midst of idolatry, immorality, indecency, and then for seventy plus years he maintained a testimony for God. He was living 1000 miles from home. There they changed his name, his curriculum and his diet. However, they could not change his heart!

(3) THE BOOK OF DANIEL IS THEOCRATIC

Israel was a theocracy. It was ruled by the Lord. In this book of Daniel, we meet some temporal rulers but only one eternal ruler. Is this not what the book of Daniel is all about? *The rule of*

God! Is this not a timely message for our age? We live in a time of instability, insecurity, and self-sufficiency. The rejection of God's rule, which started for man in the Garden of Eden, seems to be reaching a frenzied pitch. Because man rejects the rule of God, his pride drives him to do things opposite to what God has ordained.

As Renald Showers reminds us:

"The Lord regards human life as sacred, but man destroys it by abortion. God instituted marriage to be permanent, but man divorces and suggests that marriage be abolished. God says that the fear of the Lord is the beginning of wisdom, but man forbids any reference to God in the classroom. God established sex to be used within the bonds of marriage, but man perverts sex through pornography, fornication, adultery and homosexuality. Man reels from one crisis to another but instead of admitting that his rebellion against God is the cause of his problem, he stands unbowed before the God of the universe."

Now is this not the problem that all of us battle with?

Do you recall the words of Frank Sinatra's song?

"I did it my way!"

Do you recall the words of A.A. Pollard's hymn?

"Have Thine own way, Lord."

Which is it for you? Your way or God's way?

Now this message of God's rule over the realm of man is conveyed to us in two ways. Here is a book that stresses:

(a) THE REIGN OF THE LORD

Look at the two key phrases in the book of Daniel. The first is found in Chapter 2 verse 28 and the second in Chapter 4 verse 25. If you bring these two phrases together, you have the key to the book.

"There is a God in heaven ... the Most High ruleth in the kingdom of men."

The whole point is that the God of the Bible, who is the Christian's God, is sovereign over the affairs of men and of nations.

Here is something that we can trace throughout this book. Look at God's rule:

1. In relation to JEHOIAKIM: *"The Lord gave Jehoiakim, king of Judah into his hand"* (Chapter 1:2). Who gave? *"The Lord gave!"* Nebuchadnezzar thought he captured the city. The *"Babylonian Daily News"* probably had the headline: *"Nebuchadnezzar conquers King of Judah"*. No, he did not! God gave it to him. The Sovereignty of God in the affairs of men.

2. In relation to NEBUCHADNEZZAR: *"Thou, O king, art a king of kings: for the God of Heaven hath given thee a kingdom, power, and strength, and glory"* (Chapter 2:37). Do you see it? Nebuchadnezzar said: *"I have got all this!" "Is not this great Babylon, that I have built?"* (Chapter 4:30) How did Nebuchadnezzar, a wicked, despotic king come to the throne of Babylon? It is simple. The God of Heaven gave it to him.

3. In relation to BELSHAZZAR: *"God in whose hand thy breath is"* (Chapter 5:23). In this Chapter, Daniel is explaining mystery and preaching prophecy - and he declares God's authority over Belshazzar.

What is this book teaching us? The kingdoms of this world are passing away and the Kingdom of the Most High is going to abide - and through all the long centuries, through all that is taking place, the Most High rules. Does that not thrill your soul? We all know about despots. We call them by different names: Hitler, Mussolini, Saddam Hussein, Gaddafi, but Daniel shows us God's sovereignty in dealing with despots. Under the sovereign rule of God, the biggest of men will be humbled and brought to the dust. Do you know why? ***Heaven Rules! God Rules!***

Look at Eastern Europe. Did you ever think you would live to see the Berlin Wall down? Communism reeling?

What about what is happening in the Middle East? How will history interpret these events? People pressure! How will believers interpret these events? God ruling!

Note, then, the Reign of the Lord. Note also:

(b) THE NAME OF THE LORD

What is the name that is most frequently used of God in this book? *"The Most High."* (See Chapter 3:26; 4:2, 17, 24, 25, 32, 34 and 7:18 22, 25, 27) Do you know when that was first used? Away back in the book of Genesis! Lot had been taken captive. Abraham set out in pursuit. He rescued Lot and the enemies' goods were taken. The King of Sodom tried to do a deal with Abraham and, in response, Abraham said: *"I have lift up mine hand unto the LORD, the most high God, the possessor of Heaven and earth"* (Genesis 14:22). The phrase: *"the most High God"* is the translation of the Hebrew name *"EL ELYON"* - *"the possessor of Heaven and earth"*. God can dispose of His property as He pleases. This is the message of the book of Daniel - *"the Most High ruleth"*.

Behind the political intrigue, the rise and fall of nations, the appearance and disappearance of despots, there is a Hand that is shaping, a Heart that is planning, a Sovereign God who is accomplishing His will - for Heaven Rules.

(4) <u>THE BOOK OF DANIEL IS PROPHETIC</u>

When we talk about prophecy, what do we mean? Well, prophecy is history written in advance. We live in an age in which men like to pry into the future. A lot of money is spent on fortune tellers, consulting the horoscopes and listening to quack prophets. Yet God claims to be the only One able to foretell the future. He says: *"I am God, and there is none like Me, declaring the end from the beginning, and from ancient times the things that are not yet done"* (Isaiah 46:9-10). Only God could possess such knowledge.

Is this not exactly what Daniel declared to Nebuchadnezzar? *"The great God hath made known to the king what shall come to pass hereafter"* (Chapter 2:45). God alone could reveal such a secret.

Now, prophets had a two-fold function. They were both *forth-tellers* and *foretellers*. They possessed both insight and foresight. Their predictions were not the deductions of reason but were imparted to them by the Holy Spirit. Peter reminds us: *"For the prophecy came not in old time by the will of man: but holy men of God spake as they were moved by the Holy Ghost"* (2 Peter 1:21). Now, if the predictive element in prophecy can be seen in other books of the Bible, it is especially prominent in Daniel.

You see, it is Daniel who predicts:

(a) THE FIRST ADVENT OF CHRIST

Look at Chapter 9 and verses 20 to 27. Here Gabriel is giving to Daniel vital information about a period of seventy weeks. It is not necessary for us to go into detail here, but can you see clearly that the total number of weeks between the decree *"to restore and to build Jerusalem unto the Messiah the Prince"* is 69 weeks? Or, if you like 483 years. Each of those years consisted of 360 days and so the total number of days is 173,880 days. Now when did this period begin? It began with the construction of the city (verse 25) When was that? Well, it was in the book of Nehemiah – Nehemiah 2 verses 1 to 5 - that Artaxerxes decreed that Nehemiah could return to rebuild the city. This command was issued during the 20th year of Artaxerxes' reign. The *Encyclopaedia Britannica* sets this date as 14th March 445 B.C. Now this is the decree that this verse 25 is talking about.

Sir Robert Anderson, who founded Scotland Yard and who was a brilliant Bible scholar, points out that if you take 14th March 445 B.C. when the decree to rebuild Jerusalem went forth and add to it 173,880 days, you come to 6th April A.D. 32 - and it was on this very day that the Lord Jesus made His triumphal entry into the city of Jerusalem and presented Himself to the nation as their Messiah Prince. Of course, it was on this day that the Pharisees plotted to murder Christ and within a few short days, He was, in the language of Daniel 9 verse 26, *"cut off, but not for Himself"*. When He died on the Cross, He received nothing that was due Him. No honour, no respect, no love and no acceptance. John says: *"He came unto His own, and His own received Him not"* (John 1:11). Instead, Christ received what He did not deserve, the sins of the world.

Is God's Word not amazing? A precise prediction concerning the First Advent of Christ in this book – and also predictions of:

(b) THE SECOND ADVENT OF CHRST

Look at Chapter 2 and verse 44. There is a reference in this verse to: *"these kings"*. What kings? Kings who are symbolized by the ten toes of the image seen by Nebuchadnezzar. Revelation 17 verse 12 also refers to *"ten kings"*. I submit to you that this lies in the future. Never in the past did Rome survive under ten heads. More than that, never in the past did Rome survive under ten heads at one given time. More than that still, never in the past did Rome survive under ten heads at one given time and then been smitten by the Lord Jesus. The stone in Nebuchadnezzar's dream is Christ. This would be confirmed by Psalm 118 verse 22 and Luke 20 verse 17. When in the past did this smiting stone shatter those earthly kingdoms? On the contrary, Rome hit Christ. A Roman officer sentenced Him to death; a Roman soldier scourged Him, and Roman soldiers nailed Him to the Cross, but there is a day coming when Christ will destroy the revived Roman Empire pictured in this image and establish His kingdom. *That* kingdom will be something unlike anything we have ever known.

"In the days of these kings shall the God of heaven set up a kingdom, which shall never be destroyed" (Chapter 2:44).

What a moment that will be when:

"Jesus shall reign where'er the sun
Doth his successive journeys run;
His Kingdom stretch from shore to shore,
Till moons shall wax and wane no more."

What a book this is! Authentic, historic, theocratic, prophetic, and:

(5) <u>THE BOOK OF DANIEL IS DRAMATIC</u>

Indeed how fast moving are the events that are recorded in this book, most of them involving Daniel!

Three times in the book, he is called *"greatly beloved"* by God – Chapter 9 verse 23; Chapter 10 verse 11 and Chapter 10 verse 19. Here was a man who spent almost his entire career - from the time he was a teenager until he was a very old man - in positions of influence and authority, in highly visible public life.

Is there anything inappropriate about a godly person being elevated to a position of responsibility and trust by an ungodly government or by a pagan king? Well, Daniel was promoted. Yet, such a life is not without its dangers, but when tensions arose between serving the Lord and serving the King, Daniel and his friends did not waver for a moment. Can you see:

(a) The Loyalty of the Four in Chapter 1

You know, *God always proves His man before He promotes him.* What a test this was! Probably some of these foods (being forced on Daniel and his three friends) were prohibited by Leviticus 11. They were defiled and not to be eaten by the Jews. In Babylon, all wine was offered as a toast to the gods. *"But Daniel purposed in his heart that he would not defile himself with the portion of the king's meat, nor with the wine which he drank"* (Chapter 1:8). I believe that Daniel had a daily quiet time. There was a time each day when he meditated on the Word of God. From that spiritual reservoir, he drew convictions that enabled him to make a right decision when the crisis came. There is a tremendous lesson here. If you stand your ground over a little issue, then you are likely to stand your ground over a big one. Your character is formed in small decisions on little issues and this enables you to stand later when the big crunch comes.

(b) The Loyalty of the Three in Chapter 3

Nebuchadnezzar, because of the dream and because he had been told that he was represented by the *'head of gold'*, ordered a gigantic golden statue to be erected. It was 90 feet high and 9 feet wide. When the state band played, everyone had to bow down. So they did, apart from Shadrach, Meshach and Abednego. They would not bow, they would not budge, in fact they would not burn!

Look at Chapter 3 verse 16: *"We are not careful to answer thee in this matter"*. You see, they had a clear word from God that said: *"Thou shalt not make unto thee any graven image"* (Exodus 20:4). They did not have to think about it or have a committee meeting! Is this not what the world is crying out for? People who have convictions and who are not going to change their convictions on the basis of their circumstances.

Athanasius of Alexandria was one of the early church fathers. We are indebted to him for maintaining the purity of the doctrine of the deity of Jesus Christ. He would not relinquish his stand against a popular heresy of the day.

Someone came to him and said: *"Athanasius, don't you know that the Emperor is against you, the bishops are against you, the church is against you, the whole world is against you?"*

Do you know what Athanasius said?

"Then Athanasius is against the whole world!"

Are you bold enough to stand when the heat is on? Are you bold enough to stand for God when it matters?

(c) The Loyalty of the One in Chapter 6

There is a change of world power. Babylon, the head of gold in the image, has been replaced by the Medo-Persian Empire represented by the breast and arms of silver. Daniel, probably now about 86 years of age – for he was born in 625 B.C. - is faced with another test. ***Stop praying or start preparing for death.***

Would *you* be willing to die for prayer? Daniel was. When it came to choosing prayer and death or no prayer and life, Daniel chose prayer and death. *"Now when Daniel knew that the writing was signed, he went into his house; and his windows being open in his chamber toward Jerusalem, he kneeled upon his knees three times a day, and prayed, and gave thanks before his God, as he did aforetime"* (Daniel 6:10). The result? The lions' den.

Spurgeon once said: *"It was a good thing the lions did not try to eat Daniel. They would never have enjoyed him, because he was 50% grit and 50% backbone!"*

What *"lions"* are you facing? Do you believe that God is *"able to deliver you"*? *"Is thy God able?"* (Chapter 6:20).

What a man! What a testimony! What consistency! What transparency! Daniel's life was an open book

Daniel honoured God and God honoured Daniel. Is this not the unchanging principle of Scripture? *"Them that honour Me, I will honour"* (1 Samuel 2:30). Are you honouring God? In your personal life? In your business life? In your social life?

From teenager till pensioner, from captive to president, from lowest to highest, not one record of anything against him. That should make us so ashamed, but it should also encourage us. For, if Daniel could live to please God, so can we.

We have a Living Saviour and a Sovereign God, but also an Indwelling Spirit and a Completed Bible - and so are even more privileged than he was.

"The most High ruleth in the kingdom of men." So declares Chapter 4 verses 17, 25 and 32.

What matters most is that He rules and reigns in our hearts, so that in the Babylon of our day, we will be Christians of the calibre of Daniel.

What does the old hymn say?

Standing by a purpose true,
Heeding God's command,
Honour them, the faithful few!
All hail to Daniel's band!

Dare to be a Daniel,
Dare to stand alone!
Dare to have a purpose firm!
Dare to make it known.

Many mighty men are lost,
Daring not to stand,
Who for God had been a host
By joining Daniel's band.

Many giants, great and tall,
Stalking through the land,
Headlong to the earth would fall,
If met by Daniel's band.

Hold the Gospel banner high!
On to vict'ry grand!
Satan and his hosts defy,
And shout for Daniel's band.

May the Lord give us grace to do so for His glory!

CHAPTER 11

Hosea

Charles Swindoll in his book: *"You and Your Problems"* tells the following story:

"It was a quiet house on a quiet street in Houston, Texas. It was quiet because no-one was there. The Lockshin family - father, mother, daughter and sons - had left for Russia. Recently-filled prescription bottles still stood in bathroom cabinets on that day in 1986 when Arnold Lockshin's mother-in-law discovered the family's absence. Books on Marxism still occupied their place on bookshelves. Bicycles still leaned against the garage wall where Michael and Jennifer had left them after a neighbourhood ride. Lauren and Arnold's wedding album was left behind too, along with the children's drawings and Arnold's old scientific publications. This was defection, only it wasn't America's freedom that was being sought, but the Communist regime of Russia."

Charles Swindoll goes on to explain:

"This was unfathomable to most Americans. As unfathomable as another kind of defection is to many Christians - defection from the Lord Jesus Christ. How, after tasting the fruits of freedom in the United States, could anyone want to eat the butterless bread of a Communist government? Likewise, how, after experiencing the freedom of Christ's love, could anyone willingly hold out their wrists to sin's shackles?"

Yet, Christian defections and backsliding happen all the time.

Hosea is pre-eminently *a book for the backslider*. Here Hosea pictures God as a loving Husband yearning for the return of His wayward wife. The Lord says in this very book: *"My people are bent to backsliding from Me"* (Chapter 11:7).

Do you recall the charge that the Lord of the Lampstands brings against the church at Ephesus? *"Nevertheless I have somewhat against thee, because thou hast left thy first love"* (Revelation 2:4). Spiritual decline and defection! It was evident in the nation of Israel - *"They kept not the covenant of God, and refused to walk in His law"* (Psalm 78:10). It was evident in the disciples - *"Then all the disciples forsook Him, and fled"* (Matthew 26:56) and *"From that time many of His disciples went back, and walked no more with Him"* (John 6:66). It was evident in the churches in the New Testament - *"How turn ye again to the weak and beggarly elements, whereunto ye desire again to be in bondage?"* (Galatians 4:9). It was also evident in individuals. People like Samson, David, Solomon, Jonah, Peter, and Demas. Indeed of how many of us can it be said: *"Gray hairs are here and there upon him, yet he knoweth not"* (Hosea 7:9)?

Do William Cowper's lines sum up your current spiritual condition?

> *"Where is the blessedness I knew,*
> *When first I saw the Lord?*
> *Where is the soul refreshing view,*
> *Of Jesus and His Word?"*

Hosea is the first of the twelve *"Minor Prophets"* of the Old Testament. They are called *"minor"*, not because their message is unimportant but simply because of the length - the shortness - of their content.

They were Minor Prophets preaching a major message!

As we come to Hosea, let us think about:

THE PERSON

Hosea's name means *"salvation"*. It is interesting to observe that the names *"Joshua"* or *"Jehoshua"* (Numbers 13:16) and *"Jesus"*

(Matthew 1:21) are derived from the same Hebrew root as Hosea. We know very little about Hosea's background except that he was *"the son of Beeri"* (Chapter 1:1). Yet, there is a sense in which we know him at a deeper level than any of the other Minor Prophets. He has been called: *"The Prophet of the Sorrowing Heart"*, and that title fits him well. Hosea's message sprang from the depths of his own domestic tragedy.

So much for the person, what about:

THE PLACE

Hosea addresses the Northern Kingdom of the ten tribes as: *"Israel"*, *"Samaria"*, *"Jacob"* and *"Ephraim"*. The name *"Ephraim"* is used because that tribe was the largest of the ten. So here is Hosea and he is preaching to the Northern Kingdom before the fall of Samaria in 722 B.C.

That brings us to:

THE PERIOD

We get that in Chapter 1 verse 1: *"In the days of Uzziah, Jotham, Ahaz, and Hezekiah, kings of Judah, and in the days of Jeroboam the son of Joash, king of Israel"*. Did you notice the mention of Hezekiah here? The fact that Hosea was still ministering at the time when Hezekiah reigned in Judah settles it that he lived on through the fifty years or so in Israel between the death of Jeroboam the Second and the Assyrian invasion. That invasion took place when Hezekiah reigned in Judah - see Isaiah 36 verse 19. Although Hosea mentions only one king of Israel - Jeroboam, the son of Joash - the reference to the four kings of Judah places his ministry during the reigns of the last seven kings to rule over Israel. That is, from King Jeroboam the Second to King Hoshea. (See 2 Kings 14:23-29 and 17:1-4).

Now, what kind of period was this? Well, to understand the book, we need to put ourselves in the day and age in which Hosea lived. The prophet Amos had completed his ministry and soon Isaiah and Micah would begin to preach. But they would be preaching to the Northern Kingdom and it was up to Hosea to pick up the mantle of Amos and concentrate on the apostate nation of Israel. In the words of Sidlow Baxter: *"This period from Jeroboam the Second on to the captivity was the 'awful last lap' of iniquity in Israel's downward drive"*.

Loyalty to the throne was extinct. The land was filled with murder and bloodshed, adultery and sexual perversion. Drunkenness was widespread, accompanied by utter indifference to the Lord. There was no settled foreign policy. Those in power vacillated between alliance with Egypt and appeasement of Assyria.

Yet, against the background of Israel's *unfaithfulness*, there stands the *faithfulness* of God.

Bible scholars tell us that there is a key word that unlocks this whole prophecy. It is a great Hebrew word: *"chesed"*. It is found in Chapter 2 verse 19; Chapter 4 verse 1; Chapter 6 verse 6, and Chapter 10 verse 12. It means *"lovingkindness, mercy, or loyal love"*. However, that does not exhaust the word for it really has no English equivalent. It is a *"covenant word"* used to describe those with whom you have a covenant relationship. It does mean *"love"*, but it has a lot of the word *"loyalty"* in it also. You see, true love is not true love unless it is loyal. It means *"unswerving love and undying devotion"*. It means we are so committed to someone that we go on loving them whatever happens. The old English word *"troth"* that is sometimes used in marriage ceremonies comes close to what we are trying to say.

Today, many people enjoy love with someone for a while and then drop them for someone else. That is not true love. That is not *"chesed"*. That is not a *"stay-with-it"* love. That is not the kind of love that is portrayed in this book. Rather, the book of Hosea depicts the covenant love of God for His bride, the nation of Israel. The Lord had to say through Hosea's messages: *"What is happened to our marriage?"* He assured them of His loyal love but was certain He was receiving very little back in return. Now that brings us to:

THE PATTERN

The Pattern of the book. The book divides into two unequal parts. The first three chapters belong together in contrast to those that follow. They are narrative, whereas the remainder are messages. The first three chapters set before us a page of domestic history - *the Tragedy of Hosea's Home Life*. The rest of the book is an exposition of this. The domestic history, the domestic tragedy, in which Hosea was involved is the basis for a series of messages dealing with *the Tragedy of Hosea's Home Land.* You see, in order for Hosea to understand God's feelings, God took him through an extraordinary experience.

Do you remember that from the loneliness of not having a wife - see Chapter 16 verses 2 and 5 of his prophecy - Jeremiah learned how God was feeling about the nation? Ezekiel was told - in Chapter 24 verses 16 and 18 of his prophecy - that his wife would die, but he must not weep for her, all in order to show Judah that the Lord had been bereaved of His wife.

Now, in the same way, Hosea was taught how the Lord felt by obeying some unusual instructions with regard to his marriage situation.

So, the first section of this book is *Personal*: the last section of the book is *National*. The first section is all about *Hosea's Marriage*; the last section of the book is all about *Hosea's Message.*

(1) PERSONAL SECTION: HOSEA'S MARRIAGE - Chapters 1-3 - The Faithless Wife & Her Faithful Husband

These first three chapters of the book give us the background to the story.

It begins with:

(a) THE STRANGE MARRIAGE

Perhaps you think that *your* marriage is strange! The story is told how that years after conducting a marriage ceremony, the pastor met the former bridegroom. The pastor had been late in arriving for the wedding and had kept everyone waiting. He said to the groom: *"That was some fright I gave you that day!"* The groom replied: *"Yes! And I've still got her!"*

But what a strange marriage this was! Hosea says in verse 2 of Chapter 1: *"God told me to marry a prostitute"*. *"Go, take unto thee a wife of whoredoms."*

Here we encounter something of a problem! Not every Bible scholar agrees on the kind of woman Hosea married. There are two views. Hosea either married a pure woman who later became a prostitute or he married a prostitute who bore him children. Leviticus 21 verse 7 explicitly prohibited a priest from marrying a prostitute. The words: *"Go take unto thee a wife of whoredoms"* or *"Take yourself a wife of harlotry"* can be understood prophetically, that is looking to the future. It seems best to see Gomer as chaste and pure at the time of marriage to Hosea, only later becoming an immoral woman.

But that interpretation still leaves a problem! Why would God instruct Hosea to do this, knowing that Gomer would turn out to be immoral? Well, by marrying someone who would turn out to be unfaithful, Hosea could understand the anguish in God's heart over the Northern Kingdom. God had often compared His relationship with Israel to that of a marriage - see, for example, Isaiah 62 verse 5 and Jeremiah 3 verse 14. However, in Hosea's day, God's people were constantly committing spiritual adultery. His own marriage would become a visible example of his message to Israel.

This reminds us that sometimes God brings His choicest servants into the most puzzling of circumstances. Some Christians have the idea that as long as we are committed, faithful and obedient, we will be free from stress and unaffected by the trials and perplexities that affect others. Nothing could be further from the truth! Do you recall Job? He was *"perfect and upright, and one that feared God, and eschewed evil"* (Job 1:1), yet the Lord called him to go through an awful sequence of material, physical and spiritual traumas. Yet even Job's experiences pale into insignificance compared to those of the

Lord Jesus. He was absolutely perfect, yet was *"despised and rejected of men; a man of sorrows, and acquainted with grief"* (Isaiah 53:3).

Do not think it strange if the Lord allows some trial to cross *your* pathway. That was Hosea's experience, for this story begins with A Strange Marriage – and then:

(b) THE SYMBOLIC CHILDREN

Children are brought before us and these children were symbols or representations of what was coming. Each child was given a name which carried with it some prophetical meaning. The first child was called *"Jezreel"*. The name means *"to be scattered"*. This name predicted two events. Firstly, the setting aside of the house of the northern king named Jehu who went too far in his bloodletting. His story is told in 2 Kings 10. Secondly, it also predicted the Assyrian invasion at which time the entire Northern Kingdom would be scattered. The second child was called *"Lo-Ruhamah"*. The name of this child means *"no more mercy"*, indicating that God's judgment was just around the corner. Along with this baby, however, came the promise that God would spare Judah, the Southern Kingdom from this coming Assyrian invasion. The third child was a boy named *"Lo-ammi"*. This name means *"Not my people"*. God declared: *"Ye are not My people, and I will not be your God"* (Chapter 1:9).

So what have we got here? In the name of the first child, Jezreel, we see the nation *disciplined*. In the name of the second child, Lo-Ruhamah, we see the nation *deprived*. In the name of the third child, Lo-ammi, we see the nation *disowned*. These children summarize how the Lord was dealing with the nation. The names of the three children were important to the message.

Then, we see:

(c) THE SINFUL WIFE

In the case of Gomer's firstborn, we are told: she *"bare him a son"* (Chapter 1:3). But, in the case of the second child and in the case of the third child, Hosea is not mentioned. Was Gomer already being unfaithful? Was she beginning to fulfil the sad prediction that God had made when He told Hosea to marry her? What a heartbreak it must have been to this young preacher as he heard the whispers that circulated about his wife! Perhaps the children mentioned the men that came by the house when he was away!

One day, Hosea came home and found a note from Gomer to say that she was leaving him to be with the man she really loved. In Chapter 2 verse 5, we hear her say: *"I will go after my lovers"*.

Can you imagine the emotions that tore the heart of Hosea apart? I wonder, do *you* know anything about these emotions? Has *your* marriage fallen apart because of an unfaithful spouse? Well, let me encourage you - the Lord knows how you feel.

What does the hymnwriter say?

> *"Jesus knows all about our struggles;*
> *He will guide 'til the day is done:*
> *There's not a Friend like the lowly Jesus:*
> *No, not one! no, not one!"*

Can you see Gomer now? She is disgraced, derelict, and destitute. Who knows how many men she had slept with? Who knows into what degradation she had plunged? But, finally, word had reached Hosea that the woman he loved was to be sold in the slave market - and do you know what God said to him? Look at the first verse of Chapter 3: *"Then said the LORD unto me, Go yet, love a woman beloved of her friend, yet an adulteress"*. In verse 2, Hosea purchases her at the slave market.

Do you know what that is? That is:

(d) THE STEADFAST HUSBAND

Could *you* do what Hosea did? He went to the slave market looking for his wife. Slaves were sold naked! Can you see Hosea making his way among them, looking for Gomer and scarcely able to recognise this wretched woman with her sunken eyes and ravaged body? The going rate for a slave, laid down in Exodus 21, was 30 shekels of silver, but Gomer was being sold at a discount. She was not just *"shop-soiled"* or *"second-hand"*. Rather, she was a disgusting *"leftover"*. Nobody wanted her, whatever the asking price, but Hosea bought her for 15 shekels of silver. He bought her back. He brought her home. He assured her of his forgiveness and love - and we have every reason to believe that Gomer repented of her sins and became a faithful wife.

The 17th Century preacher and writer, John Bunyan, said: *"I preached what I did feel, what I smartingly did feel"*. Can you see that Hosea did the same? In the sorrowing, loving heart of Hosea, we see a picture of the sorrowing, loving heart of God. In the unfaithfulness of Gomer, we see the unfaithfulness of Israel. Thus we move from the Personal Section to the:

(2) NATIONAL SECTION: HOSEA'S MESSAGE - Chapters 4-14 - The Faithless Nation & the Faithful Lord

Raymond Brown says: *"Hosea's grief became his gospel"*. His message grew out of his marriage. No doubt, all the neighbours talked about Gomer's sins and pointed an accusing finger at her. But now Hosea points a finger at them and reveals their sins. Do you see that Hosea talks about:

(a) THE NATIONAL SIN

His message reads like today's newspaper. At the outset the Lord told Hosea: *"The land hath committed great whoredom, departing from the LORD"* (Chapter 1:2). Later, God says to them: *"Thou hast gone a whoring from thy God"* (Chapter 9:1). Spiritual unfaithfulness is compared to sexual impurity - and God hates both. Look at verse 2 of Chapter 4. There are references to swearing, lying, killing, stealing and committing adultery. Verse 11 refers to wine. These sins and many more were rampant in the nation. To make matters worse, the nation tried to cover her sins with a shallow *"religious revival"*.

Listen to the people in the opening verses of Chapter 6:

"Come, and let us return unto the LORD: for He hath torn, and He will heal us; He hath smitten, and He will bind us up. After two days will He revive us: in the third day He will raise us up, and we shall live in His sight. Then shall we know, if we follow on to know the LORD: His going forth is prepared as the morning; and He shall come unto us as the rain, as the latter and former rain unto the earth."

Hosea is a master preacher for do you see how he pictures the spiritual condition of the nation? He talks about:

1. THE MORNING CLOUD

Their love for the Lord was, according to the Lord Himself in verse 4, like a morning cloud and like early dew. Early in the morning, the dew looks like sparkling jewels, but as soon as the sun comes up, the dew is gone. Israel's devotion to the Lord was temporary, and not lasting. God says that Israel's love was just like the morning fog, shallow, superficial, transient, temporary. Now, they possessed all the trappings of a thriving religion. The sacrifices were regularly offered – see Chapter 4 verse 15 and Chapter 5 verse 6 - but this was the outward cloak that hid infidelity. *Appearances were kept up when actualities had ceased.* However, a religious veneer only fools the undiscerning!

Is *your* devotion like the morning cloud? Could the Risen Lord address you as He addressed Sardis? *"Thou hast a name that thou livest, and art dead"* (Revelation 3:1). How much reality is behind your profession? How much life is behind your façade? Are you living off yesterday's spiritual momentum? Are you doctrinally sound but inwardly dead?

Is it not so easy to come and sing His praise and seek His face and share His Word, so easy to go through all the mechanics of worship and yet our hearts are actually far from Him?

Then there is another illustration:

2. *THE HALF-BAKED CAKE*

In Chapter 7 verse 8, we read: *"Ephraim, he hath mixed himself among the people; Ephraim is a cake not turned"*. What housewife has not had the humiliating experience of a cake cooked on the outside, but uncooked inside? The cake referred to here was cooked on a griddle, and not having been turned, it was burned on one side and uncooked on the other. This set out Israel's condition: overdone on *ritual,* underdone on *righteousness;* overdone on *sacrifices,* underdone on *sanctification;* overdone on the *external,* underdone on the *internal.*

Is this not the same with us? As J. Oswald Sanders reminds us, we are:

"Overdeveloped in some respects, underdeveloped in others. All of us are only partially sanctified, because we have not turned some parts of our lives to the fire of the Holy Spirit. Some are strong in Bible knowledge, but weak in spiritual grace. Some are generous in nature, but violent in temper. Some are strong for the fundamentals, but weak in Christian love. One-sided development is true of us all. We tend to cultivate our strong points and neglect our weak points."

The reassuring fact for us is that the fire under the cake still burns. It is up to us to turn the unfinished, imperfect part of our characters to the fire of the Holy Spirit and allow Him to bring balance into our lives.

In this connection, we should remember what was said about the Lord Jesus in John 1 verse 14: *"full of grace and truth"*. His life was in perfect balance.

Here is a third picture:

3. *THE SILLY DOVE*

Look at Chapter 7 verse 11: *"Ephraim also is like a silly dove"*. In what way were the people *"silly"*?

Israel's privilege had been to dwell alone. Centuries earlier the declaration had been made: *"Israel then shall dwell in safety alone"* (Deuteronomy 33:28). However, she snatched every opportunity to make alliances with the surrounding nations, imbibing, in ever increasing manner, the spirit and worship of their gods. How solemn the divine assessment and the divine announcement in Hosea 4 verse 17: *"Ephraim is joined to idols; let him alone"*.

The warning is plain, the examples are numerous.

Do you remember Lot who *"pitched his tent toward Sodom"* (Genesis 13:12)?
Do you recall Solomon who *"loved many strange women"*? They *"turned away his heart after other gods"* (1 Kings 11:1, 4).
What about Peter, warming his hands with the enemies of Christ (Mark 14:54)?
What about Demas? He *"loved this present world"* (2 Timothy 4:10).

Worldliness shows itself in a lifestyle conformed to the spirit and standard of the age. Satan wants us to become *"conformed to this world"* (Romans 12:2). We are either transformers or conformers! A transformer is someone who is being transformed by the power from within and a conformer is someone who is conforming to the pressure from without.

The nineteenth century Scottish divine, Thomas Guthrie, wrote these searching words:

"If you find yourself loving any pleasure better than your prayers, any book better than the Bible, any house better than the house of God, any table better than the Lord's table, any person better than Christ, and any indulgence better than the hope of heaven, take alarm."

Here is a fourth powerful illustration:

4. THE GRAY HAIRS

"Gray hairs are here and there upon him, yet he knoweth not" (Chapter 7:9).

Ephraim's deterioration began with an unholy alliance: *"Ephraim, he hath mixed himself among the people"* (Chapter 7:8). This had led to idolatry: *"They have gone a whoring from under their God"* (Chapter 4:12). Idolatry led in turn to immorality. Do you see what was happening? The whole fabric of the nation was weakening. Israel was becoming senile and the tragedy was that they did not know it.

What do *"gray hairs"* speak of? Do they not speak of the decline of life? Those gray hairs come unfelt, unknown. Few go gray overnight. Is it not the same spiritually? Backsliding never begins with a bang. It begins quietly, slowly and subtly.

Donald Grey Barnhouse says: *"Withering is a low process, barely perceptible at first either to the one who is being withered or to those who look on"*.

George Sweeting says: *"Collapse in the Christian life is rarely a blow-out. It is usually a slow leak"*.

Theodore Epp of *"Back to the Bible"* says: *"Backsliding starts in such a subtle way that most of us are not aware of it. Many of us may be backslidden and may not realize it"*.

Are you taking it for granted that you are still walking with God? Joseph and Mary lost a whole day of fellowship with Jesus because they were *"supposing Him to have been in the company"* (Luke 2:44). They supposed something of which they should have been sure - and then it took them even longer to find Him again.

We should be at pains to discover whether we are going gray spiritually. When was the last time we had a spiritual check-up? When last did we look searchingly at ourselves in the mirror of the Word of God? When last did we measure ourselves by the divine standard? The tragedy of our condition might be that we might be gray spiritually and not know it. Do you recall what was said of Samson? *"He wist not that the LORD was departed from him"* (Judges 16:20). He lay in the lap of the seductive Delilah, divulging the secret of his strength. It led to him losing his strength and his sight and his service. This is one of the most tragic expressions in the whole Bible: *"He wist not that the LORD was departed from him"*. Gray hairs!

A final illustration:

5. THE DECEITFUL BOW

Hosea says: *"They return, but not to the most High: they are like a deceitful bow"* (Chapter 7:16). That is, you could not depend on them.

What a picture of the nation's sin! Is this a picture of *your* sin? Like Hosea's wife, God's people had played the harlot and judgment was to be swift and sure. Not only does God through Hosea reveal the National Sin, there is also:

(b) THE NATIONAL SUFFERING

Hosea tells them that suffering is coming in at least three areas. In the words of David Pawson, there is going to be:

Barrenness: Hosea says that there will be miscarriages, and some women will not be able to conceive. Others will lose their babies when they are born. (See Chapter 9:11-14)

Bloodshed: An enemy will attack and kill many of them - and God will not defend them. (See Chapter 10: 14-15)

Banishment: Ultimately, this enemy will be victorious and evict them from the land. (See Chapter 10:6)

"Indeed I tremble for my country, when I reflect that God is just." Thomas Jefferson wrote those words about the U.S.A. and as the prophet Hosea surveyed the kingdom of Israel, he would have agreed. Hosea could see Assyria coming upon the nation and taking it into captivity.

He pictures this judgment as the coming of a swift eagle (Chapter 8:1); the wrath of a whirlwind (Chapter 8:7) and the burning of a fire (Chapter 8:14). The nation is going to be scattered (Chapter 8:8 and Chapter 9:17) and they will reap more than they have sown (Chapter 10:12-15).

Do you know something? ***The backslider is always punished***. The book of Proverbs says: *"The backslider in heart shall be filled with his own ways"* (Chapter 14:14) and: *"The way of transgressors is hard"* (Proverbs 13:15). This is what Israel was - a backslider. Hosea cries *"Israel slideth back as a backsliding heifer"* (Chapter 4:16).

We should ponder the words:

> *"Sin will take you further than you want to go,*
> *Sin will keep you longer than you want to stay,*
> *Sin will cost you more than you want to pay."*

The Christian who breaks his vows with the Lord does not lose his salvation, but he does lose his joy, his power and his usefulness. He suffers from his sins and he suffers the discipline of God. Remember David – he sowed one sin of lust and what a harvest of tears he reaped!

Why did God permit Israel to be judged by wicked Assyria? Because He loved His people! Hebrews 12 teaches that chastening is an evidence and an expression of God's love for His people.

God cannot let them off, but at the same time God cannot let them go.

Do you want to see something of the emotion of God? We hear His own words in Chapter 11 verse 8: *"How shall I give thee up, Ephraim? How shall I deliver thee, Israel?"* What a powerful expression of the feelings of God!

Israel like Gomer had played the harlot and the Lord like Hosea, but infinitely more so, was deeply distressed. Did you ever think of the grief and hurt that an unfaithful wife or husband brings to their partner? Then you have a glimpse of the sorrow that our sin brings to God.

Your sin not only breaks His law - it breaks His heart.

Backslider, the Lord may chasten you, but He loves you. He says: *"Turn, O backsliding children ... for I am married unto you"* (Jeremiah 3:14).

Do you need to return to the Lord? Do you need to say with the Psalmist: *"I will declare mine iniquity; I will be sorry for my sin"* (Psalm 38:18)?

However, the book of Hosea does *not* end on a gloomy note for we see here not only the *National Sin* and the *National Suffering*.

We also see:

(c) THE NATIONAL SALVATION

In spite of their *persistence* (Chapter 11); their *past* (Chapter 12) and their *punishment* (Chapter 13), they would be *pardoned* (Chapter 14). Hosea sees the future glory of the nation. Just as his wife was brought back from slavery and restored to his home and heart, so the nation would one day be restored to her land and to her Lord. Of course, this will happen when Jesus Christ returns to the earth to establish His kingdom and fulfil the promises made to the fathers.

The ultimate fulfilment of these blessings in Chapter 14 must be during the Millennial period, since Israel has not and will not repent in the manner of these verses until after the Tribulation. In Hosea 14 verse 2 the people are encouraged to cry: *"Take away all iniquity, and receive us graciously"* and, according to Zechariah 12 verses 10 to 13, such a confession will be made when they look upon the one *"whom they have pierced"*.

Nonetheless, we must not miss the personal message here.

Do you know what it is?

Backsliders may return to the Lord and know His *Forgiveness*: *"I will heal their backsliding, I will love them freely"* (Chapter 14:4).

Backsliders may return to the Lord and know His *Freshness*: *"I will be as the dew unto Israel"* (Chapter 14:5).

Backsliders may return to the Lord and know His *Fragrance*: *"The scent thereof shall be as the wine of Lebanon"* (Chapter 14:7).

Backsliders may return to the Lord and know His *Fruitfulness*: *"I am like a green fir tree. From Me is thy fruit found"* (Chapter 14:8).

Do you remember when you really loved the Saviour?
Do you recall when it was spring time in your soul?
When you knew something of the freshness of first love?

Are those things just memories?
Have other things crowded out His place in your heart?
Have you gone back? Not externally but in your heart?

Do you hear His voice: *"O ... return unto the LORD thy God"* (Chapter 14:1)?

We all, I am sure, have friends who have lost interest in the things of God. I had such a friend – someone who had been a great blessing to me. A Christian who was consistent in his walk with God and his witness for God. Someone who had a genuine interest in and a burden for lost souls. A friend to whom I often turned for spiritual counsel and guidance.

Then he defected and lost interest in the things of God.

His path and mine never seemed to cross until a few years ago.

At his godly father's funeral, I gently prodded him spiritually. I encouraged him to *"return unto the Lord"*. As I walked to my car, his response brought an ache to my heart and a tear to my eye.

The words of the hymnwriter came to my mind:

"Oh, the years of sinning wasted!"

Are you where he is?

Whatever the reason, have you left your *"first love"*?

Do you need to take decisive steps to be alone with the Lord?

Will you take those steps right now?

CHAPTER 12

Joel

Ray Stedman in his book: *"Adventuring Through the Bible"* refers to J.R.R. Tolkien's three volume epic: *"The Lord of the Rings".* He explains that it is a novel of momentous events on a vast scale in a place called Middle Earth. The armies of powerful kings clash in horrific battles. Towering spiritual forces engage in a cosmic struggle of good versus evil. Yet, when the book has ended, we learn that all the sweeping events of the story, including the fate of Middle Earth, hinged on the actions of the humblest, smallest creatures of all, a small band of creatures, three feet in height, called hobbits. Says Stedman: *"The theme of the book is clear: never underestimate the power of the smallest things".*

The little book of Joel is only three chapters long and it is often underestimated. That is tragic because this is one of the most powerful books in the Word of God. You see, just as the fate of Middle Earth hinged on the actions of the little hobbits, so the fate of our world hinges on the prophecies in the little book of Joel.

Do you recall that Hosea's message grew out of a personal heartbreak in his own family? Well, Joel's message grew out of a national calamity - the invasion of a plague of locusts.

In order to see this book in its proper setting, we should notice a few things by way of introduction:

1. The Person of the Book

We have very little information about Joel except that he was, according to Chapter 1 verse 1: *"the son of Pethuel".* As the prophet's name means: *"Jehovah is God"*, his parents may well have chosen it as a declaration of their faith. Although his residence is not given, most likely he came from Judah and lived in Jerusalem.

2. *The Period of the Book*

Unlike Isaiah, Hosea, Amos and others, Joel's prophecy is not explicitly located in a distinct period in Judah's history. However, most Bible scholars believe that he wrote sometime between 838 and 756 B.C. There are a couple of reasons for saying this. Firstly, he made no mention of either the Assyrian or Babylonian invasions of Israel. Secondly, although no king is mentioned in the book, Joel does mention *"Tyre and Zidon"* (Chapter 3:4) and *"Egypt and Edom"* (Chapter 3:19) who were Israel's enemies during the reign of King Joash. This would coincide with the time that Queen Athaliah had the royal seed of Judah murdered. The account is given in 2 Kings 11. After the death of King Ahaziah, Queen Athaliah, the King's mother, sought to have all her grandchildren put to death. However, the baby Joash was hidden by his aunt, Jehosheba, and by Jehoiada the high priest in the Temple complex. Seven years later, Joash was crowned King of Judah and Queen Athaliah was slain by her own people. So, this book could have been written just prior to Joash's coronation in 835 B.C.

Keep in mind that when Joel is writing this book, he is writing to the nation of Judah and especially to the city of Jerusalem – see Chapter 3 verses 1 and 17. He is prophesying against the Temple, its priesthood and its offerings (Chapter 1:9). When he mentions the name *"Israel"*, he is not referring to the ten tribes of the Northern Kingdom but rather to the twelve tribes during *"the day of the LORD"* (Chapter 3:2, 14).

This brings us to:

3. *The Point of the Book*

The whole point of the book is *"the day of the LORD"*. This phrase is used some five times in Joel: Chapter 1:15; 2:1, 11, 31 and 3:14. Although it has a reference to the local judgment God would bring on Judah, it speaks of a future day when God will intervene in judgment upon the world.

Thus Chapter 2 verse 31 must be speaking of a future day of judgment because the sun was not darkened nor the moon turned into blood during Joel's day. Again, Chapter 3 verse 14 does not speak of Joel's day but a future day of judgment upon the enemies of Israel. You see, the plague in Joel's day - described in Chapter 1 - and the invasion beyond Joel's day - described in Chapter 2 - was a prototype of an awesome *"day of the LORD"* in the future.

To understand what is meant by *"the day of the LORD"*, we need to get a few of *"the days"* of Scripture into perspective. As Bible scholars have often pointed out, there is:

The Day of Man or *Man's Day*

The phrase is used in 1 Corinthians 4 verse 3 in reference to *"man's judgment"*. Paul says: *"But with me it is a very small thing that I should be judged of you, or of man's judgment: yea, I judge not mine own self"*. J. N. Darby translates it: *"But for me it is the smallest matter that I should be examined of you or of man's day. Nor do I even examine myself"*. We are living right now in man's day, the day when God is largely silent and when man has so much to say. Any judgment passed on Paul was merely human judgment. Paul was not nearly so concerned with the opinion of a human court in this, man's day, as in the judgment of that higher Court in a coming day.

The Day of Christ

Do you recall Paul's words to the Philippian believers? *"Being confident of this very thing, that He which hath begun a good work in you will perform it until the day of Jesus Christ"* (Philippians 1:6). In 1 Corinthians 1 verse 8, Paul mentions this day again: *"That ye may be blameless in the day of our Lord Jesus Christ"*. It is the day when we will be caught up to meet the Lord in the air and will be assembled at the Judgment Seat to receive reward and blessing.

The Day of the Lord

This day is said to be: *"a day of darkness and of gloominess"* (Joel 2:2). It is a time of judgment. The expression *"the day of the LORD"* is found time and again in the Old Testament: Isaiah 2:12; 13:6, 9; Ezekiel 13:5; 30:3; Joel 1:15; 2:1, 11, 31; 3:14; Amos 5:18, 20; Obadiah 15; Zephaniah 1:7, 14; Zechariah 14:1 and Malachi 4:5. It is found three times in the New Testament: 1 Thessalonians 5:2; 2 Thessalonians 2:2 and 2 Peter 3:10. The *"day of the LORD"* refers to the direct intervention of God in the affairs of men after the Rapture of the church. It probably covers the Tribulation, the Millennial Kingdom and the Great White Throne Judgment. It is not only a time of judgment on the wicked, but a time of blessing for the redeemed of Israel and the church.

There is another day we need to mention and it is called:

The Day of God

Peter mentions this day when he says: *"Looking for and hasting unto the coming of the day of God, wherein the heavens being on fire shall be dissolved, and the elements shall melt with fervent heat"* (2 Peter 3:12). The day of God seems to be the eternal day. Very little is said about it in the Bible. We only know that for all of eternity, God will be all in all.

So, we need to keep these different days in mind: the Day of Man, the Day of Christ, the Day of God, but Joel deals primarily with the Day of the Lord, that future day when the nations will be judged and Christ shall return to set up His glorious kingdom.

It seems that Joel refers to three important events here each of which he calls a *"day of the LORD"*.

He sees the plague of locusts as <u>*an immediate day of the Lord*</u> in Chapter 1.

He sees the invasion of Judah by Assyria as <u>*an imminent day of the Lord*</u> in Chapter 2 verses 1 to 27.

He sees the final judgment of the world as _the ultimate day of the Lord_ in Chapter 2 verse 28 to Chapter 3 verse 21.

So, Joel is moving here in three circles. He begins with a recent locust plague that had devastated the land. Then he enlarges his vision and sees the coming Assyrian invasion. Finally, he focuses on the end times. What he has to say earlier about the coming invasion of the Assyrians looks forward to and is a picture of the fearful events of the last days. Indeed, the plague in Joel's day and the invasion of the Assyrian army are both prototypes of that awesome day of the Lord which is yet future.

(1) THINGS PRESENT: Chapter 1

When you are in a crisis, you hear all kinds of voices explaining what is going on and telling you what to do. The optimists will say: *"This crisis is not going to last! Be brave!"* The pessimists will say: *"It is going to get worse - and there is no escape. We're done for!"* The alarmists will see the enemy behind every tree! The scoffers will question the news reports and shrug their shoulders saying: *"What difference does it make anyhow?"*

Joel, however, was a realist who looked at life from the standpoint of the Word of God. As the first chapter opens, we note that:

(a) THERE WAS DEVASTATION

The whole country was in the grip of a fearful locust plague. Indeed, these invaders are described as: *"a nation"* (Chapter 1:6). Now, in our country, we have no idea of what locusts can do. Locusts are like big grasshoppers. In a swarm of locusts there may be up to 600 million insects and the swarm can cover 400 square miles. They can eat up to 80,000 tons of food a day. Thus when they descend on an area, all vegetation ceases. They can travel substantial distances each day and they can lay 5,000 eggs per square foot. Their appetite is voracious and their heads look like those of horses. Someone has described the locust as *"the incarnation of hunger!"*

One lady was speaking to another lady on a Monday morning. She said: *"I had the locust preacher yesterday for dinner".*

The other lady said: *"You mean - the local preacher, do you not? Locusts are things that eat all before them and leave nothing behind."*

The other lady said: *"Yes, that was him!"*

The appetite of the locust is never satisfied. They devour all vegetation in their path. Moses had taught, back in Deuteronomy 28 verses 38 and 39, that locusts and crop failure could be a source of divine judgment.

Do you see how Joel describes them in Chapter 1 verse 4 ? The four different names here - palmerworm, locust, cankerworm, caterpillar - could be the four stages of development of the locust or Joel could be describing here four different species of locust. Over eighty species are known to exist in the East.

The picture is clear - locusts, locusts and more locusts. There had been widespread devastation. Joel is asking the question: *"Hath this been in your days, or even in the days of your fathers?"* (Chapter 1:2). This could be a reference to the locusts in Egypt in Exodus 10. The result? The land was stripped bare. It was a national tragedy.

We can make an application to our day! Are *we* not living in days of national and international tragedies? The day of the tsunami, the day of the missing airplane and the day of the overturned ferry. Floods, volcanoes, earthquakes have devastated so many lives.

The problem was this. Many people could see the *locusts*, but they could not see the *Lord*. They could count the material loss, but they could not see the spiritual truth.

An old commentator looked at the four different names used here in verse 4 and applied them to God's people. The four chief passions were lust, vainglory, gluttony and anger.

What was the outcome of the activities in verse 4? Barrenness!

What is the swarm of locusts that is bringing barrenness to your life? Is it lethargy? Have you a half-hearted attitude? Perhaps it is laxity. Are you careless about your walk with the Lord? Could it be that it is lukewarmness? What is it that has brought devastation to your spiritual life?

There was devastation – and then:

(b) THERE WAS LAMENTATION

Do you see what the Lord says in verse 13 of Chapter 1? *"Gird yourselves, and lament, ye priests: howl, ye ministers of the altar: come, lie all night in sackcloth, ye ministers of my God."*

Joel addresses several different groups of people as he describes the terrible plague and its devastating results. The ***old men*** in Chapter 1 verses 1 to 4 are asked if they can remember such a tragedy from the years gone by. No! They cannot. In fact, they will tell their children and even their great-grandchildren about the awful event. Joel next turns to the ***drunkards*** in verses 5 to 7 who weep and howl because the vineyards have been ruined and their supply of drink is gone. Is it not sad when people can weep over a loss of luxuries and sinful pleasures and yet not over the loss of basic necessities? Joel then turns to the ***worshippers*** in verses 8 to 10 who go to the Temple empty-handed because there are no sacrifices to bring. He addresses the ***farmers*** in verses 11 and 12 who are howling because their crops are all ruined. Finally, Joel turns to the ***priests*** in verses 13 and 14 and tells them to fast and pray.

Here we reach the heart of the matter. It was because of sin that God was punishing the nation. So long as the people obeyed Him, He would send the rain and the harvest, but if they turned away from Him, He would make the Heavens like brass and destroy their fields (Deuteronomy 11:10-17 and 2 Chronicles 7:13-14).

Is it not *so* easy to drift along from day to day, taking our blessings for granted, until the Lord permits a national calamity to occur, reminding us of our total dependence on Him? Do you need to be reminded of that? God did not have to send great battalions to Judah to bring the people to their knees. All He needed - a swarm of little insects! They did the job. Will the Lord send something to our country to bring it to its knees?

(c) THERE WAS PROCLAMATION

Do you see it in verse 14 of Chapter 1? *"Sanctify ye a fast, call a solemn assembly, gather the elders and all the inhabitants of the land into the house of the LORD your God, and cry unto the LORD."*

Remember what was said about the Queen sitting on the throne. God had promised David: *"There shall not fail thee a man upon the throne of Israel"* (1 Kings 9:5). He allowed them to have a King but not a Queen. However, Queen Athaliah was on the throne - and what a treacherous Queen she was! ***National sin had been committed and national repentance was required.*** This plague was not just a freak of nature. This was God speaking to the nation.

At such a time of national calamity, is there not a place for national prayer and fasting? We need to waken up to the fact that God wants to speak to us through the events of our lives. He wants to bless us, but we will not listen. Is this not our problem? Has the Lord ever allowed events in your life to awaken you to your need of Him?

(2) THINGS IMMINENT: Chapter 2 verses 1-27

In Chapter 2, Joel's vision focused on the future, but on the nearby future - the day of the Assyrian. In Chapter 3, he focuses on the future, but the far distant future - the day of the Antichrist. But, he sees it all as *"the day of the LORD"*. The one was a type of the other. Unless Joel had some other attack in mind, about which we know nothing, he was probably referring to the Assyrian invasion, during the reign of King Hezekiah which took place in 701 B.C. The story is told in Isaiah Chapters 36 and 37. The Lord allowed the Assyrians to ravage the land, but He miraculously delivered Jerusalem from being taken.

You will notice that Joel speaks here about:

(a) THE ALARM

He says: *"Blow ye the trumpet in Zion, and sound an alarm in My holy mountain"* (Chapter 2:1). This was real war, so Joel commanded the watchmen to blow the trumpets and warn the people. What we have here in Chapter 2 is almost a repetition of the plague of locusts in Chapter 1. Is Joel using the locusts to describe the Assyrian soldiers? Just as the locusts had destroyed everything edible before them, so this army would use a "scorched earth policy". They would devastate the towns and the land. (See Isaiah 36:10 and 37:11, 18) The locusts looked like miniature horses, but the Assyrians would ride real horses and conquer the land. This whole section pictures the onward march of a ruthless, relentless and resistless army. All of this was highly descriptive of the Assyrians. Yet this invasion of Israel, dreadful as it would be, would be nothing compared with the invasion of Israel in the end times.

Do you see what Joel is doing here? He seems to be moving back and forward from one invasion to the other. The one was the shadow: the other was the substance. The nearer invasion, terrible as though it would be, was merely illustrative of the later invasion. Thus the trumpet was sounded.

In the light of the fact that the *"end times"* are upon us, do we not need to sound the trumpet? Do you recall what Paul said of the believers in Thessalonica? *"From you sounded out the Word of the Lord"* (1 Thessalonians 1:8). Could that be said of us? Are we trumpeting out the gospel?

(b) THE ADMONITION

Do you see what the Lord says in Chapter 2 verses 12 and 13? *"Turn ye even to Me with all your heart, and with fasting, and with weeping, and with mourning: and rend your heart, and not your garments, and turn unto the LORD your God."* Watching someone tear their clothes can be impressive, but that was not good enough for the Lord.

This exact phrase: *"Rend your heart"* is not used anywhere else in the Bible but its meaning is clear.

The heart of the people's problems was the problem of the people's hearts.

Said Jeremiah 17 verse 9: *"The heart is deceitful above all things, and desperately wicked"*. This was where the change was needed. King Hezekiah led them in that change. Sadly, however, it was only superficial for they returned to their evil ways.

In the light of end time prophecies, *"What manner of persons ought ye to be in all holy conversation and godliness?"* (2 Peter 3:11). So often, all we offer in worship is a postured pretence, a shameful sham and a sick stench in the nostrils of the Lord.

(c) THE ASSURANCE

The assurance was that if there was true repentance, God would work for Israel, with Israel and through Israel. What faith Joel had! He says: *"The LORD will answer ... His people"* (Chapter 2:19). Do you recall that in one night God killed 185,000 Assyrian soldiers and Sennacherib went home a defeated king? (See Isaiah 37:36) Here God promises to drive away the army of locusts and the army of Assyria and restore the pastures again. In fact, God will give them bumper crops and restore to them the *"years that the locust hath eaten"* (verse 25). Why will God do this? Not because they deserve it, but that they and the heathen might know: *"I am in the midst of Israel, and that I am the LORD your God, and none else"* (verse 27)

There is a principle here that we need to grasp. It is a promise to all who return to the Lord with sincere and broken hearts. God will restore those wasted years if there is a brokenness of spirit.

So, Joel has described *Things Present* and *Things Imminent*. Now he turns to the future to talk about:

(3) <u>THINGS DISTANT: Chapter 2 verse 28 to Chapter 3 verse 21</u>

Joel describes a series of events relating to *"the great and the terrible day of the LORD"* (Chapter 2:31). He talks about what will happen before that day, during that day and after that day.

(a) Before That Day: The Spirit is Poured Out

Says Chapter 2 verse 28: *"It shall come to pass afterward, that I will pour out My spirit upon all flesh"*.

We need to consider these words from - Israel's Point of View.

"It shall come to pass afterward." After what? After the events in verses 18 to 27 when the Lord heals the nation after the Assyrian invasion. But, look at how Peter explains this word in Acts 2 verse 17. He says: *"And it shall come to pass in the last days, saith God, I will pour out of My Spirit upon all flesh"*. So Peter interprets *"Afterward"* as *"the last days"*. Now, *"the last days"* begin, according to Hebrews 1 verse 2, with the ministry of Christ on earth and will conclude with *"the day of the LORD"*, that period of time that is called *"the great tribulation"* (Matthew 24:21). Many Bible scholars think that this particular time is brought before us in Revelation Chapters 6 to 19 and that it will climax with the return of Christ to earth to deliver Israel and establish His kingdom – see Isaiah 2:2-4; Zechariah 12-14 and Revelation 19:11 to 20:6. Joel promised that before the *"day of the LORD"* would come, there would be a remarkable outpouring of the Holy Spirit, accompanied by signs in the Heavens and on the earth.

Do you recall that during the Old Testament period, the Holy Spirit was given only to special people who had special jobs to do? People like Moses and the prophets (Numbers 11:17); the judges (Judges 3:10) and great men like David (1 Samuel 16:13). But here is the promise through Joel that the Spirit will come upon *"all flesh"* - men and women, young and old, Jew and Gentile. *"And it shall come to pass, that whosoever shall call on the name of the LORD shall be delivered"* (Chapter 2:32).

We need to consider these words from - the Church's Point of View.

The question is: Was Joel's prophecy fulfilled completely, partially or not at all on the day of Pentecost? Well, look again at Acts 2. Listen to Peter's words in verses 14 to 21. Is Peter saying that Joel's prophecy was fulfilled at Pentecost? I do not believe he is. In fact, Peter never used the word *"fulfilled"* or any word which suggested fulfilment. What then did Peter mean? Well, look at the context. Peter was answering the accusation that the believers were drunk and in order to counter the Jewish mockers Peter says: *"But this is that"*. In other words: *"Stop your mocking, for this is similar to what Joel said would happen when God pours His Spirit on all flesh prior to the Kingdom Age"*. If this were a fulfilment of Joel's prophecy, Peter would have said *"This is a fulfilment"*. He said no such thing!

Moreover, Joel said that God would pour His Spirit out *"upon all flesh"* (Chapter 2:28). That certainly did not happen at Pentecost!

But, there is another reason why Joel's prophecy was not fulfilled at Pentecost. Peter goes on to quote Joel and he says: *"I will shew wonders in heaven above, and signs in the earth beneath; blood, and fire, and vapour of smoke: the sun shall be turned into darkness, and the moon into blood"* (Acts 2:19-20). Did that happen at Pentecost? Not at all! No, what happened at Pentecost was but the beginning of God's blessing on Israel. Had the nation received Christ instead of arresting the apostles and killing Stephen, the promised *"times of refreshing"* would have come with the return of Christ and the establishment of His kingdom (Acts 3:19-26).

Joel is telling us that during the last days of Israel's history, during the Tribulation period, the Spirit of God will work in mighty power in the saving of both Jews and Gentiles, and there will be mighty wonders and signs in the Heavens – see Zechariah 12:10 and 13:1 and Romans 11:26. Indeed, these are recorded in Revelation 6 verses 12 and 13.

(b) During That Day: Judgment is Poured Out

You can see from the opening verse of Chapter 3 that the Jews will be back in their land, delivered from the captivities in Gentile nations. All the nations will gather together to fight Jerusalem. The prophet Joel sees the nations massing against Israel. North, east, south and west, they encircle the land. They are determined to uproot the nation of Israel and rid the world, once for all, of the hated Hebrew people.

The Lord says in verse 2: *"I ... will plead with them there for My people and for My heritage Israel"*. In verse 12, we read: *"Let the heathen be wakened, and come up to the valley of Jehoshaphat: for there will I sit to judge all the heathen round about"*. There are: *"Multitudes, multitudes in the valley of decision"* (verse 14).

Is this not the same judgment that Christ speaks of in Matthew 25? At this judgment, He will separate the *"sheep"* from the *"goats"*, those who have helped Israel in the time of trouble from those who have been set for her destruction. Joel lists some of the sins that the Gentiles have committed against the Jews - scattering them among the nations, selling them into slavery, treating them like cheap merchandise for which people cast lots, plundering the land of its wealth, and taking what belonged to the Lord and using it for their own gods.

It is worth noting that God refers to the Jews as: *"My people"* and: *"My heritage"* and to the land as *"My land"* (verse 2). The wealth is *"My silver"* and *"My gold"* (verse 5). God has not forsaken Israel! The promises of God to Israel cannot be broken. Indeed, if God could not hang onto Israel, He could not hang onto us either.

Joel is saying: *"Nations, prepare for Judgment"* (Chapter 3:1-8); *"Nations, prepare for War"* (Chapter 3:9-15) and *"Nations, prepare for Defeat"* (Chapter 3:16).

In Chapter 3 verse 2, when God promises to *"plead"* with the nations, this does not mean that He will beg them to repent. The word *"plead"* can be translated: *"execute judgment"*, as in Isaiah 66 verse 16 and Jeremiah 25 verse 31. In verse 13, the battle is compared to a ripe harvest of grapes. This is generally called "the battle of Armageddon", described in Revelation 14 verses 14 to 20, when the armies of the nations of the world unite against the Lord and His Christ and gather to destroy Jerusalem. (See also Psalm 2 and Zechariah 12-14) Then: *"the LORD also shall roar out of Zion"* (verse 16).

When the Lamb becomes a Lion, the nations had better tremble. Do you see that phrase *"the valley of decision"* in verse 14? The Hebrew word for *"decision" ("charute")* has a basic meaning of *"to decide and sharpen or to cut"*. It is speaking about God's decision to cut these huge armies into pieces as one would mow down grain with a sharp threshing instrument. Christ will defend His land, His people, and His holy city. God knows what the nations have done to the Jews and He will one day settle accounts. There is coming a day of reckoning!

(c) After That Day: Blessing will be Poured Out

As Joel preached, the people could see the dry fields, the starving cattle, and the empty barns. They could see and hear the locusts as they ravaged the country. But, Joel is picturing a time when wine, milk, and water shall flow in ceaseless measure in the land. This is, of course, the kingdom age when Jesus Christ shall sit on David's throne in Jerusalem, and when the land shall be healed and the blessing of God restored.

Can you see here:

The Restoration of the Land

Look at verses 18 and 19. The Lord gave the land to Israel as an everlasting possession in an unconditional, eternal covenant with Abraham. The record is given in Genesis 17 verses 7, 13 and 19. This is known as the Abrahamic Covenant. When the King comes to reign, the land will be like the Garden of Eden for beauty and fruitfulness. *"He will make her wilderness like Eden, and her desert like the garden of the LORD"* is the promise of Isaiah 51 verse 3. There will be wonders in *animal life*, as the wolf dwells with the lamb and the leopard lies down with the kid (Isaiah 11:6). There will be wonders in *agricultural life*, as the desert rejoices and blossoms as the rose (Isaiah 35:1). Still again, there will be wonders in *physical life*, as life-spans are extended (Isaiah 65:20).

What a day it is going to be when the King comes to reign!

The Residents of the Land

The book draws to a close with these words: *"But Judah shall dwell for ever, and Jerusalem from generation to generation, for I will cleanse their blood that I have not cleansed"* (verses 20-21).

What good would it be to have a restored land if it were populated with a sinful people? When the Lord returns, He will pour out His Spirit on the house of David and Jerusalem. Declares Paul: *"All Israel shall be saved"* (Romans 11:26). *"In that day there shall be a fountain opened to the house of David and to the inhabitants of Jerusalem for sin and for uncleanness"* (Zechariah 13:1).

The Religion of the Land

In verse 17, God says: *"So shall ye know that I am the LORD your God dwelling in Zion, My holy mountain"*. Mount Zion, where the Temple stood, was a very special place to the Jews because it was the place God chose for His own dwelling. (See Psalm 48; Psalm 87 and Psalm 132:13) Today, the Jewish people have no temple on Mount Zion. Instead, a Muslim Mosque stands there. But, God promises that He will restore Zion and dwell there in all His glory. (See Isaiah 4 and Isaiah 51:3) Can you see the blessings that will be outpoured after this day?

Do not overlook how the book ends. It says: *"For the LORD dwelleth in Zion"* (verse 21). That is:

The Reign of the Lord

The prophecy of Joel begins with *tragedy* - the invasion of the locusts, but it ends with *triumph* - the reign of the King of Kings and Lord of Lords.

Today, we are living on the threshold of that *"great and terrible day of the LORD"*. We are living in the day of man, when man judges and runs the affairs of this planet - and not for better but for worse. But, the day of Christ is about to dawn and we shall be: *"caught up together ... to meet the Lord in the air"*. Then the Lord will make those final moves on earth that will bring an end to man's mismanagement of earth's affairs.

The *"day of the LORD"* is imminent.

Will you, then, accept the challenge in these last days to give all-out service to the Lord? *"Occupy till I come"*, is the instruction of Luke 19 verse 13.

Will you pray with anticipation for the coming of Christ's kingdom: *"Thy kingdom come"* (Matthew 6:10)? Those words can be *applied evangelistically* - for His kingdom to come in the hearts of the lost. They should be *interpreted prophetically* - the King will come to set up His kingdom!

Will you sing with Frances Ridley Havergal?

"Oh, the joy to see Thee reigning,
Thee, my own beloved Lord!
Every tongue Thy name confessing,
Worship, honour, glory, blessing,
Brought to Thee with one accord;
Thee, my Master and my Friend,
Vindicated and enthroned,
Unto earth's remotest end,
Glorified, adored and owned!"

CHAPTER 13
Amos

Try and picture this scene. It is about 30 to 40 years before the fall of Israel to Assyria. We are visiting the city of Bethel where King Jeroboam the Second has his private "chapel" and where Amaziah is his priest. The nation of Israel is enjoying peace and prosperity. In fact, it is living in luxury. The impressive service is about to begin and Amaziah is in charge. Suddenly, we hear a commotion outside the chapel. *"Woe to them that are at ease in Zion"*, cries a voice. *"God will send judgment on this wicked nation."* We rush outside and there we find a rustic hill preacher from Tekoa, named Amos. He is not a prophet in the professional sense, for his father was not a prophet, neither did he attend the prophetic schools (Chapter 7:14). But, he is God's man with God's message and he is warning that judgment is coming to Israel. He uses the word *"captivity"* several times in his book – see Chapter 5 verses 5 and 27, Chapter 6 verse 7 and Chapter 7 verse 17.

Now, who is this shepherd farmer and what message is he bringing to Israel? Well, let us think for a moment about:

THE MAN

<u>*His Name*</u>

"Amos" means *"burden"* or *"burden bearer"*. He is not to be confused with Amoz, the father of Isaiah, whose name is mentioned in Isaiah 1 verse 1. Being a mid-8th Century prophet, Amos was a contemporary of Jonah (mentioned in 2 Kings 14:25), Hosea (Hosea 1:1) and Isaiah (Isaiah 1:1). He hailed from Tekoa, which lay twelve miles south of Jerusalem, six miles south of Bethlehem, and overlooked the Dead

Sea. Amos, therefore, belonged to Judah, the Southern Kingdom of the divided nation. The name: *"Tekoa"* is interesting. It is thought to mean *"the pitching of tents"*. Amos may not have had any permanent dwelling. The shepherds and their families would have lived in a small cluster of tents. Amos was what we might call *"a rough diamond"*, plain and straightforward in his life and speech.

His Job

He was a herdsman and also looked after sycamore trees. Dressing sycamore figs meant slitting the fruit in two to encourage ripening. This may all point to Amos being a general farm labourer, a "Jack of all trades". Sycamore figs tended to be the food of the poor. Moreover, his work as a shepherd would have put Amos in the social basement! Some Rabbis rated a shepherd no better than a heathen man. So can you see this man? He did not have a great job. He had no religious training. He was not an obvious candidate for preaching, but under God's hand and by God's grace, he was exactly the right man for the job.

Can you imagine the impression his appearance would make at Bethel or Samaria? Well, imagine a Scottish highlander coming from a little croft standing on the steps of St. Paul's Cathedral, announcing the judgment of God to England! Can you picture the reaction? Yet here is Amos, a country preacher, a *"cowboy"* with the burden of the Lord upon him, wending his way north past Jerusalem, on out of Judah across the border into the sister kingdom of Israel and on north to Bethel to preach God's judgment.

He was sure of:

His Calling

Look at verse 15 of Chapter 7: *"The LORD took me as I followed the flock, and the LORD said unto me, Go, prophesy unto My people Israel"*.

Here was a man with *A Divine Call*: *"The LORD took me"*.
Here was a man with *A Divine Charge*: *"Prophesy"*.
Here was a man with *A Divine Commission*: *"Unto My people Israel"*.

Amos had not been trained in any of the schools of the prophets. He had no academic or theological training, but then, God is sovereign in His choice of servants. He is not tied to any bishop's hands. He is not bound to any set of officials. He is not restricted in His workings to any recognized ministerial order.

A man with God's call has a note of authority about him: *"Now therefore hear thou the word of the LORD"* (Chapter 7:16).

When Amos marched north around 760 B.C. and when he delivered his messages from God, and then when he wrote them down, he became the first of the writing prophets.

So much for the man, now think about:

THE AGE

The opening verse tells us the age in which he served. He prophesied *"in the days of Uzziah king of Judah, and in the days of Jeroboam the son of Joash king of Israel, two years before the earthquake"*. It was during the reign of Jeroboam the Second that the territory of Israel was enlarged. The prophecy given by Jonah the prophet, in 2 Kings 14 verse 25, came to fruition. Still again, these were days when there was no significant world empire. Neither Egypt nor Syria, neither Assyria nor Babylon was a power of such magnitude as to pose an out- and-out threat to the region.

Thus it was:

A Time of Prosperity

The height of fashion was to have a second home, what was called a "summerhouse" to which you could go in the heat of the summer. They were usually located up in the hills. The growth of commerce had resulted in an ever-increasing wealthy upper-class. The people rested on beds of ivory, dined on fine wines and choice calves, and were enjoying a high standard of luxury. These good conditions were, however, not so good, for in such times people forget God and worship pleasure.

As someone has said: *"Prosperity is good campaigning weather for the devil"*.

<u>*A Time of Peace*</u>

Assyria was the *"big boy of the day"*, but Jonah's visit to Nineveh had effectively postponed their threat to Israel for some time.

<u>*A Time of Poverty*</u>

Propserity did not mark everyone in the nation. Amos spoke often of the poor and needy. In Chapter 2 verse 6, for example, he declares: *"They sold the righteous for silver, and the poor for a pair of shoes"*.

The calloused heart of the rich made it:

<u>*A Time of Persecution*</u>

The rich sold the poor like cattle and cheated them in court (see Chapter 5:12-13). It was the apathy - *"they are not grieved for the affliction of Joseph"* (Chapter 6:6) - and the antagonism - *"which oppress the poor, which crush the needy"* (Chapter 4:1) - of the wealthy who called themselves *"the people of God"* that angered Amos the most.

Although Amos does not mention it much, it was:

<u>*A Time of Perversion*</u>

Morally: there was illicit sex as a father and son went *"in unto the same maid"* (Chapter 2:7). There was the excessive use of alcohol (Chapter 6:6).

Yet:

Religiously: these cruel, calloused people *"were in church every Sunday"*. The land *"oozed"* with religion. This is what infuriated Amos. It is always sickening to see injustice or immorality join hands with Christianity and make it appear that they are friends.

If sin is a welcome guest in your house, you will never be welcomed in God's house in Heaven (Revelation 22:14-15). These people went to "church" but did not carry "church" with them back into the world.

Israel *needed to learn that a civilization built on dirt cannot stand.*

A Time of Probation

The end was coming for the Northern Kingdom and Amos knew it. The judgment of God was about to fall and Amos preached it:

"And the LORD said unto me … The high places of Isaac shall be desolate, and the sanctuaries of Israel shall be laid waste; and I will rise against the house of Jeroboam with the sword" (Chapter 7:8-9).

"I saw the Lord standing upon the altar: and He said, Smite the lintel of the door, that the posts may shake: and cut them in the head, all of them; and I will slay the last of them with the sword: he that fleeth of them shall not flee away, and he that escapeth of them shall not be delivered. Though they dig into hell, thence shall Mine hand take them; though they climb up to heaven, thence will I bring them down: And though they hide themselves in the top of Carmel, I will search and take them out thence; and though they be hid from My sight in the bottom of the sea, thence will I command the serpent, and he shall bite them: And though they go into captivity before their enemies, thence will I command the sword, and it shall slay them: and I will set Mine eyes upon them for evil, and not for good" (Chapter 9:1-4).

Forty years after he preached, in 722 B.C., the Assyrians marched on Israel and removed the Ten Tribes to Assyria.

The Man, the Age, but what about:

THE TRUTH

What was it that Amos preached?

"For thus Amos saith, Jeroboam shall die by the sword, and Israel shall surely be led away captive out of their own land" (Chapter 7:11).

That was the burden of the prophet's message. God was going to judge the nation and the king and sent them into exile. Why?

There was an absence of true worship: *"Come to Bethel, and transgress; at Gilgal multiply transgression"* (Chapter 4:4).
There was a lack of justice: *"Ye have turned judgment into gall, and the fruit of righteousness into hemlock"* (Chapter 6:12).

It is interesting to observe that in this book Amos looks in different directions:

(1) AMOS LOOKS OUTWARD - Chapters 1-2

Amos delivers God's message in an interesting way. Comparing this account with a map of ancient Israel, you find that Amos goes round the boundaries of Israel in various directions, delivering a message concerning all the neighboring nations. Destruction of all these surrounding nations sounded good to Israel and she rejoiced in it, not realising that she was the real target of God's anger and wrath.

Now this section contains eight songs, called: *"The Doom Songs"*.

Notice here that:

(a) Judgment is Pronounced upon the Gentiles

Amos starts by condemning Israel's neighbours.

There is a pattern here in each of these pronouncements. Mark:

The Authority

Do you see it every time? *"Thus saith the LORD"* (Chapter 1:3, 6, 9, 11, 13 and Chapter 2:1). You would think that they could hear a lion roar or the thunder roll and know that danger was at hand. God was speaking, thundering from Jerusalem. *"The LORD will roar from Zion"* (Chapter 1:2). Judgment always begins at the house of God. He had sent drought to the land so that even fruitful Carmel was withering, but it did not bring the people to their knees. So He called a common farmer to preach to His people and warn them. The phrase *"Thus saith the LORD"* or its equivalent appears thirty nine times in this book.

The Announcement

"For three transgressions … and for four" - first used in verse 3 of Chapter 1 - is a Jewish idiom that means: *"an indefinite number that has finally come to the end"*. The measure of the sin of the people was full. Literally, it had overreached itself. The sin of these people had reached breaking-point. They had gone beyond the limit of God's patience.

The Accusation

Do you see the word *"because"* each time? Amos begins in Chapter 1 verse 3 with **Syria** and accuses them of awful cruelty in war. Next, in verse 6, he moves down the west coast to the ancient land of Philistia or what is now called **Gaza**. Again, he reminds Israel that God has judged this land. Why? Because the people have participated in the slave trade. Then, in verse 9, he moves back up the coast to **Tyre**, on the northwest side of Israel. There he says that God judged Tyre because the people had broken their agreements. In verse 11, he continues on to the land of **Edom**. *"Thou shalt not abhor an Edomite"*, God had declared in Deuteronomy 23 verse 7. *"He is thy brother."* But, the Edomites forever hated the Hebrews. Edom is accused of not showing pity to Israel but rather maintaining an unforgiving spirit. Sadly, this is something that multitudes of believers know all about! Amos then moves, in verse 13, up the east side of Israel to the land of **Ammon**, what is known today as Jordan. Ammon is judged for bitter cruelty and selfish greed. As he travels south, he pronounces God's judgment on **Moab** for cruelty to Edom – in verse 1 of Chapter 2. Next, he comes, in verse 4, to the Southern Kingdom of **Judah**. He declares that because Judah has despised God's law, judgment has fallen on the nation. Finally, in verse 6, he turns to **Israel**, to the heart of the ten northern tribes of Israel and declares that God is going to judge them because of the corruption and injustice that was in their hearts.

Before we turn to God's messages to Judah and Israel, we should pause and reflect on these judgments on the Gentile nations. Though they were not under the law of Moses, these nations were responsible to God for what they did and ***responsibility brings accountability***.

God sees what the nations do and He judges them accordingly. He moved against the inhumane cruelty of these greedy, warlike peoples. The same God is alive today. We look out at *"man's inhumanity to man"*. We see child abuse. We see one nation invading another nation. We see rape and murder and exploitation on every hand. People ask: *"Is there a God?"*; *"Does He care?"* and *"If so, why does He not do something?"* World news may give the impression that evil leaders are getting away with terrible crimes, but God is still on the throne and will punish evil doers in His good time.

(b) Judgment is Pronounced on the Jews

"I don't know why you preach about the sins of Christians", a church member said to the preacher. *"After all, the sins of Christians are different from the sins of unsaved people."*

"Yes", replied the preacher. *"They are worse!"*

Can you imagine that as Amos was delivering this blistering message of judgment against all the surrounding neighbours of Israel and even against Judah, the people of Israel were shouting: *"Amen!"*? They were delighted to hear that their enemies were going to get it! Now, however, this mighty man of valour, this God-called prophet, this fire-and-brimstone preacher, this prophet of thunder, turns on his heels and points his finger right in the face of *Israel* and gives *them* a message.

The story is told of an old country Christian who was a bit overweight. This old boy would sit Sunday after Sunday, smiling and nodding as the pastor preached about swearing, drinking, smoking and cursing. One Sunday, however, the pastor preached against the sin of gluttony. This boy was incensed! After the service, he stomped up to the preacher and said: *"You have ceased to be a-preaching and you have started to be a-meddling!"*

Church people love it when we preach to somebody else, when we lash out at sinners. It is when we *"quit a-preaching and go a-meddling"* that we get into trouble.

Well, Amos gets into *"meddling"*, for notice the charges he brought against Israel. These included:

INJUSTICE: Chapter 2 verses 6-7

The poor could not get fair justice in the courts because of the greed of corrupt judges who were always ready to accept a bribe. *"They sold the righteous for silver, and the poor for a pair of shoes"* (Chapter 2:6). James Montgomery Boice warns: *"There is no seeking after God that is not at the same time a seeking after justice. Anything else is hypocrisy."*

IMMORALITY: Chapter 2 verses 7-8

A father and a son were visiting the same prostitute. These may have been cult prostitutes who were part of the heathen, idolatrous worship. At the temple in Bethel, the worshippers had sexual relations with male and female prostitutes, believing that this would secure blessing for their crops. No wonder judgment was coming!

INTOXICATION: Chapter 2 verse 8

While lying upon the clothes illegally taken from the poor, the rich drank wine that they purchased by fines illegally imposed upon the poor and they did this *"in the house of their god"*. Not only that, look at verse 12: *"But ye gave the Nazarites wine to drink; and commanded the prophets, saying, Prophesy not"*. Do you see what was happening? Deliberate attempts were made to seduce these believers, who had taken a vow to abstain from intoxicating drink, from their allegiance to the Lord. It is a sad day when you get Christians encouraging other believers to drink!

INGRATITUDE: Chapter 2 verses 9-12

The Lord had led His people out of Egypt. He had cared for them in the wilderness and had destroyed other nations so the Jews could claim their inheritance in Canaan. God had poured out His blessings upon Israel, but how did Israel react to them? They corrupted the land. They rejected the message of the prophets. They forced the Nazarites to break their holy vows.

Bribery, greed, adultery, immorality, selfishness, ingratitude, drunkenness, and the rejecting of God's revelation. No wonder Amos cries: *"Behold, I am pressed under you!" "I am pressed under this burden of sin."* (Chapter 2:13)

There is no alternative. Judgment is coming and no-one will be able to escape.

"Therefore the flight shall perish from the swift, and the strong shall not strengthen his force, neither shall the mighty deliver himself: Neither shall he stand that handleth the bow; and he that is swift of foot shall not deliver himself: neither shall he that rideth the horse deliver himself. And he that is courageous among the mighty shall flee away naked in that day, saith the LORD" (Chapter 2:14-16).

Amos looks outward, and then:

(2) AMOS LOOKS INWARD: Chapters 3-6

Having announced judgment to the nations, Amos now looks within the hearts of the people and explains why this judgment is coming. Please remember that Israel was enjoying a time of peace, prosperity, and "religious revival". People were attending religious services and bringing generous offerings. But, the true servants of God do not look at the outward appearance. They look at the heart. In these four chapters, Amos delivers three sermons, each one prefaced by this phrase: *"Hear this word"* (Chapter 3:1; 4:1 and 5:1).

The first message declares *Israel's guilt in the present*.
The second message stresses *Israel's sin in the past*.
The third message emphasises *Israel's punishment in the future*.

Notice, then, that Amos deals with:

(a) ***THE PRESENT: Chapter 3***

"How can our God send judgment upon us?" the people were asking. *"Are we not His chosen people?"*

But, that was the very reason for the judgment. Where there is privilege, there must also be responsibility. ***Increased privileges means increased responsibility.*** Israel had been supremely favoured and, therefore, was supremely responsible. Do you hear what the Lord says in Chapter 3 verse 2? *"You only have I known of all the families of the earth: therefore I will punish you for all your iniquities."* Here they were rejoicing in their privileges, thinking that God would say: *"You only have I known - therefore I will prosper you"*. But, No! God says: *"I will punish you for all your iniquities"*. Israel was an *"elect nation"*. God had chosen them, called them and blessed them, but that involved responsibility. They were responsible to love God and obey Him. If they failed to do so, God was responsible to chasten them and restore them to Himself.

The doctrine of election is not an excuse for sin. It is rather an incentive to holiness.

We should be so humbled by His grace and so amazed by His love – *"Behold, what manner of love the Father hath bestowed upon us"* (1 John 3:1) - that our hearts should want to do nothing else but worship and serve Him. Privilege always brings with it responsibility. *"For unto whomsoever much is given, of him shall be much required"* (Luke 12:48).

Amos describes the relationship between God and His people as two walking together. He asks: *"Can two walk together, except they be agreed?"* (Chapter 3:3)

Incidentally, you cannot *"walk together"* with someone in romance unless they are saved.

You cannot *"walk together"* with someone in business unless they are saved.

You cannot *"walk together"* with someone in evangelism unless they are saved.

Amos is using an argument from cause and effect:

If two people are walking together, they must have made an appointment together.

If a lion roars, he has prey (verse 4).

If a bird is in the trap, somebody set the trap (verse 5).

If the trumpet sounds, calamity is near (verse 6).

If the prophet is preaching, then God must have sent him (verse 7) - and God had sent Amos to declare judgment on Israel. The Assyrians are coming to destroy the nation (verses 9-15) and the *"lovely services"* at Bethel will not hold them back. The luxurious homes of the wealthy will all be destroyed.

(b) THE PAST: Chapter 4

Do you hear what he says in verse 1? *"Hear this word, ye kine of Bashan, that are in the mountain of Samaria."* Do you know to whom Amos was talking? He was speaking to the upper-class women of Samaria. These *"society women"* lounged about all day, drinking wine and telling their husbands what to do. Now, Amos did not use this image because these women were overweight and looked like cows! Rather, because by their sins they were fattening themselves up for the coming slaughter. You see, they were marked by Luxurious Living The word *"luxury"* comes from a Latin word that means *"excessive"*. It originally referred to plants that grow abundantly. Then it came to refer to people who have an abundance of money, time and comfort which they use for themselves as they live in aimless pleasure.

Ralph Waldo Emerson wrote in his own journal: *"Our expense is almost all for conformity. It is for cake that we all run in debt"*. Now, it is not a sin to be rich and to have the comforts of life. *It is not a problem to own things; the problem comes when things own us.* The wealthy in Israel had everything that money could buy, but they did not have the things that money cannot buy - the things of the Lord that make life worthwhile.

There was not only luxurious living but there was also Worthless Worship. Do you see verses 4 and 5? *"Come to Bethel, and transgress."* Do you see what Amos is doing? He was making fun of their worship because it was not from the heart but rather strictly for show. They were indulging in what Gareth Crossley calls: *"A perverted religion formed of a mishmash of pagan ceremonies and a corrupted form of Jehovah worship"*.

The Lord hates worship that is merely a performance but not a living experience.

A.W. Tozer was right to say:

"For the true Christian, the one supreme test for present soundness and ultimate worth of everything religious must be the place our Lord occupies in it."

In the current trend toward *"user friendly"* services, our constant concern should be: *"What would glorify the Lord?"*

Entertainment is no substitute for worship.
Tickling people's ears is no substitute for touching God's heart.
Amusing ourselves is no substitute for delighting Him.

The people of Israel "loved" going to religious meetings, but they did not love the God they claimed to worship. I wonder: Like the Jews in the days of Amos, are we only going to Bethel and sinning?

Is it not interesting that God had sent warnings to the nation, but they would not listen? Five times in Chapter 4, God says: *"Yet have ye not returned unto Me saith the LORD"* (verses 6, 8, 9, 10 and 11).

Do you see what God sent?

1. Famine: A Food Shortage (verse 6)
2. Drought: A Water Shortage (verses 7-8)
3. Ravaged Crops (verse 9)
4. Sickness (verse 10)
5. Defeat in war (verse 10)
6. Catastrophe (verse 11)
7. Ultimate Judgment (verses 12-13)

Through these disciplines, the Lord had tried to speak to His people and bring them to repentance, but they still would not return to Him. What more could God do? He would come Himself and deal with them: *"Prepare to meet thy God, O Israel"* (verse 12). The Lord of Hosts would come with the Assyrian army and take the people away like cattle being led to the slaughter.

So Amos deals with the Present and the Past, and then:

(c) THE PROSPECT: Chapter 5 verse 1 to Chapter 6 verse 14

Do you see how Chapter 5 begins? *"Hear ye this word which I take up against you, even a lamentation, O house of Israel."* This lamentation was a funeral dirge over the death of the nation of Israel. Can you see here the prophet weeping? Amos weeps as he contemplates the judgments coming on his people. The scope of that judgment is indicated in verse 3 and suggests that 90% of the people would die. This is why Amos time and time again uses the word: *"Seek!"* Do you see it? Verses 4, 6, 8 and 14. Amos was saying: *"Don't seek religious services; seek the Lord"*.

There were some in the nation who were saying: *"The day of the LORD will come and then God will deliver us"* (verses 18-20). They did not realize that the day of the Lord would be a time of judgment for *them* as well as for their enemies. They are like Christians today who *"long for"* the return of Christ, yet may not be prepared to meet Him. Perhaps they have not made amends with a brother or sister in Christ. Perhaps they have not warned their loved ones about coming judgment.

In verse 24, we have the key verse of the book: *"But let judgment run down as waters, and righteousness as a mighty stream"*. Was this not the concern of the Lord in the day of Amos? That His people be righteous in their character and just in their conduct?

Amos longed to see the nation obeying God and executing His justice in the land. But, in Chapter 6, Amos continues to weep over the sins of the people.

There was:

Indifference - verses 1-2. *"Woe to them that are at ease in Zion."*
Indulgence - verses 3-7. *"Lie upon beds of ivory, and stretch themselves upon their couches."*
Insolence - verses 8-14. *"Have we not taken to us horns by our own strength?"*

Do you see the word: *"Therefore"* in verse 7 of Chapter 6? That introduces God's response to Israel's sins and brings us to the final section of the book where:

(3) *AMOS LOOKS FORWARD: Chapters 7-9*

In the closing part of his book, Amos beholds five visions. From these visions, he discovers what God will do to the nation.

(a) The Vision of the Grasshoppers

In Chapter 7 verses 1 to 3, the grasshoppers are about to destroy the crop, but Amos intercedes and the Lord stops them.

(b) The Vision of Fire

In verses 4 to 6, this second vision seemed to depict the same general disaster - the coming of the Assyrian army into Israel. But, Amos intercedes and judgment is restrained. Next was:

(c) The Vision of the Plumb-line

This is recorded in verses 7 to 17. A plumb-line was an instrument used to test whether a wall was straight and true. Buildings that are seriously *"out of plumb"* are unsafe and should be demolished. God is measuring Israel and she does not conform to His Word. Therefore, judgment is coming.

Can you imagine the stir that Amos created through such preaching? Indeed the *"state priest"*, Amaziah, could take no more. He interrupted, saying in effect: *"You are not patriotic. Take your soapbox and go back to the hills to preach"*. But Amos was not afraid. Boldly, he cried: *"Amaziah, you will pay for your compromise and sins, because your wife will become a harlot and your family will die by the sword"*.

Is Amos not the kind of prophet-preacher we need in our nation today?

A pastor who preached the Word faithfully every Sunday was not liked by the affluent in his congregation. They came to him and asked him to resign. He said: *"I will respond to your request next Sunday!"* At the close of the morning service that following Sunday, the pastor said: *"My answer to the request that I resign is found in the words of a song - 'I shall not be moved!'"*

Do you recall Charles Wesley's lines?

> *"Shall I, to sooth the unholy throng,*
> *Soften Thy truth or smooth my tongue,*
> *To gain earth's gilded toys or flee*
> *The cross endured, my Lord, by Thee?"*

(d) <u>The Vision of the Basket of Summer Fruit</u>

This is found in Chapter 8 verses 1 to 14. You see, this fruit that was dead ripe would ruin quickly in hot lands. What was the vision saying, but that judgment was imminent?

Finally, there was:

(e) <u>The Vision of the Lord</u>

This is contained in the first ten verses of Chapter 9. The vision begins in verse 1 with the Lord standing upon the altar. Why is God at the altar? He is there because judgment begins, as Peter tells us in 1 Peter 4 verse 17, at the house of the Lord.

Do you see what God plans to do? Look at verses 8 and 9:

"Behold, the eyes of the Lord God are upon the sinful kingdom, and I will destroy it from off the face of the earth; saving that I will not utterly destroy the house of Jacob, saith the Lord. For, lo, I will command, and I will sift the house of Israel among all nations, like as corn is sifted in a sieve, yet shall not the least grain fall upon the earth."

The good seed, the believing remnant, will be saved, but the chaff will be burned up.

Is it not interesting how this book closes? Both Joel and Amos picture a glorious Millennial future when Israel, at last, will be restored to the land. Verse 11 is quoted in Acts 15 verse 16 at the first church conference. Today God is calling out of the nations a people for His name, the church, but when the church is completed, then He will return and restore the tabernacle (*"house"*) of David and establish the Jewish kingdom. The land will become fruitful again, and the people will be blessed forever.

God has established an irrevocable covenent with Abraham and with David. Today, some are preaching Replacement Theology and are saying that all the blessings given to Israel will find their fulfilment in the Church. Strange that the Church would get all the blessings regarding Israel, but none of the curses!

There is a future for Israel.

What did the hymnwriter declare?

> *"O, the King is coming,*
> *The King is coming!*
> *I just heard the trumpets sounding,*
> *And now His face I see;*
> *O, the King is coming,*
> *The King is coming!*
> *Praise God, He's coming for me."*

If you believe that, you will not be *"at ease in Zion"*!

CHAPTER 14
Obadiah

The story is told of a flight attendant who was on the same plane as the former heavy-weight boxing champion, Muhammad Ali. Everyone in the aircraft was seated for take-off. This flight attendant, however, noticed that the former world champion did not have his seatbelt fastened. She approached him and asked him kindly: *"Excuse me, Sir, but would you mind fastening your seatbelt?"* The story goes that Muhammad Ali looked up with that saucy grin of his and said in a slow gravelly voice: *"Superman don't need no seatbelt"*. Without missing a beat, the flight attendant packed a punch with this sharp reply: *"Superman don't need no plane either - so how about fastening up?"*

Of course, Ali was only joking. If a person really believed he was Superman, he would be seriously deluded. He would be like the ancient Edomites in this book of Obadiah who had been self-deceived by their own pride.

The truth is, however, that we all have the same tendency.

A.W. Tozer described the kind of Christians the Lord longs for us to be as:

"Men and women who have stopped being fooled about their own strength and are not afraid of being caught depending on their all-sufficient Lord."

Obadiah may be a small book, but it deals with the biggest sin - ***pride***. The age of the book is unknown, but the sin is the oldest of all sins. It turned an angel into a devil (Isaiah 14:12-15); depopulated Heaven (Revelation 12:9); emptied Eden (Genesis

3:23) and caused the Saviour to die. It keeps hearts closed to God's salvation and thereby populates Hell.

G. Campbell Morgan says: *"Pride of heart is that attitude of life which declares its ability to live without God"*.

Is this not what Edom sought to do? You see, this prophecy of Obadiah, the shortest book in the Old Testament, is the story of two nations and two brothers. This book deals with the family feud traced back to Jacob and Esau in Genesis 25 and 27. Their descendants were known respectively as the children of Israel and the children of Edom. The Edomites could not forget and would not forgive family differences of bygone history. They refused to help when Moses requested passage through their territory as the Israelites journeyed to the Promised Land. They did not grieve when the Israelites got into difficulty. Rather, they gloated over their setbacks, looted their property and betrayed them into the hands of their enemies.

They prided themselves in what they thought was the invincible mountain of Petra. There is a reference to this in verse 3: *"The pride of thine heart hath deceived thee, thou that dwellest in the clefts of the rock, whose habitation is high; that saith in his heart, Who shall bring me down to the ground?"* However, Obadiah's words were to come true. They were to become a nation reduced to nothing.

"Obadiah" means *"servant of the Lord"*. The Bible refers to other men with the same name. Little is known about any of them and we know very little about this particuler prophet. We have no knowledge of the prophet's hometown, family or experience. But, keep this in mind. It is the *message* not the *messenger* that is important. It is God who speaks through His servant and it is God who will bring His purposes to pass.

The background to this book is very difficult to determine, though we know it is tied to the Edomite assault on Jerusalem described for us in verses 10 to 14. Obadiah wrote shortly after this attack. There were four significant invasions of Jerusalem in Old Testament history. They are described in 1 Kings 14;

2 Chronicles 21; 2 Kings 14, and 2 Chronicles 36. Only two fit with the historical data that is given here. The first possibility is the invasion by the Philistines and Arabians in 848 B.C. – as recorded in 2 Chronicles 21. The second is the invasion by the Babylonians in 586 B.C. – as recorded in 2 Chronicles 36. Most of the experts who have tried to tie Obadiah's prophecy into his nation's history suggest that it points towards what happened when the Babylonians ravaged Jerusalem in 586 B.C. – so we assume that Obadiah has 586 B.C. in mind.

So, try and picture this scene. The time is 586 B.C. The place is Jerusalem. The event is the destruction of Jerusalem by the Babylonian armies. We see the angry soldiers as they wreck the walls, slay the people and burn the city. But, we see something else. We see a group of neighbouring citizens, the Edomites, as they stand on the other side and encourage the Babylonians to ruin the city. *"Rase it, rase it"*, they are calling. (Psalm 137:7). *"Dash their little children against the stones and wipe out the Jews."*

Who are these people who desire such terrible things? They are brethren to the Jews. The Edomites were the descendants of Esau, Jacob's older brother. Do you recall that God chose Jacob and rejected Esau. Esau moved to the mountains in the south and established the Edomite kingdom Idumea. They remained enemies. Now, Obadiah is foretelling Edom's certain doom.

Do you know something? Anti-Semitism eventually brings the judgment of God. Nations that curse and persecute Jews will reap what they sow. Why? Because they are attacking a people with whom the Lord has a long-standing, unconditional and irrevocable covenant (Genesis 12:1-3). On the other hand, nations that bless the Jews will enjoy God's blessing.

This book of Obadiah falls into three sections:

(1) PREDICTION - verses 1 to 9 - WHAT WILL HAPPEN

Obadiah tells the Edomites that the nations are going to destroy them. Unlike thieves and robbers who just take the things they are interested in, they will take everything including their very territory (verses 5-6).

Ginsburg, the great Hebrew scholar, translated Obadiah verse 6 like this: *"How are the things of Esau stripped bare!"* In other words, they are laid out in the open for you to look at for the first time. Obadiah puts the microscope down on Esau, and when you look through the eyepiece, you see Edom.

In these verses:

(a) God's Sovereignty needs to be Recognised

Jeremiah had already announced the doom of Edom in Chapter 49 verses 7 to 22 of his prophecy. In fact, there are some quotations from this prophecy here in Obadiah. This is the *"report"* or *"rumour"* that Obadiah had heard and to which he refers in verse 1. The Lord was going to avenge Israel and destroy Edom. The Lord had told Obadiah that an ambassador from a nation allied with Edom was visiting the other nations to convince their leaders to join forces and attack Edom. Actually, it was the Lord who had ordained this change in policy and what appeared to be another diplomatic visit was the working out of His purposes against Edom. This was the beginning of the fulfilment of verse 7: *"The men that were at peace with thee have deceived thee"*.

John Wesley said he read the newspaper *"to see how God was governing His world"*, and that is certainly a biblical approach. Remember the words of Daniel 4 verse 17: *"The most High ruleth in the kingdom of men, and giveth it to whomsoever He will"*. Now, this *does not* mean that God is to blame for wicked decisions that government officials make, but it *does* mean God is on the throne and working out His perfect will. Does this not bring encouragement to your heart? We often grieve as we watch world events and the suffering that one nation inflicts on another. We wonder at times why God permits certain things to happen, but God is in control. He sees the big picture and He knows the end from the beginning. He puts down and He raises up.

(*b*) *Edom's History needs to be Scrutinised*

The prophecy was directed against Edom. This little country bordered Judah in the north, ran south all the way to the Gulf of Aqaba and bordered the desert in the east. It was about twenty to thirty miles wide and about a hundred miles long. Edom was a wild, rugged, mountainous and almost inaccessible land. It had cliffs that had towered as high as 5,000 feet above sea level. Its deep ravines were easily defended. Its major cities were Bozrah in the north, Teman in the south and Sela or Petra in the centre. The city of Petra was thought to be impregnable because of its precarious position and difficulty of access.

The name *"Edom"* means *"red"*. It was the name that was given to Esau because he had red hair (Genesis 25:25). He sold his birthright for some of Jacob's *"red"* pottage or stew. In order to clarify the identity of Edom, go back to Genesis 36 verse 1: *"Now these are the generations of Esau, who is Edom"*. Look also at verse 8 of the same chapter: *"Esau is Edom"*. Esau is Edom and Edom is Esau. The Edomites were those who were descended from Esau, just as the Israelites are those who are descended from Jacob.

The long warfare between the Israelites and the Edomites began in the womb of Rebekkah:

"And the children struggled together within her; and she said, If it be so, why am I thus? And she went to enquire of the LORD. And the LORD said unto her, Two nations are in thy womb, and two manner of people shall be separated from thy bowels; and the one people shall be stronger than the other people; and the elder shall serve the younger." (Genesis 25:22-23)

From the very beginning, these two brothers were struggling against each other. Esau was an outdoor fellow who loved to hunt. Jacob would rather stay in the house and learn to cook. He was, as we might say now, tied to his mother's apron strings. However, Jacob had a spiritual discernment that Esau did not have. Esau was a man of the flesh and did not care for spiritual things. In fact, he so discounted his birthright that he traded it to Jacob for a bowl of soup. Jacob and Esau lived in a state of perpetual antagonism -

as did their descendants. It is so sad when a family is wrecked by bitterness, division and antagonism.

Israel was instructed not to hate Edom because they were related. *"Thou shalt not abhor an Edomite; for he is thy brother"* was the command given in Deuteronomy 23 verse 7. The Edomites, however, had a fierce hatred of Israel. They were Israel's most persistent enemy. They refused to allow the Israelites passage through their land on the way to Canaan - Numbers 20 verses 14 to 21 - and this hostility lasted for centuries. Ezekiel 35 verse 5 speaks about a *"perpetual hatred"*.

Conflict was seen in the days of Saul (1 Samuel 14:47); the days of David (2 Samuel 8:13-16); the days of Joab (1 Kings 11:16), and the days of Solomon (1 Kings 11:17-22). Instead of coming to Israel's aid, Edom always allied themselves with the surrounding nations to oppress Israel. They failed to recognize that this hostility to the Jews was hostility to God and that their anti-Semitic policies had sown the seeds of their destruction. *"There is none understanding in him"* cried Obadiah in verse 7.

Is history not repeating itself? Think of the hatred that characterizes the Arab and Muslim nations that surround Israel today. Although they are related by blood, they hate the Jews with a passion equalled only by that of Edom of old. These anti-Semitic nations make alliances with one another, make common cause with Russia, and will even side with the Antichrist against Israel. What they do not understand is that their bitter hatred of the Jews will ultimately bring them to grief.

(c) Man's Arrogancy needs to Neutralised

Look at verse 3: *"The pride of thine heart hath deceived thee"*. Edom was a small nation, but it was a proud one. Do you see what they were proud of?

They were Proud of their Security

They are described as: *"thou that dwellest in the clefts of the rock, whose habitation is high; that saith in his heart, Who shall bring me down to the ground?"* (verse 3). This land of Edom, today part of Jordan, was also known as the land of Seir (Genesis 32:3). Like the eagles, the Edomites lived in the rocks and looked down from the heights with disdain on the nations around them. Edom felt invincible and impregnable because of her natural defences. Their attitude was the attitude of those involved with the Titanic! When that ship left Southampton on her fateful maiden voyage, a passenger by the name of Mrs. Albert Caldwell asked a crewman if the ship was really unsinkable. Do you know what he said? *"God Himself could not sink this ship!"* This was the spirit that prevailed in Edom.

They were Proud of their Prosperity

Located on several major trade routes, Edom was able to amass riches.

They were Proud of their Diplomacy

Obadiah speaks about the *"men of thy confederacy"* in verse 7. By that, he means their allies. Edom had evidently established a network of allies among the surrounding nations. They knew how to win friends and influence people!

They were Proud of their Army

In verse 9, Obadiah refers to their *"mighty men"*. Yet, none of them could save Edom when the Lord decreed that its cities would become a slaughterhouse.

Are you seeing how proud this small nation was?

They were Proud of their Philosophy

Verse 8 records the words of the Lord: *"Shall I not … even destroy the wise men out of Edom, and understanding out of the mount of Esau?"* In keeping with their free-thinking, the Edomites gained a reputation for shrewdness and worldly wisdom. Do you recall that Eliphaz, one of Job's friends, was, a Temanite, and thus from

Edom? (See Job 4:1) The Herods, unprincipled statesmen known for cleverness, scheming and lack of ideals, were Edomites. But, Obadiah says, the wise men of Edom were destined for the sword.

Pride! We tend to be easy on pride but God never is. Do you know what the book of Proverbs says? *"Every one that is proud in heart is an abomination to the LORD"* (Proverbs 16:5). *"These six things doth the LORD hate: yea, seven are an abomination unto Him,"* (Proverbs 6:16-19). Do you know what is number one on God's hate list? *"A proud look!"*

Why is pride singled out in this way? Because it dethrones God and replaces Him with man. We can be proud of our education, our ability, our achievements, our possessions, our homes, our children, our titles, our positions in business, society or in the church.

The word *"pride"* itself occurs some forty-eight times in Scripture and the word *"proud"* about fifty-seven times. An equivalent phrase is: *"lifted up his heart"* which is frequently mentioned in the Bible.

There are different forms of pride:

There is Pride of Face: the multi-million cosmetic industry is evidence of that. Women are induced continually to buy perfume and paints, cosmetics and creams, all guaranteed to produce artificial beauty.

There is Pride of Race: some think that because they are born in a certain country they are *"the people"*.

There is Pride of Grace: and *"spiritual pride is the most arrogant of all brands of pride"*. This was, for example, the form of pride afflicting Jehu when he haughtily said to Jehonadab: *"Come with me, and see my zeal for the LORD"* (2 Kings 10:16).

The story is told of C. H. Spurgeon who one Sunday preached a masterly sermon. As soon as he had finished his message, the devil whispered to him: *"Spurgeon, that was a fine sermon. You preached magnificently"*. For a brief moment, he agreed with the devil. Leaving his pulpit, he was met by a loyal deacon at the foot of the pulpit stairs who started to say: *"Mr. Spurgeon, that was a masterpiece!"* Spurgeon, however, interrupted the well-meaning deacon by saying: *"My friend, you're too late. The devil told me that a few moments ago"*.

There is no part of life that is ring-fenced against pride. It is even possible to be proud of one's supposed humility. Someone has said: *"Every day and in a thousand ways, I am tempted to make myself the centre of the universe!"* Are there not echoes of that in us all? Yet the Bible says: *"God resisteth the proud, but giveth grace to the humble"* (James 4:6).

The poet makes the point:

"Oh, why should the spirit of man be proud?
Like a fast-flitting meteor, a fast-flying cloud,
A flash of lightning, a break of the wave,
He passes from life to his rest in the grave."

(d) <u>Scripture's Typology needs to be Emphasised</u>

Now, when we refer to *"typology"*, what do we mean? According to Baker's *"Dictionary of Theology"*: *"a type is a shadow cast on the pages of Old Testament history by a truth whose full embodiment or antitype is found in the New Testament revelation"*. A type is a figure or picture of something to come.

You see, what is so important about these two men and these two nations is this: they set before us a similar struggle described in the New Testament, namely the Christian's struggle between the flesh and the spirit. Do you recall Paul's words in verse 17 of Galatians 5? *"For the flesh lusteth against the Spirit, and the Spirit against the flesh: and these are contrary the one to the other: so that ye cannot do the things that ye would."* These are the two natures of the believer, the new nature and the old nature. They are opposed to each other. Esau pictures the flesh, the old nature, that part of man's nature wherein his natural desires have free rein. Jacob pictures the Spirit, the new nature.

Think about this. One Sunday morning, your new nature wants to gets up, go to church to hear the Word and remember the Lord. But, your old nature, your Esau nature, fights it. *"You are tired"*, an inner voice says. *"You've had a tough week. Don't get up so early. Have a rest."*

Have you ever known that struggle? The old nature wants to look at a filthy programme and the new nature says: *"Those scenes will pollute your mind"*. Conflicts like these exist in a thousand different scenarios every day of life. This conflict is illustrated for us in Esau and Jacob, in Edom and Israel.

(2) DENUNCIATION - verses 10-14 - WHY IT WILL HAPPEN

First of all, the prophet declares that God would judge Edom and take away everything the nation boasted about and depended on for security. Then, in this second section, Obadiah explains why God was judging Edom. It was because Edom had done *three unforgiveable things*: Encouraging Judah's foes; enjoying Judah's fall and enslaving Judah's fugitives. Do you notice that Edom's three evils are introduced with the words: *"Thou shouldest not"* in verses 12, 13 and 14?

(a) There was Encouragement for Judah's Foes

In 586 B.C., Nebuchadnezzar, the king of Babylon, mounted a massive attack against Judah, concentrating his fiercest fire on Jerusalem. He *"slew their young men with the sword … and had no compassion upon young man or maiden, old man, or him that stooped for age … and all the vessels of the house of God, great and small, and the treasures of the house of the LORD, and the treasures of the king, and of his princes; all these he brought to Babylon. And they burnt the house of God, and brake down the wall of Jerusalem, and burnt all the palaces thereof with fire, and destroyed all the goodly vessels thereof. And them that had escaped from the sword carried he away to Babylon"* (2 Chronicles 36:17-20). Can you picture it? It was the darkest day in

Hebrew history. Jerusalem and the Temple lay in ruins. What did the Edomites do? They applauded and helped the conquerors.

Do you see what Obadiah says in verse 11? *"In the day that thou stoodest on the other side, in the day that the strangers carried away captive his forces, and foreigners entered into his gates, and cast lots upon Jerusalem, even thou wast as one of them."* The Edomites could have thrown their weight behind their neighbours. Instead, they opted to sit on their hands and let the Babylonians do their worst. The Lord says: *"You were just like one of them"*. By not helping Judah, the Edomites were as guilty as those who were ravaging Jerusalem. Indeed do you know what the Edomites were doing while Jerusalem was under attack? They were shouting: *"Rase it, rase it, even to the foundation thereof"* (Psalm 137:7).

Is that not an interesting phrase: *"In the day that thou stoodest on the other side"*? Does that not remind you of the priest and the Levite in the parable of the Good Samaritan? The wounded man was lying on the road. *"By chance there came down a certain priest that way: and when he saw him, he passed by on the other side. And likewise a Levite, when he was at the place, came and looked on him, and passed by on the other side"* (Luke 10:31-32). You would have expected these two religious workers to do something for the victim at the side of the road, but as far as they were concerned, he was a nuisance to avoid.

In March 1964, twenty-eight year old Catherine Genovese arrived home at her apartment building in Kew Gardens, New York. She had worked the late shift and it was now three in the morning. A man approached her out of the darkness and began stabbing her repeatedly. She screamed out: *"He stabbed me! Help me!"* A neighbour opened his window and shouted: *"Let that girl alone!"* The attacker ran away, leaving Catherine wounded. When no-one came out of the building to help her, the attacker returned. She fought him, but he continued stabbing her, then he sexually assaulted her. He took $49 from her purse and left her in the hallway of the apartment building. The assault lasted about thirty minutes. At least a dozen neighbours were aware of the attack and heard the cries for help. Only after the attacker left, did one of those neighbours finally call the police. Catherine died in the ambulance on the way to hospital.

"Thou stoodest on the other side!" "And passed by on the other side!" If we go through life, wanting to have our own way, then the people who need us will be nuisances to us. However, if we go through life, seeking to share the love of the Lord, then every nuisance will become an opportunity for ministry to glorify the Lord.

(b) There was Enjoyment at Judah's Fall

Do you see verse 12? *"Neither shouldest thou have rejoiced over the children of Judah in the day of their destruction."* While Judah was reeling, the Edomites were rejoicing. They were cheering on the Babylonians as they tore the city apart.

Can you imagine it?

"That will teach these despicable Jews a lesson", someone would have called out.

"Come on Edom", another probably shouted. *"What are we waiting for? Let's get in on the action. This is the day we have been hoping for."*

For the Jews, this was a day of distress, but for the Edomites, it was a day of delight. In their pride, they looked down on the Jews and gloated over their misfortune. Do you recall the counsel that is given to us in the book of Proverbs? *"Rejoice not when thine enemy falleth, and let not thine heart be glad when he stumbleth: Lest the LORD see it, and it displease Him and He turn away His wrath from him"* (Proverbs 24:17-18).

At times are we like the Edomites? Are we *"silent spectators"* when our brothers fall into difficulty? Do you know a Christian who has fallen into sin or some difficulty? What is your attitude to them? Are you helping them - or do you delight in digging out the details and spreading the news? Do you know a neighbouring church which is declining in numbers and whose very existence is threatened? Do you feel a smugness, a satisfaction, a superiority about that? What about some preacher of the Gospel who has fallen? Do you kick him when he is down or do you extend a helpful brotherly hand?

(c) There was Enslavement for Judah's Fugitives

This was the crowning act of wickedness. It was bad enough for people to do nothing to help their brothers, and then it was worse to stand and rejoice at their brothers' calamities, but when they gave aid to the enemy - that was carrying this *"family feud"* too far.

Do you see what was happening? When the Jews were trying to escape from the city of Jerusalem, the Edomites stood at the forks in the roads, waiting to capture them and hand them over to the Babylonians. The Babylonians then hauled them away to slavery.

Look at verse 14:

"Neither shouldest thou have stood in the crossway, to cut off those of his that did escape; neither shouldest thou have delivered up those of his that did remain in the day of distress."

Do you recall what the prophet Jehu said to King Jehoshaphat? *"Shouldest thou help the ungodly, and love them that hate the LORD?"* (2 Chronicles 19:2). As the Lord's people, we must love our enemies and pray for them (Matthew 5:44), but we certainly should not assist sinners in opposing and persecuting believers. To do so is to turn traitor in the army of the Lord.

Can you see Edom's sin? Well, look, finally, at Edom's doom:

(3) CONSUMMATION - verses 15-21 - HOW IT WILL HAPPEN

God said concerning Edom: *"Thou shalt be cut off for ever"* (verse 10). At the time Obadiah wrote this prophecy, Edom seemed far more likely to survive than Judah. However, history has strikingly endorsed this prophecy.

In other words:

(a) A Just Retribution will be Executed

Verse 15 begins: *"The day of the LORD is near upon all the heathen"*. This judgment has a near and a far fulfillment. Like so many other prophecies, Obadiah's words would have a partial fulfilment for Edom and a later fulfillment for the end-time foes of Israel. As we have noted in other books, the *"day of the LORD"* is a time when God will pour out His wrath upon a wicked world, judge the nations and then establish His kingdom, thus fulfilling the promises made to Israel. However, this phrase was also used to describe God-ordained calamities sent to punish people at any time – and these judgments were foretastes of the future worldwide *"day of the LORD"*.

Do you see the reasoning behind the punishment? Verse 15 continues: *"As thou hast done, it shall be done unto thee: thy reward shall return upon thine own head"*. God would treat them the way they had treated the Jews. Scholars call it *"poetic justice"*.

They were traitors to the Jews - therefore their own allies would betray them: verse 7.
They plundered and looted - so their nation would be robbed: verses 5-6.
Edom was violent - so they would be cut off completely: verses 9-10.
Edom wanted the Jews to be destroyed by Babylon - so she would be destroyed by Babylon: verses 10 and 18.

It would seem that the Edomites fell before Babylon some five years after they had helped that nation to destroy Jerusalem. (See Jeremiah 27:3-6 and Malachi 1:3) By the third century A.D., their name had perished.

However, in the end times, all nations, including a latter day Edom, will come up against the nation of Israel. The re-birth of the state of Israel in our day heralds the approaching fulfilment of Obadiah's end time prophecy. The ancient arena is fast becoming the modern arena. The old land of Edom is now part of the modern country of Jordan which joins with other Arab nations in their hostility towards Israel. No doubt this nation will play its part in the battle of Armageddon, on the side of the Beast, in seeking to exterminate the Jewish people once and for all, fully and forever. But, they will not succeed. For *"as thou hast done, it shall be done unto thee"* (verse 15). God will see to it that justice is done and retribution will be executed.

If on the one hand a just retribution will be executed, on the other hand:

(b) A Joyous Restoration will be Experienced

Do you notice the first word of verse 17? *"But!"* Mark well the *"buts"* of the Bible. They are hinges on which great events and doctrines turn. Note this one: *"But upon Mount Zion shall be deliverance, and there shall be holiness; and the house of Jacob shall possess their possessions"*. The Lord *did* deliver His people from Babylonian captivity and He *will* again deliver them in the last days and establish His kingdom.

The word *"shall"* appears no less than twelve times in the last verses: verses 17, 18, 19, 20 and 21. It is a word of *certainty*. It stresses the fact that what God has promised, He will most certainly perform.

What has God promised?

Rescue - verse 17.
Revenge - verse 18.
Restoration - verses 19 -20.
Reign - verse 21.

Not even during the great days of David and Solomon did Israel possess more than a tenth of the total land grant that is hers under the Abrahamic Covenant. But, she will!

"And the kingdom shall be the LORD'S" (verse 21).

What a wonderful way to end this brief book!

Today, the King has been rejected and David's throne is empty in Jerusalem. The Jews are in the sad condition described in the book of Hosea. They are without king, priest, sacrifice or priesthood. But, when Christ returns, the nation will look upon Him whom they have pierced. They will be cleansed and forgiven, and the kingdom will be established.

As predicted in Daniel 2, Christ the Stone will come down and crush all the kingdoms of the world. No matter what may happen to the affairs of Israel as the Gentile nations seek to control her or capture her, you can be sure that God will watch over this people and will one day give them their promised kingdom. *"And in the days of these kings shall the God of heaven set up a kingdom, which shall never be destroyed"* (Daniel 2:44).

In the words of the hymnwriter:

"Jesus shall reign where'er the sun,
Does its successive journeys run,
His kingdom stretch from shore to shore,
Till moons shall wax and wane no more."

Are you saved? Is your family saved? Have you a relative not yet saved? Are you just letting them go to Hell?

"O, give us all a passion,
For souls as ne'er before,
To warn men and to tell them,
The Judge is at the door."

May God give us a passion for souls to warn them of coming judgment and of their need to prepare to meet their God!

CHAPTER 15

Jonah

There is a great deal of ignorance about the twelve preaching prophets whose writings are found at the end of the Old Testament. Ignorance among people generally and, what is sadder, ignorance even among Christians.

However, there is one name that does stand out among these ancient worthies, not because of his preaching but because of his association with the most criticized fish in the Mediterranean. Who has not heard of Jonah?

This book of Jonah is one of the strangest books in the Bible:

Jonah was a prophet, yet there is no prophecy in his book except the one sentence that he preached in Nineveh!
He was a missionary, yet he did not want to go to the mission field!
He saw a great revival, yet he was so unhappy that the revival came!

Who was this man? When did he live? Did he even exist?

The name *"Jonah"* means *"dove"* and his father's name *"Amittai"* means *"truthful"* Nothing is known about him apart from what is in this book and the historical statement in 2 Kings 14 verse 25: Jeroboam *"restored the coast of Israel from the entering of Hamath unto the sea of the plain, according to the word of the LORD God of Israel, which He spake by the hand of His servant Jonah, the son of Amittai, the prophet, which was of Gath-hepher"*. This village was located about three miles north-east of Nazareth, the hometown of the Lord Jesus. So Jonah lived during the reign of King Jeroboam the

Second, the king who ruled the Northern Kingdom of Israel from 790 to 750 B.C.

Now, before we launch into this book, it may help us to understand a little about:

Jonah and His Cities

Nineveh: Nineveh was then the capital of Assyria and was located in what we now know as Northern Iraq. It was rated the greatest city of the ancient Near East, surrounded by massive walls 100 feet high and wide enough to take three chariots abreast. It was 500 miles north-east of where Jonah lived, so even getting there would have meant a long and dangerous journey. Nineveh was renowned for its paganism, idolatry, immorality and violence. Its vicious leaders thought nothing of cutting off the fingers, lips and noses of those who opposed them.

Tarshish: Tarshish was far from Israel, located in what is now known as Spain.

Joppa: Joppa was then a seaport. It is now called Jaffa and is a thriving town in the land of Israel.

Jonah and His Contemporaries

Elisha was Jonah's predecessor. In fact, Jonah may have been one of Elisha's disciples, learning much from this "man of God". Amos, Hosea and Isaiah were all Jonah's successors.

Jonah and His Critics

The book of Jonah is one of three Old Testament books especially hated by Satan. These three are:

Genesis: this book predicts the incarnation of Christ as the seed of the woman - see Genesis 3 verse 15.
Daniel: this book predicts the glorious second coming of Christ to destroy His enemies - see Daniel 7 verses 9 to 12.

<u>Jonah</u>: this book predicts in type form the death and resurrection of Christ - Matthew 12 verses 38 to 41.

There is no question about it. Jonah was a real person and a genuine prophet. Listen to what the Saviour says: *"For as Jonas was three days and three nights in the whale's belly; so shall the Son of Man be three days and three nights in the heart of the earth"* (Matthew 12:40). The main reason we believe in a real, historical Jonah is that our Lord Jesus believed in a real, historical Jonah. Christ related Jonah to His own resurrection. If Jonah's experience was not historical, such an association would not have made sense. Was Christ deceitful? Did the Saviour tell us a lie when He said that Jonah was in a fish's belly three days and three nights? Of course not! Jesus Christ is the *"Truth"* and His Word cannot be broken.

If the story of Jonah is fictional, so too is the Gospel. Look again at verse 40 of Matthew 12. The Saviour said: *"For as Jonas was ... so shall the Son of Man be"*. Some Christians might say: *"What does it matter?"* It matters a lot! The Psalmist posed a question many years ago: *"If the foundations be destroyed, what can the righteous do?"* (Psalm 11:3). The Bible's account about Jonah is not incidental to our faith - it is fundamental. If the book of Jonah is not true, then what confidence can we have in the Gospel records? Deny the historical authenticity of Jonah and you will deny the authenticity of the resurrection of Jesus Christ.

The story is told of a young girl who was studying oceans at school. The teacher tried to reassure the class: *"I don't want you ever to be afraid of going out into the sea, because there are no sea creatures that can swallow you whole"*.

The little girl raised her hand and said: *"I learned in church that a great fish swallowed Jonah whole"*.

The teacher scoffed at the girl and said: *"That could never happen. It's impossible"*.

The girl answered: *"When I get to Heaven, I'll ask Jonah myself and find out if it was true"*.

The teacher asked: *"What if Jonah didn't get to Heaven?"*

To this, the little girl said: *"Then you can ask him!"*

Actually, the book of Jonah is not simply about a great fish. In fact, the fish is mentioned only four times.

Again, the book of Jonah is not just about a great city. In fact, the city of Nineveh is mentioned only nine times.

The book of Jonah is not even about a reluctant prophet, even though Jonah is mentioned about eighteen times.

The book of Jonah is primarily about a great God who is mentioned thirty eight times in these four short chapters.

If you eliminate God from this book, the story does not make sense.

This book is all about *the will of God - and how we respond to it.*
This book is all about *the love of God - and how we share it.*

There are four movements in the book corresponding to the four chapters.

In Chapter 1: Jonah and the Storm.
In Chapter 2: Jonah and the Fish.
In Chapter 3: Jonah and the City.
In Chapter 4: Jonah and the Lord.

Chapter 1: Running FROM God - Jonah Protesting

The book begins by recording that Jonah was instructed by God to go to Nineveh. Verse 3, however, declares: *"But Jonah rose up to flee unto Tarshish from the presence of the LORD"*. Instead of going to Nineveh, Jonah ran in the opposite direction. Three times in the first ten verses we read the phrase: *"fled from the presence of the LORD"*. Jonah knew that he could not escape the omnipresence of God. There is no place where God is not. Psalm 139 makes that clear: *"Whither shall I go from Thy Spirit? Or whither shall I flee from Thy presence?"* (verse 7). O. Palmer Robertson says: *"Trying to get away from God is like trying to get away from air"*. Impossible! This expression in Jonah 1 simply means that Jonah resigned his prophetic office. He was determined not only to ensure that he did not undertake this responsibility, but that he would not be available in the future for any other such undertaking. Thus he became a backslidden prophet.

It is as if Jonah said: *"Here am I, send him! I'm on my way to Tarshish"*. What a contrast that was to Isaiah! God asked: *"Whom shall I send, and who will go for us?"* Isaiah's response was: *"Here am I; send me"* (Isaiah 6:8).

Are you like Isaiah or Jonah? It may be that Nineveh for some is *reconciliation*. To other believers, it may be *repentance*. Still others may be called to the Nineveh of *restitution*. Where are you headed?

There are really only two roads in the Christian life:

One leads to *Nineveh*: the other to *Tarshish*.
The way to Nineveh is the way to *revival*: the way to Tarshish is the way to *ruin*.
One road is *obedience* to the will of God: the other is *disobedience* to His will.

Now what was:

(a) THE CAUSE OF HIS BACKSLIDING

"Jonah rose up to flee ... from the presence of the LORD" (verse 3). Why? He was <u>God's man</u> with <u>God's message</u>. Why should he run from God?

Was it the ***unknown***? Think about it. What if the Lord called *you* to go to, say, Brazil? How would you feel? With the people and the culture so different? Perhaps Jonah was afraid that he would become ***unpopular***? After all, he was popular in Israel, because his prediction had been fulfilled that the nation would regain her lost territory from her enemies (2 Kings 14:25). Are *you* running away from God's will because you are afraid of being unpopular? Perhaps Jonah was ***unconcerned***. History tells us that the Assyrians were a cruel and heartless people who thought nothing of burying their enemies alive, skinning them alive or impaling them on sharp poles under the hot sun. *"If the city of Nineveh is going to be overthrown, then let it be overthrown"*, argues Jonah. *"I would rather disobey God than see my enemies saved from defeat."* If that was Jonah's attitude, then that was wrong. Look at what he says after the revival in Nineveh? *"I fled before unto Tarshish: for I knew that Thou art a gracious God, and merciful, slow to anger, and of great kindness, and repentest Thee of the evil"* (Chapter 4:2). Nineveh was the capital city of an enemy nation and Jonah had a sneaking suspicion that God might pardon it. In that case, Israel's enemy might be able to strike. It was his sense of patriotism for his own country and his prejudice against another country that made Jonah flee.

What is the reason for *your* disobedience? Do you feel inadequate? Are you fearful? Are you prejudiced?

When you stand before the Saviour and gaze with undimmed eye upon that brow which was pierced, when you look upon those hands and feet that were marred, what excuses will you make for not giving His message of redeeming love to a lost world?

(b) THE COURSE OF HIS BACKSLIDING

Do you notice that it was downward? It is both *perilous* and *ominous* when a Christian starts going down. Do you see Jonah's steps downward? Down to Joppa and down into the ship (verse 3); down into the sides of the ship (verse 5); down into the sea (verse 15) and down into the great fish (verse 17).

Disobedience always leads downward.

Any journey that is away from God is always downward - and to go down is both easy and hard. Easy, because no self-effort is required, but hard, because of the consequences.

Things seemed to work out for Jonah, even in his backslidden state. Satan can make disobedience very convenient and very easy! You see, Jonah had the money for the fare. A ship was waiting for him. He seemed to be at peace, for he was able to sleep in the storm. It seems that when you are trying to run away from God, you can always find a ship that is willing to take you!

Some believers think that because they *"find a ship"*, it is providential and, therefore, must be all right. It is amazing how skilful the devil is in his manipulative powers and subtle ways.

Sometimes, one spouse says to another: *"We need to separate for a time. I need some space!"* That almost always means that there is someone else involved. In other words: *"they find a ship going to Tarshish"*.

Sometimes, a young Christian girl marries an unsaved man. The boy just seemed to come along and it appeared the right thing to do. *"She just found a ship going to Tarshish."*

A man gets into financial trouble because: *"He found a ship going to Tarshish."*

The truth is this - any time we want to run away from the will of God, we will find a ship and the devil will make sure it is running on time!

But, do you see:

(c) THE CONSEQUENCE OF HIS BACKSLIDING

Charles Spurgeon said that God never allows His children to sin successfully, and Jonah is the proof of that statement. *"For whom the Lord loveth He chasteneth, and scourgeth every son whom He receiveth"* (Hebrews 12:6). Spurgeon also said: *"It may hard going forward, but it is harder going backward"*. Donald Grey Barnhouse commented: *"When you run away from the Lord, you never get to where you are going and you always pay your own fare"*.

Running away from the Lord is always a costly business. Do you see what Jonah lost here? He lost God's voice, for the Lord now speaks in thunder and lightning. He lost his power in prayer and even his desire to pray. The heathen were praying, but Jonah was sleeping. He lost his testimony with the men on the ship. He lost his influence for good, because he was the cause of the storm. He almost lost his life.

We always pay dearly when we flee from the Lord. Ask the girl who married the unsaved man - he was lying when he said he would never abandon their marriage. Ask the teenage girls who have fled home. Ask the man whom the Lord called to preach and who, instead of going, attempted to head for some distant Tarshish. Jeremy Taylor, the 17th Century English preacher, said: *"God threatens terrible things if we will not be happy"*. He was referring to being happy with God's will for our lives, being happy in Him. It cost Jonah spiritual peace, joy and contentment. What is it costing *you*? Will you say with Jonah: *"Here am I, send him!"*? Or, will you say with Isaiah: *"Here am I, send me!"*?

Are these your words?

> *"Mine are the hands to do the work;*
> *My feet shall run for Thee;*
> *My lips shall sound the glorious news;*
> *Lord, here am I, send me."*

<u>Chapter 2: Running TO God - Jonah Praying</u>

In Matthew 12 verse 40, the *Authorised Version* translates the Greek word *"ketous" as "whale"*, but the word really means *"a sea monster"* or *"a great fish"*. It may have been a whale – and there are numerous validated stories of men being swallowed by whales and surviving the ordeal. It does not really matter. You see, the point of the story is not so much the great fish but the great God. <u>Too much discussion about the great fish turns into a red herring!</u> Why is it that we always think we have to explain the miraculous? What happened to Jonah was a miracle! Take away the miraculous from Jonah and you destroy the miracle of the Gospel, the death, burial and resurrection of Jesus Christ.

Now, let us be honest. After all the problems Jonah had caused and had brought upon himself, the sailors, and ultimately the Lord, you would have thought that God would have either let him go or else finished him off. But, no!

Jonah had gone down of his own accord. Down to Joppa, down into the ship, down into the sides of the ship - three steps down.

God had brought him down into the sea, then down into the fish and now God brings him down further still.

"I went down to the bottoms of the mountains" (Chapter 2:6). Jonah was down about as far down as he could go.

In that beautiful Psalm 116, the Psalmist says: *"I was brought low, and He helped me"* (verse 6). Brought low and then saved. Jonah was brought low, brought down, then he was brought up in more senses than one! *"The LORD spake unto the fish, and it vomited out Jonah upon the dry land"* (Chapter 2:10).

When Jonah was writing this story, he was looking back and attempting to put himself into the situation again to show us how he really felt. Can you imagine what it must have been like? Can you imagine a place more filthy? More horrible? More depressing than the one where Jonah was - in the belly of a fish, in the dreadful sea, all alone cast away from mankind? Yet, it was there that Jonah was motivated at last to pray.

Chapter 2 begins with the words: *"Then Jonah prayed"*.

When did Jonah pray? *Why* did Jonah pray? *What happened* when Jonah prayed?

(a) WHEN did Jonah RETURN to Prayer?

"Then Jonah prayed unto the LORD his God out of the fish's belly"

(Chapter 2:1). *Then! Then! Then!* But why did Jonah not pray before this? Well, because he was out of the habit of praying. His act of disobedience resulted in Jonah getting out of the habit of praying. The Psalmist said: *"If I regard iniquity in my heart, the Lord will not hear me"* (Psalm 66:18). *"If I cherish a life of disobedience, then when I pray the Lord does not hear me – and so I give up"*. John Bunyan said: *"Prayer will make a man cease from sin or sin will entice a man to cease from prayer"*. Have you got out of the habit of praying? Is it because of sin in your life?

"Then Jonah prayed unto the LORD his God out of the fish's belly, and said, I cried by reason of mine affliction unto the LORD, and He heard me" (Chapter 2:1-2).

Are we not all a bit like Jonah? Which of us has not tried to manage his own affairs until everything began to go wrong? We were at our wits' end, with no way of escape – and then we *"remembered the LORD"* (Chapter 2:7). Then we prayed. Is it not amazing that some of us wait until we are in a *"fish's belly"* before we call out to the Lord? Is that where you are? In a fish's belly? Are you in a confusing situation? Does there seem to be no way out? Are you saying: *"What will I do? My hopes are dashed! My life is ruined!"* Take encouragement from Jonah. He records: *"I cried by reason of mine affliction unto the LORD, and He heard me"*.

(b) WHY did Jonah RESORT to Prayer?

What was the reason for his prayer? Well look at verse 3 of Chapter 2: *"For Thou hadst cast me into the deep, in the midst of the seas; and the floods compassed me about: all Thy billows and Thy waves passed over me"*. Jonah recognised the chastening hand of the Lord. Who sent out the *"great wind"* (Chapter 1:4)? The Lord. Who appointed the *"great fish"* (Chapter 1:17)? The Lord. ***The adversity God sent moved the lips of Jonah.***

Can you not recall incidents and situations in your life which made you desperate for God to intervene? When nothing else causes us to call upon the Lord, adversity has a way of stimulating our lips and bending our knees in prayer. It was affliction that made Jonah pray.

The Psalmist also learned this same painful lesson: *"Before I was afflicted I went astray: but now have I kept Thy word"* (Psalm 119:67).

(c) WHAT did Jonah RECEIVE in Prayer?

"And He heard me" (Chapter 2:2). Jonah received an answer! Look at Jonah. He disobeyed the Lord. He disregarded the Lord, but the Lord not only listened to his voice – He also responded to his prayer. Verse 10 records that the Lord spoke to the fish and: *"it vomited out Jonah upon the dry land"*.

It is interesting that in this prayer Jonah:

Recalled God's Word

The whole of this chapter is a selection of verses from the Psalms. Jonah simply prayed the Word of God. He quotes from Psalm 18 verse 6; from Psalm 42 verse 7; from Psalm 16 verse 10 and from Psalm 3 verse 8.

Do *you* know God's Word well enough to recall when you are in dark circumstances? To pray the Word of God is a great way to pray!

Remembered God's Mercy

In verse 4, Jonah declares: *"I am cast out of Thy sight; yet I will look again toward Thy holy temple"*. Jonah looked to the place of mercy, for back in 1 Kings 8 verse 38, Solomon spoke about a man spreading *"forth his hands towards this house"*. He continued: *"Then hear Thou in Heaven Thy dwelling place, and forgive"*. Do we need to say: *"I will look again"*?

Here is a man renouncing his sin, remembering his vow and re-consecrating his life to the Lord (Chapter 2:8-9).

Recognised God's Sovereignty

Jonah cries: *"Salvation is of the LORD"* (Chapter 2:9). Jonah could not save himself, but the Lord spoke to the fish and the fish spewed Jonah onto the shore.

Thus Chapter 2 concludes and Chapter 3 commences: *"And the word of the LORD came unto Jonah the second time"*.

Do you see the third picture?

Chapter 3: Running FOR God - Jonah Preaching

"The victorious Christian life", said George H. Morrison, is a: *"series of new beginnings"*. When we fail, the enemy wants us to believe that our ministry is ended and that there is no hope of recovery. However, our God is the God of the second chance. Where would any of us be were that not the case? *"The word of the LORD came unto Jonah the second time."*

There are two very graphic pictures that are brought before us in this passage.

(a) THE PEDESTRIAN PREACHER

Can you see him? Walking up and down like a street vendor, Jonah begins to declare the destruction of the city: *"Yet forty days, and Nineveh shall be overthrown"* (Chapter 3:4). The word *"overthrown"* literally means *"overturned"*. Nineveh would be turned upside down. It simply meant that Nineveh would be totally destroyed just like Sodom and Gormorrah in Genesis 19. This message was *short, simple, searching* and *startling*.

Was this all Jonah said? We are not sure. We are told in verse 5: *"So the people of Nineveh believed God"* – so did he spend time telling the people about the true and living God? They would need to know something about this God of Israel in order to exercise sincere faith. Did Jonah expose the folly of their idolatry? Did he recount his personal history to show them that his God was sovereign and powerful? Again, we are not sure. What we do know is that Jonah obeyed God. He went to Nineveh. He declared the message that God gave him - and God did the rest.

Remember that 2 Kings 14 verse 25 describes Jonah as a *"prophet"*. There was:

1. _A Fidelity about His Preaching_

God said to Jonah: *"Preach unto it the preaching that I bid thee"* (Chapter 3:2). Verse 4 records: *"And he cried, and said, Yet forty days, and Nineveh shall be overthrown"*. He made no attempt to spin God's Word into something the Ninevites might find more user-friendly. No, here was a man who sensed his obligation to be faithful to the Word of God and thus warn the people. What an example Jonah is for all preachers! You see, we live in age when society and the pew tend to dictate to the preacher. Social pressures attempt to mould the servant of God, but the true servant of Christ must always *"preach the Word"* (2 Timothy 4:2). Some of the congregation may not like that, but then we preach not what will please but what is before us in this Bible. Our attitude should be that of Paul: *"If I yet pleased men, I should not be the servant of Christ"* (Galatians 1:10). As the servant of Christ, you are to preach the Word of God faithfully and fearlessly.

Was this not Jonah's brief? Is this not your brief? Jonah had been to the other side of the precipice. Some scholars believe that he actually died and was raised back to life. Now he returned as a warning sign to the Ninevites that if they went over that spiritual precipice on which they stood, there was no way back. Do *we* believe that? Have we grasped that? Do you believe that there is no way back for that loved one of yours if they go over the precipice into Hell? Are you, therefore, marked by _*fidelity*_?

2. _An Expectancy about His Preaching_

Somehow I do not think Jonah was surprised when, after he preached: *"the people of Nineveh believed God"* (Chapter 3:5). They looked at Jonah. He was a horrifying sight to behold. *"God punishes sin"*, they said. *"Look at the man - he is discoloured!"* But the fact that Jonah was alive at all caused them to say: *"God pardons sinners"*. You see, Jonah was preaching out of personal experience about the reality of God's judgment. He had experienced it. No wonder he preached, expecting God to work.

A young student came to C. H. Spurgeon on one occasion and

said: *"Mr. Spurgeon, I have been preaching around the countryside for some time now, but I don't see souls saved like you do".*

Spurgeon looked at the young man and said: *"Do you expect to see souls saved every time you preach?"*

He replied: *"Why no, Sir".*

Spurgeon said: *"Well, that is why you don't see them saved!"*

Do you know what our problem is? We go around not expecting anything to happen!

Do you see what happened here?

(b) THE PENTITENT PEOPLE

The people *"believed God"* and proved their faith by their works of contrition. And - God forgave them! This was undoubtedly one of the greatest revivals in history. Is it not amazing what happened when one man got right with God! When one man corrected his ways, he changed his world. Can you see it? One sentence and Nineveh was brought to its knees.

J. Edwin Orr tells how in 1859 a schoolboy in Coleraine was under deep conviction of sin. Not being able to continue his studies, he was sent home by his teacher in the company of another boy. On their way home, the two boys noticed an empty house and they entered it to pray. At last, the unsaved boy got saved and immediately returned to the classroom to tell his teacher. *"I am so happy I have the Lord Jesus in my heart"*, he said. That simple testimony had its effect on the class and boy after boy stepped outside. The teacher looking out of the window noticed the boys kneeling in prayer around the schoolyard. The teacher was overcome, so he asked the converted schoolboy to comfort them. Soon the school was in strange disorder. Ministers of the Gospel were sent for and remained at the school all day, dealing with sinners. Pupils, teachers, parents and neighbours were converted and the school was occupied until eleven o'clock that night. *"One sentence empowered by the Spirit of God and Coleraine was awakened."*

May it please God to do it again! The cry of our heart should be: *"Lord, send us another mighty revival!"*

If you or I had been writing this story, we would probably have closed it at the end of Chapter 3. We all like to have a happy ending, but Jonah adds this last chapter to show himself *"warts and all"*. Here we see Jonah:

Chapter 4: Running AGAINST God - Jonah Pouting

Instead of *rejoicing,* Jonah is *resenting.* Instead of *singing,* he is *sulking.*

In Chapter 1, Jonah is like the Prodigal Son: doing his own thing and going his own way. In Chapter 4, he is like the elder brother: critical, selfish, sullen, angry and unhappy with what was going on. How many angry saints there are in the Church! Some of them have carried *"chips on their shoulders"* for years and will do so to the grave, but what they forget is that they will carry them right to the Judgment Seat of Christ!

Can you see Jonah:

(a) LAMENTING OVER A CITY

Geographically, Jonah was outside Nineveh. *Chronologically,* he was in days of revival. *Spiritually,* he was almost back to square one again.

"But it displeased Jonah exceedingly, and he was very angry" (Chapter 4:1). With whom was he *"very angry"*? Sad to say - with the Lord Himself! Why was he so displeased and angry? Because the Lord had not destroyed the city of Nineveh, because the Lord had shown mercy to repenting sinners. Jonah was thoroughly a Jew and the very idea that Gentiles, especially those in wicked Nineveh, could experience the saving grace of God was repugnant to him. He could not stand the blessing of God resting on others.

Are there prejudices we need to sacrifice? Can we rejoice when God is blessing others? Other lands, other Christians, other churches, other circles than ours? Do we rejoice?

Do you see Jonah now? He comes before the Lord and says in effect: *"I knew it would turn out like this!"*

Warren Wiersbe says:

"It took God longer to prepare His servant and get him to obey His will than it did for the entire godless city of Nineveh to repent."

Things have not changed much, have they? It takes God longer to get believers right than it does to get sinners to repent.

How patient God is with us! How patient He was with Jonah, for now we see Jonah:

(b) LEARNING FROM A GOURD

What was a gourd? Some think it was a castor oil plant. Certainly, Jonah needed a good dose of castor oil! It was probably a fast-growing perennial plant which reached a height of some 8-10 feet. It looked like a palm tree with large leaves and it protected Jonah from the sun.

But look at verses 7 to 11:

"But God prepared a worm when the morning rose the next day, and it smote the gourd that it withered. And it came to pass, when the sun did arise, that God prepared a vehement east wind; and the sun beat upon the head of Jonah, that he fainted, and wished in himself to die, and said, It is better for me to die than to live. And God said to Jonah, Doest thou well to be angry for the gourd? And he said, I do well to be angry, even unto death. Then said the LORD, Thou hast had pity on the gourd, for the which thou hast not laboured, neither madest it grow; which came up in a night, and perished in a night: And should not I spare Nineveh, that great city, wherein are more than sixscore thousand persons that cannot discern between their right hand and their left hand; and also much cattle?"

What a stark contrast between Jonah and God!

Jonah was concerned about a _Plant_: God was concerned about a _People_. Jonah was concerned over something for which he had _not laboured_: God was concerned over His _Creation_.
Jonah was concerned about something which is _Temporal_ – the gourd lasted only a night: God was concerned about souls which are _Eternal_.

The truth was that Jonah seemed to care more about *plants* than about *people*!

Could the same be said of you? Of me? Do we care more about the items in our gardens, the produce in our fields, the contents in our homes, the stock in our business, than we do about never-dying souls and the spread of the Gospel to them?

Do you know what God is concerned about?

Souls: *"And should not I spare Nineveh?"*
Souls in Great Cities: *"That great city."* The population was one million.
The Souls of Little Children in Great Cities: *"That cannot discern between their right hand and their left hand."*

What does the chorus say?

"Jesus loves the little children,
All the children of the world,
Red and yellow, black and white,
All are precious in His sight,
Jesus loves the little children of the world."

Remember the words of the Lord Jesus: *"Suffer little children, and forbid them not, to come unto Me: for of such is the kingdom of Heaven"* (Matthew 19:14).

Oh, how compassionate is our God! What about us? What about you?

Will you seek to labour for Christ in your Nineveh so that on that future day you might be able to say: *"Behold, I and the children whom the LORD hath given me"* (Isaiah 8:18)?

CHAPTER 16

Micah

What's in a name? In the Bible, names are often very significant. The book of Genesis, for example, contains the story of a man named *"Methuselah"*, a famous name because Methuselah is the oldest man in Scripture and probably the oldest men who ever lived. Do you recall that when Methuselah was born, his father Enoch give him a name that proved not only significant but also prophetic? In Hebrew, the name means: *"When he dies, it will come"*. Methuselah lived 969 years - and the very year in which he died was the year of the great flood of Noah. Now, this book of Micah is another example of the significance of names in the Bible. In Hebrew, *"Micah"*, which is a shortened form of *"Micaiah"*, means: *"Who is like the Lord?"* In the last chapter, Micah uses a play on his own name, saying: *"Who is a God like unto Thee?"* (Chapter 7:18).

R. G. Lee says:

"The name of the prophet was suited to his character. God was everything to him. He had a high view of the holiness, righteousness and compassion of God. To judge by his writings, he was a man of powerful personality, of calm, sane judgment, tender-hearted yet faithful, and for all this he gave God the credit and the glory."

No doubt, you are familiar with certain sections of the book of Micah. There is the one that concerns beating swords into ploughshares and spears into pruning hooks and the reign of peace that will come when Christ returns (Chapter 4:3). Then there is the passage that you will have heard from Micah read at the Carol services: *"But thou, Bethlehem Ephratah, though thou be little among the thousands of Judah, yet out of thee shall He come forth unto Me that is to be ruler in Israel; whose goings forth have been from of old, from everlasting"* (Chapter 5:2). That prediction was made some 700 years before the birth of the Lord Jesus. Then there is that classic statement in Chapter 6 verse 8: *"What doth the LORD require of thee, but to do justly, and to love mercy, and to walk humbly with thy God?"* Of course, there is that remarkable statement at the end of the book which has been made into a number of hymns: *"Who is a God like unto Thee, that pardoneth iniquity?"* (Chapter 7:18).

All memorable statements but, as David Pawson says: *"They are usually taken out of context and used as pretexts. We need to put the whole book into context, time and place"*.

So, let us consider:

THE PLACE

Micah was a native of the village of Moresheth Gath (Chapter 1:1, 14), a village about twenty four miles south-west of the city of Jerusalem. Keep in mind that Galilee, the northern part of Israel, was called: *"Galilee of the Nations"* because international traffic went through it. The south was more Jewish and it had far fewer international visitors. If you take an east/west cross-section in the south, you have the Mediterranean Sea at one side and the Dead Sea at the other. The Dead Sea is a lot lower than the Mediterranean. Now, Micah came from Moresheth Gath which was situated between the Philistines and the Jews. As such, he could look up to the corrupt city of Jerusalem and down to the Gaza Strip.

THE PERIOD

Micah exercised his ministry during the reigns of three kings of Judah: Jotham (750-732 B.C.); Ahaz (735-715 B.C.) and Hezekiah (715-686 B.C.). He probably preached for about seventeen years, starting before 732 B.C. and continuing until after 715 B.C. This means that he was a contemporary of Isaiah in Judah and Amos and Hosea in Israel. By this time, of course, Israel was divided following the death of Solomon. The ten tribes of the north had separated, calling themselves *"Israel"*, and the two tribes in the south were known as *"Judah"*. Micah was the only prophet who directed his preaching to both the Northern and the Southern Kingdoms, but the burden of his prophecy was for Judah.

So, here are Isaiah and Micah preaching at the same time.

Isaiah came from an upper class, wealthy background, but Micah was a simple country man with a heart for the ordinary people who were being exploited.

Isaiah preached in the *city*: Micah preached in the *country*.

Isaiah was God's messenger in the *palace*: Micah was God's messenger to the *people*.

Isaiah dealt with *political matters*: Micah dealt with *personal matters*.

THE PURPOSE

The purpose of Micah's prophecy was, in the words of Sidlow Baxter, to set forth the theme of ***"Present Judgment but Future Blessing"***.

Micah was a country man living a simple life out in the fields and hills, but he was burdened about what was happening all around him. In the Bible, cities were always seen as dangerous places. The concentration of sinners makes sin worse. So, vice and crime are normally worse in the city than in the surrounding country. What was happening in Judah was this: the corruption in Jerusalem was beginning to touch the country towns in which Micah laboured. Property was being taken by violence: *"They covet fields, and take them by violence; and houses, and take them away"* (Chapter 2:2). Debts were being collected by force: *"Ye pull off the robe with the garment from them that pass by securely as men averse from war"* (Chapter 2:8). Priests and prophets were corrupt: *"The priests … teach for hire, and the prophets … divine for money"* (Chapter 3:11). Justice was being perverted by the nation's leaders: *"Ye heads of the house of Jacob, and princes of the house of Israel, that abhor judgment, and pervert all equity"* (Chapter 3:9).

Witchcraft and paganism were rife throughout the land (Chapter 5:12-14). False weights and deceit were being frequently used in trade (Chapter 6:10-12). Family relationships had broken down with awful consequences. *"Trust ye not in a friend, put ye not confidence in a guide ... a man's enemies are the men of his own house"* (Chapter 7:5-6).

Micah saw the coming judgment of God upon Israel under Assyria in 722 B.C. as well as the fall of Jerusalem and Judah under the Babylonians in 586 B. C. He sought to call the Jews back to faithful worship of Jehovah and sincere obedience to His covenant, but they refused to listen. He was the prophet of social justice. His heart went out to the helpless, but the people would not repent.

The simplest way to divide this book is by the threefold use of the expression: *"Hear ye"*. Chapter 1 verse 2: *"Hear, all ye people"*. Chapter 3 verse 1: *"Hear, I pray you"*. Chapter 6 verse 1: *"Hear ye"*.

So, these sections begin with the rebuke for sin and the announcement of judgment. Then each section closes with the promise of blessing in the Messiah – See Chapter 2 verses 12 and 13, Chapter 5 verses 10 to 15 and Chapter 7 verse 20.

As has been said, the central thought of the book is: ***"Present Judgment but Future Blessing"***.

Look at:

THE FIRST SERMON – Chapter 1 verse 1 to Chapter 2 verse 13

Micah wastes no time in getting to his message. The Lord has spoken to him and warned him that the sins of the people are so great that He must send judgment. Do you see that he names the capital cities in the opening verse? Jerusalem, the capital of Judah in the Southern Kingdom, and Samaria, the capital of Israel in the Northern Kingdom. In fact, in this first message Micah names twelve cities and points out their sins. The sins of the cities were polluting the whole nation. Does that not sound up-to-date? Judgment was coming. The Court was convened, the judge had arrived, and the defendants were named.

Here there is brought before us:

(a) THE REVELATION OF COMING JUDGMENT

God points an accusing finger at His own people, Israel and Judah. Today, when a judge enters a courtroom, everyone in the courtroom rises. It is a symbol of respect for the judge and the law the judge represents, but no judge ever came to court in the manner described by Micah. *"Behold, the LORD cometh forth out of His place"* (verse 3). This phrase *"cometh forth out of His place"* means: *"to come forth for battle"*. God opens the court and declares war.

A judge comes to court to see to it that justice is done. The judge is not allowed to take sides. However, when God comes to judge the nations, He has all the evidence necessary. He does not have to call any witnesses. God is angry at His people because of their sins. That is why His coming makes the earth split and the mountains melt so that the rock flows like melted wax or like a waterfall (verse 4).

The *"wound"* in verse 9: *"Her wound is incurable"* is the stroke of judgment. It is described as *"incurable"*, that is, there would be no recovery from it. God's rod to inflict the stroke was Assyria - and after the Assyrians had laid low the Northern Kingdom of Israel, they also invaded the Southern Kingdom of Judah. This ninth verse is in advance of the event: *"It (the stroke) is come unto Judah: he is come unto the gate of My people, even to Jerusalem"*.

When the Northern Kingdom went into Assyria in 722 B. C., Sennacherib invaded the Southern country of Judah in 701 B. C., but they could not take the city because of the prayers of Isaiah and Hezekiah. God intervened and in one night one hundred and eighty-five thousand soldiers were slain. Sennacherib then returned to the house of his god, but he was slain by his two sons.

In verses 10 to 16, the unfamiliar names are names of places in the locality where Micah was reared. There is a reference to *"Shephelah"*. The Hebrew Bible mentions *"Shephelah"* several times. The word means *"low"* and refers to lowlands, a region of perhaps 12 to 15 miles in Judea. Micah is describing the ruin of the southern part of Judah by the invading Assyrians in 701 B.C. They swept through the land and destroyed these cities, but they could not take Jerusalem because God protected it.

Micah does a play on words here and he shows how each city will become the very opposite of the meaning of its name. For example, *"Saphir"* in verse 11 means *"beautiful"*, but the citizens would endure public disgrace. In verse 14, there is a reference to *"Moresheth-gath"*. This was Micah's own city. The name means *"betrothed"* and brides were given farewell gifts. Verse 14 declares that presents would be given to this place. In other words the town would no longer belong to Judah but would *"leave home"* and belong to the invaders.

David Pawson says that if Micah were preaching in London, he would say something like this.

"Hammersmith will be hacked to pieces. Battersea will be battered for all to see. Barking will be set on by wild dogs and sheep will graze over what is left of Shepherd's Bush. Vultures will feed on the corpses at Peckham."

This is how Micah speaks about local places. He takes the name of each town and he twists that name so that it becomes a message of judgment.

How could God do this? Were they not His special people? Was the land not His love-gift to them? Yes, the people were and yes, the land was. *That* is why He was punishing them! *"You only have I known of all the families of the earth: therefore I will punish you for all your iniquities"* (Amos 3:2).

Privilege brings responsibility and responsibility brings accountability.

Observe:

(b) THE REASONS FOR COMING JUDGMENT

What were some of the sins that God would judge? ***Idolatry.*** Do you see that verse 5 talks about *"the high places of Judah"*? The people insisted on worshiping: *"the works of thine hands"* (Chapter 5:13). People still do that today! We may not carve out statues and bow before them, but we certainly live for the things we have manufactured - cars, clothes, houses, money. What we serve and what we sacrifice for is the thing that we worship.

In Chapter 2 verse 1, we see the sin of ***covetousness***. People would lie awake at night thinking up new ways to get "things" and then get up early to carry out their plans. Paul says in Colossians 3 verse 5: *"covetousness ... is idolatry"*. Many people today have an insatiable appetite to get more *"things"*. Do you recall the warning of the Lord Jesus? *"Take heed, and beware of covetousness: for a man's life consisteth not in the abundance of the things which he possesseth."* (Luke 12:15).

The people were not only covetous, but they used ***illegal means*** to get what they wanted - fraud, threats, and violence. The rich took advantage of the poor and the rulers did not obey the Law of God. They practised the world's version of the Golden Rule: ***"Whosoever has the gold, makes the rules"***.

Do you know what the name of this sin is? ***Materialism*** and it affects *us* big time today. Parents rob children of time and companionship by working at several jobs, so that they can make more money to buy more *"fun"*. Believers rob the Lord of *"tithes and offerings"* that are rightfully His, so that they can enjoy the good life. We forget the words of the Lord Jesus in Matthew 6 verse 33 and instead put everything ahead of the kingdom of God.

How did Micah respond to the sins of the people and the judgment of God? He wept and mourned. *"Therefore I will wail and howl"* (verse 8). He was like a broken man at a funeral. He saw his fellow countrymen rushing down a slippery slope and if they would not weep for themselves, he would do so for them.

Do you recall the lamentations of Jeremiah? *"Oh that my head were waters, and mine eyes a fountain of tears, that I might weep day and night for the slain of the daughter of my people!"* (Jeremiah 9:1).

Do you recall Paul's great burden for his fellow Jews? *"I have great heaviness and continual sorrow in my heart. For I could wish that myself were accursed from Christ for my brethren"* (Romans 9:2-3).

Have we the same kind of heart-broken concern today? How do we react when we read of an escalating divorce rate? A Christian leader who has a moral lapse? Fellow believers who show signs of losing their first love? Do we climb up to the judge's bench or fall down at the mourner's bench?

How did the people react to Micah's preaching? They tried to stop him! In Chapter 2 verse 8, they rise up like an enemy. Back in verse 6, they say: *"Prophesy not"*. In other words: *"Stop preaching such terrible things. You know they will not happen to us. We are God's people"*. But Micah says: *"I must preach. The Spirit of God compels me"*. Micah knew that the people did not want honest preaching. They preferred their drunken false prophets who lived as wickedly as the people did. *"If a man walking in the spirit and falsehood do lie, saying, I will prophesy unto thee of wine and strong drink; he shall even be the prophet of this people"* (Chapter 2:11).

<u>THE FURTHER SERMON - Chapter 3 verse 1 to Chapter 5 verse 15</u>

Do you see that this section begins with the same charge to hear? *"Hear, I pray you, O heads of Jacob, and ye princes of the house of Israel."*

Notice that in these chapters Micah speaks of:

(a) THE COMING RETRIBUTION: Chapter 3

Do you know the story of the Greek philosopher, Diogenes? He went about the countryside carrying a lantern. Even in broad daylight he carried his lantern to arouse curiosity and provoke questions. People would ask: *"Why are you carrying a lantern in the daytime?"* and Diogenes would reply: *"I'm looking for an honest man"*.

Like Diogenes, Micah has been tramping around the Southern Kingdom of Judah, searching for godliness. However, he finds only oppression, corruption, bribery and injustice. Micah exposes the mess in Jerusalem and he says that the reason for God's judgment on His people is because those who have authority have forgotten that they are responsible to God.

Look at verse 12: *"Therefore shall Zion for your sake be plowed as a field, and Jerusalem shall become heaps"*. I suppose we could call this - the collapse of civilization! Why was this?

Well, look at Chapter 3 and notice that Micah addresses:

CORRUPT POLITICIANS

In the first four verses, there are leaders who were not only permitting the wealthy to exploit the poor, but were doing it themselves. They fleeced the poor, scraping them to the bone, stripping away everything they had. Do you see where Micah starts? At the top. When you clean out a fishpond, you start at the top, because the dead fish always rise to the top! When a country goes sour, it starts at the top and dribbles down to the bottom.

Micah told the leaders that the Assyrians were not their enemy. He laid the blame for the decline and destruction *at their own feet*. *"You are the cause of this"*, he said. *"You are the real enemy of this country"*.

For something similar, remember the words of Elijah to Ahab in 1 Kings 18 verse 18: *"I have not troubled Israel; but thou, and thy father's house, in that ye have forsaken the commandments of the LORD"*. When God sought to bring about revival under King Hezekiah, He started with King Hezekiah. The revival in Nineveh started when the king repented in sackcloth and ashes.

Paul tells us in Romans 13 verse 4 that the political leaders are God's ministers. They are responsible to the Lord. The tragedy in Judah was that instead of defending the sheep they were devouring them.

Ron Dunn speaking of U.S.A could easily have been speaking of the United Kingdom when he said:

"This seems to be the place we have come to in our country. They have thrown the Bible out of the schools and left it in the motels. They handcuff the policemen and let the criminals go free. The Supreme Court can't come to a satisfactory decision concerning pornographic literature in the malls, but they have no difficulty in ruling out prayer in the schools."

Do we not need to follow the exhortation of Paul in 1 Timothy 2 verses 1 and 2 and pray for our leaders that our country might be led in righteousness.

COMPROMISING PREACHERS

What were the preachers doing in Micah's day that brought about the denunciation of God? The very same thing preachers are doing in our day - preaching what the people want to hear. The establishment wanted to hear *"Peace"* so the prophets said: *"Peace"*, even though Assyria the superpower to the north was eying Judah. You see, these preachers were willing to say anything as long as there was adequate remuneration. *"Judge for reward ... teach for hire ... divine for money"* (Chapter 3:11). How different was Micah! He says in verse 8: *"But truly I am full of power by the Spirit of the LORD, and of judgment, and of might, to declare unto Jacob his transgression, and to Israel his sin"*.

Do we realize that this is the only thing that can give life-changing power to preaching today? Spurgeon said: *"It were better to speak six words in the power of the Spirit than to preach seventy years of sermons without the Spirit"*.

COMPLACENT PEOPLE

All of this corruption and pollution was permeating the country and yet the people leaned upon the Lord and said: *"Is not the LORD among us? None evil can come upon us"* (verse 11). In other words: *"Micah, you talk about all this corruption and this immorality - why the Lord is with us! We are trusting in God, we believe in God. Nothing can happen to us"*. You see, to all outward appearances, the religious life of the country was flourishing, but the endless activity in the Temple and elsewhere hid widespread sin.

Ron Dunn says that several years ago there was in the city of Chicago a group of policemen who became bandits. They would go out and rob a store, then return to their hiding places, put on their uniforms, and investigate their own crime. I wonder, is that we are doing? Says Jeremiah 7 verse 8: *"Behold, ye trust in lying words, that cannot profit"*. Has the church become a hideout for multitudes of Christians who during the week are living Christless, godless lives and then think because they come to church on Sunday morning, God is going to overlook it all. ***He will not do it!***

As far as Judah was concerned judgment was coming, but Chapter 4 takes up a wonderful new theme. One day there will be peace on the earth and righteousness will reign, for there is:

(b) THE COMING RESTORATION: Chapter 4

Do you see how this chapter begins? *"But in the last days."* The period known as *"the last days"* began with the ministry of Christ (Hebrews 1:1-2) and they climax with His return to establish His kingdom on earth. You see, the pendulum is swinging here from predictions of coming judgment to previews of the Messianic age. This passage describes a scene yet to come. Nations today will never forget how to make war, never beat their swords into ploughshares, never turn their spears into pruning hooks - until the coming of the King. The words of Micah here in verse 3 are almost identical to the words of Isaiah 2 verse 4, speaking of a similar time.

These words are inscribed on the pedestal of a bronze statue in the United Nations garden. The statue depicts a strong man literally hammering a sword into a farmer's plough. It was a gift from the Soviet Union, presented in 1959, three years after Soviet Premier

Nikita Khrushchev promised the West: *"We will bury you"*. So much for world peace! At least until the Messiah comes!

A kingdom is coming in which there will be multilateral disarmament and this kingdom is going to be established on earth. Did you know that when you are praying the *"disciples' prayer"* this is what you are praying for? *"Thy kingdom come. Thy will be done in earth, as it is in Heaven"* (Matthew 6:10).

You say, how can this happen? It can happen because of:

(c) THE COMING RULER: Chapter 5

Keep in mind here that Micah is shifting his focus time and time again. Sometimes he sees his people in his day, then he sees his people in *"the last days"*. Here in Chapter 5, he is shifting his focus again, this time to the coming of the Messiah.

Do you see here:

The First Advent of the Lord Jesus

Look at Chapter 5 verse 2.

Would you for a moment:

> *"Turn your eyes upon Jesus,*
> *Look full in His wonderful face"*

Do you see *His Eternality*? He is the eternal God *"whose goings forth have been from of old, from everlasting"*.

Do you see *His Humanity*? *"Shall He come forth unto Me."* Christ stepped out of eternity into human history, sent by the Father to be the Saviour of the world.

Do you see *His Humility*? *"But thou Bethlehem Ephratah."* The name *"Bethlehem"*, means *"House of bread"* and the name *"Ephratah"* means *"fruitful"*. There, David had been born. There, Christ would be born. In this little town the Lord of Glory, the second person of the Godhead, would become man. You see, when God chose to become a man He did not choose to be born in Athens, Alexandria, Babylon, Rome, London, Paris or Washington. He chose to be born in Bethlehem, in a humble stable or cave.

But, Micah looks ahead not just to His first coming but to:

The Second Advent of the Lord Jesus

Having gone to Calvary as the great shepherd of the sheep, He will retain His shepherd character when He returns.

You know, in the Old Testament the sheep was always slain for the shepherd, but in the New Testament the Shepherd was slain for the sheep.

> *"When blood from a victim must flow,*
> *This Shepherd, by pity was led,*
> *To stand between us and the foe,*
> *And willingly died in our stead."*

The Lord Jesus will reign as Shepherd. God's ideal Old Testament king was David, the shepherd king. In the Hebrew Scriptures the whole idea of kingship is wrapped up in the idea of a shepherd, one who pastors, protects and provides.

In Psalm 22, we see the Suffering Shepherd.
In Psalm 23, we see the Sustaining Shepherd.
In Psalm 24, we see the Sovereign Shepherd.

Micah could see *"our Lord Jesus, that great shepherd of the sheep"* (Hebrews 13:20), standing and feeding His flock, with no-one daring to interfere. *"He shall stand and feed in the strength of the LORD, in the majesty of the name of the LORD His God; and they shall abide: for now shall He be great unto the ends of the earth"* (verse 4).

Micah concludes Chapter 5 by declaring that Israel's future enemies would be defeated (verses 5-6); the Jewish remnant would be blessed (verses 7-9) and the nation would be purged (verses 10-15).

THE FINAL SERMON – Chapter 6 verse 1 to Chapter 7 verse 20

Do you see again how it begins? *"Hear ye now what the LORD saith."* Micah is moving his focus again from the dim and distant future and he is bringing the people back to the present. Do you recall that the opening chapters of the book condemned the sins of the people? Now the prophet appeals for their repentance. Micah began his prophecy with a trial scene and now he returns to it.

God has a controversy with His people, and Micah wants them to keep some things before them:

(a) GOD'S GOODNESS IN THE PAST

"State your case against Me" says the Lord. *"I have a complaint against you"*, announces the Lord. *"I have done all I could do for you, yet you have rejected Me. I brought you out of Egypt. I led you in the wilderness. I protected you from your enemies. What more could I have done?"*

Is it not astonishing that we *also* neglect the Lord as if He wearies us?

As John Phillips says:

"He is the most fascinating, absorbing person in the universe. Yet we yawn in His face and gave our attention to our puny business matters and pitiful little pleasures as if they were the most important things in the universe."

(b) GOD'S DEMANDS IN THE PRESENT

What would it take to get right with God? Look at verses 6 and 7 of Chapter 6. There are references to *"burnt offerings"*, to *"thousands of rams"* to *"ten thousands of rivers of oil"*. There is even a reference to: *"my firstborn"*! Yet these were all external things and Micah swept aside Judah's reliance on them. God does not want extravagant gifts and sacrifices. He wants our hearts! He wants obedient hearts - and when He has our heart, He has our all.

Psalm 51 verses 16 and 17 declare: *"Thou desirest not sacrifice; else would I give it: Thou delightest not in burnt offering. The sacrifices of God are a broken spirit: a broken and a contrite heart, O God, Thou wilt not despise"*.

Micah 6 verse 8 has been called: *"the greatest saying of the Old Testament"*. Here Micah is pleading with the Jews to repent on the grounds that they are God's people. *"O My people"* (verses 3 and 5).

What are God's demands?

To be Considerate: "To do justly"

Did you know that this is how the Bible describes God? *"A God of truth and without iniquity, just and right is He"* (Deuteronomy 32:4). Of course, the people in Micah's day ignored this, for they stole other people's property; they perverted the course of justice and they engaged in financial chicanery.

Are *you* doing justly? When you fill in your tax return? When you pay your employee less than he or she deserves? When you keep your child away from school without good reason? When you travel on public transport without paying the correct fee?

To be Compassionate: "To love mercy"

A man was having his portrait painted and said to the artist: *"I hope this will do me justice!"* The artist replied: *"It's not justice you need – it's mercy!"*

Do you recall that word *"chesed"*, mercy, that we noted in the book of Hosea? Albert Barnes, the 19th Century American Bible scholar said: *"Nowhere do we imitate God more than in showing mercy"*.

To be Contrite: "To walk humbly with thy God"

Augustine maintained: *"For those who would learn God's ways, humility is the first thing, humility is the second thing and humility is the third thing"*.

Consider the life of the Lord Jesus Christ.

Did He not do justly? Did He not love mercy? Did He not walk humbly with His Father?

Here is Micah telling his people that God has a controversy with them, pleading with them to repent and reminding them of God's Goodness in the Past, God's Demands in the Present and:

(c) GOD'S PLANS IN THE FUTURE

Speaking in the latter part of Chapter 6, God says in effect: *"You had better repent because judgment is coming"*.

Sadly, the Israelites refused to obey God, and the tragedy of Israel's sinfulness overwhelmed Micah's soul. He cried in the opening verse of Chapter 7: *"Woe is me!"*

However, Micah has faith in God. *"Therefore I will look unto the LORD; I will wait for the God of my salvation: my God will hear me"* (verse 7).

He turned away from the sins of his people to meditate on the faithfulness of God. God will *punish* sin, but Micah saw a day when God will *pardon* sin. The prophet could see end-time Israel restored and God making good His promises to Abraham, Isaac and Jacob. Israel's *future is bright* and Israel's *foes are beaten*.

Do you remember the meaning of Micah's name? ***"Who is like God?"*** Who indeed!

Look how the prophecy concludes:

"Who is a God like unto Thee, that pardoneth iniquity, and passeth by the transgression of the remnant of His heritage? He retaineth not His anger for ever, because He delighteth in mercy. He will turn again, He will have compassion upon us; He will subdue our iniquities; and Thou wilt cast all their sins into the depths of the sea. Thou wilt perform the truth to Jacob, and the mercy to Abraham, which Thou hast sworn unto our fathers from the days of old" (verses 18-20).

As someone has put it: *"God has cast our sins into the deepest ocean and has put up a sign - 'No fishing!'"*

Well may we ask with Micah: *"Who is a God like unto Thee?"*

Well may we sing:

Great God of wonders! All Thy ways,
Display Thine attributes divine;
But the bright glories of Thy grace,
Above Thine other wonders shine:
Who is a pardoning God like Thee?
Or who has grace so rich and free?

Such deep transgressions to forgive!
Such guilty, daring worms to spare!
This is Thy grand prerogative,
And in the honour none shall share:
Who is a pardoning God like Thee?
Or who has grace so rich and free?

Pardon, from an offended God!
Pardon, for sins of deepest dye!
Pardon, bestowed through Jesus' blood!
Pardon, that brings the rebel nigh!
Who is a pardoning God like Thee?
Or who has grace so rich and free?

CHAPTER 17
Nahum

Queen Victoria was celebrating sixty years on the British throne when Rudyard Kipling published his poem entitled: *"Recessional"*. Not everyone in Great Britain liked the poem because it punctured national pride at a time when the Empire was at its peak. *"Recessional"* was a warning that other empires had vanished from the stage of history and the British Empire might follow in their train. God was still the Judge of the nations. Kipling wrote:

> *"Far-called, our navies melt away;*
> *On dune and headland sinks the fire:*
> *Lo, all our pomp of yesterday*
> *Is one with Nineveh and Tyre!*
> *Judge of the Nations, spare us yet,*
> *Lest we forget, lest we forget!"*

The prophet Nahum would have loved the poem, especially Kipling's reference to Nineveh. It was Nahum who wrote this Old Testament book that vividly describes the destruction of Nineveh, the event that marked the beginning of the end of the Assyrian Empire.

The book of Nahum is neglected and considered obscure. It is not a book that many Christians read. It is not a book to which many preachers would turn.

Yet, every portion of Scripture is indispensable and has its own contribution to make to our spiritual growth and nourishment.

Paul reminds us: *"All Scripture is given by inspiration of God, and is profitable for doctrine, for reproof, for correction, for instruction in righteousness: that the man of God may be perfect, throughly furnished unto all good works"* (2 Timothy 3:16-17).

This little prophecy of Nahum is no exception!

In what way is it profitable? Well, let me try and set the scene by pointing out:

1. TWO PROPHETS

Do you recall the other prophet who was associated with Nineveh? *Jonah!* He prophesied during the era of King Jeroboam the Second who reigned from 790 -750 B.C. in the Northern Kingdom. *Nahum* appeared on the scene about 100 or so years later, preaching during the reign of King Manasseh (695-642 B.C) in the Southern Kingdom.

Now it is interesting that two of the Minor Prophets deal wholly with Nineveh. *Jonah* had preached in the streets of Nineveh and the Ninevites had learned through him that God is *"slow to anger"* (Jonah 4:2). But, revivals are only transitory and soon the Ninevites went to greater lengths of sin than ever before. They must learn now through *Nahum* that God is *"a jealous God"* (Exodus 34:14).

Jonah's message had been: *"Now is the accepted time!"*
Nahum's message was: *"Now it is too late!"*

Jonah had revealed God was the *God of the Second Chance.*
Nahum revealed that God was the *God of the Final Word.*

Between them, these two prophets underlined the truth of Paul's words to the Romans: *"Behold therefore the goodness and severity of God"* (Romans 11:22).

Now, as with prophecy of Jonah, there is a question that underlines the book of Nahum which has troubled Christians down through the generations:

The prophecy of *Jonah* asks: "Does God control nature?"
The prophecy of *Nahum* asks: "Does God control history?"

The Bible says that it is God who draws the atlas of history. When Paul preached in Athens to the Greeks, he said: *"God ... hath made of one blood all nations of men for to dwell on all the face of the earth, and hath determined the times before appointed, and the bounds of their habitation"* (Acts 17:26).

God allots every nation its place in time and space. God can allow a nation to rise and become an empire and God can also bring it to an end.

Many scholars believe that God brought the British Empire to an end when she washed her hands of the Jewish people in 1947. Indeed, within five years the Empire had gone.

Does God control history? ***"History is His story."***

2. *TWO PERIODS*

Nahum does not mention a single king in this little book, so we have to try and determine the time of his ministry from internal evidence.

There are two periods mentioned in the book. The earlier one is found in Chapter 3 verses 8 to 10. Verse 8 begins with a question: *"Art thou better than populous No?"* In verse 9, we read: *"Ethiopia and Egypt were her strength, and it was infinite; Put and Lubim were thy helpers"*. Records verse 10: *"Yet was she carried away"*. *"No"* was No-Amon or Thebes, the capital of Upper Egypt, and this city was destroyed by the Assyrians in 663 B.C.

The latter period, of course, was the destruction of Nineveh by the Babylonians in 612 B.C. This is predicted in Chapter 3 verse 7: *"And it shall come to pass, that all they that look upon thee shall flee from thee, and say, Nineveh is laid waste"*.

Nahum would thus fall in between the dates of 663 B.C. and 612 B.C.

3. *TWO PLACES*

The book concerns two places – Nineveh and Judah.

Nineveh was then the capital of Assyria and located in what we now know as Northern Iraq. It was rated the greatest city of the ancient Near East, surrounded by massive walls which were 100 feet high and wide enough to take three chariots abreast. In Jonah's day, the population of the city was about one million and in Nahum's day, it would be more.

The other place that is mentioned in the book is Judah – See Chapter 1 verse 15. You see, this was not a message of warning to Nineveh. They had heard God's warning from Jonah some 100 or so years earlier. No, there was no hope for Nineveh. God's patience had run out and His judgment was about to fall. Rather, this was a message of hope for Judah, to encourage them to trust God in an hour of great danger and in a day of crisis.

We know very little about Nahum. His name means *"Comfort"* or *"Consolation"*, and some think it is a shortened form of *"Nehemiah"* which means *"Comfort of Jehovah"*. He is identified, in verse 1 of Chapter 1, as a native of Elkosh, but it is difficult to determine where this is. Some suggest that it was on the Tigris River, north of Nineveh. Others believe that it was in Northern Galilee. Others say it was Capernaum, *"Caper-Nahum"* meaning *"place of Nahum the prophet"*. Still others, that it was in Judah between Jerusalem and Gaza. Sidlow Baxter, for example, says: *"This much is certain. Nahum addresses Judah and the impression left on the reader's mind is that he also wrote from Judah"*.

4. *TWO PROPHECIES*

We have discovered in reading the Prophets that we must distinguish between those parts which relate primarily to events which have long since been fulfilled and those which have to do entirely with what is still future. Keeping that in mind, look at verse 11 of Chapter 1. *"There is one come out of thee, that imagineth evil against the LORD, a wicked counsellor."* The expression: *"wicked counsellor"* is literally: *"counsellor of Belial"*. The leader being addressed is, according to Chapter 3 verse 18, the King of Assyria and this verse in Chapter 1 suggests Satanic influence on the leadership. Did Nahum have in mind Rab-shakeh who, a few years earlier had come from Assyria to terrify Jerusalem – see 2 Kings 18 and 19 and Isaiah 36 and 37. He was certainly a *"counsellor of Belial"*, *"a man of sin"*. What was he known by? His mouth. It was this man who placed Jehovah on the same level as the *"gods of the nations"* (Isaiah 36:18). What a picture he is of the *"man of sin"* who is yet to appear on the stage of history! He will be someone who will defy the living God. He will meet with the same end as the Assyrian host, for Paul says: *"Then shall that Wicked be revealed, whom the Lord shall consume with the spirit of His mouth, and shall destroy with the brightness of His coming"* (2 Thessalonians 2:8).

Yes, Nineveh is fallen, is fallen! God will not acquit! His government is righteous. He is the stronghold of the godly. Says John in Revelation 1 verse 7: *"Behold, He cometh with clouds; and every eye shall see Him"*. Wrongs shall be righted and in that day the cry will be: *"The kingdoms of this world are become the kingdoms of our Lord, and of His Christ"* (Revelation 11:15).

The book of Nahum has only three chapters and it is divided easily between them:

Chapter One announces the certainty of Nineveh's overthrow.
Chapter Two depicts the siege and capture of the city.
Chapter Three tells of the wickedness that provoked such judgment.

Notice then:

(1) NINEVEH'S JUDGMENT IS DECLARED - Chapter 1

Israel had been destroyed by the Assyrians and Judah had been threatened by the Assyrians, but now the judgment of the Assyrians is declared. Though Assyria had been blessed by God in the days of Jonah (780 B.C.) and used by God in the punishment of Israel (722 B.C.), as described in 2 Kings 17 verse 6, nonetheless, her sins will not be overlooked. This people who had known God, and had been blessed by God, had now rejected God and will be punished by God. Look at verse 8: *"With an overrunning flood He will make an utter end of the place thereof, and darkness shall pursue His enemies"*. Nahum describes Nineveh's judgment as an engulfing flood and darkness from which none can escape.

The message of Nahum can be viewed almost as a court scene. First of all, we have a portrait of the One who judges in court, God. This is followed by a description of the judgment and finally the reason for such a heavy sentence.

How do we see God?

The story is told of a school teacher who asked her young pupils to draw a picture of what was important to them. At the back of the room, Johnny began to labour over his drawing. Everybody else finished and handed in their picture, but he was still drawing. The teacher graciously walked back, put her arm around Johnny's shoulder and said: *"Johnny, what are you drawing?"* He did not look up, he just kept on working feverishly at his picture.

The teacher asked again: *"What are you drawing?"*

"God!"

"But Johnny", the teacher said gently, *"no-one knows what God looks like!"*

The little boy answered: *"They will when I'm through!"*

An amusing story, but - what is *your* concept of God? How do you view God? How do you see God? Have you a balanced view of God?

We like to think of God as a God of forgiveness, mercy, grace and compassion - and He certainly is. However, if that is the only side to God that we see, we will end up with a *"fuzzy"* image of God, perhaps even a false god who is indifferent to the sins of men. That is not the God of the Bible.

Nahum's prophecy may not make for *"entertaining reading"*, but this prophecy does a marvellous service for us in setting the balance of who God is and what God is like.

Note that Nahum sets before us:

(a) THE GREATNESS OF GOD

On 7th January 1855, the minister of New Park Street Church, Southwark opened his morning sermon as follows: *"The highest science, the loftiest speculation, the mightiest philosophy, which can ever engage the attention of a child of God is the name, the nature, the person, the work, the doings and the existence of the great God whom he calls his Father"*.

Would you agree with that statement from C. H. Spurgeon?

I wonder, have we lost sight of the holiness, the glory, the majesty and the might of our God? If so, the result is that we have a low view of worship.

Well, Nahum puts the balance where it ought to be. For this opening chapter declares who and what God is. What a remarkable way to begin:

"The burden of Nineveh. The book of the vision of Nahum the Elkoshite. God is …"

"God is!" The Holy Spirit deems certain truths to be self-evident, the first and foremost being that God is.

Do you believe in the existence of God? Do you believe in the reality of God?

Here is one of the things that separates the Christian from the atheist and the agnostic.
The atheist insists: *"There is no God!"*
The agnostic shrugs his shoulders and says: *"I just don't know!"*
What a contrast with the believer who comes with an emphatic: *"Yes, the Lord is!"*

You see, this opening chapter is a study on theology, a study of God. It's a far different picture from the one the average person in our country has of God today. Do you want to see the God of the Bible? Well, look at these opening verses. Here we see:

1. *<u>His Jealousy: Chapter 1 verses 2 to 3</u>*

Says Nahum: *"God is jealous"*. The Lord Himself says: *"I the LORD thy God am a jealous God"* (Exodus 20:5). Our God is a jealous God. This word *"jealous"* often baffles us, but remember there is a sinful jealousy and a rightful jealousy. Jealousy is a sin if it means being envious of what others have, but it is a virtue if it means cherishing what we have and wanting to protect it. Envy is wanting what someone has: jealousy can be wanting what is rightfully yours. A faithful husband and wife are jealous over one another and do everything they can to keep their relationship exclusive.

"Jealous" and *"zealous"* come from the same root - for when you are jealous over someone, you are zealous to protect the relationship.

When studying the book of Hosea, we learned that the Lord was *"married"* to Israel in a covenant relationship. Any breach of that covenant aroused His jealous love. He will not share His people with false gods any more than a husband would share his wife with his neighbour.

Nineveh was a city given over to idolatry and God's jealous love burned against their wilful breaking of His law. God is jealous over His glory, His name and the worship that is due to Him alone.

2. *<u>His Fury: Chapter 1 verse 2</u>*

Nahum continues: *"The LORD revengeth; the LORD revengeth and is furious"*. In verse 6, Nahum describes God's *"indignation"* as so fierce and powerful that it is *"poured out like fire"* with the power to shatter the rocks. That word *"indignation"* comes from a Hebrew term that can be literally translated as: *"foaming at the mouth"*.

Have you ever considered this attribute of God's anger?

God was angry - very angry - at Aaron when he led the people into idolatry (Deuteronomy 9:20).
In the Wilderness wanderings, Israel sinned against God in such a way that they provoked Him to anger (Psalm 78:58-59).
When Solomon turned his heart away from God, we read: *"The LORD was angry with Solomon"* (1 Kings 11:9).
Yet, verse 3 of Nahum 1 declares: *"The LORD is slow to anger"*. In fact, He had given Nineveh over 100 years of mercy, but they had gone too far in their idolatry, brutality and robbery. The Lord then had to judge them.

A.W. Pink says:

"There are more references in Scripture to the anger, fury and wrath of God than there are to His love and tenderness."

Some people picture God as more of a Santa Claus than the Creator, Father, King and Judge He truly is. They cannot bear the thought of God having to discipline or to punish someone. They want to reshape their image of God into something more genial, warmer, and softer.

Does God really get angry with sinful men?

The Psalmist says:

"Kiss the Son, lest He be angry, and ye perish from the way, when His wrath is kindled but a little. Blessed are all they that put their trust in Him" (Psalm 2:12).

"God judgeth the righteous, and God is angry with the wicked every day" (Psalm 7:11).

Do we *really* believe in God's wrath? Do we *really* believe that God will judge the world some day? Do we *really* believe that He will send sinners to the Lake of Fire, including members of our families? We believe it in our heads, but do we *really* believe it in our hearts?

The reason these questions need to be asked is because we often lack any real urgency in our evangelism.

On 8th July 1741, Jonathan Edwards, the 18th Century American preacher and theologian, preached a message in Enfield, Connecticut entitled: *"Sinners in the Hands of An Angry God"*. He said this:

"God's wrath towards you burns like fire; He looks upon you as worthy of nothing else, but to be cast into the fire ... It is nothing but His hand that holds you from falling into the fire every moment. It is to be ascribed to nothing else, that you did not go to hell last night; that you were suffered to awake again in this world, after you closed your eyes to sleep. And there is no other reason to be given, why you have not dropped into hell since you arose in the morning, but that God's hand has held you up."

No wonder that, as Jonathan Edwards preached that message, the elders threw their arms around the pillars of the building and cried: *"Lord, save us, for we are going down to the pit of hell!"*

Can the question be posed: Is Nahum correcting your view of God?

3. *<u>His Majesty: Chapter 1 verses 3 to 6</u>*

Does God have the power to judge? Of course He does! Look at His power in nature. In winds and storms, in rains and droughts, on land and sea. *"Who can stand before His indignation?"* is a question in verse 6. The answer, of course, is obvious. *No-one!*

Nations today seem to forget the power of the Lord. They act as though there is no God. But, you can be sure that the day of judgment will come - and in that day no amount of atomic bombs or fighter planes will make any difference.

4. *<u>His Reliability: Chapter 1 verse 7</u>*

Nahum says: *"The LORD is good, a strong hold in the day of trouble"*. The same God who is jealous, angry at sin, majestic and powerful is a refuge for His people.

Do you recall the words of the hymn?

> *"Where could I go? Oh, where could I go?*
> *Seeking a refuge for my soul,*
> *Needing a friend to help me in the end,*
> *Where could I go, but to the Lord?"*

Do you see those words: *"strong hold"*? The meaning is: *"a fortified place or refuge"*. Are you facing trouble? Have you fled to this refuge? Do you recall those glorious words in Deuteronomy 33 verse 27? *"The eternal God is thy refuge, and underneath are the everlasting arms"*. The Psalmist declares: *"I will say of the LORD, He is my refuge and my fortress: my God; in Him will I trust"* (Psalm 91:2). He says in an earlier Psalm: *"The LORD is my rock, and my fortress, and my deliverer; my God, my strength, in whom I will trust"* (Psalm 18:2).

Have you learned through experience that God is your *guaranteed* refuge? He is *reliable.*

5. His Equity: Chapter 1 verses 8 to 14

The Assyrians tried to use their wisdom against God and His people. Nahum says: *"What do ye imagine against the LORD? He will make an utter end: affliction shall not rise up the second time"* (verse 9). All Assyrian attempts to foil God's judgment would end in futility. The affliction of God's people would not be allowed to occur again. Assyria's end was determined.

Are you getting a glimpse of the greatness of God? Do you see His Jealousy, His Fury, His Majesty, His Reliability, His Equity – and then will you notice:

6. His Mercy: Chapter 1 verse 15

In the last verse of the chapter, there is the picture of the herald who announces that Nineveh is fallen and that the Assyrian army is defeated. *"Behold upon the mountains the feet of him that bringeth good tidings, that publisheth peace!"*

The Greatness of God, and also:

(b) THE GOODNESS OF GOD

Nahum says: *"The LORD is good"* (verse 7). This almost seems to be out of place after Nahum's opening salvo against Nineveh, but it is not. You see, we need to keep in mind that Nahum's prophecy was given for Judah's encouragement. Here God's people were being given the assurance that their deadly enemy was to be wiped out, while they remained secure and free to worship Him without fear of invasion.

Here is something about God that we need to know. *God is good.*

The Psalmist says: *"Good and upright is the LORD"* (Psalm 25:8) and again: *"O taste and see that the LORD is good"* (Psalm 34:8).

It is interesting to notice that when Nahum said: *"The LORD is good"*, he was in the midst of prophesying judgment. So often when things go well for us, we say: *"Isn't God good!"* Then, when trouble crosses our pathway, we doubt the goodness of God. However, ***God is eternally, immutably and unchangeably good***.

Has some dire circumstance caused you to doubt God's goodness toward you?

One of God's faithful missionaries, Allen Gardiner, experienced many physical difficulties and hardships during his service for the Saviour. Despite his troubles, he said: *"When God gives me strength, failure will not daunt me"*. In 1851, at the age of 57, he died of disease and starvation while serving on Picton Island at the southern tip of South America. When his body was found, his diary lay nearby. It bore the record of hunger, thirst, wounds and loneliness. The last entry in his little book showed the struggle of his shaking hand as he tried to write legibly. It read: *"I am overwhelmed with a sense of the goodness of God"*.

What about you? Even in the storms of life, does your faith look up amid the trial and cry out: *"The Lord is good"*?

Nahum thus speaks here about the Greatness of God and the Goodness of God, and then he speaks about:

(c) THE GOVERNMENT OF GOD

There may not be much *Gospel* in Nahum, but there is a great deal of *government*.

John Phillips reminds us: *"It is as much a truth in Scripture that God rules as it is that He redeems"*.

We can see the rule of God here in relation to:

The Destruction of Nineveh

In these closing verses of Chapter 1, Nahum describes the fall of Nineveh with two pictures: a great flood of waters that sweeps everything away and a fire of dry thorns that burns like stubble.

Twice, in verses 8 and 9, Nahum says this: God *"will make an utter end"*. You see, His purposes in grace and mercy were now to be replaced by His purposes in judgment and wrath.

History tells us that Nabopolassar, King of the Babylonian invasion forces, besieged the city for three years, leading three massive attacks and failing each time. Because of this, the Assyrians inside Nineveh rejoiced and began holding drunken parties. Suddenly, however, the Tigris River overflowed its banks and sent its wildly churning waters against the walls of the city. Soon it had washed a hole into which rushed the Babylonians - and the proud city was destroyed.

Do we need to grasp this truth: *"The Most High ruleth in the kingdom of men, and giveth it to whomsoever He will"* (Daniel 4:17).

The Deliverance of Judah

Can you imagine how happy the people of Judah and the surrounding nations were when they heard: *"Nineveh has fallen. The Assyrian Empire has been broken"*?

Yes, the Lord had used Assyria to chasten Judah in the past, but that would not happen again. This time God would break the yoke that Assyria had put on Judah - and Assyria would attack them no more.

Today, God's long patience with Israel's enemies aggravates the national sin of her foes. The Lord acts so slowly that people have come to the conclusion that either there is no God, or, if He is there, He does not care. They think that they can get away with their sins forever. But, ***God waits and God warns***. Wicked nations misinterpret God's patience. They can only see the *silence* of God and forget His *sovereignty*.

As Nahum said: *"The LORD ... will not at all acquit the wicked"* (Chapter 1:3).

(2) NINEVEH'S JUDGMENT IS DESCRIBED - Chapter 2

It is almost as if Nahum was watching the events unfold on television, so graphic is the detail!

Here he describes:

(a) THE SIEGE OF THE CITY

The fascinating thing is that the people who came up to destroy Nineveh wore scarlet uniforms just as Nahum had prophesied - even though such uniforms were unheard of in Nahum's day. *"The shield of his mighty men is made red, the valiant men are in scarlet"* (verse 3). He saw also how they entered in through the river gates - *"The gates of the rivers shall be opened"* (verse 6) - and described the city of blood. Verse 4 declares: *"The chariots shall rage in the streets, they shall justle one against another in the broad ways: they shall seem like torches, they shall run like the lightnings"*, but this should not be regarded as a prophecy of the modern car! It only pictures the chariots in the streets of the city. *"Huzzab"* in verse 7 probably refers to the Queen being led away in humiliation.

(b) THE SACK OF THE CITY

Do you notice the repeated reference to lions in verses 11, 12 and 13? You see, the lion was the emblem of Assyria. Visit the Assyrian room in any large museum and you will see statues of lions. Nahum is asking: *"Where are your lions now? Where are your rulers? Where are your champions?"* Nahum was calling Nineveh a toothless lion.

Now, in the Bible, the Assyrians were not only people who were actual enemies of Israel, but they were also a type of a people yet to come - a society that would threaten the peace of the earth and play an important part on the stage of world history in the last days. Who are these people? Well, look at verse 13 where God says: *"Behold, I am against thee, saith the LORD of hosts"*. An *identical* declaration against *Russia* was made by God when He said: *"Behold, I am against thee, O Gog"* (Ezekiel 38:3 and again in Ezekiel 39:1).

We do not know what the future holds for Russia, but we do know that God only sets His face against a people as a last resort and as a result of long defiance and deliberate provocation.

Is Russia the Assyria of our day? Is Russia equally determined to rule the world? Is Russia equally ruthless in war? Is Russia equally boastful of its power and culture? Is Russia equally antagonistic to God and the Jew? Then Russia will equally be the eventual target of God's wrath.

(3) NINEVEH'S JUDGMENT IS DESERVED - Chapter 3

Nahum is now ready to explain the reasons for God's judgment on Assyria. He talks here about:

(a) THEIR MURDEROUS FORM

This was a city that was founded and maintained on murder, bloodshed and constant warfare.

One of the kings of Assyria, Sennacherib, wrote of his enemies:

"I cut their throats like lambs. I cut off their precious lives as one cuts string. Like the many waters of a storm, I make the contents of their gullets and entrails run down upon the wide earth. Their hands I cut off."

(b) THEIR MORAL FAILURE

Nahum compares Nineveh to a harlot. You see, the chief deity of Nineveh was Ishtar, goddess of sexual passion, fertility and war. Psalm 115 describes false gods and then, in verse 8, declares: *"They that make them are like unto them: so is every one that trusteth in them"*. People become like the god they worship, for what we *believe*, determines how we *behave*. The Assyrians were ensnared by this evil goddess and were under the influence of lust, greed and violence.

(c) THEIR MAJOR FALLACY

They felt they were better than No-Ammon, or Thebes, in Egypt and believed that what happened there, could not happen to them.

Well, what happened to Nineveh? Well, today it is a desert!

Do you see in the closing verses:

(d) THEIR MISERY FINALIZED

In verse 15, Nahum could see the city stripped and as desolate as a landscape after a locust plague: *"There shall the fire devour thee; the sword shall cut thee off, it shall eat thee up like the cankerworm: make thyself many as the cankerworm, make thyself many as the locusts"*.

What a powerful reminder that the Lord judges the sins of nations and the sins of individuals!

As the book of Hebrews declares: *"It is a fearful thing to fall into the hands of the living God"* (Hebrews 10:31).

Our God is indeed a consuming fire, but can we leave Nahum

by referring again to verse 7 of Chapter 1: *"He knoweth them that trust in Him"*. God does not need a computer to record your name. Actually, He has you written on His heart. He has written your name on the palms of His hands. The palm of the hand is the tenderest part facing us as we look at it. The thought is this - our thoughts of God are intermittent, but His remembrance of us is constant. He knows you.

Are you not glad that God knows who you are?

Is it not unbelievable? The God who made Heaven and earth knows your name. He knows the very hairs on your head by number (Matthew 10:30). He knows you intimately.

If God numbers the hairs on your head, do you not think that He is up-to-date on the larger issues of your life?

Do you not think that He knows exactly how you feel - and cares deeply? ***God knows you.*** He perceives you.

He knows your fears. He sees your tears.

Have you ever heard the old saying: "Out of sight, out of mind"? You are never out of His sight and you are never off His mind.

"The LORD is good, a strong hold in the day of trouble; and He knoweth them that trust in Him."

A. W. Tozer says:

"With the goodness of God to desire our highest welfare, the wisdom of God to plan it, and the power of God to achieve it, what do we lack?"

The answer is - Nothing!

How good that, with the Psalmist, we can say: *"This God is our God for ever and ever: He will be our guide even unto death"* (Psalm 48:14).

CHAPTER 18

Habakkuk

On 11th March 2011 at 2:46 pm. a massive earthquake struck Japan. Several lives were lost, but the greatest loss of life was yet to come as the earthquake triggered massive tsunami waves, some as high has 90 feet, that swept across low-lying cities. 16,000 people were killed.

Why?

How often that question comes in life and how difficult it is to find an answer!

Why does a good God allow tragedy to come to His children?
Why should that young beautiful girl be stricken with an incurable disease?
Why should the innocent child of devoted parents be born physically and mentally handicapped?

Have you ever looked out upon this world with its injustice and violence and asked the question: ***'Why?'***?

Why doesn't God do something?
Why is God silent?
Why do the wicked triumph?
Why does God stand back and allow the earth to be ploughed and ploughed again by the wicked?
How can God remain aloof so long?

As we read the book of Habakkuk, we are confronted with:

1. DIFFICULT PROBLEMS

One of the modern Christian myths, that ought to be silenced, is that when you trust Christ as your Saviour, all your problems disappear. *They do not!* It *is* true that your basic spiritual problem, your relationship with the Lord, has been solved. Your sins are forgiven. God's righteousness is imputed to you. However, with that solution comes a whole new set of problems that you did not face when you were an unbeliever.

Habakkuk was *"The Questioning Prophet"*. He has been called: *"The Doubting Thomas of the Old Testament"*. He seems to have been more concerned with solving a problem than with delivering a prophecy.

As Habakkuk surveyed the situation in the land of Judah, he wrestled with this question: *"Why did God allow the wickedness in his homeland to continue?"*

Even worse was this second question: *"How could God allow a bad nation to be judged by an even worse nation?"*

Indeed, we could summarize the teaching of this book by Habakkuk's two questions and God's two answers.

Question Number 1: ***Why does God not punish wicked Judah?***
Answer: ***Judah will be punished by the Chaldeans – Chapter 1***

Question Number 2: ***Why does the Lord use godless pagans to chastise His own covenant people?***
Answer: ***The Chaldeans whom God raised up to punish Judah will themselves be punished – Chapter 2***

Thus the prophet is grappling with these serious questions. He is watching his society crumble at its very core, only to feel as if God is deaf and dumb to the situation.

Job struggled to find the reason for personal suffering.
Habakkuk struggled to find the reason for national suffering.

Esther teaches us that God is a God of providence.
Habakkuk teaches us that God is a God of providence even if that providence is perplexing.

2. *A DEFINITE PERIOD*

Habakkuk was living in a dark hour of history. His book begins: *"The burden which Habakkuk the prophet did see"*. Did you catch it? *"The burden which … the prophet did see."* In other words, this was not only a burden which Habakkuk sensed in his heart, it was a burden which he saw with his eyes. Everywhere he looked, he saw the plight of his people. Habakkuk knew that the kingdom of Judah was rapidly deteriorating. Ever since the untimely death of King Josiah, who had attempted to lead the nation of Judah back to God, things had only got worse. The religious reforms Josiah made were soon forgotten, and his son, Jehoiakim, went on to lead the nation further away from God and closer to disaster. A godly father does not always produce a godly son. This is often observed in the Bible - and it is to be observed with Josiah and Jehoiakim.

The words of verses 5 and 6 lead us to the conclusion that Habakkuk ministered in the years leading up to the invasion of Judah by Nebuchadnezzar. This invasion took place in 605 B.C. His bitter lament in these opening verses may reflect a time period shortly after the death of Josiah in 609 B.C., a time period in which the godly king's reforms were quickly overturned by Jehoiakim.

Jehoiakim was the king who heard the Word of God and then cut it with his knife and threw it into the fire. By his actions, recorded for us in Jeremiah 36, he declared: *"We will not have God and we will not have God's Word"*.

It seemed to Habakkuk that the wicked were winning. He would agree with the Psalmist when he said: *"The wicked walk on every side, when the vilest men are exalted"* (Psalm 12:8). Habakkuk was living in a time when society was falling apart. Jeremiah lived at that same time. They were contemporaries and they were watching the internal decay of their nation.

Are we living in a similar period in history? Indeed, we are! Corrupt governments and corrupt morals. How does the poet put it?

> *"Truth forever on the scaffold,*
> *Wrong forever on the throne."*

Do you ever wonder about our nation?

3. ***A DESPONDENT PROPHET***

We can understand this, can we not? Would *you* not be despondent if you knew that *your* nation was about to be taken into captivity? Here is this man of God, Habakkuk, living on the eve of the captivity of his people. The Babylonians were about to come down on the nation of Judah, the Southern Kingdom, and destroy it. They were going to take the people of God captive to the land of Babylon. The Temple of the Lord would be ransacked and destroyed.

We know nothing about Habakkuk apart from this book.

Do you see <u>His Name</u>?

His name means *"to embrace"*. His great ministry was, as Martin Luther once said: *"to take the people of Judah into his arms and carry them to the Lord"*.

Do you see <u>His Burden</u>?

That word *"burden"* conveys the idea of something heavy, a load to be lifted. He was burdened about the nation's sin - and God's seeming indifference to act in judgment. But, the message of judgment he had to deliver became a great burden as well.

Do you know something?

No-one is ever greatly used of God - who does not have a burden. Nothing great is ever going to be done for God - unless someone has a burden.

Are we burdened because of our *Nation's Sins*?
Are we burdened because of our *Broken Homes*?
Are we burdened because of our *Lukewarm Churches*?
Are we burdened because of our *Lost Families*?

We should be burdened because we are not burdened.
We should be concerned because we are not concerned.
We should be troubled because we are not troubled.
We should be disturbed because we are not disturbed.

Evan Roberts, who was so greatly used in the 1904 Revival in Wales, bowed himself over a church pew and prayed: *"O God, bend me, bend me, bend me"*. God answered his longing heart and met him in such revival blessing that the whole of Wales was affected.

A man burdened, a man broken, a man blessed.

Now, what is unique about Habakkuk's writing is that it has no direct message from God to His people. Instead it records what Habakkuk and the Lord said to each other and then the prophet's eventual response to their dialogue.

The book lends itself very readily to three divisions marked off by the three chapters.

Chapter 1 - Faith is *Puzzled,* the believer is *Tested*.
Chapter 2 - Faith is *Patient,* the believer is *Trusting*.
Chapter 3 - Faith is *Praising,* the believer is *Triumphing*.

Chapter 1: the prophet is *Worried with Conditions*.
Chapter 2: the prophet is *Watching with Confidence*.
Chapter 3: the prophet is *Worshipping with Contentment*.

Chapter 1: the prophet *is Sighing*.
Chapter 2: the prophet is *Silenced*.
Chapter 3: the prophet is *Singing*.

CHAPTER 1: THE PROPHET IS WONDERING

As we read this chapter, we observe that Habakkuk told God exactly what he was thinking. At first, he complained that God was doing too little. Then he complained that God was doing too much. God could not win!

Do you see that this prophet believed in interrogatory prayer? *Intercessory prayer* is when you ask God for things: *interrogatory prayer* is when you ask God questions.

Three questions seem to be on Habakkuk's mind here.

(a) *IS GOD INDIFFERENT?*

In verse 2, Habakkuk cries out to God: *"O LORD, how long shall I cry, and Thou wilt not hear! Even cry out unto Thee of violence, and Thou wilt not save!"*

He cries to God and he hears no answer. He faces a problem common to us all - the problem of unanswered prayer. So, in his bewilderment and pain he cries out: *"Lord, how long do I have to keep this up? When are You going to do something?"* Do you see how he expresses himself in this verse? The word *"cry"* is used twice to indicate the intensity of Habakkuk's prayer. The first word *"cry"* (*"Shawa"*) means: *"to cry for help"*. Habakkuk was asking how long he would have to wait until God sent an answer to his plea for help. The second word for *"cry"* (*"Zaag"*) is a more intense word for help and means: *"to scream, to cry with a loud voice and a disturbed heart"*.

Apparently, Habakkuk had prayed about this matter for some time. He asked: *"O LORD, how long shall I cry?"* He had prayed, cried, begged and pleaded with God, only to feel as if his prayer was unheard, as well as unheeded. Habakkuk had poured his heart out to God and had prayed that God would do something about the violence, strife and injustice in the land, but God did not seem even to hear his prayer.

Have you ever walked in the same shoes as this prophet Habakkuk?

Have there been times in your life when you have cried out and called out to God, only to walk away feeling as if your prayer rose no higher than your head?

Here is a man who has a burden. He is weighed down about the sins of his people. He is perplexed about the ways of God in a world of war and sin - and what does he do?

This burdened prophet takes his burden to the Lord.

Prayer is the place where burdens are lifted. Prayer is the place where burdens change shoulders. We transfer the burden from our shoulders and place it upon the shoulder of our Burden-bearer, the Lord Jesus Christ. He loves to carry our burdens!

Yet, there are those times when we bring our burden to the Lord and it seems that God is nowhere to be found. We pray, we plead, we persist, but there seems to come no answer. Have you been to that place? Are you there now? Here is a word of encouragement:

Keep pleading. Keep praying. Keep persisting.
God's delays are not God's denials.
When God seems silent today, it is because He is going to speak someday.
When prayer seems unheard, unheeded and unanswered, do not give up. Rather, look up.

(b) IS GOD INACTIVE?

Do you see how verse 3 opens? *"Why dost Thou shew me iniquity, and cause me to behold grievance?" "Why?"* In other words, Habakkuk was saying: *"God, You are inactive. Why don't You judge the sins of the people?"*

Habakkuk lived in a nation that had known a spiritual revival. Josiah, the king, had brought about a great reformation. He had cleansed the Temple, then the city and then the country. However, it had not lasted. Revivals seldom do! Judah had gone back to their sins again.

Habakkuk names them. One was *violence*. A sin that is widespread today! Another sin was *iniquity*. It means vanity. It means that the ungodly were prospering. The prophet also mentions *grievance*. It means misery. The people were being exploited. The poor were being exploited by the rich. The people were experiencing *"spoiling"*. The word means *"destruction"*. The family was being destroyed. The home was being destroyed. The nation was being destroyed. Foundations were shaking. Then there is a reference to *"strife"*. It means: *"disputes and fightings"*. It goes along with *"contention"*. Strife and contention - is that not a description of society today? Habakkuk also listed the sin of *injustice*. He declares: *"Therefore the law is slacked"*. The Hebrew word for *"slacked"* means *"paralyzed"*. The law could do nothing.

Yet, through all of this, God seemed to be unconcerned. You see, what troubled Habakkuk more than *man's sin* was *God's silence*. Why does God not *do* something?

Have *you* ever asked that question? Why is it that God permits certain things to happen? Why is the Christian church what she is today? Why has God not answered the prayers of His faithful people? We have been praying for revival for years - why does God not answer? Why has God not saved my loved one? Why is God apparently sitting idly by, allowing our nation to run full-throttle into self-destruction, devastation, and damnation?

Why?

Well, let me remind you that sometimes God lets us get exactly what we deserve. Do you recall God's Word to a wicked society in the book of Genesis? *"My Spirit shall not always strive with man"* (Genesis 6:3). In other words, God will sometimes allow man to lie in the bed he has made for himself.

People do not want the Bible. They do not want Gospel-preaching churches. They do not want standards. They do not want absolutes. They do not want the Ten Commandments. God says: *"Fine! If you do not want them, you can have what you want"*. They then face the consequences of rejecting God's way. How then can we rightfully blame God for allowing us to reap what we have ourselves sown?

Yet, on the other hand, God's ways are *often* mysterious. It was William Cowper who penned the words:

> *"God moves in a mysterious way*
> *His wonders to perform;*
> *He plants His footsteps in the sea*
> *And rides upon the storm."*

Is God inactive? No! God gives the prophet an answer in verses 5 to 11 of Chapter 1. Do you see what He says in verses 5 and 6?

"Behold ye among the heathen, and regard, and wonder marvellously: for I will work a work in your days, which ye will not believe, though it be told you. For, lo, I raise up the Chaldeans, that bitter and hasty nation, which shall march through the breadth of the land, to possess the dwellingplaces that are not theirs."

God *was* still on the throne. God *was* still in control. God controlled not only Israel, but also His enemies, the Chaldeans. Every nation on earth is under the hand of God.

What does the chorus say?

> *"He's got the whole world in His hands."*

However, Habakkuk's prayers may have stirred up an even bigger problem, the issue of the Babylonians. It was one of those situations where Habakkuk could have said: *"I wish I'd never asked the question!"*

God was going to use the Babylonians as His instrument to chasten His people - and answer the prophet's prayer. But not in the way he expected!

Habakkuk was crying out: *"Lord, are You indifferent?"* and *"Are You inactive?"* God comes back and says: *"I'm working! I'm working!"* The Chaldeans were to be God's instrument of judgment on Judah - and God's answer to the prophet's prayer.

Was this the answer that Habakkuk was expecting? No! He was hoping that God would send a revival to His people. His prayer was: *"O LORD, revive Thy work in the midst of the years"* (Chapter 3:2). He wanted God to judge the evil leaders and establish righteousness in the land. Then, the nation would escape punishment and the people and the cities would be spared. The answer given by God, however, was that judgment was coming – and coming by the hands of the Chaldeans. Imagine praying for revival in our own land - and God answering our prayer by allowing our land to go into captivity!

God works mysteriously! Mysteriously, and yet He works perfectly. God knows exactly what He is doing!

Habakkuk needed to claim Romans 8 verse 28, did he not? *"And we know that all things work together for good to them that love God, to them who are the called according to His purpose."*

Habakkuk did not have the book of Romans, but he did have the God of the book of Romans!

You see, even though we cannot understand His actions, God does all things perfectly. Do you believe that?

Can you say with the poet?

My Father's way may twist and turn
My heart may throb and ache,
But in my soul I'm glad to know,
He maketh no mistake.

My cherished plans may go astray,
My hopes may fade away,
But still I'll trust my Lord to lead,
For He doth know the way.

Tho' night be dark and it may seem
That day will never break,
I'll pin my faith, my all, in Him,
He maketh no mistake.

There's so much now I cannot see,
My eyesight's far too dim,
But come what may, I'll simply trust,
And leave it all to Him.

For by and by the mist will lift,
And plain it all He'll make,
Through all the way, tho' dark to me,
He made not one mistake.

A M Overton.

You see, we only see a few frames in the total picture of God's programme, but the Lord knows the whole story. He sees it all from beginning to end. We need to remember: *"The secret things belong unto the LORD our God"* (Deuteronomy 29:29). God is working all things together for our good – and He can employ the use of anyone or anything to accomplish His will, His work, His plan or His purpose.

In this case, God enlisted the unusual source of wickedness to judge wickedness. This raised the question:

(c) IS GOD INCONSISTENT?

Do you see what Habakkuk says in verses 12 and 13? The prophet is saying: *"Lord, I know we are in sin, but they are worse. We know the true God. They - the Babylonians - don't! How can they come down upon us?"*

"Thou art of purer eyes than to behold evil, and canst not look on iniquity: wherefore lookest Thou upon them that deal treacherously, and holdest Thy tongue when the wicked devoureth the man that is more righteous than he?" (verse 13).

"Can a holy God just sit and watch His own people being caught like fish or trampled like insects?" (See verse 14).

Habakkuk predicts the response of the Chaldeans: *"They will just say, 'Our gods have given us the victory. Jehovah is not the true God.'"*

Do you ever wrestle with the problems of life? Does it ever seem to you that the Lord does not care? Does it appear at times that He has forsaken His people?

Look at verse 12: *"Art Thou not from everlasting, O LORD my God, mine Holy One? We shall not die, O LORD"*. God would not permanently cast off the people with whom He had made an irrevocable covenant.

You see, no matter what happened, no matter how bad it might be, God would not belie, belittle, or betray His own character and nature.

Regardless of your plight, problem, or predicament, God has not, will not and cannot flee you, forsake you, forget you or fail you.

Habakkuk says: *"Lord, I don't understand this, but You are mightier than I am. All I can do is patiently wait for You to reveal Your truth to me"*.

And so we see:

CHAPTER 2: THE PROPHET IS WAITING

Instead of becoming an atheist or an agnostic, Habakkuk went to his watchtower to pray, meditate and wait on the Lord. Think of:

(a) THE PATIENCE THAT IS REQUIRED

"What's the trouble, Dr. Brooks?"

That was the question once put to Phillips Brooks, the famous American preacher. The inquirer had come upon him, pacing his study floor like a caged lion.

"The trouble? I am in a hurry and God isn't! That's the trouble!"

What does the poem say?

"Patience is a virtue, possess if you can
Seldom found in woman - and never in a man."

Yet Habakkuk is told: *"Though it tarry, wait for it"* (Chapter 2:3). The prophet learns what we must learn. He learns that God is never in a hurry. He learns that God *will* work, but in His own schedule, by His own system, and with His own standard.

Waiting on God is the crucible of the Christian life.

This is the area which is easy to preach, but hard to practise.

We are willing to wait as long as God hurries up!
We are willing to wait as long as God gives us the answer we have been waiting for - and He does it in the allotted time.

We expect instant answers to our prayers.
We expect instant salvation for our loved ones.
We expect instant healing of illness.
We expect in our personal lives instant guidance for every obstacle, every situation and every decision that we have to make.

Even when we ask God for patience, we say: *"God, give me patience - and do it now!"* We are people with little patience.

Habakkuk was, however, different. Although he sought answers to his perplexity concerning God's dealing with Judah, he *was* patient for he says: *"I will stand upon my watch, and set me upon the tower, and will watch to see what He will say unto me"*.

He is told: *"Wait for it"* (verse 3). Faith is nourished by the waiting. Waiting on God.

Like Habakkuk, have you some problem or some perplexity? What have you done with it? Have you brooded over it? Have you talked to others about it? Have you gossiped about it? Or, have you said: *"I am going to the watch tower. I am going to the heights. I am going to look to God and to God alone. I am waiting only on Him."*?

(b) THE PROPHECY THAT IS RECORDED

God said in effect: *"It is all right, Habakkuk. I have heard your prayer.*

I understand your perplexity. Here is my answer: the Chaldeans, whom I am going to raise up to punish Judah, will themselves be completely routed and destroyed".

So, this prophecy from verse 5 to verse 20 is all about the demise of the Babylonians. Five times here in Chapter 2, God says: *"Woe"*. The word means: *"calamity and destruction"* and God pronounces these judgments on the nation of Babylon.

There was the Woe against Selfishness – verse 6.
There was the Woe against Covetousness – verse 9.
There was the Woe against Ruthlessness – verse 12.
There was the Woe against Drunkenness – verse 15.
There was the Woe against Godlessness – verse 19.

Do you see what God says to Habakkuk in verse 2? *"Write the vision, and make it plain upon tables, that he may run that readeth it"* Do you realize that we would not be studying Habakkuk today had he not written down what God told him, what God showed him?

Habakkuk is to write down the revelation of God and post it plainly, publicly and permanently, so that generation after generation would read it, whether they walked by it, or ran by it.

Prophecy was being recorded. Babylon was going to be destroyed by the Medo-Persian Empire – and so it was on 13th October 539 B.C. The record is given in Daniel 5:25-31. However, do not stop there for this prophecy has a future aspect to it. Do you see verse 3? It says: *"It will surely come, it will not tarry"*. The writer to the Hebrews, inspired by the Holy Spirit, changed the *"it"* to *"He"* (Hebrews 10:37). Thus we read: *"For yet a little while, and He that shall come will come, and will not tarry"*. The *"He"* is the Lord Jesus. Do you know what is going to happen when Christ comes? He will destroy Satan's diabolical world system of which the Babylonians were a symbol in Habakkuk's day.

You see, during the Tribulation period, Babylon will again represent the evil religious and political systems, like the Babylon of old. The political system will destroy the religious system, the ecumenical church headed by the Pope of Rome, which in turn will be destroyed by Christ at His coming in glory.

What a promise is this! *"He that shall come will come, and will not tarry."*

To quote John Phillips:

"Prophecies concerning the second advent of Christ have slumbered in the womb of time for thousands of years. Today, they are stirring into remarkable life and end-time events will unfold swiftly when the 'appointed time' comes."

But how are we to live in the meantime?

(c) THE PRINCIPLE THAT IS REVEALED

God answered Habakkuk's perplexity, by setting forth an unchanging principle that runs throughout the Word of God. God shows the prophet that there are two types of people in the world. Look at verse 4 of Chapter 2: *"Behold, his soul which is lifted up is not upright in him: but the just shall live by his faith"*. The first half of the verse can be rendered like this *"Behold the proud - his soul is not upright in him"*. These are the first group of people - the sinners. These were the Chaldeans who were a type of all mankind. You see, the proud trusts in himself, but the just, the believing Jew, lives by his faith. The second type of person is the righteous person who has been justified.

The Hebrew language had no word for *"faith"*. The word translated *"faith"* in this passage is *"emunah"* which means *"firmness, faithfulness, fidelity"*. That does not mean that the Old Testament believers were not people of faith. Nor does it mean they were not justified by faith. We read, for example: Abraham *"believed in the LORD; and He counted it to him for righteousness"* (Genesis 15:6). When Abraham put his trust in God, God reckoned His own righteousness to him, counting him a justified man.

The word translated *"faith"* denotes faithfulness. Justifying faith will reveal itself in faithful living before the Lord. Here is how we are to live in a world that is filled with chaos, confusion and corruption: *"The just shall live by his faith"* This fourth verse is the hinge on which the rest of this book, as well as the rest of the Bible, swings. It is the secret to a successful Christian life. Indeed the New Testament writers quote this verse three times, bringing to us three different aspects of the Christian life.

In the book of Romans, the emphasis is on *"the just"* (Romans 1:17). It was this truth that brought about the conversion of Martin Luther and consequently became the watchword of the Reformation. Luther was trying to earn salvation by works. His testimony was this: *"I was a good monk, and I kept the rules of my order so strictly that I may say that if ever a monk got to Heaven by his monkery it was I"*. It was when Luther was appointed to lecture in theology and particularly on the book of Romans that the Gospel dawned in his own soul.

"The just shall live by feelings"? No!
"The just shall live by fastings"? No!
"The just shall live by fear"? No!

"The just shall live by faith."

Luther said: *"This text was to me the true gate of Paradise to my soul"*.

What about you? Have you ever exercised faith in Christ and been declared righteous before God?

In the book of Galatians, the emphasis is on: *"shall live"* (Galatians 3:11).

In the book of Hebrews, the emphasis is on: *"by faith"* (Hebrews 10:38). You see, many of the Hebrew Christians, who had been justified by faith in Christ, considered turning back to their old Jewish religion because of persecution. So the writer seeks to encourage them to persevere until the Lord came – and the promise is given that His Coming would not be long.

Are you facing persecution? Are you encountering severe trials?

Are you tempted to go back? To give up?

The Lord is saying: ***"Trust Me"***.

When the doctor's report is not good: *"The just shall live by his faith"*.
When the love of your life walks out: *"The just shall live by his faith"*.
When the money is gone and the food runs out: *"The just shall live by his faith"*.
When the threat of nuclear war is a daily reality and when the whole world falls apart: *"The just shall live by his faith"*.

CHAPTER 3: THE PROPHET IS WORSHIPPING

When we come to this third chapter, what a changed man Habakkuk is!

Instead of being *puzzled*, he is *praising*.
Instead of *wondering*, he is *worshipping*.
Instead of *sighing*, he is *singing*.

Do you notice that he worships the Lord:

(a) BY PRAYING

The chapter opens with the words: *"A prayer of Habakkuk the prophet upon Shigionoth"*. He is praying fervently, for that word: *"Shigionoth"* means: *"expressive of profound and strong emotions"*. A related word is found in the heading to Psalm 7. He has been moved deeply by the revelation that God gave him in Chapter 2 and now he carries his burden to God in prayer. He says: *"Lord, I see that You are working in this world"*. He says: *"Lord, continue that work. Keep it alive and finish it"*. Habakkuk knew that Judah's revival could only come after judgment and cleansing had taken place. He is really saying: *"Whatever I and my countrymen may have to suffer is of no concern, as long as the work is revived and kept alive"*.

Are *you* concerned about the condition of the church, the state of the world, your own spiritual life? Does that concern express itself in prayer? C. H. Spurgeon said: *"Whether we like it or not, asking is the rule of the kingdom"*.

(b) BY PONDERING

He reviews the history of Israel and the wonderful works of the Lord.

He sees His God as:

The God of *Majesty* in verses 3 to 5.
The God of *Might* in verses 6 to 12.
The God of *Mercy* in verses 13 to 15.

He knew that God had worked in the past and, therefore, he could trust Him to work in the present and in the future. Do you see what Habakkuk writes at this point? He says, for the third time in the book: *"Selah"* (verse 13). Do you know what it means? *"There, what do you think of that?"* It means to pause, to mediate and think on God.

Do you need to do that? Is your faith being tested? Is it being tried by the circumstances of life? Do you need to pause and get a glimpse of the greatness of your God? You see, the thing that lifted Habakkuk from the valley to the mountaintop was his understanding of the greatness of his God.

(c) BY PRAISING

Some scholars believe that Habakkuk was not only a prophet but also a member of the Levitical orchestra in the temple. Certainly, there is a reference as the book closes: *"To the chief singer on my stringed instruments"*.

Do you recall how Habakkuk began his book?
He began it, in verse 3 of Chapter 1, with the question: *"Why?"* The age-old problem of *Unchecked Perversity*.
Then he moved, in verse 13 of Chapter 1, to the question: *"Wherefore?"* The *"Wherefore"* of *Inactive Providence*! God sees but seemingly He does not do anything.

But, see that Habakkuk has now come from the *"Why?"* and the *"Wherefore?"* to the *"Yet"* of Chapter 3 verse 18: *"Yet I will rejoice in the LORD, I will joy in the God of my salvation"*.

Habakkuk does see a time when God withdraws His hand of blessing and extends His hand of cursing. But, in the <u>midst of despair</u>, he found a <u>multitude of delights</u>.

He cries:

"Although the fig tree shall not blossom, neither shall fruit be in the vines; the labour of the olive shall fail, and the fields shall yield no meat; the flock shall be cut off from the fold, and there shall be no herd in the stalls: Yet I will rejoice in the LORD."

Today, he would cry:

"Although the bank account is depleted, the fridge is empty and the heating is broken, yet I will rejoice in the Lord."

Do you know why?

Now comes the explanation: *"I will joy in the God of my salvation"*. It is the testimony of personal experience. God is *"the God of my salvation"*. Since Habakkuk has God, he has all. Everything he needs for time and everything he needs for eternity.

The story is told of a husband and his wife and their little boy. The wife became very ill and died as a result of her illness. The day she was buried, the husband and the young son returned home. As the day wore on, the darkness came and bedtime approached. The little boy asked if he could sleep with his father - and they went into the room to sleep together that night. After they had committed themselves to the Lord, they crawled into bed and turned out the lights. The little boy then called out to his father:

"Daddy, it is dark in here. I'm lonely and I miss Mummy. Daddy, you don't have to turn the lights on, but if you would turn over in the bed with your face toward me, I would feel so much better!"

That father said to his young son in the darkness of that room: *"Yes, I'll will do that"*. He turned towards his son.

Though that little boy could not see him, he knew that his father was looking at him. He was comforted and was able to sleep through the darkness of the night because he knew that his father's face was turned toward him.

There are times when the *"Whys?"* and the *"Wherefores?"* of many a providence will perplex us, but as long as we know that our Heavenly Father is looking on us, planning for us, ministering to us, we can make it through the darkest of nights.

Like the deer in verse 19, we will be able to walk securely, living victoriously over our circumstances.

Habakkuk has come full circle.

He began in the *valley*, asking: *"Why, Lord?"*
He was lifted by a *vision*: *"The just shall live by his faith"*.
Finally, he walked *victoriously*, living above his circumstances, rejoicing in the God of his salvation.

All his questions have been answered; all his doubts have been removed; all his fears have been banished.

His *problem* has been swallowed up by *praise*, because God was still on the throne.

Habakkuk looked beyond the impending judgment to the Coming Cyrus and then to the Conquering Christ. Verse 13 of this final chapter declares: *"Thou wentest forth for the salvation of Thy people, even for salvation with Thine anointed"*.

God is Ruling and Christ will Reign.

Will you then ***Rest in Him***? *"For the just shall live by his faith."*

In the darkness, trust Him!

CHAPTER 19

Zephaniah

Imagine someone saying to you: *"You are so judgmental!"* Would you consider it a compliment or an insult? Undoubtedly, an insult. The concept of judgment has fallen on hard times. Yet, the fact remains that God, the God of the Bible, is very judgmental. You see, while our culture insists that all issues should be viewed in shades of grey, in terms of morality, God insists on viewing the world and the human race in the very stark terms of black and white; evil and good; sin and righteousness; wrong and right; goats and sheep, and Hell and Heaven. As we come to the book of Zephaniah, we encounter a very *judgmental prophet* who speaks for a *judgmental God.*

There are no shades of grey in Zephaniah. There is no compromise. It is all judgment.

Some people would like to rewrite the Bible and leave out the references to God's judgment, but the Bible is God's truth to us. It is His revelation of Himself, so that we can know Him and respond to Him.

If we would know God, we must know Him in His many dimensions. You see, some people think that the Old Testament presents a God of judgment, while the New Testament presents a God of love. In fact, we find hundreds of references to the love and mercy of God in the Old Testament, while in the New Testament, we see many references to the justice and judgment of God.

Now, we see all these facets of the character of God revealed in this book of Zephaniah.

The name *"Zephaniah"* means: *"hidden of the Lord"* or *"he whom the Lord hides"*. For this reason, some scholars have said that he was born in the latter part of Manasseh's reign and that his parents gave him this name for his life being spared during the atrocities of King Manasseh. 2 Chronicles 33 verse 6 records that the King: *"Caused his children to pass through the fire in the valley of the son of Hinnom"*. They were evidently sacrificed to the god Molech, under the King's direction. Zephaniah was hidden by the Lord so that he could avoid the slaughter.

This man was no ordinary preacher. Verse 1 reveals that he was the great, great-grandson of *"Hizkiah"* and most translations translate *"Hizkiah"* as *"Hezekiah"*. King Hezekiah was one of Judah's most famous rulers. Zephaniah thus had royal blood in his veins, but, more importantly, he had the fire of God in his belly and he had the message of God upon his lips.

The background for Zephaniah's prophecy was a time of political, spiritual and moral upheaval. Think of the situation:

1. POLITICALLY

The nation of Assyria was losing its world power and Babylon instead was becoming the leading world empire. Zephaniah tells us that when he prophesied, it was: *"in the days of Josiah, the son of Amon, king of Judah"* (Chapter 1:1). So, Zephaniah exercised his ministry during the reign of godly King Josiah (640-609 B.C.).

It was during the reign of King Josiah that Judah was reformed and Zephaniah's preaching may have played a vital part in initiating Josiah's desire for a national reformation.

2. SPIRITUALLY

Hezekiah, referred to in verse 1, was a godly king of Judah. Hezekiah, however, was succeeded by Manasseh (696-642 B.C.). He reigned for 55 years and was the most wicked king in Judah's history. He revived Baal worship, made his son pass through the fire, observed times, used enchantments and dealt with mediums and wizards. Amon (642-640 B.C.), Manasseh's son, took the throne after his father's death and continued the idolatry of his father. He was assassinated by his servants only two years into his reign. Amon was succeeded by his son Josiah who was only eight years old when he began to reign over Judah. At the age of sixteen, he *"began to seek after the God of David his father"* (2 Chronicles 34:3), then, at the age of twenty, he started a great reformation in the land, destroying the idols and judging the false priests and prophets.

However, revival cannot be legislated. Outwardly, this revival was impressive: inwardly, it fell far short of what was needed. The people got rid of the idols in their homes but not those in their hearts! It was *legislation not dedication*. It was *reformation not regeneration*. The people went along with what they were required to do, but their hearts were not in it.

Now, it was during Josiah's reign that Zephaniah preached. Internal evidence seems to suggest that he prophesied just before Josiah's reforms which took place in 622 B.C.

3. PROPHETICALLY

As regards the *Prophets*: Zephaniah, Jeremiah and Habakkuk were contemporaries and they have been called the *"eleventh hour prophets to Judah"*.

As regards the *Prophecy*: this book is all about *"the day of the Lord"*. Some people confuse *"the day of the Lord"* with *"the Lord's day"*. Christians often call Sunday: *"the Lord's day"* because Sunday, the day the Lord Jesus rose from the dead, is when believers gather together for worship and to celebrate His death and resurrection. But, what the Bible calls *"the day of the Lord"* is something else altogether, like the difference between a horse chestnut and a chestnut horse.

This subject - *"the day of the Lord"* - is found time and again in the Old Testament. It is mentioned by name at least eighteen times in the Old Testament - Isaiah 2:12; Isaiah 13:6,9; Jeremiah 46:10;

Ezekiel 13:5; Ezekiel 30:3; Joel 1:15; Joel 2:1, 11, 31; Joel 3:14; Amos 5:18, 20; Obadiah 15; Zephaniah 1:7, 14; Zechariah 14:1 and Malachi 4:5 - and three times in the New Testament - 1 Thessalonians 5:2; 2 Thessalonians 2:2 and 2 Peter 3:10.

The phrase: *"the day of the Lord"* has a twofold meaning. Presently, it refers to God's judgments on Judah and Jerusalem. In this book, the *"day of the Lord"* would be the Babylonian invasion and the final ruin of the city and Temple. Prophetically, it refers to that future day of judgment when God will pour out His wrath upon the whole world as described in Revelation 6 to 19. Another term for this period is: *"the time of Jacob's trouble"* (Jeremiah 30:7), *"the tribulation"* that is so vividly described in Revelation 6 to 19. So, *"the day of the Lord"* has an immediate fulfilment and an ultimate fulfilment. Immediately, it refers to God's judgments on Judah. Ultimately, it is that time when God will send tribulation to the world, judge the nations, save His people Israel and then establish His righteous kingdom.

When we read carefully this book, we soon see that what Zephaniah has to say falls into three parts:

In the *first part,* the prophet seems to be looking inward.
In the *second part,* he is looking outward.
In the *last part,* he is looking forward.

(1) THE PROPHET IS LOOKING INWARD: Chapter 1 verse 2 to Chapter 2 verse 3

Sidlow Baxter writes:

"A glance through these verses will show us at once that everything here refers to the judgment that is coming on Judah."

Thus, we read:

"I will also stretch out Mine hand upon Judah, and upon all the inhabitants of Jerusalem" (Chapter 1:4).

"It shall come to pass at that time, that I will search Jerusalem with candles, and punish the men that are settled on their lees" (Chapter 1:12).

Notice the word "because" in verse 17. *"I will bring distress upon men, that they shall walk like blind men, because they have sinned against the LORD."*

Why is all the terrible calamity described in the previous verses coming on Judah? *"Because they have sinned against the LORD."*

So, the prophet announces that judgment is coming and nothing will escape.

"The day of the Lord" is:

(a) DESERVED

Judah had felt the blessing of God's *"mighty hand and ... outstretched arm"* (Deuteronomy 26:8) when He delivered them from the Egyptians. But now God's privileged people, because of their wickedness would be judged by His same hand. Jeremiah 21 verse 5 records the words of God: *"I Myself will fight against you with an outstretched hand and with a strong arm"*.

Do you notice that the prophet mentions five types of wickedness for which Judah would be judged?

1. There was Immorality

Zephaniah mentions *"the remnant of Baal"* in verse 4 - and Baal worship was licentious in the extreme. The name *"Baal"* means *"master or lord"* and is often used synonymously with idolatry. The name *"Chemarims"*, also found in the fourth verse, refers to foreign priests brought into Judah to conduct Baal worship. The religion of Baal was extremely sensual. Open immorality was, according to 1 Kings 14 verse 23, practised *"on every high hill"* and *"under every green tree"*.

2. There was Astrology

Verse 5 refers to: *"Them that worship the host of heaven upon the housetops"*. You see, they erected family altars on the flat roofs of their houses and burned incense in the morning and evening to the sun, moon and stars. These practices are described in Jeremiah 19 verse 13 and again in Jeremiah 32 verse 29.

Many today who are involved in astrology deny that they *worship* the stars, but many practise horoscope readings and lead their day according to those predictions. Opinion polls have established that the stars influence many lives. Even some Christians consult their daily or weekly horoscopes!

3. There was Insincerity

Zephaniah continues, by referring to: *"Them that worship and that swear by the LORD, and that swear by Malcham"* (verse 5). The name *"Malcham"* is the same as Molech (Leviticus 18:21) and Milcom (1 Kings 11:5), the national god of the Ammonites.

What these Judeans were guilty of was this - *syncretistic worship*. They were hypocrites and compromisers. They wanted a foot in both camps - and the Lord promised to cut them off!

Is it possible that *you* claim to be a believer but you are involved in an organization that embraces ancient religious systems, condemned in the Bible? If so, God has a word for you: *"Get out, keep out and stay out!"* Remember the words of the Apostle: *"Be ye not unequally yoked together with unbelievers"* (2 Corinthians 6:14).

4. There was Apostasy

Look at what the prophet says in verse 6: *"Them that are turned back from the LORD"*. There is a term to describe such people – *"apostasy"*. The word means *"a falling away"*, a deliberate and total abandonment of the faith previously professed but not possessed.

This was not just an issue for Zephaniah's day. It is an issue in our own day. Apparently, apostate teachings are finding fertile ground in which to germinate in some churches and Bible colleges today. One particular survey of ministers in training in the U.S.A. discovered that 56% rejected the virgin birth; 71% rejected life after death; 54% rejected the bodily resurrection of the Lord Jesus and 98% rejected Christ's return to earth.

Do you see now why judgment was coming on Judah? Immorality, astrology, insincerity and apostasy – and then a fifth sin:

5. There was Infidelity

There were *"those that have not sought the LORD, nor enquired for Him"* (verse 6). The same could be said of many Israelis today! According to the Israeli preacher David Levy, 45% of Jews living in Israel are secular Jews who do not practise their religion. These unbelievers have no interest in God whatsoever.

Do you know something? Within 50 years of Zephaniah's prediction, judgment fell on Judah. Its judgment was total. Its captivity was complete. Nothing went untouched when the day of the Lord came.

Zephaniah sets out the basis on which the day of the Lord was deserved. The day is also:

(b) DECLARED

In verses 7 to 13 of Chapter 1, Zephaniah declares the coming judgment. He says: *"Hold thy peace at the presence of the Lord GOD: for the day of the LORD is at hand"* (verse 7).

Do you notice that the judgment is described, in verses 7 and 8, as a sacrifice to which the Lord had already invited His guests? Judah was to be the sacrifice! The hated Babylonians were the guests. They would slaughter the nation and devour it like an animal sacrificed in the Temple.

Zephaniah then mentions seven groups of people who were going to suffer the judgment of God.

They are:

The princes - verse 8
The king's posterity – verse 8
The plunderers – verse 9
The people in general – verse 10
The polluted merchants – verse 11
The passionless people – verse 12
The property of the wealthy – verse 13.

Do you see what verse 13 says? *"They shall build houses, but not inhabit them; and they shall plant vineyards, but not drink the wine thereof."* The Lord was not going to allow them to enjoy the houses that they had obtained through ill-gotten gain. In Amos 5 verse 11, the same warning is given.

Do you recall the admonition that Paul gives, so relevant to all of us who live in this materialistic age? *"But they that will be rich fall into temptation and a snare, and into many foolish and hurtful lusts, which drown men in destruction and perdition. For the love of money is the root of all evil"* (1 Timothy 6:9-10).

There is nothing wrong with owning things - the problem comes when things begin to own us!

So, you can see that this *"day of the Lord"* is *deserved* and *declared* and then this *"day of the Lord"* is:

(c) DESCRIBED

Verse 14 begins: *"The great day of the LORD is near, it is near, and hasteth greatly"*. The word *"near"* is emphatic, stressing how quickly it will come. The coming invasion of the dreaded Babylonians was rapidly approaching.

To describe *"the day of the Lord"*, Zephaniah piled up words and phrases expressing doom and gloom and set them out in a series of five couplets. Do you see them in verses 15 and 16?

"A day of wrath."

"A day of trouble and distress."
"A day of wasteness and desolation."
"A day of darkness and gloominess."
"A day of clouds and thick darkness."
"A day of the trumpet and alarm."

You can hear the cries of the captives and the shouts of the warriors. You can see the victims' blood poured out like cheap dust and *"their flesh like dung"* (verse 17).

What a scene of destruction and carnage! All because the nation refused to submit to the word of the Lord!

This is but an illustration of what will happen in the end times when God's judgment falls on a wicked world, only that final *"day of the Lord"* will be far more terrible.

Many years ago, a gentleman bought an expensive barometer in the city of New York. That evening, he brought it home, unpacked it and hung it on his wall. The needle of the barometer was pointing towards: *"hurricane"*. So he took off the wall, shook it, put it back, but still the needle pointed towards: *"hurricane"*.

Again, he took it down, shook it, put it back up, but still the needle remained unchanged. That evening, he decided to write a nasty letter to the store where he had purchased the barometer. In the letter, he pointed out that the barometer was faulty, for its needle was always pointing to: *"hurricane"*. The next morning, on his way to work, he posted the letter.

That evening when he came home from his work the barometer was gone ... but so too was his house. The hurricane had come!

There is coming a tempest upon this world, the like of which this world has never seen.

It was not escapism but a sound knowledge of Scripture which prompted Horatius Bonar to sing:

"I see the fair moon veil her lustre,
I see the sackcloth of the sun,
The shrouding of each starry cluster,
The threefold woe of earth begun.

I see the last dark bloody sunset,
I see the dread Avenger's form,
I see the Armageddon onset,
But I shall be above the storm."

Every true believer will be above the storm. We are not going through! We are going up!

(d) DELAYED

The Lord offers them the possibility that even at this late stage judgment can be delayed and turned away by repentance. Is this not the message that all the prophets have? If the people will humble themselves, God will hear and forgive and show them mercy in return.

Do you notice that Zephaniah called upon a godly remnant to: *"Seek the LORD ... seek righteousness, seek meekness"* (Chapter 2:3)? If the faithful remnant continued in righteousness: *"it may be ye shall be hid in the day of the LORD's anger"* (verse 3). The Lord *did* spare a godly remnant that stayed true to Him throughout the seventy years of captivity. Warren Wiersbe calls them: *"a company of the concerned"* who became the nucleus of the restored nation when they returned to the promised land.

Will this not happen again during the Great Tribulation? God will protect a remnant of Jewish believers from the final *"day of the Lord"*. This protection is described in Revelation 7 verses 3 to 8 and again in Revelation 12 verse 13 to 17. Verse 6 of Revelation 12 says: *"And the woman fled into the wilderness, where she hath a place prepared of God"*. The Roman Catholic Church says that the woman is Mary! The Amillennialists say that the woman is the Church! Not so! The woman is Israel! Many Bible scholars believe that the faithful Jews of the last days will flee to the city of Petra, south of the Dead Sea. One thing is sure, God will prepare a special place where this Jewish remnant will be cared for and protected. Do you recall what Zephaniah's name means? *"He whom the Lord hides"* - a promise that not all believers will be exterminated by the Antichrist's *"Gestapo"*.

Thus, in this opening section, the prophet is looking inward to the judgment that is coming on Judah.

(2) THE PROPHET IS LOOKING OUTWARD: Chapter 2 verse 4 to Chapter 3 verse 8

Zephaniah looks away from Judah and Jerusalem to the surrounding nations. In this section, he speaks about:

(a) THE CONQUERORS OF JUDAH

The prophet names the various Gentile nations around Judah and announces that God will also judge *them* for their sins. Though they were never given God's Law as were the Jews – *"He sheweth His word unto Jacob, His statutes and His judgments unto Israel. He hath not dealt so with any nation: and as for His judgments, they have not known them"* (Psalm 147:19-20) - the Gentiles were still responsible before God. God had revealed Himself to them in creation and conscience. Romans 1 and 2 make this clear. In addition, these nations had not always treated the Jews kindly and now the time had arrived for the Lord to judge them.

It is interesting that these nations correspond to the four points of the compass – and remember that Zephaniah's vision extends to the end times. As in the past, so in the present, Israel is surrounded by anti-Semitic nations who are seeking her destruction.

Who are they?

1. To the West: Philistia – Verses 4 to 7

Philistia had five major cities during Zephaniah's day, four of which are mentioned as being marked out for judgment - Gaza, Ashkelon, Ashdod and Ekron.

All of this had an initial fulfilment in the time of Nebuchadnezzar, but it will be re-enacted in the end times.

2. To the East: Moab and Ammon – Verses 8 to 11

Both these nations were the descendants of backslidden Lot. The sad story of their origin is recorded in the last few verses of Genesis 19. As nations, they had mistreated God's people and had proudly *"magnified themselves"* (verse 8). Therefore, God would humble them. Their lands would be ruined. Their idols would prove powerless. When the end times arrive, Jordan will again have become an active foe of Israel - and all Zephaniah's predictions will have their final fulfilment.

3. To the South: The Ethiopians – Verse 12

It seems that Ethiopia was included in this prophecy, because they were allied to Egypt. Egypt was a perpetual foe of Israel - and Egypt received judgment at the hands of Nebuchadnezzar. We know from Ezekiel 38 and 39 that Ethiopia will be an ally of Russia when Russia invades Israel.

4. To the North: Assyria - Verses 13 to 15

Assyria dominated the ancient world from 883 to 612 B.C., but Zephaniah prophesied that the Lord would *"destroy Assyria; and .... make Nineveh a desolation, and dry like a wilderness"* (verse 13). This took place in 612 B.C. Today, Nineveh is a tourist attraction and the only things she has to show are her ruins!

Now, since the initial predictions about the destruction of these nations have come true, is it not reasonable to assume that the final predictions about the destruction of these same nations will also come to pass? God's promise to Abraham, in the opening verses of Genesis 12, still stands. Those who bless Israel, God will bless. Those who curse Israel, God will curse. The nations that have sinned against God by mistreating the Jews can expect the Lord to judge them.

So Zephaniah speaks about the conquerors of Judah, but then he speaks about:

(b) THE CAPITAL OF JUDAH – Chapter 3 verses 1 to 7

If God judges the sins of the heathen, how much more will He judge the sins of Judah, the *"holy nation"* (Exodus 19:6) of God? Look how Chapter 3 commences: *"Woe to her that is filthy and polluted, to the oppressing city!"* Jerusalem's troubles are the result of her people's rejection of God's Word and their departure from the Lord.

Here were a people who could see God's judgment day after day, but they did not take it to heart. They saw God punish other nations, but they said: *"It will never happen here!"* Well, it did happen! In 606 B.C., the Babylonians came and destroyed the nation, the city and the Temple.

Says Proverbs 14 verse 34: *"Sin is a reproach to any people"*, but that is especially the case when it is committed by the people of God.

What happens to a nation that was founded on Biblical principles when it abandons the gold standard of the Word of God?

Well, look at the United Kingdom. Look at the United States. God's Word has been rejected and the warning of coming judgment has been despised. *"Woe!"* is the warning that comes from God.

Notice, however, that Zephaniah does not end his prophecy with *gloom,* but rather with *gladness. "The day of the Lord"* extends beyond the judgment of the Great Tribulation and the Lord's return and includes the entire Messianic Kingdom. You see, Zephaniah reminds us that Israel's greatest days are yet to come.

The prophet is not just looking inward and looking outward, in the final section:

(3) __THE PROPHET IS LOOKING FORWARD – Verses 8 to 20__

God will one day re-gather His people. He will punish the Gentile nations. He will restore Israel and Judah to their land. Verse 8 is certainly a prediction of the Battle of Armageddon, when all nations shall gather against Jerusalem in the last days. *"My determination is to gather the nations, that I may assemble the kingdoms, to pour upon them Mine indignation, even all My fierce anger: for all the earth shall be devoured with the fire of My jealousy"*.

The Lord Jesus will return and judge these nations, and then establish His kingdom. You see, the prophet is looking forward to:

(a) ISRAEL'S RESTORATION

He saw the exiled Hebrew people coming from *"beyond the rivers of Ethiopia"* (verse 10) - the upper Nile region of southern Egypt, Sudan and northern Ethiopia. The Jews of our day have already trekked from there to the re-born state of Israel.

Notice also that Israel's final restoration will be a time of blessing for the Gentiles, who will be cleansed and able to praise and worship the Lord aright. *"For then will I turn to the people a pure language, that they may all call upon the name of the LORD, to serve Him with one consent"* (verse 9).

(b) ISRAEL'S REPENTANCE

Verse 11 declares: *"In that day shalt thou not be ashamed for all thy doings, wherein thou hast transgressed against Me"*. When the Jews see Christ, they will mourn over their transgressions. Says Zechariah 12 verse 10: *"And they shall look upon Me whom they have pierced, and they shall mourn for Him, as one mourneth for his only son, and shall be in bitterness for Him, as one that is in bitterness for his firstborn"*. It will be a time of deep repentance and confession that will lead to salvation. The pride of race, religion, and ritual so characteristic of the Jews down through the centuries will be a thing of the past.

J.C. Hoover was a missionary to the Jews in Denver, Colorado. One day, he was travelling in a car with a Jewish Rabbi. As they drove up to the synagogue, the Rabbi said to his friend: *"Mr. Hoover, you Gentile Christians are looking for the second coming of your Saviour, Jesus Christ, and we Jews are looking for the first coming of our Messiah. Who knows but He might be the same person!"*

The Rabbi then paused for a moment and then said: *"Mr. Hoover, how do you think we will recognise our Messiah?"*

Quietly and reverently, the missionary read those words of the prophet: *"And they shall look upon Me whom they have pierced".*

The Rabbi was silent as he got out of the car and slowly walked into the synagogue.

The day is coming, when Israel, although blind at present, will recognize the Lord Jesus as the Messiah, and He who was crucified by them will then be received by them.

So the prophet is looking forward to Israel's restoration and repentance, and also to:

(c) ISRAEL'S REJOICING

"Sing, O daughter of Zion: shout, O Israel; be glad and rejoice with all the heart, O daughter of Jerusalem" (verse 14).

Why will Israel rejoice?

Israel will rejoice because of Christ's Return: for *"the LORD hath taken away thy judgments"* (verse 15). The charges against the nation will be forgiven.

Israel will rejoice because the Lord has removed her foes: *"He hath cast out thine enemy"* (verse 15).

Israel will rejoice because: *"the LORD is in the midst of thee"* (verse 15).

Israel will rejoice because the nation will: *"not see evil any more"* (verse 15). *"In that day it shall be said to Jerusalem, Fear thou not"* (verse 16).

What joy lies ahead for the nation of Israel! Down through the long centuries, they have been hounded and hunted from country after country and in country after country. They have known no rest or safety. At times they have prospered in the land of their exile, but sooner or later anti-Semitism has always reared its head and the tale of their woes has begun again.

But, Zephaniah saw a day when all that will be over. He saw Israel as a merry people, rejoicing, singing, and shouting with joy.

God is with them. Even more, He holds them to His heart, like a loving mother holds a baby. He even sings to them. Look at verse 17: *"The LORD thy God in the midst of thee is mighty; He will save, He will rejoice over thee with joy; He will rest in His love, He will joy over thee with singing"*.

Do you know that our God is a *singing God*? God the Father sings here to the Jewish remnant entering the kingdom. God the Son sang at the close of the Passover Feast in the Upper Room (Matthew 26:30). Hebrews 2 verse 12, quoting Psalm 22 verse 22, says that He will sing again: *"I will declare Thy name unto My brethren, in the midst of the church will I sing praise unto Thee"*. God the Holy Spirit sings today through the hearts and lips of Christians who praise God in the Spirit (Ephesians 5:18-21). Is this fruit of the Spirit - joy - evident in *your* life?

(d) ISRAEL'S REDEEMER

"The LORD thy God in the midst of thee is mighty; He will save" (verse 17).

For centuries, the Jewish people have taken hope and comfort in the promise that Messiah will one day come and bring world peace; secure the land of Israel for them, and rebuild the Temple on its historic site in Jerusalem. Well, Zephaniah assured them that Christ will one day be visibly present in His glorious person to fulfill all the promises He has made to the nation. That has not yet happened, but Zephaniah assures us it most certainly will.

It is interesting that the book of Zephaniah begins with a King and ends with a King. The prophet referred to a *Past King,* his relative Hezekiah, but now he looks forward to a *Promised King,* the Lord Jesus.

Are you looking forward to the coming reign of Jesus Christ? Do you pray with anticipation for it? Do you live in the light of it?

At the service of the Coronation of our Queen, a close friend of the Royal Family sat close to the Queen Mother. She later told how that during the Coronation service, when it came to the moment when that stripling of a girl was crowned Queen, she turned and looked at the face of the Queen Mother. She saw the tears streaming down her cheeks. The crown was placed upon the one who had the right to wear it, the only one!

Have *you* crowned the Lord Jesus? Have you crowned Him *"Lord of all"*? Have you placed the crown upon His head? If so, has the action of a moment become the attitude of a lifetime?

The hymnwriter penned these powerful words:

"I can hear the chariots rumble, I can see the marching throng,
And the flurry of God's trumpets spells the end of sin and wrong,
Regal robes are now unfolding, Heaven's grandstand's all in place,
Heaven's choir is now assembled, Start to sing 'Amazing Grace'.

O, the King is coming, the King is coming,
I just heard the trumpet sounding,
And now His face I see,
O, the King is coming, the King is coming
Praise God, He's coming for me!"

CHAPTER 20

Haggai

It was the Lord Jesus who said:

"Father ... I have glorified Thee on the earth: I have finished the work which Thou gavest Me to do" (John 17:1, 4).

The Lord Jesus was characterised by commitment – and those who follow Him should also be characterised by commitment.

Jonathan Edwards said:

"I go to preach with two propositions. First, every person ought to give his life to Christ. Second, whether or not anyone else gives Him his life, I will give Him mine."

That is commitment.

Today, however, *"commitment"* is a bad word, especially in the local church.

A lack of commitment was an issue in Haggai's day. The mood of God's people at this time was one of apathy and indifference. Can you imagine the scene at this building site in Jerusalem? Fifteen years have passed since any work has been done. The weeds and nettles have grown over the foundation of the Temple and the general impression is one of desolation and neglect. Then God stirred His people through the preaching of Haggai and Zechariah and they got about the task of rebuilding the Temple.

There are six books in the Old Testament which have to do with the period of time covering the Captivity of the Jews in Babylon and their return to Israel, the land of promise. Three of these books are in the <u>*historical section*</u> of your Bible: Ezra, Nehemiah and Esther. The other three books are in the <u>*prophetical section*</u> of your Bible: Haggai, Zechariah and Malachi.

As we come to Haggai, we should think about:

1. THE PERSON

Haggai's name means *"festal one"* and it has been suggested that Haggai was born on a feast day. In Chapter 2 verse 3, he poses a question: *"Who is left among you that saw this house in her first glory?"* Some feel that Haggai himself had seen the glory of Solomon's Temple before it was destroyed. This would make him over 70 years of age when writing this prophecy. Haggai only spoke for three or four months and then his ministry was finished. His book is the second shortest book in the Old Testament, with only Obadiah being shorter.

2. THE PLACE

The prophecy begins: *"In the second year of Darius the king, in the sixth month, in the first day of the month, came the word of the LORD by Haggai the prophet unto Zerubbabel"*.

<u>*The Time was right*</u>: The sixth month, the first day of the month, in the second year of Darius - so that would be 520 B.C.

"Came the word of the LORD by Haggai the prophet" – you can see <u>*the Man was right.*</u>

"Unto Zerubbabel ... governor of Judah" - so <u>*the Place was right*</u>.

3. THE PERIOD

The last three books of the Old Testament take us into the post-exilic period.

Do you recall that in 538 B.C. Cyrus issued a decree that the Jews could return to their homeland. The early section of Ezra records that about 50,000 responded under the civil leadership of Zerubbabel and the spiritual guidance of Joshua the high priest. In 535 B.C. they began to rebuild the Temple, but opposition from without and discouragement from within caused the work to cease. For 15 years (535 B.C to 520 B.C.), not another brick was added to the building.

Then Haggai and his contemporary Zechariah were commissioned by the Lord to stir up the people to not only rebuild the Temple but also to reorder their spiritual priorities. This is recorded in Ezra 5 and 6. As a result, the Temple was completed four years later in 516 B.C.

This is:

4. THE PURPOSE

The aim of the book is to encourage the people of God to get back to the rebuilding of the Temple. It is to stimulate God's people to get back to the work of the Lord once again.

R.G. Lee, the famous American preacher, says:

"Haggai's message is full of stirring words for us today. If, as a church, we thought more of the Lord's work than of our comfort, there would be no lack of means to carry the work forward."

5. THE PATTERN

The book falls into four parts with the dates of each prophecy given by Haggai firmly fixed. Verse 1 of Chapter 1, as has been said, is set in the second year of Darius. This was 520 B.C. Haggai then delivers four prophecies within four months of each other.

1. The First Message was preached on 29th August 520 B.C. (Chapter 1:1).
2. The Second Message was preached on 17th October 520 B.C. (Chapter 2:1).

3. The Third Message was preached on 18th December 520 B.C. (Chapter 2:10).
4. The Fourth Message was preached on 18th December 520 B.C. (Chapter 2:20).

Thus we have *four messages* preached within a period of *four months* and those messages were directed to Zerubbabel, the governor of Judah, to Joshua the high priest, and to the people of Judah.

Here is Haggai with the shortest ministry of any prophet - only four months. But, it resulted in some of the greatest work. It was the Lord's work that was being done.

Let us look at each of these four messages:

The First Message was Directed to the Hands of the People: Chapter 1

We could summarize this first message with the word: *Practical.*

Look at verses 5, 7 and 8:

"Now therefore thus saith the LORD of hosts; Consider your ways."

"Thus saith the LORD of hosts; Consider your ways. Go up to the mountain, and bring wood, and build the house; and I will take pleasure in it, and I will be glorified, saith the LORD."

One of the key words of the prophecy is the word: *"Consider"*.

"And now, I pray you, consider from this day and upward, from before a stone was laid upon a stone in the temple of the LORD" (Chapter 2:15).

"Consider now from this day and upward, from the four and twentieth day of the ninth month, even from the day that the foundation of the LORD's temple was laid, consider it" (Chapter 2:18).

These people were to give careful thought to their ways and take a good hard look at their lifestyle.

Notice that the chapter beings with:

(a) THE REBUKE TO THE PEOPLE

God begins to speak in verse 2. *"Thus speaketh the LORD of hosts, saying, This people say, The time is not come, the time that the LORD's house should be built."*

It is interesting that God did not refer to them as *"His people"* but as *"this people"*. If anyone during those fifteen or so years had posed the question: *"Do you not think we ought to do something about starting work on God's house again?"*, the people would have said: *"Oh, the time is not right!"* Then they would have come up with all sorts of excuses as to why the time was not right.

It was Billy Sunday who called an excuse: *"the skin of a reason stuffed with a lie"* and Benjamin Franklin wrote: *"I never knew a man who was good at making excuses who was good at anything else"*.

A spirit of apathy and indolence had crept over the people from which they could not seem to rouse themselves. Thus the work of God remained at a standstill.

This was not something unique to the Jews of that time. For most of my ministry, I have heard various believers say: *"It is not a good time to be someone or to do something for God!"* An apathetic spirit that says: *"I cannot be bothered!"* pervades the local church today.

Could it be that apathy has crept into *your* life? Perhaps you no longer attend public worship as regularly as once you did. One growing sign of apathy is the gradual decline of the Sunday evening service. We are trying to get the unsaved out but we cannot seem to arouse the Lord's people. The Lord's Day has become the Lord's half-day. So many Christians are *"SMO"* - *"Sunday Morning Only"*. Maybe, *you* are not seen very often at the prayer meeting or the Bible Class. Could it be that *you* are no longer consistent in your personal prayer time and the reading of the Word?

"The time is not just right, the economy is bad, the family are demanding, I am just so tired."

Are *you* full of such excuses?

Some Christians not only talk like this in relation to *worship* but also in relation to *work*. When you talk about evangelism, there are some who say: *"It's not the right time to do that"* or *"It's hard to win people for the Lord"* or *"We're living in the last days"* or *"Wait till there is more unity in the assembly"*.

Is this not the way we talk? No hurry about the Lord's work and no urgency about prayer and plenty of time later for soul-winning! Is that *your* attitude?

This was the attitude of gruff old Dr. Ryland of Northampton when he rebuked the young William Carey. Carey, exercised about taking the Gospel to other lands, had referred to the *"Great Commission"* of Matthew 28. Carey said: *"Expect great things from God: attempt great things for God"*.

Said Ryland: *"Young man, sit down; when God is pleased to convert the heathen world, He will do it without your help or mine"*.

What a paralyzing idea that is!

The cults put us to shame with their enthusiasm and zeal and we stand among the ruins of the Temple and say: *"The time is not come"*.

Yet the Lord Jesus Himself declares: *"Say not ye, There are yet four months, and then cometh harvest? Behold, I say unto you, Lift up your eyes, and look on the fields; for they are white already to harvest"* (John 4:35).

Thus there is this rebuke to the people. Then, we read about:

(b) THE RESOURCES AMONG THE PEOPLE

Says the Lord in verse 6: *"Ye have sown much ... ; ye eat ... "*. Where had all their obsession with getting and having brought them? Nowhere! Their agriculture had failed: *"Sown much, and bring in little"*. The economy of the land was not sufficient to meet the people's needs: *"Ye eat, but ye have not enough; ye drink, but ye are not filled with drink; ye clothe you, but there is none warm"*. Inflation was spiralling out of control: *"He that earneth wages earneth wages to put it into a bag with holes"* (verse 6). To quote Joyce Baldwin: *"Their money disappeared like flour through a sieve!"* It reminds us of the bumper sticker that says: *"My take home pay will not take me home!"*

Now why was this the case? What was the explanation?

Look at verses 9 and 10:

"Ye looked for much, and, lo, it came to little; and when ye brought it home, I did blow upon it. Why? saith the LORD of hosts. Because of Mine house that is waste, and ye run every man unto his own house. Therefore the heaven over you is stayed from dew, and the earth is stayed from her fruit."

God says:

"When you stopped building, I stopped blessing. If you want My blessings, then get back to building My house. Get your priorities right and everything will fall into place. Make the main thing, the main thing."

In the words of the Saviour: *"But seek ye first the kingdom of God, and His righteousness; and all these things shall be added unto you"* (Matthew 6:33). What things? All that they needed!

It was as if the Lord was saying to them: *"You say that the time is not right to build My house. But, I notice that you give plenty of time to building and refurbishing your own houses with decorative panelling and other extras"*. Not that it was wrong in any sense for the people to furnish their homes tastefully and to provide themselves with certain comforts. The point Haggai was making was that these things had taken over their lives and had become more important to them than the things of God.

Their sense of priorities had become distorted and, as a result, the Lord had withheld His blessing.

Someone has defined *"worldliness"* as: *"that state in which our thinking is governed by the mind and outlook of the world"*. Is that not what happened in Paul's day? Do you recall what he wrote to the church at Philippi? He described young Timothy like this: *"I have no man likeminded, who will naturally care for your state. For all seek their own (interests), not the things which are Jesus Christ's"* (Philippians 2:20-21). As Paul looked around him in Rome, believers generally were characterized by that self-seeking spirit that degrades the Lord Jesus to second place. Living for time instead of eternity; living for self instead of for God.

Can that not so easily happen to us? Our homes and families, our jobs and careers, our interests and pleasures, can all displace and jeopardize the work of God in our lives to such an extent that the Lord Himself becomes marginalized. Is this what has happened to you? Has your life become so cluttered with other things that the Lord is now secondary? Have you no time available for reflection on the things of God? Has the Lord to compete with all these other things to get a foothold in your life?

The Lord is saying to you: *"Consider your ways"*. He is saying: *"Give very careful thought in reflecting on your priorities. Make the proper adjustments and follow the Lord's will"*.

It seems these people *did exactly that! "All the remnant of the people, obeyed the voice of the LORD their God, and the words of Haggai the prophet"* (verse 12).

You see, this was:

(c) THE RESPONSE OF THE PEOPLE

Verse 14 records: *"The LORD stirred up the spirit of Zerubbabel ... and the spirit of Joshua ... and the spirit of all the remnant of the people; and they came and did work in the house of the LORD of hosts, their God".*

This could not have been easy. For 15 years the Temple had been desolate. But on 21st September 520 B.C., just 23 days later, the work of God was resumed. Judah had responded to Haggai's message, but it took three weeks to plan the work and prepare the materials.

They responded *promptly*. In less than a month after Haggai had delivered his message, they had resumed the work.

Let me pose this challenge - When God's Word stirs you, do you obey promptly or are you merely a sermon taster, just a *"hearer of the Word"*? (James 1:22- 23).

They responded *properly*. Zerubbabel, the civic leader, and Joshua, the spiritual leader, take the initiative. You see, a people can only rise as high as the leadership is willing to take them. If the elders and the deacons are not in attendance at the Bible Study and Prayer Meeting, how can they expect the remainder of the flock to be there?

Do you see here the effect of God's Word? The work resumed.

How quickly situations can change when the Spirit of God is present. Is this not what we desperately need today? The Spirit of God to stir our spirit with an all-consuming zeal for the work of God and the Gospel of Christ?

We need to pray with Amy Carmichael:

> *"Give me the love that leads the way,*
> *The faith that nothing can dismay,*
> *The hope no disappointments tire,*
> *The passion that will burn like fire;*
> *Let me not sink to be a clod*
> *Make me Thy fuel, O Flame of God."*

The Second Message was Directed to the Hearts of the People: Chapter 2 verses 1 to 9

We could summarize this second message with the word: *Emotional.*

Emotions were running high. This second message came just 27 days after they had started building. Morale was declining because the older people were making comparisons with Solomon's Temple.

You see:

(a) THE PAST

In verse 3 of Chapter 2, the past is brought before us. There is a reference to: *"this house in her first glory"*.

When they laid the foundation some 15 years earlier, the older men had wept because they remembered the glory of Solomon's Temple (Ezra 3:12), and now some of the people were discouraged because the new Temple lacked splendour and glory. *As the walls went up, the people's spirits came down.* Zerubbabel's Temple was not as glorious as the Temple of King Solomon. The old men were saying: *"Call this is a Temple? You should have seen the Temple we had!"*

We are all familiar with the *"good old days"* syndrome, the tendency to look back to the past through rose-coloured spectacles.

Warren Wiersbe wrote:

"We can learn from the past, but we are not to live in the past."

A wee granddaughter was listening to her grandmother reading the great stories of the Bible. Looking up into her face, she said: *"Granny, wasn't God exciting then!"* Is that how you feel? Do you think God is no longer exciting? Do you believe that all His great deeds are in the past?

Too many believers look to the past, but what is God doing in your life today? Is your experience of Him richer than it was twenty years ago? It should be, for: *"Every day with Jesus"* should be: *"sweeter than the day before"*.

Haggai refers to the past. He also refers to:

(b) THE PRESENT

Someone has said that *"encouragement is oxygen to the soul"* and Haggai encouraged them to finish the project. The message he brought them was this: *"Be strong (take courage) ... and work: for I am with you, saith the LORD of hosts"* (verse 4).

Zerubbabel was told: *"Be strong"*.
Joshua was told: *"Be strong"*.
All the people were told: *"Be strong"*.
A threefold repetition: *"Be strong"*.
They were to get on and finish the work they had begun.

It is easy to begin anything, whether a building, a project or a particular calling, but to continue and finish it - that is the important thing.

Is this the message *you* require to hear? Is your morale low? Have you written out your resignation? Are you ready to give up? If so, ask yourself: *"Whom am I serving?"*

These people should have been encouraged because they had:

1. The Presence of God

"Be strong ... and work: for I am with you, saith the LORD of hosts: according to the word that I covenanted with you when ye came out of Egypt" (verses 4 and 5). God had covenanted to shepherd them during the forty years in the wilderness and to give them the land of Canaan.

Is this not the confidence that we have in the Lord's work? The

Lord is with you, as you teach the children, reach the lost, and visit the sick.

2. The Power of God

They had God's presence and they had God's power. *"My Spirit remaineth among you: fear ye not"* (verse 5). Apart from the power of the Holy Spirit, our labours are in vain. Says Paul to the Philippians: *"It is God which worketh in you both to will and to do of His good pleasure"* (Philippians 2:13). If we are too strong in ourselves, the Lord cannot use us. That is what ruined King Uzziah. *"He was marvellously helped, till he was strong"* (2 Chronicles 26:15).

As you step forward, seeking to build God's spiritual temple (1 Corinthians 3:17 and 6:19) out of the ruins of fallen humanity, be encouraged. The Lord is with you and the Lord is in you.

But, Haggai also focuses on:

(c) THE FUTURE

In verses 6 to 9, we read:

"For thus saith the LORD of hosts; Yet once, it is a little while, and I will shake the heavens, and the earth, and the sea, and the dry land; And I will shake all nations, and the desire of all nations shall come: and I will fill this house with glory, saith the LORD of hosts. The silver is Mine, and the gold is Mine, saith the LORD of hosts. The glory of this latter house shall be greater than of the former, saith the LORD of hosts: and in this place will I give peace, saith the LORD of hosts."

"I will shake … I will shake." Just when will this shaking take place? Well, surely this prophecy about shaking all nature is prophetical in scope. Does this not refer to the Messiah's Second Advent when God will *"shake the heavens and the earth"* (Haggai 2:21 – see also Joel 3:16, Matthew 24:29 and Revelation 16:18, 20) and will destroy Gentile world powers (Haggai 2:22 - see also Daniel 2:34-35, 44-45 and Hebrews 12:26-27). Violent shaking indeed!

A people in the care of a covenant-keeping God, who is able to shake all nature and all nations with equal ease, need not fear. The Lord says: *"I will shake all nations, and the desire of all nations shall come"* (verse 7). In both Jewish and Christian tradition, this phrase: *"the desire of all nations"* has been generally interpreted as a Messianic title of Christ. Whether people recognize it or not, He is the One for whom the human heart yearns. All creation groans and travails in longing for Him (Romans 8:19-22). He is the only One who could fulfil their desire for peace on the earth (verse 9).

In verses 7 and 9, *two glories* are mentioned. It appears that the *glory referred in verse 7* is the glory that Christ brought to the Temple in Jerusalem when He was taken there in Luke 2 verses 21 to 24. *The glory in verse 9* refers to the glory of the Millennial Temple that will function during Christ's reign on earth – see Isaiah 60 verses 1 to 5 and Ezekiel 40 to 48. This Temple will be built after the shaking of verse 6.

The Lord came in *grace* to the courts of Zerubbabel's Temple, but one day He will come in *government*. Ezekiel's Temple will be one of peace when the Lord Jesus reigns as King of kings and Lord of lords for one thousand years.

The Third Message was Directed to the Holiness of the People: Chapter 2 verses 10 to 19

We could summarize this third message with the word: *Spiritual.*

God not only demands that we serve Him, but also demands that our service be unspoilt by sin. Although the people had turned to the Lord on 21st September 520 B.C., the effects of God's past judgments were still being felt. He had smitten the land with: *"blasting and with mildew and with hail"* (verse 17). This past judgment had not produced national repentance for the Lord said: *"Yet ye turned not to Me"* (verse 17).

The people may have thought themselves holy because they were back in the Holy Land and the Holy City, offering sacrifices on the restored altar in Jerusalem, but, in fact, they were *defiled* because of their *disobedience*. They had expected God's blessing the very day they began the work on the Temple, but now it was December and things were still difficult.

Haggai explained why the Lord had not blessed them. They were still unclean. You see, as one Bible scholar has said:

(a) CLEAN DOES NOT MAKE DIRTY CLEAN

In verse 11, an instruction is given: *"Ask now the priests concerning the law"*. Do you see the first question? *"If one bear holy flesh in the skirt of his garment, and with his skirt do touch bread, or pottage, or wine, or oil, or any meat, shall it be holy?"* (verse 12). The *"holy flesh"* was that portion set aside to be sacrificed to the Lord. Often a priest carried the sacrifice in his robe, which meant, according to Leviticus 6 verse 27, that his garment became holy. So Haggai questioned the priests: *"If the holy flesh touched other food, was holiness transferred to them as well?" "The priests answered and said, No."* Holiness cannot be transferred to items of food. Clean does not make dirty, clean. A healthy person cannot pass on his good health to a sick person.

But:

(b) DIRTY DOES MAKE CLEAN DIRTY

Do you see the next question: *"If one that is unclean by a dead body touch any of these, shall it be unclean? And the priests answered and said, It shall be unclean"* (verse 13). The Law of Moses - Leviticus 22 verses 4 to 7 - taught that moral cleanness cannot be transmitted but moral uncleanness can. In other words, holiness is not catching but uncleanness is. You cannot give someone your holiness or health, but you can give someone your uncleanness and sickness.

Dirty people building a clean Temple made the new Temple dirty in God's sight.

No wonder the Lord said: *"So is this people, and so is this nation before Me"* (verse 14). Have we grasped the principle that God is not so much concerned about *what we do* for Him, but *whether we are clean* to do it? Do we realize that sin hinders the work of God? Do we recognize that sin robs us of the blessings of God?

It was the sin of the people that brought about the destruction of Jerusalem and the captivity of the nation.

It was sin that hindered the rebuilding of the Temple and the renewing of the nation.

Remember the words of Proverbs 14 and verse 34: *"Righteousness exalteth a nation: but sin is a reproach to any people"*.

Here is the challenge for us all: Are we serving the Lord with unclean hands and hearts? Are we living as if God winked at sin? Do we think that because we are working for the Lord that He will continue to bless us?

Note that once the nation had been cleansed, God promised to bless them. He gave them His Word: *"From this day will I bless you"* (verse 19).

The final message was preached the same day as the third message was preached and this final message was directed to the governor personally.

The Fourth Message was Directed to the Hopes of the People: Chapter 2 verses 20 to 23

We could summarize the fourth message with the word: *Prophetical*.

Haggai announced that Israel's enemies would be judged and the long-expected Messianic blessing would come to the nation. In other words, there would be:

(a) THE GREAT TRIBULATION

Perhaps Zerubbabel saw the great empires around him and feared for the tiny remnant of the Jews. Circumstances have a way of discouraging us as we seek to build the work of the Lord. But, God encouraged the governor's faith: *"I will shake the heavens and the earth"*. In other words: *"Do not be afraid of these kingdoms. I will overthrow them and destroy them"*.

Were the nations around Jerusalem larger and stronger? Rest assured that the Lord would care for His people Israel as He always had done in the past. The same God who enabled Moses to defeat Egypt and the same God who enabled Joshua to conquer Canaan would protect His people so that His purposes could be fulfilled through them.

Israel will endure until the last days and then the Lord will defeat her enemies and establish her in her kingdom. Notice also:

(b) THE GLORIOUS ELEVATION

Look at how the book ends. *"In that day ... will I take thee, O Zerubbabel, My servant ... and will make thee as a signet: for I have chosen thee"* (verse 23).

The word *"signet"* speaks of authority and honour. The signet was used as a person's signature. It was used to validate royal authority within the document sealed – see 1 Kings 21 verse 8. It was used as a guarantee to fulfil a future promise – see Genesis 38 verse 18. In Biblical times, it was worn on the right hand (Jeremiah 22:24) or around the neck. You see, God was saying: *"Zerubbabel, you are as a signet, a very precious jewel, to Me. I have chosen you. Do not give up"*.

Zerubbabel was of the royal line. He was the grandson of King Jehoiachin (also known as *"Jechonias"* in Matthew 1 verse 12 and *"Coniah"* in Jeremiah 22 verse 24). He was an ancestor of the Lord Jesus, his name being listed in the genealogy of Christ in Matthew 1 at verse 12. In fact, these words spoken to Zerubbabel find their ultimate fulfilment in His descendant, the Lord Jesus. God gave His royal signet ring, His seal of authority and placed it on the finger of Jesus Christ and He will, finally, rule all the nations of the world.

What a word of encouragement in a day of darkness! A word of encouragement that speaks not only to the people of Jerusalem as they build the Temple, but that speaks to us today, in our age of darkness, as the events of the world lead us closer and closer to the climax of history, *"the day of the Lord"*.

God wants *us* to know that *today* is the *time for building*. He says: *"Be strong ... and work, for I am with you, saith the LORD of hosts"* (Chapter 2:4). We are working on a *"Temple"* for God's glory, but it is not made of stone and cedar. The church body is the temple of the Holy Spirit.

Are you doing all you can to build the house of the Lord? Or, are you sitting among the ruins saying: *"The time is not come, the time that the LORD's house should be built"* (Chapter 1:2)? The obligations face us today. Souls are perishing today. Others need a helping hand today. How will you respond?

Will you continue to put self ahead of God?

Will you continue to look back instead of looking ahead?

Will you continue to cover your sin instead of confessing it?

Will you continue to live for time instead of eternity?

Grasp the wonderful promises in this book: *"I am with you"* (Chapter 1:13); *"Fear ye not"* (Chapter 2:5); *"From this day will I bless you"* (Chapter 2:19) and *"I have chosen you"* (Chapter 2:23).

Rise up and do the work of the Lord!

The words of the hymnwriter should challenge us:

Facing a task unfinished
That drives us to our knees,
A need that undiminished
Rebukes our slothful ease,
We, who rejoice to know Thee,
Renew before Thy throne
The solemn pledge we owe Thee,
To go and make Thee known.

Where other lords beside Thee
Hold their unhindered sway,
Where forces that defied Thee
Defy Thee still today,
With none to heed their crying
For life, and love, and light,
Unnumbered souls are dying
And pass into the night.

We bear the torch that flaming,
Fell from the hands of those
Who gave their lives proclaiming,
That Jesus died and rose,
Ours is the same commission,
The same glad message ours,
Fired by the same ambition,
To Thee we yield our powers.

O Father who sustained them,`
O Spirit who inspired,
Saviour, whose love constrained them,
To toil with zeal untired,
From cowardice defend us,
From lethargy awake!
Forth on Thine errands send us,
To labour for Thy sake.

CHAPTER 21

Zechariah

Some years ago, the city of Chicago was given an original statue by Pablo Picasso to adorn the plaza outside the City Hall. As the statue was being erected, it was heavily screened from the curious gaze of the passers-by. When it was finished, it stood there in the plaza, thickly veiled. The day came, however, when the Mayor unveiled the statue to the astonished gaze of the citizens of that city and of the wider world. There it stood in all its glory, the latest offering at the altar of art, Chicago's own gigantic Picasso.

Now, what the Mayor did for Chicago when he unveiled the statue, the book of Zechariah does for us.

This book has been called the *"book of the Revelation of the Old Testament"* or the *"Apocalypse of the Old Testament"*, meaning that it parallels the New Testament book of Revelation or *"the Apocalypse"*. You see, the Greek word which is translated: *"Revelation"* is: *"apokalupsis"* which literally means: *"an unveiling"*. Visions, symbols and prophecies of end times abound in Zechariah – and this book draws aside the veil. As such, it is very appropriate that this book appears almost at the end of the Old Testament.

George Robinson has called Zechariah: *"the most Messianic, the most truly apocalyptic and eschatological of all the writings of the Old Testament"*.

Consider, by way of introduction:

1. THE PERSON

Sometimes we read through names found in the opening verses

of a book without considering their significance, but Hebrew names often carry a weight of meaning. Zechariah is called the son of Berechiah, the son of Iddo. In the book of Ezra - Chapter 5 verse 1 and Chapter 6 verse 14 - he is called the son of Iddo. It seems that Zechariah's biological father died as a young man, and his grandfather reared him as his own son. Iddo was, according to Nehemiah 12 verse 4, one of the priests who returned from Babylon with Zerubbabel and Joshua. This means that, like Jeremiah and Ezekiel, Zechariah was also a priest. Indeed, from this time onwards, the priesthood takes the lead in the nation as to its government.

You see, the history of the Jews falls into three main periods.

First, from Moses to Samuel, we have Israel under the *Judges*.
Then, from Saul to Zedekiah, we have Israel under the *Kings*.
But now, from Joshua and the return of the "remnant" down to the destruction of Jerusalem in A.D. 70, we have Israel under the *Priests*.

The meaning of these three names is interesting:

"Zechariah" means: *"God remembers"*.
"Berechiah" means: *"God will bless"*.
"Iddo" means: *"Appointed time"*.

Putting all of these together, we have the message of the book in capsule:

"God will remember to bless His people in His appointed time."

So much for The Person, notice:

2. *THE PLACE*

Ezra 5 begins with these words: *"Then the prophets, Haggai the prophet, and Zechariah the son of Iddo, prophesied unto the Jews that were in Judah and Jerusalem in the name of the God of Israel, even unto them"*.

If the key word of the prophecy of Haggai is: *"From this day will I bless you"* (Haggai 2:19), then the keyword of the prophecy of Zechariah is found in Chapter 1 verses 14 to 16:

"So the angel that communed with me said unto me, Cry thou, saying, Thus saith the LORD of hosts; I am jealous for Jerusalem and for Zion with a great jealousy. And I am very sore displeased with the heathen that are at ease; for I was but a little displeased, and they helped forward the affliction. Therefore thus saith the LORD; I am returned to Jerusalem with mercies; My house shall be built in it, saith the LORD of hosts, and a line shall be stretched forth upon Jerusalem."

The Lord was going to comfort Zion and prove to the nations that Jerusalem was indeed His chosen city. Jerusalem is the centre of all things geographically, spiritually and prophetically.

3. THE PERIOD

The timeline is much the same as the book of Haggai. Haggai's four prophecies were all given in the second year of Darius the king: on the first day of the sixth month; on the twenty-first day of the seventh month and, the final two, on the twenty-fourth day of the ninth month. The book of Zechariah begins in the eighth month of the same year. Thus Zechariah begins his ministry two months after Haggai delivers his first message to the people. Haggai's ministry was given over a few months. Zechariah's ministry lasted longer. Chapter 7 verse 1 refers to the fourth year of Darius. Zechariah most likely continued his ministry until the Temple was completed around 516-515 B.C.

The prophecies given by Zechariah, however, span the centuries from the rebuilding of the Temple, through the times of the Gentiles to their fullness, on to the glorious return of the Lord and the setting up of His kingdom.

4. THE PURPOSE

Haggai's purpose was to rebuild the Temple. He was used to start the revival, while Zechariah was used to keep it going strong with a more positive emphasis, calling the people to repentance and reassuring them of future blessings.

I suppose we could put this way: ***the purpose was to encourage them for the present and enlighten them for the future***.

Zechariah's visions were of greater scope than those of his fellow preacher.

John Phillips says:

"He soared on eagle's wings far beyond his own day and age, seeing the coming of the Greeks, the coming of the Romans, the crucifixion of Christ, the scattering again of the Hebrew people, the events of the last days, the rise to power of the Beast, the ultimate horrors awaiting Jerusalem and the final return of Christ to impose upon this planet a righteous reign for God."

Just a word about:

5. THE PROPHECY

1. *It is Prophetic*

This *"Apocalypse of the Old Testament"* relates both to Zechariah's immediate audience as well as to the future. In each of the three main sections, the prophet begins historically and then moves forward to the time when the Messiah returns to the temple to set up His earthly kingdom. Now sometimes this can leave us in confusion as to the time period that is being considered. We need to be careful.

These Old Testament prophets saw two mountains. They prophesied first with regard to things relating to their own generation, then they saw the second mountain which was a coming, literal, earthly Messianic kingdom when the King would return in power and great glory. But, what they did not see was the valley in between - the Church period, the Age of Grace. The Church was a New Testament entity. They saw the message

God gave for their own generation, then spanned the centuries and saw the coming of the King in great power. In considering these prophecies we must make a distinction between the *near meaning* (the first mountain) and the *distant meaning* (the second mountain).

The first two sections were written during the rebuilding of the Temple and the last section seems to have been written considerably later. The first six chapters have an immediate reference to the *"Jewish Remnant"* now back in the land, while the last section refers to Israel in the last days.

2. *It is Messianic*

One pervading Person dominates the prophecy - the Messiah.

Lamoyne Sharpe says:

Christ is -

The Angel of the Lord – Chapter 1
The Array of Fire around Jerusalem – Chapter 2
The Advocate to assure deliverance of the accused – Chapter 3
The Anointed One for Priestly Administration – Chapter 4
The Appointed Priest and the Authoritative King – Chapter 6
The Abiding Lord – Chapter 7
The Approaching King – Chapter 9
The Afflicted Shepherd – Chapter 11
The Associate of God – Chapter 13
The Appearing King to usher in His kingdom – Chapter 14

Here were two men, Haggai and Zechariah, raised up by the Lord to inspire and give life to the waning zeal of the Jewish leaders and people. Zechariah's book divides into three sections:

(1) PICTURES CONCERNING ISRAEL'S FUTURE: Chapters 1 to 6

This section is *Apocalyptic*. It has to do with visions and symbols and prophecies. But, notice that it begins with:

(a) THE VISITATION OF THE LORD – Chapter 1 verses 1 to 6

You can see here *the Man that God Appoints*: According to Chapter 2 verse 4, he is a young man. The Hebrew word for *"young man"* means: *"a lad or youth"*. This youth and Haggai, who perhaps was in his late sixties, were working side-by-side to accomplish the same goal. You know, the Lord can use both the young and the old in His work. The old should not despise the young and the young should not despise the old. The deciding factor is not age, education, experience or prestige but - Has he been called of God? If so, then he is *God's man for the hour.* I wonder has God been stirring *your* heart for His work? Are you available to Him?

You can see here *the Message that God Ordains*: A preacher's first sermon is usually difficult but in Zechariah's case it was doubly difficult, because of the theme – *Repentance!* God commanded His young servant to call the discouraged, dispirited, disconsolate people to turn from their wicked ways and obey His Word. Look at verse 3: *"Turn ye unto Me … and I will turn unto you"*. Israel had returned to the Land but not to the Lord! You can go to church without meeting with the Lord! Zechariah began with a pointed sermon. He reminded them that it was because their forefathers would not listen to the prophets that the exile had happened. It was a timely reminder. Zechariah cries: *"Don't make the same mistakes or you will be in trouble too"*. Occasionally, we hear evangelists calling sinners to repent, but when was the last time you heard a preacher calling saints to repent?

Vance Havner says:

"The last word of our Lord to the church is not the Great Commission, although the Great Commission is indeed our programme to the end of the age, but our Lord's last word to the church is - Repent."

Is this not what the Risen Lord says to the church at Laodicea? *"Be zealous therefore, and repent"* (Revelation 3:19). It is one thing to ask God to bless us, but it is quite another to be the kind of people God can bless!

But notice, too:

(b) THE VISIONS OF THE PROPHET – Chapter 1 verse 7 to Chapter 6

Scholars are divided as to how many visions Zechariah received. I think he had a series of eight visions. God gave them to him to encourage the remnant in Jerusalem and motivate them to finish rebuilding the Temple.

These visions focus primarily on God's ministry to Israel and His judgment on the Gentile nations that have afflicted Israel. One Bible scholar has described these visions in the following way:

Vision No. 1: The Vision of Comfort – Chapter 1 verses 7 to 17

This was a vision of horsemen and the myrtle trees. Israel is symbolised as a grove of lowly myrtles in a shadowed place in the valley. It may be a time of despair and darkness for Israel presently, but an Unseen One stands among them, watching symbolically, mounted in power on horseback and backed by other riders on horses.

Job 1 and 2 reveal that Satan goes *"to and fro in the earth"* and walks *"up and down in it"*. 1 Peter 5 verse 8 describes him as: *"a roaring lion ... seeking whom he may devour"*. However, is it not comforting to know that God also has His *"spiritual spies"* out, checking upon this old sinful world?

Israel, though downtrodden, is under the watchful eye of the covenant-keeping God.

We see here: *Divine Sympathy*.

Vision No. 2: The Vision of Conquest – Chapter 1 verses 18 to 21

It was a vision of horns and carpenters. A horn in Scripture is usually a symbol of power. The vision of the four horns takes in the four world powers that over the centuries participated in the scattering of Israel. These are the four world powers seen in the Image of Daniel 2. Babylon, Medo-Persia, Greece and Rome.

These Gentile powers that scattered Israel remain unconcerned about the fate of the Jewish people. However, the vision of the craftsmen summoned to destroy the horns is a reminder that God has His own instruments at hand and is quite able to bring Gentile world power to nought.

We see here: <u>*Divine Safety.*</u>

<u>*Vision No. 3: The Vision of Conditions – Chapter 2*</u>

This was a vision of a Measuring Line. In the vision there is a man with a measuring line in his hand. As this man goes out to measure the city of Jerusalem, the interpreting angel says to the prophet: *"Jerusalem shall be inhabited as towns without walls for the multitude of men and cattle therein. For I, saith the LORD, will be unto her a wall of fire round about, and will be the glory in the midst of her"* (verses 4-5).

This wonderful description of the coming peace of Jerusalem is followed by a description of days of blessing that are to come upon Israel in the future.

A causal glance at the headlines on any day of the week is proof that these days have not yet come for Israel. However, those days *will* come. God has given His word on it. The Lord assured Israel: *"He that toucheth you toucheth the apple of His eye"* (verse 8).

The Jewish people are precious to God. Woe betide any nation that harms them!

We see here: <u>*Divine Security*</u>.

<u>*Vision No. 4: The Vision of Cleansing – Chapter 3*</u>

In this vision, Zechariah sees Joshua, the high priest, dressed in filthy clothing and standing before God in Heaven. He is being accused by Satan because of his soiled clothing. Christ Himself, however, rebukes Satan. He removes Joshua's dirty clothing and dresses him in clean apparel. Joshua then is challenged to serve the Lord with his whole heart.

If we were applying this in the Gospel, we would say that Joshua was cleansed, then he was clothed, then he was crowned. Joshua is then challenged to serve the Lord with all his heart.

What does this all mean? Just this - God promises that what He had done for this one Jew, He would one day do for the whole nation.

We see here: *Divine Salvation*.

Vision No. 5: The Vision of Communication – Chapter 4

This was a vision of a Candlestick. Here Zechariah sees a sevenfold golden candlestick supplied by a reservoir of oil. On either side of the lampstand was a carved olive tree. This vision points to the day when the nation of Israel will experience a spiritual awakening that will make her a light to the world.

Oil in Scripture always refers to the Holy Spirit - and do you see what verse 6 says? *"Not by might, nor by power, but by My Spirit, saith the LORD of hosts."* Not by military might, not by political power, but by the Spirit of God!

Do you want to burn brightly in this dark world of sin? Then you will need to know the enabling power of the Spirit of God.

We see here: *Divine Sufficiency*.

Vision No. 6: The Vision of Condemnation – Chapter 5 verses 1 to 4

This was a vision of a Flying Roll. Zechariah saw a flying scroll. It measured some fifteen feet wide by thirty feet long. As it flew over the land, it was pronouncing a curse because of Judah's sins against God and man.

Sin will yet be judged among the Hebrew people. In the coming Tribulation, the nation of Israel will be refined.

We see here: *Divine Scrutiny*.

Vision No. 7: The Vision of Control – Chapter 5 verses 5 to 11

This was a vision of a Woman in the ephah. You see, what Zechariah saw was a flying bushel basket, covered by a heavy lead top piece. Two women appeared and they carried off the ephah with its burden to Babylon.

What does it mean? It means that sin will have its focal point once more in the very place where much of it began, back in Babylon.

Historically, it was at Babel that organized rebellion against God commenced – with the Tower of Genesis 11.

Prophetically, the book of Revelation hints at the rebuilding of Babylon and the final overthrow of the Beast's Empire.

We see here: *Divine Severity*.

Vision No. 8: The Vision of Command – Chapter 6 verses 1 to 8

This was a vision of four chariots with red, black, white and dappled-grey horses which go throughout the whole earth to do God's will. You see, God has a worldwide command and control of history. Revelation 6 makes the very same point. God is still on the throne. He puts down one nation and pulls up another, fulfilling His redemptive purposes for the world. This should bring comfort to the heart of every child of God.

We see here: *Divine Sovereignty*.

It was at this point that three men arrive from Babylon. They were merchants bringing silver and gold for the Temple but Zechariah was told to take some of it and make a crown and then have a coronation for Joshua in the Temple.

Does this not anticipate the day when the Lord Jesus as the Priest-King of Psalm 110 will be owned by the restored, redeemed and repentant nation of Israel? No wonder the cry rings forth: *"Behold the man!"* (verse 12) as they look upon Him as their true and long- rejected Messiah.

These then were Pictures Concerning Israel's Future. Zechariah was carried down the centuries to see in broad, sweeping outline the plans and purposes of God in connection with His people, Israel.

(2) PROBLEMS CONCERNING ISRAEL'S FASTS: Chapters 7 and 8

This section is *historic*. These chapters record a visit from some Jews to ask about their fasts in the commemoration of the fall of Jerusalem.

Notice:

(a) THE QUESTION ASKED

Look at verse 3 of Chapter 7. *"Should I weep in the fifth month, separating myself, as I have done these so many years?"*

You see, since the fall of Jerusalem in 586 B.C. the Jews had observed four annual fasts to commemorate recent tragic events:

- the taking of Jerusalem by Nebuchadnezzar in the fourth month - Jeremiah 52 verse 6.
- the burning of the Temple in the fifth month - Jeremiah 52 verse 12.
- the murder of Gedaliah the governor in the seventh month - Jeremiah 41 verses 1 and 2.
- the siege of Jerusalem in the tenth month - 2 Kings 25 verse 1.

Now, with the rebuilding of the Temple going so well, the Jews wanted to know if it was still necessary for then to *"weep in the fifth month"* to commemorate the burning of the original Temple.

I suppose this raises the whole question of traditions. The word: *"tradition"* simply means: *"that which is passed along"*. It comes from a Latin word that means: *"to hand over"*. Now, the basic doctrines of the Christian faith must be handed from generation to generation - see 2 Timothy 2 verse 2 and Jude 3 - but man-made traditions do not carry the same authority as the inspired Word of God.

"We have never done it that way before!" is the watchword in many churches, but do we not need to be careful lest tradition hinders the work of the Lord? Centuries ago when the first missionaries went to Moravia they were not allowed to preach in the Slavic language. Why? Because the only *"holy languages"* approved by the church were Hebrew and Latin. Church leaders had sense enough to revoke this directive, otherwise evangelism would have been impossible.

(b) THE QUESTION ARGUED

Look at verses 4 to 14. What is being explored is this: *"Why did you fast on those occasions? Were you heartbroken over what these tragedies meant to God?"* You see, to institute four feasts because of the tragedies that occurred in Jerusalem and yet not repent because of the sins that caused those tragedies was to miss entirely the whole point of God's discipline.

The attitude of the heart is important - is it not? It is easier to have a religion of habit than to have a religion of the heart. Here were people who were concerned with empty ritual but the Lord referred then to divine revelation.

(c) THE QUESTION ANSWERED

Evidently, the question about fasts touched a raw nerve. In response, Zechariah read his people a lecture. *"Thus saith the LORD"* he cried ten times in Chapter 8.

In answer to the question about fasts, God never ordained those irksome feasts. It *did not matter* to God whether they kept them or not. Do you know what *did matter* to the Lord? That they keep the Word that He had given them. All their national calamities stemmed from the fact that they had not obeyed the law of the Lord. We too as believers will be in trouble if we neglect His Word.

Here again Zechariah's vision is enlarged. He saw once more the last days and the Millennial reign when feasts would forever replace fasts and when the Jewish people would become the blessing to mankind that God always intended them to be.

The closing chapters of this prophecy all focus on the future. So, while in the first section, we have *Pictures concerning Israel's Future* and in the second section, *Problems concerning Israel's Fasts*, in the final section we have:

(3) PROPHECIES CONCERNING ISRAEL'S FATE: Chapters 9 to 14

This section is *Prophetic*. Bible Scholars believe that these prophecies were probably written some considerable time later.

They have to do with *two burdens*. *"The burden of the word of the LORD"* (Chapter 9:1) and again: *"The burden of the word of the LORD for Israel"* (Chapter 12:1). The word *"burden"* signifies a prophecy or message which the prophet carries like a load on his heart. These two burdens focus on the first and second advents of the Coming Messiah.

Notice here:

(a) The FIRST COMING of the KING - Chapters 9 to 11

There was Preparation for the King

These opening verses in Chapter 9 describe the march of Alexander the Great and his army through the area north and east of Israel. The opening verse which refers to *"the eyes of man"* suggests that the eye of the Lord is on all mankind, as well as on the tribes.

Merrill Unger suggests that as the people were watching Alexander, they were watching God at work. *"History is His story!"* But, why all this concern over the conquests of Alexander the Great? Well, his victories helped prepare the world for the coming of the Lord Jesus. By building Greek cities and by spreading Greek culture and the Greek language, he unified the world and when the Romans took over they found an Empire all prepared for them. Greek was the language of literature and our New Testament is written in the common Greek language of the people of that day.

The combination of Greek culture and Roman government, roads and laws was just what the early church needed for the spread of the Gospel. God was preparing an era for the coming of His Son.

There was the Presentation of the King

Look at verse 9 of Chapter 9:

"Rejoice greatly, O daughter of Zion; shout, O daughter of Jerusalem: behold, thy King cometh unto thee: He is just, and having salvation; lowly, and riding upon an ass, and upon a colt the foal of an ass."

Do you know when that was fulfilled? When the Lord Jesus rode into Jerusalem on what we call *"Palm Sunday"*. The event is described by all four Gospel writers - Mathew 21, Mark 11, Luke 19 and John 12. Christ was making a formal presentation of Himself to Israel as her long-promised Messiah. It is interesting that this is the only public demonstration Christ allowed during His ministry - and He did it to fulfil Scripture.

Can you see from this verse?

The Uniqueness of His Person

He is *"just"* that is justified, vindicated, acceptable to God as sinless, declared righteous.

The Uniqueness of His Purpose

He comes *"having salvation"*.

Remember the words of the chorus:

"He did not come to judge the world,
He did not come to blame,
He did not only come to seek,
It was to save He came –

And when we call Him: 'Saviour',
We call Him by His name."

<u>*The Uniqueness of His Position*</u>

He is *"lowly"*. Eternally, He was *"high and lifted up"*. The cherubims - as Isaiah 6 reveals - chanted before Him their ceaseless song, yet He became *"lowly"*. He was born in a cattle shed. He was raised in a provincial town where He worked as a carpenter. He was *"despised and rejected of men"* (Isaiah 53:3).

<u>*The Uniqueness of His Power*</u>

He would come *"riding ... upon a colt the foal of an ass"*. Alexander the Great rode a mighty white steed, but Jesus Christ rode a lowly donkey.

Our Lord's power did not need that *"outward adorning"*. He might have built a palace with a word, yet at times, He had nowhere to lay His head.

Now, unknown to Zechariah, there would be a gap between verse 9 and verse 10. The Lord would stop the Jewish clock and between the two verses insert an Age of Grace. He would give birth to the church, an entity about which the Old Testament prophets never dreamed.

(b) The FUTURE COMING of the KING – Chapters 12 to 14

Zechariah says: *"Then shall the LORD go forth ... and His feet shall stand in that day upon the mount of Olives, which is before Jerusalem"* (Chapter 14:3-4).

"In that day" - a day he explains as being: *"the day of the LORD"*. In other words, the vision of the prophet is focused on end time events.

Let me draw your attention to some of these momentous events.

There will be:

1. *AN INTERNATIONAL RENDEZVOUS*

Do you see what God says in Chapter 14 verse 2? *"I will gather all nations against Jerusalem to battle."* Do you see the emphasis? *"All nations."* Earlier, in Chapter 12 verse 3, there is a similar expression: *"All people"*.

This attack involves the armies of the world and is part of the famous *"battle of Armageddon"*, further described in Revelation 16 verses 12 to 16. Zechariah describes Jerusalem's situation using the images of a cup and a stone (Chapter 12:1-3). Now, a cup is a familiar Biblical image for judgment. *"In the hand of the LORD there is a cup"* (Psalm 75 verse 8); *"Awake, awake, stand up, O Jerusalem, which hast drunk at the hand of the LORD the cup of His fury"* (Isaiah 51 verse 17) and *"The same shall drink of the wine of the wrath of God, which is poured out without mixture into the cup of His indignation"* (Revelation 14 verse 10). You see, the plan of the nations was to *"swallow up"* Jerusalem, but when they begin to *"drink the cup"*, its contents make them sick and drunk.

History shows that every nation that has ever tried to destroy the Jews has itself been destroyed. It will be no different when the nations of the world collectively attack God's chosen people. Some of the enemy soldiers will enter the city, loot it, abuse the women and take half the inhabitants captive, but the Lord will make Jerusalem like an immovable rock that will not yield. This stone will eventually cut the invading armies to pieces.

2. *A LITERAL RETURN*

Do you see verses 3 and 4 of Chapter 14?

"Then shall the LORD go forth, and fight against those nations ... And His feet shall stand in that day upon the mount of Olives."

The Lord is going to visibly appear.

Jerusalem has been besieged so many, many times. General Allenby led British forces against the city in 1917 and took it without firing a shot. He respectfully dismounted from his horse and walked into this holy city. The Jews and Arabs fought over Jerusalem in 1948 when Israel became a state. In 1967, the Jews captured Jerusalem from the Arabs, united the city and proclaimed it the capital of the state of Israel. Moshe Dayan, the Israeli Commander, came to the Wailing Wall and declared: *"We have returned to the holiest of our holy places, never to part from it again"*.

Jerusalem's history is troubled, but the worst siege still lies ahead. By the time two-thirds of the population have perished (Chapter 13:8), the Jews will have lost all hope. It will seem as though the Arabs have finally achieved their goal - the seizure of Jerusalem and the extermination of the Jews.

But, when all seems lost, the miracle will happen: *"Then shall the LORD go forth, and fight against those nations"*.

He will return to halt the siege, to thrash the nations, to seize the Antichrist and to disarm the devil himself.

Jesus Christ will come and defend His people and defeat His enemies.

3. A NATIONAL REPENTANCE

Our Lord's goal is more than their *national preservation*. It is their *spiritual restoration*.

Do you see how Chapter 12 concludes and how Chapter 13 commences?

"And I will pour upon the house of David, and upon the inhabitants of Jerusalem, the spirit of grace and of supplications: and they shall look upon Me whom they have pierced, and they shall mourn for Him, as one mourneth for his only son, and shall be in bitterness for Him, as one that is in bitterness for his firstborn. In that day shall there be a great mourning in Jerusalem, as the mourning of Hadadrimmon in the valley of Megiddon. And the land shall mourn, every family apart; the family of the house of David apart, and their wives apart; the family of

the house of Nathan apart, and their wives apart; The family of the house of Levi apart, and their wives apart; the family of Shimei apart, and their wives apart; All the families that remain, every family apart, and their wives apart. In that day there shall be a fountain opened to the house of David and to the inhabitants of Jerusalem for sin and for uncleanness." (Chapter 12:10-14; Chapter 13:1)

The Jewish people will come under strong conviction as their eyes are opened at last to Christ, to the One *"whom they have pierced"*. Calvary in all its horror will loom up before them. Suddenly, they will realize that right there at *"the place of the skull"* outside the city of Jerusalem, they crucified their Messiah. They will mourn as they gaze, like Saul of Tarsus, on the One they pierced.

The day is coming, when Israel, although blind at present, will recognize the Lord Jesus as the Messiah. He who was crucified by them will then be received by them. *"In that day"*, the Jews will see that fountain filled with blood and avail themselves of its cleansing power.

It was William Cowper who penned these lovely words:

"There is a fountain, filled with blood,
Drawn from Immanuel's veins;
And sinners, plunged beneath that flood,
Lose all their guilty stains."

We believers have been there, but there is coming a day when Israel will be there also.

But there is something else here:

4. A UNIVERSAL REIGN

"The LORD shall be king over all the earth" (Chapter 14:9).

After the nations have been punished and Israel has been purified, the Lord will establish His righteous kingdom and reign on David's throne.

The words of Luke 1 verses 32 and 33, spoken by the angel to Mary, will be fulfilled:

"He shall be great, and shall be called the Son of the Highest: and the Lord God shall give unto Him the throne of His father David: and He shall reign over the house of Jacob for ever; and of His kingdom there shall be no end."

That will be *then*, but what about *now*?

Says Paul in 1 Corinthians 15 verse 25: *"He must reign"*.

He will reign then, but what about now?

Is the Lord Jesus reigning and holding sway in your life?

Do you pray with anticipation for the coming of Christ's kingdom?

Do you look forward to the coming reign of Jesus Christ?

Do you feel like Frances Havergal?

"Oh, the joy to see Thee reigning,
Thee, my own beloved Lord!
Every tongue Thy name confessing,
Worship, honour, glory, blessing,
Brought to Thee with glad accord;
Thee, my Master and my Friend,
Vindicated and enthroned,
Unto earth's remotest end,
Glorified, adored and owned!"

CHAPTER 22
Malachi

President Grover Cleveland came home from church one Sunday.

His wife asked him what the message had been about.

He simply answered: *"Sin!"*

His wife probed: *"Well, what did the preacher say about it?"*

The President responded: *"I don't remember, but he was against it!"*

Malachi preached about sin! He was against it!

Do you notice that the opening words of Malachi are: *"The burden of the word of the LORD to Israel by Malachi"*?

There is so much to learn from this first verse!

Malachi's ministry was called a *"burden"*. The word was used to speak of an animal carrying a heavy burden for its master. The message that Malachi delivered was heavy on his heart. Moreover, it was *"the word of the LORD"*. It was not Malachi's message. Malachi was but the delivery boy. His name means: *"My messenger"*. Notice again, it was God's message to *"Israel"*. After the captivity ended, the nation was called *"Israel"* once again.

The message that Malachi brought was *not to comfort but to convict.*

It was *not* a message of *commendation,* but one of *condemnation.*

It was *not* a message that *delighted* the people, but *discomforted* the people.

Malachi was called to perform a difficult and dangerous task. It was his duty to rebuke the people for sins they were committing. Sins were being committed by the people against God and against one another. Malachi rebuked them and then called them to return to the Lord.

The *book* of Malachi is a *small book with a big message*.

The *prophet* Malachi is a *minor prophet with a major message*.

By way of introduction, let us notice some things about this book of Malachi:

1. It is a Closing Book

It is the last book of the Old Testament. It is the 39th book of the Bible, but the last of the Old Testament. It is the last book of the Old Testament era and it marks the beginning of a four hundred year period in which God gave no fresh revelation. With this last work in the Minor Prophets, God closes the Old Testament canon.

2. It is a Connecting Book

The Book not only concludes the Old Testament, but it also connects the Old to the New. The book tells us of the messenger who would prepare the way of the Lord. In the New Testament, we see that messenger - John the Baptist.

3. It is a Co-existent Book

The prophecy of Malachi sits side-by-side with the history of Nehemiah.

The book of <u>*Ezra*</u> is all about the <u>*rebuilding of the Temple*</u>.
The book of <u>*Nehemiah*</u> is all about the <u>*rebuilding of the walls*</u>.

Things progressed rapidly under Nehemiah. The walls of Jerusalem were rebuilt and spiritual renewal took place. However, Nehemiah was called back to Persia on business and was absent from Jerusalem between 432 and 425 B.C. – see Nehemiah 5 verse 14 and Chapter 13 verse 6. It is probable that Malachi conducted his ministry during those years. The sins described in this book are certainly found in Nehemiah 13 verses 10 to 30, so the *burden of Malachi* and the *building of Nehemiah* should be considered side by side.

Nehemiah sought to *rebuild a city*: *Malachi* sought to *recall a people*.

Nehemiah focuses upon the *condition of a place*: *Malachi* focuses upon the *condition of a people*.

4. It is a Contemporary Book

A prophet preaching to people who lived 2400 years ago surely has no meaning or value for us! But, it does. Yes, Malachi's message is dated, but it is not out-of-date. While times have changed, many things have not.

Are we living in an age of *crippling doubt*? So it was in Malachi's day.
Are we living in a time when God's people are *careless and casual* about the commands of the Lord? So it was in Malachi's day.
Are we living in a day when *divorce* is rife? So it was in Malachi's day.
Are we living a day when God's people treat *stewardship* lightly? So it was in Malachi's day.

This message may have been first delivered by an Old Testament Prophet, but it still needs delivering by a New Testament preacher.

It is as contemporary as the day it was given!

5. It is a Challenging Book

The voice of the prophet was only heard in Israel in times of national apostasy. The prophets were sometimes *foretellers*, giving glimpses of things to come. They were, however, always *forthtellers* inspired by the Lord to denounce prevalent sins and call God's people to repentance.

Malachi is a call for God's people to examine the realness of their spiritual life and the sinfulness of their personal life.

Malachi predicts a returning Lord and a ready people.

Now observe six pictures of the people and the priests. Notice that here they are:

(1) DENYING GOD'S LOVE – Chapter 1 verses 1 to 5

"I have loved you, saith the LORD" (verse 2). *"Oh,"* they respond: *"Wherein hast Thou loved us"*. In other words: *"Prove it!"*

Denying God's love is the beginning of unbelief and disobedience.

One of the features of this book is the use of the word: *"Wherein?"* – see Chapter 1 verses 2, 6 and 7; Chapter 2 verse 17 and Chapter 3 verses 7, 8 and 13.

Malachi sets forth his prophecy in the form of a dispute employing the question and answer method. The Lord's accusations against His people were met by cynical questions. Their answers reveal that they felt they were doing what was right and doing nothing wrong.

Their answers said in effect: *"What do you mean? We are not guilty of these things!"*

"Wherein hast Thou loved us?" "Prove it!"

Oh, here they were. They had come back from Babylon and with blood, sweat, and tears had rebuilt the Temple, Jerusalem and other cities. They had turned their backs on centuries of idolatry and reinstituted the worship of God.

But, had God rewarded them? No!
Had He restored the kingdom? No!
Had He fulfilled the glorious promises of many a prophet? No!
Had He sent the Messiah whose coming had been prophesied by Isaiah and Zechariah? No!
Then, how could it be said that God loved them?

They denied God's love and so the Lord points to three phases of His love for them.

Notice:

(a) GOD'S LOVE IN THE PAST

In verses 2 and 3, God refers back to Jacob and Esau. *"I loved Jacob, and I hated Esau."* That statement is quoted by Paul in Romans 9 verse 13 to prove God's electing grace for Israel and for all who trust Christ for salvation, but that statement has troubled some people. *"I hated Esau."* What does this mean? Well, the verb *"hate"* must not be defined as a positive expression of the wrath of God. Rather, God's love for Jacob was so great, that in comparison His actions towards Esau looked like hatred.

Do you remember that Jacob loved Rachel so much that his relationship to Leah seemed like hatred? (Genesis 29:31 – see also Deuteronomy 21:15-17)

Do you recall what Christ said to would-be-disciples? *"If any man come to Me, and hate not his father, and mother, and wife, and children, and brethren, and sisters, yea, and his own life also, he cannot be My disciple"* (Luke 14:26). Christ was using the word *"hate"* in a similar way. You see, our love for Christ may move us to do things that appear like hatred to those we love.

Someone said to Dr. Arno C. Gaebelein, the gifted Hebrew Christian leader of a generation ago: *"I have a serious problem with Malachi 1 verse 3 where God says: 'Esau have I hated'."*

Dr. Gaebelein replied: *"I have a greater problem with Malachi 1 verse 2 where God says: 'Jacob have I loved'."*

Centuries have come and gone since the Lord spoke to Israel through Malachi, but God says to us, the church today: *"I have loved you"*. The words are in the perfect tense, meaning that God had loved them in the past and that He loved them in the present.

Are you denying God's love for you? Are your circumstances such that you wonder if God truly loves you? Is the devil telling you that He does not?

Will you think hard and long about the: *" I"* and the: *"you"*? The: *"I"* is none other than the all-powerful, all-knowing, all-present God. The: *"you"* refers to people who are undeserving, unclean and unworthy.

Will you listen to it again and marvel at the statement: *"I have loved you"*. How? By choosing us in Christ before the world began, declares Ephesians 1 verse 4. But, we cannot peer into the Councils of eternity to see the everlasting love of God. So, where do we look? To the Cross of the Lord Jesus!

As we look there, we must exclaim:

"God loved me so much that He nailed His Son to the Cross to bear the penalty for my sins!"

With Charles Wesley, we must sing:

> *"Amazing love! how can it be*
> *That Thou, my God, shouldst die for me?"*

Then there is:

(b) GOD'S LOVE IN THE PRESENT

God had delivered both Edom and Judah into the hands of the Babylonians. The Jews, He had brought back and blessed. As for

Edom, God had *"laid his mountains and his heritage waste for the dragons of the wilderness"*. Still Edom showed pride and self-will. *"Edom saith, We are impoverished, but we will return and build the desolate places"*. The result was God's curse: *"They shall build, but I will throw down"*.

Was this not what the prophecy of Obadiah was all about? Why, when the Babylonians came to take Jerusalem, the Edomites cried in effect: *"Hooray! the Jews are finished!"* (see Psalm 137:7) Since that day, *Edom* was under *God's judgment*, but *Israel* was under *God's protection*.

Do *you* not experience the tokens of God's love every day? The truths of His Word; the fellowship of His people; the wonder of His worship; the guidance of His hand; the provision of His strength - are these not simply expressions of His ongoing love?

The Past, the Present – and then there is:

(c) GOD'S LOVE IN THE FUTURE

God says, in verse 5: *"Your eyes shall see, and ye shall say, The LORD will be magnified from the border of Israel"*. Israel was God's chosen instrument by means of which He intended to be magnified in the sight of all mankind. No doubt, there is a hint here of Millennial glory, when the Lord will receive pure worship throughout the world. His name will be honoured everywhere.

"From the rising of the sun even unto the going down of the same My name shall be great among the Gentiles; and in every place incense shall be offered unto My name, and a pure offering: for My name shall be great among the heathen, saith the LORD of hosts" (verse 11).

What love is this! He loved us in the past! He loves us in the present! He never will cease loving us - He will love us throughout the unending cycles of eternity!

Do you think I should ever stand up and ask: *"Wherein hast Thou loved me?"*

I am one of the people chosen by the Lord in Christ before the foundation of the world. Why did God choose a thing like me? - *because He loved me!*

He sent His Son from Heaven to the Cross of shame to bear my sins - *because He loved me!*

He came through His Word by His Spirit and met me on the road of life and saved me - *because He loved me!*

> *"He loves me so,*
> *He loves me so,*
> *He died because He loves me so."*

Not only were the people guilty of Denying God's Love, they were also guilty of:

(2) <u>DESPISING GOD'S NAME – Chapter 1 verses 6 to 14</u>

The Lord now turns to the priests. They should have been the spiritual leaders of the land, but He accuses them of despising His name.

"A son honoureth his father, and a servant his master: if then I be a father, where is Mine honour? and if I be a master, where is My fear? saith the LORD of hosts unto you, O priests, that despise My name. And ye say, Wherein have we despised Thy name?" (verse 6).

The priests still did not get it, so the Lord, in verse 7, explains.

"Ye offer polluted bread upon Mine altar; and ye say, Wherein have we polluted Thee? In that ye say, The table of the LORD is contemptible."

"Bread" speaks of the animal sacrifices offered to God. The *"table"* speaks of the brazen altar on which these sacrifices were offered. Do you see that Malachi uses the word *"polluted"* twice? It means: *"to desecrate or defile"*.

You see, they were:

(a) Giving the WORST not the BEST

According to verse 8, they were offering the blind for sacrifice.

Do you recall God's Word in all of this?

Back in Leviticus 22, God had said: *"Whatsoever hath a blemish, that shall ye not offer: for it shall not be acceptable for you … blind, or broken, or maimed … ye shall not offer these unto the LORD"* (verses 20 and 22). Still again, God said: *"If there be any blemish therein, as if it be lame, or blind, or have any ill blemish, thou shalt not sacrifice it unto the LORD thy God"* (Deuteronomy 15:21).

Yet, these priests were ignoring what the law said and offering animals that were blind, lame and sick. Because of the condition of these animals, their owners were glad to get rid of them!

John Benton says:

"Sacrifice is the giving up of something we genuinely value in order to express our devotion to God, but the 'sacrificing' of diseased animals was like offering someone as a birthday present the contents of our dustbin."

Giving the worst not the best!

Now, let me challenge you: What are you offering the Lord? What are you giving to the Lord? In what way are you worshiping the Lord?

Campbell Morgan says:

"Sacrificing to God something which costs nothing is because you think God is worth nothing."

Are we giving our best to God in worship? Do we arrive with a heart that is prepared and eager to worship? Do we concentrate in public worship or do we allow our thoughts to wander? Do we give the ministry of God's Word a careful hearing? Or, have we allowed our familiarity with the things of God to dull our appreciation of them? Have we just lost *"the wonder of it all"*?

(b) Giving the LAST not the FIRST

God was just getting the leftovers. That is why He says in verse 8: *"Offer it now unto thy governor; will he be pleased with thee, or accept thy person? saith the LORD of hosts"*. If they had offered these defective beasts to their governor, he would have rejected them, but their view was: *Anything will do for the Lord!*

Is the Lord just getting the leftovers in your life?
If you have money left at the end of the week, you will *"tip"* the Lord.
If you have energy left, you might decide to serve Him.
If you have time left, you might come out to worship Him.

We should give the Lord the ***best*** in terms of quality. The Lord only wants unblemished lambs on His altar. If it is a *"reject"*, it is not good enough for the Lord.

(c) Giving the CHEAP not the COSTLY

Sometimes, the people would bring an unblemished lamb to offer as a sacrifice at the temple, and the priests would reason:

"It does not make sense to slaughter this perfectly good lamb. After all, it is just going to be burned on the altar. Let us sell it for a decent price and substitute a slightly blemished lamb that is cheaper. Good stewardship demands it."

But, do you see what God thought of it all? He expresses His thoughts in verse 10. As far as He was concerned, it would be better for the doors of the Temple to be shut and for the fires of the altar to be put out, rather than this charade continuing.

Remember the words of David who said: *"Neither will I offer burnt offerings unto the LORD my God of that which doth cost me nothing"* (2 Samuel 24:24).

Are you giving to the Lord your best? Are you striving to give Him the first? Does your giving cost you something?

Here is another characteristic of these people. They were:

(3) DEFILING GOD'S COVENANT – *Chapter 2 verses 1 to 16*

A covenant is an agreement between two or more people in which each pledges to do or not to do certain things. In verses 1 to 9, there is brought before us:

(a) THE LEVITICAL COVENANT`

In the Old Testament, priests were descendants of Aaron, the brother of Moses, who was from the tribe of Levi. They were called Levites and their job was to serve in the Tabernacle. They were to be set apart for two primary purposes: to sacrifice animals and to serve the Lord. Verse 5 declares that the covenant with Levi was a wonderful covenant of: *"life and peace"*, because Levi feared the Lord. However, the fear of God was conspicuously missing in the awful priests of Malachi's day. In verses 5 to 7, we have the ideal priest. He fears the Lord and obeys Him. He receives the Word and teaches it. He seeks to turn others from sin. But, the priests in Malachi's day actually led people astray. *"Ye have caused many to stumble at the law"* (verse 8). They had defiled the holy covenant. In Moses' day, the Levites had a *belief that behaved*. In Malachi's day, their ministry had degenerated into a well-paying job with *"fringe benefits and social security"*.

John Phillips says:

"Professionalism in the things of God nearly always degenerates into dead orthodoxy or faith-denying liberalism."

So, what was God going to do with them? Well, look at Chapter 2 verse 2. He says: *"I will curse your blessings"*. The word: *"curse"* simply meant: *"to ban"*. They would be banned from being blessed of the Lord. In fact, the Lord would, according to verse 3, remove them from His service.

Is it not wonderful to realize that Christ bore the curse for us at Calvary? That is the declaration of Galatians 3 verse 13. *"Christ hath redeemed us from the curse of the law, being made a curse for us."* I believe I will never be cursed, yet the Lord can cast me away. By that, I do *not* mean that I will be lost again. I will *never* be lost again, for I am eternally secure in Christ. However, *He can set me aside*. He can remove His blessing. The Lord can get on without us.

Do you recall that sad record in the book of Judges? A warning about Samson who lost his power. The Bible says:

"He awoke out of his sleep, and said, I will go out as at other times before, and shake myself. And he wist not that the LORD was departed from him." (Judges 16:20)

John Milton described Samson's situation:

"Eyeless in Gaza, at the mill with slaves,
Himself in bonds under Philistian yoke."

Is that where you are spiritually? Have you lost your sight? God's Word no longer thrills you. You have lost your strength. You are no longer an overcomer. You have lost your service. Once you were busy for Him, but not anymore. Are you under the discipline of God? Is the blessing of God being withheld from your life because your heart is not right with Him?

But notice there was also:

(b) THE MATRIMONIAL COVENANT

The question was: *"Why be faithful to God?"* That question can soon become: *"Why be faithful to your wife?"* - especially when your wife gets older and loses her appeal. *"Why not trade her in for a 'newer model'?"*

Well, this is what they were doing in Malachi's day. Men were divorcing the wives of their youth for newer *"Canaanite models"*. In Nehemiah 13, Nehemiah records: *"In those days also saw I Jews that had married wives of Ashdod, of Ammon, and of Moab"* (Nehemiah 13:23).

This practice was an abomination in God's sight.

"Judah hath dealt treacherously, and an abomination is committed in Israel and in Jerusalem; for Judah hath profaned the holiness of the LORD which he loved, and hath married the daughter of a strange god" (verse 11).

Do you notice the word *"treacherously"*? It appears five times in the passage: verses 10, 11, 14, 15 and 16. It means: *"to betray a trust, to be unfaithful to a commitment".*

Is this not what is happening all around us today? According to the latest polls, in the United Kingdom the percentage of Christian marriages that are ending in divorce is around 50%, about the same as the national average.

Someone has said:

"Fifty years ago, parents were apt to have lots of children, but nowadays children are apt to have lots of parents."

Over these past few years, the Western World has witnessed an epidemic of divorce. Probably, most of us have family or friends who have gone through divorce. There is no point in heaping guilt or condemnation on those who have already been traumatized by divorce. We cannot undo the past. We cannot "unscramble the egg". But, what is the truth concerning marriage? It is this - God hates divorce! Do you see what verse 16 says? *"He hateth putting away."* Why? Because marriage is a covenant. *"The wife of thy youth ... yet is she thy companion, and the wife of thy covenant"* (verse 14).

A Biblical marriage involved the parties obligating themselves to an unalterable and permanent relationship for life. What makes this covenant so serious is this - God is the witness of it. *"Because the LORD hath been witness between thee and the wife of thy youth"* (verse 14). His Hebrew wife was the one with whom he stood before the priest and covenanted to be faithful and true - and God looked on as a witness.

Do you remember the explanation given by Diana, Princess of Wales, for the failure of her marriage? What she said was this: *"There were three in our marriage!"* Well, there *are* three in every true marriage, and the third person is not the mistress. The third person is God Himself. God takes this covenant seriously and views it as lifelong.

The sentiments that so often we hear: *"I don't love her anymore"* or *"I don't love him anymore"* are just not valid. God says: *"Learn to love each other as I have commanded you"*. Do you know what a lasting marriage is built on? Not on romantic love! It is built on commitment.

Love in the best and highest sense is not a feeling but a commitment. A commitment to a person through thick and thin; in the good times and in the bad times; in sickness and in health, and from good looks to not so good looks. Commitment is the glue that holds the marriage together during the inevitable times of stress.

What about your home? What about your heart? What about your hearth?

Then there was something else. These people were:

(4) DOUBTING GOD'S JUSTICE – Chapter 2 verse 17 to Chapter 3 verse 6

When Judah returned to the land, she expected to experience prosperity and glory just like the days of Solomon. But this was not to be the case. In fact, she found just the opposite. Her wicked enemies lived in prosperity, while Judah suffered privation - and this caused the people to question whether God was holy and just.

Their cry was: *"Where is the God of justice?"* (Chapter 2:17) Malachi's response was: *"He is coming"*. Look at:

(a) THE COMPLAINT OF THE PEOPLE

They said: *"Every one that doeth evil is good in the sight of the LORD"* (verse 17). The leaders believed that God had prospered the wicked and had left His own righteous people in poverty and they, therefore, reasoned that the wicked must be considered good in God's eyes. They even questioned whether God was available to take action against the wicked. They asked: *"Where is the God of justice?"*

Their words were cynical and skeptical: *"We returned to the land, rebuilt the Temple and restored the worship"*, they said. *"But, look at the difficulties we are experiencing. Why is God not keeping His promises? Where are the blessings He promised through the prophets? Where is the Messiah who was to come?"*

They had become disappointed with God. He had not done for them what they had hoped. They thought that God had let them down.

It may be that you have never said such things, but you will have thought such things. We all have!

You thought that when you trusted Christ, He would give you an abundant life and relief from major problems. Instead, you seem to have more problems now than you did before.

You did not previously struggle against sin, but now it is a daily battle. It is a daily battle that you often lose.

In the past, you did not worry about pleasing God, about your use of time and money, but now you feel guilty about squandering those things.

In fact, now you feel guilty about things you did not even previously know were sinful.

Have you prayed a lot about that particular situation, about that unsaved one? But rather than things getting better, have they, in fact, got worse?

Are you wondering: *"Does it pay to serve God? What difference does it make if I follow the Lord or not? Where is the God of justice?"*

That was the Complaint of the People, but notice:

(b) THE COMING OF THE LORD

Chapter 3 begins: *"Behold, I will send My messenger, and he shall prepare the way before Me"*. The word: *"Behold"* indicates that something startling and unusual is on the verge of taking place. God promises to send His messenger - John the Baptist - who will announce *"the Messenger of the Covenant"*, the Lord Jesus.

"The Lord ... shall suddenly come to His temple" (verse 1). Do you recall that Christ did come into the Temple? He exposed its sins and purified its courts? The Gospels record that He did so twice – in John 2 verses 13 to 17 and Matthew 21 verses 12 and 13. In His ministry He revealed the sins of the religious leaders so much that they finally crucified Him.

So this prophecy was *partially fulfilled* in His First Coming, but it will be *ultimately fulfilled* at His Second Coming.

Do you see that word *"suddenly"*? It is found 25 times in the Old Testament and in every case except one - 2 Chronicles 29 verse 36 - it is connected with disaster and judgment. Do you know what time of disaster and judgment that is? Jeremiah 30 verse 7 gives it another description: *"the time of Jacob's trouble"*. A day, a time when Israel will be troubled and judged. The same period is referred to elsewhere as: *"the day of the LORD"* or: *"the great tribulation"*.

After the church has been raptured, there will be seven years of tribulation, through which the nation of Israel will be purged and refined. Then the Lord Jesus will come in His second advent and judge the world, slay Israel's enemies, and begin a reign of a thousand years of righteousness on the earth.

"Where is the God of judgment?" sneered the scoffers.
"Here He is", says Malachi as he declared the word of the Lord.

In verse 6, God declares: *"I am the LORD, I change not; therefore ye sons of Jacob are not consumed"*.

The only reason the skeptics of Malachi's day were not destroyed was the immutability of God. He was simply being true to His righteous character, true to His covenant promises. If God had not been unchanging, He would have given the skeptics what they asked for – judgment!

Could it be that you are mocking God? Disobeying God? Are you saying: *"Where is the God of judgment?"* Can I tell you: *"He is coming"*? He is coming to bring you to judgment.

First He will judge the saint at the Judgment Seat of Christ. Then He will judge the sinner at the Great White Throne.

Then these people were also:

(5) DISOBEYING GOD'S WORD – Chapter 3 verses 7 to 12

"Will a man rob God?" is the question at the start of verse 8. What a question! However, these people were robbing God. Again, they ask the question: *"Wherein?"* God explains. The people were robbing Him of the tithes that were due to Him.

Are you robbing God? Are you failing to give to God that which He requires? Have you never learnt the blessing of giving to God? Are you among the many believers who are takers but not givers?

Look here at:

(a) THE PRINCIPLE OF GIVING

Someone says: *"But this is the Old Testament!"*

Are you not happy with the tithe? Are you saying: *"There is no express command to tithe given to the church in the New Testament?"* Are you suggesting for one moment that the *"grace-giving"* that Paul talks about in the Corinthian letter is less than 10%?

Actually, the law of Moses prescribed several tithes that would have amounted to somewhere between 20 to 25 % - see Leviticus

27 verses 30 to 33; Numbers 18 verses 20 and 21 and Deuteronomy 12 verse 17, and Chapter 14 verses 22, 28 and 29.

One thing is sure - *When a Christian grows in grace, he grows in giving.*

Yet, is God saying to us: *"Ye have robbed me"*?

Deuteronomy 8 verse 18 declares:

"But thou shalt remember the LORD thy God: for it is He that giveth thee power to get wealth".

William MacDonald has made this very piercing statement regarding the lack of stewardship in the church of Jesus Christ today:

"We rob God in this sense, often times the Lord's own money is not available to Him."

Can you imagine the possibility that God's own money is not available to Him, because the believers in Malachi's day or the believers in our day are so tight-fisted? They will not let go of it and allow the Lord to use it.

Thus there is set out the Principle of Giving – and also:

(b) THE PROMISE OF BLESSING

God says: *"Prove Me now herewith"* (verse 10). This is the only time in the Bible when God says: *"Prove Me. Put Me to the test".*

God says that when we open up our wallet, He opens up His window.

You see, giving is not only God's way of raising money. It is God's way of growing Christians.

Tithing is not God's way of getting something from you. It is God's way of giving something to you.

However, God's blessing is to be the *result* of tithing *not the reason* for tithing.

It pays to give, but if you give because it pays, it won't pay!

Mary Crowley, who founded Home Interiors, Inc., was a devout Christian who used her wealth as well as her talents to extend the kingdom of God and help others. At one time, she had very little materially. She did not even have a car. She and her two children walked faithfully every Sunday to the services at the First Baptist Church of Dallas in Texas. Members of the congregation often picked them up and gave them a ride to church.

During those years, she faithfully tithed her meagre income to the Lord. In time, her home-decorating talents and business mind resulted in exceeding wealth. When prosperity came, she continued her faithful stewardship.

She wore around her neck, two small gold shovels. One was larger than the other.

When people enquired about their meaning, she would answer:

"The little shovel is mine. I can shovel it out. The big one is God's. He shovels it in ten times faster".

But can you see the state Israel were in?

Denying God's love.
Despising God's name.
Defiling God's covenant.
Doubting God's justice.
Disobeying God's Word.

There was a further sin. They were:

(6) <u>DISREGARDING GOD'S CHARACTER – Chapter 3 verse 13 to Chapter 4 verse 6</u>

They were always questioning what God said. *"Wherein? Wherein? Wherein?"* Now they were at it again. You see, there was:

(a) THE QUESTION OF DEVOTION

Many were saying it was vain to serve God. They were saying that the proud were blessed and happy.

However, there were others. There was a minority, a faithful remnant.

Says Chapter 3 verse 16:

"Then they that feared the LORD spake often one to another: and the LORD hearkened, and heard it, and a book of remembrance was written before Him for them that feared the LORD, and that thought upon His name. And they shall be Mine, saith the LORD of hosts, in that day when I make up My jewels."

There were those who encouraged one another by saying: *"Don't listen to these scoffers. Don't give up serving the Lord. He will reward those who serve Him and He will judge those who scorn Him"*.

Who are you with? Into which group would we be placed? Have you said: *"Serving You, Lord, is a waste of time"*?

(b) THE QUESTION OF DISTINCTION

In verse 5 of Chapter 4, God declares: *"Behold, I will send you Elijah the prophet before the coming of the great and dreadful day of the LORD"*. Note the use of the word: "day". Malachi mentions the word *"day"* four times in the six verses of this chapter. There will be a distinction. It will be a <u>day of burning for the rebellious</u> (verse 1), but a <u>day of blessing for the remnant</u> (verse 2).

But, there is another distinction here. Do you see the title of the Lord Jesus in verse 2? *"The Sun of righteousness."* When He returns visibly to the earth, Christ will be like the noonday sun breaking through the gloom of the dark night of the world. But, before the sun arises, the morning star will appear. Christ says, in Revelation 22 verse 16: *"I am ... the bright and morning star"*.

Today, we know the morning star as the planet Venus, the second planet from the sun and the brightest object in the night sky. Depending on where it is in its orbital path, the morning star can be seen to rise as much as three hours before the sun.

There will two stages of the appearance of the Lord Jesus. First, He will appear as the morning star, coming for His own. Then, at a later period, He will appear as the shining sun, coming in all His power and glory and visible to all the world.

This is the question - How do we get ready for a Coming Lord?

(c) THE QUESTION OF DUTY

How are we to live in the light of these cataclysmic events?

Well, according to verse 4, God's Word should regulate our thinking:

"Remember ye the law of Moses My servant ... with the statutes and judgments."

According to verse 5, God's Work should dominate our living.

The final verse in the Chapter, the final verse in the book, the final verse in the Old Testament is verse 6:

"And he shall turn the heart of the fathers to the children, and the heart of the children to their fathers, lest I come and smite the earth with a curse."

Thus the Old Testament ends.

At the end of the first book of the Old Testament, we read of a: *"coffin"*.

At the end of the final book of the Old Testament, we read of a: *"curse"*.

These two words really indicate that until then all was failure.

But, at end of the New Testament we read: *"And there shall be no more curse"* (Revelation 22:3).

What makes the difference? More accurately, *who* makes the difference? Jesus Christ.

His message to us is: *"Occupy till I come"*.

Thus we conclude our second stage of: *"A Journey through the Bible"*.

It is surely appropriate to do so with the touching words of the poet:

Perhaps today, the clouds will part asunder,
Reveal a glory, brighter than the sun,
And we shall view with transport, joy and wonder,
The Hope of earth and Heaven's beloved One.

Perhaps today, the world's last taunt shall grieve us,
And Satan, foiled, his final dart shall cast,
And all our flesh's frailties shall leave us,
And disappointment evermore be past.

Perhaps today, from weary beds of anguish
God's suffering saints shall breathe their final sigh,
In glory rise, no more on earth to languish,
To meet their great Deliv'rer in the sky.

Perhaps today, the trump of God resounding,
Shall wake the sleepers from their beds of clay,
And we with them our longed-for Lord surrounding,
Shall see His glorious face—perhaps today!

Also available by Denis Lyle:

From Earth to Glory - Psalm 23
ISBN 9781872734484

Denis Lyle has taken a very fresh and inspiring approach to Psalm 23. *From Earth to Glory* focuses on the Lord as the Shepherd. The illustrations throughout the narrative are fascinating and the spiritual lessons from them give value to the book.

The reading and studying of *From Earth to Glory* will most certainly be of spiritual help and blessing.

Norrie Emerson

Available from:

www.ritchiechristianmedia.co.uk

Also available by Denis Lyle:

A Journey Through the Bible - Genesis to Esther
ISBN 9781872734552

As Denis Lyle takes the reader on *A Journey Through the Bible,* the Journey is both enlightening and edifying. In coming to know more about each book, the reader will come to know more about the Divine Author. I warmly commend this Volume to you.

Fraser A Munro

Available from:

www.ritchiechristianmedia.co.uk